WILFRID LAURIER UNIVERSITY DUPL

W9-DIZ-422

The Globalization Decade

THE GLOBALIZATION DECADE

A Critical Reader

Edited by Leo Panitch, Colin Leys, Alan Zuege
and Martijn Konings

DISCARD
WLU BRANTFORD CAMPUS

The Merlin Press
Fernwood Publishing

© this collection, The Merlin Press, 2004
The authors assert the right to be identified as the
authors of this work

First published 2004 by The Merlin Press Ltd.
PO Box 30705
London WC2E 8QD
www.merlinpress.co.uk

British Library Cataloguing in Publication Data
is available from the British Library

National Library of Canada Cataloguing in Publication Data
The globalization decade: a critical reader / edited by Leo Panitch ... [et al.]
Includes bibliographical references.
ISBN 1-55266-088-5
1. Globalization – Political aspects. 2. Globalization. 3. Capitalism.
I. Panitch, Leo, 1945-
JZ1318.G5773 2002   327.1   C2002-903650-X

Published the UK by The Merlin Press
ISBN: 0850365163

Published in Canada by Fernwood Publishing
ISBN: 1552660885

All rights reserved. No part of this publication may be
reproduced, stored in a retrieval system, or transmitted,
in any form or by any means, electronic, mechanical,
photocopying, recording or otherwise, without the
prior permission of the publisher.

Printed in Great Britain by Antony Rowe Ltd., Chippenham

CONTENTS

THE GLOBALIZATION DECADE:
AN INTRODUCTION

Alan Zuege, Martijn Konings, Colin Leys and Leo Panitch

The Globalization Decade brings together some of the most original and influential analyses yet made of the realities of neoliberal globalization, the new international order that was consolidated during the 1990s. The foundations of globalization's 'long decade' were, of course, laid much earlier. Capital's drive to become truly global was re-started under American leadership at the end of World War II, and gathered economic momentum throughout the whole post-war period, expressed most visibly in the increasing size and mobility of multinational corporations. Neoliberalism itself became a full-fledged political project in the 1980s, when Reagan and Thatcher launched their offensive to impose the discipline of global competition on everyone, from workers and peasants to national states and corporations north and south. But it was only in the 1990s that globalization became a fully accomplished fact, to which the world has been adjusting – or failing to adjust – in the first years of the twenty-first century. The essays here explore both the historical roots of these processes and their broad social context. They all view globalization in its totality: not as a mere series of 'reforms' giving free rein to transnational companies but as a radical programme to reshape the entire economic, political, legal and ideological landscape of capitalism. They link the economics of global capitalism both to its geopolitical dimensions and to its intimate repercussions on daily life.

Taken together, these essays accomplish three things. They provide a critique of the dominant intellectual and political fashions in the globalization debate, challenging both orthodox and left perspectives; they analyze the processes driving market liberalization as well as its human and ecological costs; and they point creatively towards democratic and egalitarian alternatives. Cutting across academic disciplines and specialized debates, they take up the following themes: the re-emergence of a world market in capital and the possibility of its control; technological and organizational changes in production and the ascendancy of a new financial order at the centre of neoliberal globalization; the changing class configurations and social relations associated with this; the inequalities and deflationary pressure inherent in the neoliberal economic program; the futility of social democratic models to harness the global market for progressive purposes and economic growth; and the political transformations and contradictions involved in managing the globalization process in the domestic and international spheres.

Long before the opening of the globalization decade, the 'organic intellectuals' of capitalism – in banks, think-tanks, university departments of economics, etc. – espoused market liberalization as the solution to the inefficiency and indiscipline that they claimed had set in across the industrialized world. The origins of the severe political and economic crises that deepened in the early 1970s were attributed to the unchecked growth of trade union power, interventionist government and national protectionism. Across the advanced economies, industry and finance abandoned a strategy of negotiation in favour of confrontation, seeking to reverse the postwar gains of working classes and social movements through a comprehensive programme of rollbacks, privatizations and liberalizations. This new agenda, embraced by global elites, was pressed forward in the 1980s by Wall Street bankers and Washington policy-makers in particular, demanding that governments everywhere to dismantle the political and economic constraints on capital constructed through decades of struggle and compromise.

At first, neoliberals tapped into the sense of fear and powerlessness of those they called on to surrender to international competition, claiming that globalization was inevitable and irreversible. According to them new technologies and the expanding scale and mobility of capital had unleashed economic forces that could no longer be contained by nation states. The neoclassical models advanced by 'Chicago School' economists purported to offer assurance that employment, trade and currency equilibrium would be secured by the mechanisms of the self-regulating market. States that exposed themselves to the rigour of international competition would eventually come to share in the fruits of enhanced efficiency and higher rates of growth, whereas those which tried to impede the free flow of capital on the basis of 'unenlightened' notions of the general interest or, even worse, 'special interests', would be disciplined harshly by the market.

By the 1990s, these neoliberal postulates were accepted by many others in diverse fields, from pop historians to postmodern geographers, who coined euphemistic phrases like the 'death of distance' to depict a 'borderless' and 'weightless' economy which could no longer be captured by established intellectual frameworks – a myth brilliantly demolished in the now famous essay here by Ursula Huws. But to reject such myths does not mean falling prey to the tendency, fashionable on the social-democratic centre-left, of supposing that globalization's importance has been exaggerated. Those who subscribe to this tendency have maintained that capital remains 'embedded' in specific national social formations and that international financial flows are not dissimilar from what they were at the beginning of the twentieth century. Denying that global pressures force national institutions to converge on a standard liberal economic pattern, they insist that the role of the state has even been enhanced in some respects, as globalization puts a premium on the capacity of states to forge 'social pacts' and 'public–private partnerships' in competitive strategies to enhance labour productivity. On this view, neoliberalism is seen mainly as a wrong theory, and its influence on policy circles as unfortunate and unnecessary. However, as Gregory Albo points out in his essay, the impact of neoliberal policies is not confined to a few countries; all forms of national capitalism are in different ways and to different degrees being deeply modified by it.

The papers collected here thus challenge both the neoliberal account, in which economic globalization is portrayed as the working out of a pure logic, devoid of social content and disconnected from political processes; and the social democratic account, which minimizes the significance of globalization in order to try to show how national states can accommodate to it. An important contribution of this volume is to transcend the false dichotomy of political authority and market power that underlies these debates.

'Taking globalization seriously' (as Hugo Radice's essay insists we must do) requires foregrounding its social and political as much as its economic dimensions. Gérard Duménil and Dominique Lévy's essay, for example, recognizes the significance of the increasingly integrated and liberalized international market in capital, as reflected in the vast growth in international trade and foreign direct investment as well as short-term capital flows; the revolution in information technology; the 'networked' multinational corporation; and the ethos of shareholder capitalism. But they also show that the emergence of this complex set of structures has by no means been the smooth, homogenizing and harmonizing process predicted by orthodox economic models. The contradictions of neoliberalism, repeatedly revealed in financial crises, trade asymmetries and seemingly unending 'structural adjustments', attended by mass unemployment and sheer coercion, have made the 'long decade' of globalization a time of immiseration for much of the world's population. The marketization of society has resulted in the creation of large private monopolies, destroyed essential labour market institutions, sparked speculative capital movements resulting in stock market instability, and caused economic downturns by restricting demand. The lives of those most dependent on social security have everywhere become much harder.

Conversely, the fact that even neoliberal regimes have ultimately been unable to scale down welfare expenditures has more to do with the contradictory consequences of neoliberal policies (e.g. a rise in unemployment) and the resistance it generates, than with any institutionally entrenched commitment to the welfare state. Even the strongest corporatist 'models of capitalism' – from Swedish Social Democracy to the Rhineland Model to the 'Third Italy' – have buckled under the pressure of international competition. Corporatist institutions have certainly not been dismantled, but their function has been dramatically altered: now they function almost exclusively as a means of legitimation for unpopular policies, rather than as channels of even limited representation.

What is especially significant about the essays collected here, however, is that they do not see nation states as helpless victims of the rise of global markets. On the contrary, they show how nation states have been active participants in shaping these markets, and how in the process they have in turn been profoundly restructured and conditioned *by* them. They challenge the prevailing illusion that globalization results from disembodied technologies and impersonal market forces, showing instead that the ways new technologies were used and new markets were created in even the most mobile and 'fungible' financial assets of all, such as 'derivatives', were ultimately the product of political choice and social agency.

In the mainstream literature – trapped within a conceptual framework pitting states versus markets – *political* globalization is seldom discussed, and seems as mysterious as its economic counterpart. Even today, the connection between globalization and states is often discussed purely as a matter of a decline in national sovereignty. Market liberalization in fact relied heavily on national states to dismantle the barriers to capital that had been built up over the postwar period; and the resulting instability of emerging world markets, and the international tensions and political disorder they have generated, have further increased the burden on states, since they have to manage these contradictions. And as they have taken up this responsibility, the growing visibility of political regulation and the coerciveness of state interventions have displaced the contradictions of globalization ever more clearly onto national and international political processes.

Of course, the 'external' constraints on domestic policy-making are real enough; the changing role of the state is indeed generalized and enforced by the workings of world markets. A dynamic of competitive liberalization across the advanced economies was triggered by early moves to restore an open international economic order, including the development of the London Eurodollar market in the 1960s and the liberalization of financial services in New York beginning in the early 1970s. As the essays here forcefully demonstrate, the resulting integration of world markets does exert a constant disciplinary pressure on domestic policy-making and limits the room to manoeuvre of states as they compete for mobile capital. But these external pressures are only part of the story. The multifold transformations implied by political globalization cannot be adequately measured in degrees of state autonomy; they affect the very *form* of state autonomy. New channels of state activity have been opened up, while others have been closed down and the terrain of political conflict has been changed.

Untangling this requires opening up the 'black box' of the nation state. The essays by Panitch and Tsoukalas take up this task, drawing on the work of Nicos Poulantzas in the classic 'state theory' debates of the 1970s to track the changing 'institutional materiality' of the state in the management of the globalization process. They reveal how a dramatic internal reorganization of the state has accompanied and followed the globalization process. What this means is that taking *political* globalization seriously involves first of all recognizing that the erosion of autonomous domestic bases of accumulation and national bourgeoisies has transformed the structure of political representation and social compromise. As capital has become increasingly mobile it has gained in structural power vis-à-vis labour, but it has also become more dependent on global sources of accumulation. Correspondingly, then, nation states have increasingly abandoned their former role of reproducing domestic social compromises through 'welfare state' regulation to embrace the economic requirements that come with being part of the new global economy, and to share with other states and international institutions the political responsibilities for managing the global system.

This reorganization is what is meant by the 'internationalization of the state'. There is no 'world state' developing to oversee globalization; on the contrary, international corporations that worked so hard to escape regulatory constraints and welfare costs at the national level have no wish to recreate them at a higher level. Instead, the internationalization of the state entails, on the one hand, a *reordering* of the relative status and influence of government departments in favour of those which mediate relations with the world economy – treasuries, central banks and trade ministries – relative to departments of employment, social services, and the like. On the other hand, it involves a partial *fragmentation* of the state, associated with the rise of trans-governmental regulatory networks, as the demands of an integrating world economy bring officials from domestic agencies into regular contact with their regulatory counterparts abroad. This does not, however, necessarily translate into an assertion of greater state independence from the social forces these agencies seek to represent within the policy process – as the scandals from Berlusconi to Blair to Bush over state-business ties testify. Nor are internationalization pressures confined to those ministries directly implicated in global governance. All branches of the state, from education to local government, now have a part to play in reorienting their social constituencies to the demands and discourse of international competitiveness.

An important related development is the expanding *ideological* role played by government agencies. This signals a broader shift in the legitimation function of the contemporary capitalist state, as this function comes into sharper contradiction with the state's accumulation functions in the international sphere. Under conditions of globalization the maintenance of social cohesion and the mobilization of popular 'consent' present new challenges. Powerful domestic agencies of the state have insulated themselves from popular pressures in order to remain responsive to the exigencies of the world economy, placing them further from the reach of democratic institutions. Liberal democracy looks increasingly thin, as parliamentary institutions are bypassed, political parties are hollowed out and the public sphere is drastically curtailed and penetrated by market forces. The universal message of international competitiveness, echoed today by all nation states, represents an ideological strategy to overcome these tensions by tying the 'national interest' to success in the global marketplace.

The radical restructuring of domestic political processes has been accompanied by an equally dramatic transformation of international political and legal processes. International law and interstate agreements, in the form of a dense web of hundreds of bilateral trade and investment treaties, as well as broader regional and multilateral frameworks, have become principal tools for widening and deepening the liberal economic order, and consolidating it in more permanent forms. This international juridification is matched by domestic economic regulation. Together they show how, contrary to the popular rhetoric of 'free trade' and 'deregulation', liberal markets in fact require an ever more complex system of codification to make them work. International institutions like the IMF and World Bank endorse these trade and investment treaties, while also playing an increasingly direct role in prying open the economies of the 'south' for Western commercial interests via 'structural adjustment'. Using the lever of debt, this involves measures that target the very policy instruments used to protect vulnerable third world industries, which once protected the industries of many countries in the north too, at the comparable stage of their own development.

Political globalization has also transformed the imperial system and the interstate structures that oversee the management of the world economy. Peter Gowan argues that the end of the Cold War marked a break in the international order and undermined the original justification for the American-centred 'protectorate system' which formerly cemented the Western alliance against the threat of Communism and Soviet power. With the Cold War over, the new overriding strategic goal of the US policy establishment became the preservation and enhancement of the United States' place at the apex of the global system. American capitalism now penetrated the rest of the world's social systems, the might of the US military was unparalleled, and American dominance in international finance and other important economic sectors was maintained. This new imperial project involves a dual role for the American state: on the one hand, the manager of a world capitalist order – a role it alone can currently play; and on the other, the embodiment of the American national interest – and an all too often chauvinist identity.

In 2004, at the end of the 'long decade' of globalization, the practical legacy of neoliberal globalization can be measured against the pollyanna-ish predictions of its backers. Today the claims of the globalizers, that economic integration would spread prosperity and welfare across the planet, ring hollow. Of late even the tiny minority of shareholders, fund managers, multinational executives and developing world elites who have reaped the lion's share of the benefits have been feeling the chill of globalization's contradictions. Growth in many parts of the world remains anaemic, social inequality within and between nations has dramatically increased, and waves of instability ripple through the international financial system. And the latest political promise of the imperial managers of the global system – to bring 'democracy' to the Middle East, Central Asia and beyond – is entirely lacking in credibility. In reality, they continue to support local despots wherever their neoliberal prescriptions can be forced upon unwilling societies. They selectively target for attack the political regimes lying at the fringes of the neoliberal order (from Yugoslavia to Iraq and Venezuela), along with the populist movements which arise to resist that order (whether left-leaning anti-globalization mobilizations or religious and ethno-nationalist backlashes).

The invisible hand of the global market is now frankly backed by the iron fist of internal state repression and imperialist war, and the world is a manifestly less secure and more dangerous place for the majority of its inhabitants. One of the great strengths of the essays in this collection is that the human costs of the neoliberal agenda are always at the centre of their concern: from Manfred Bienefeld's prescient warning of the prospect of social disintegration across the developing world, and the resulting threat of global polarization; to Wally Seccombe's analysis of the devastation wrought by 'shareholder capitalism' on workers, their families and communities; to Elmar Altvater's dissection of the 'growth obsession' and its callous disregard for ecological destruction and the marginalization of those left behind in the race for global position.

The evolving anti-globalization, anti-imperialist and anti-war movements are powerful evidence of the limits of the neoliberal message, and of the diminished social base of the globalizers' project. While the essays here do not offer blueprints for progressive alternatives, some important guidelines do emerge from them. At a minimum they make it very clear that efforts to construct a new social compromise parallel to that of the 'golden age' of post-war capitalism, only adapted to globalization through 'progressive competitiveness', are doomed to fail. The 'modernized' social-democratic parties that have been in office in various European countries throughout much of the second half of the 'long' globalization decade have been unable to deliver on their 'Third Way' promise of a high-tech, high-wage economy, supported by investments in education and public services. In practice there has been a continued slide towards increasingly liberalized labour markets, producing a growing class of the working poor, a steady drift towards individualism, a scapegoating of public sector workers for the failure of ill-conceived government plans, and intensified social divisions.

Instead of seeking to accommodate neoliberal globalization by trying to adjust domestic institutions and social relations to the requirements of global capital, the starting point must be strategies that involve the reimposition of controls on capital movements, as Jim Crotty and Gerald Epstein argue in the essay repub-

lished here – and as many contemporary analysts of all persuasions, from Soros
to Stiglitz, have subsequently come to agree. But this cannot mean merely going
back to the capital controls of the Bretton Woods era, which the 1970s showed
were too weak to withstand the economic and political power of increasingly
internationalized capital. The key long-term condition for an alternative to globalization is democratic investment control within each state, the exact opposite
of the goal sought in recent multilateral negotiations. Moreover such control
must go beyond the kind of quantitative controls on capital inflows and outflows
allowed under Bretton Woods, let alone beyond the Tobin Tax on capital flows
advanced by many on the left.

A campaign for democratic capital controls is required, one which puts on
the agenda what international investment is for and should be for. Nor can we
pretend that controls over foreign investment can be divorced from the need
for democratic control over private domestic investment. This will not be adequately addressed by notions of 'pension fund socialism', or labour investment
funds that offer tax breaks to the workers who put their money into them. More
daunting still, but nevertheless unavoidable, is the need to confront the implications of the 'growth obsession'. The left's call for a return to the unprecedented
rates of growth of the postwar era simply ignores the ecological unsustainability
of such a project, the costs of which are already being experienced everywhere.
The needs of the world's impoverished and excluded cannot be met by continually intensifying the exploitation of the world's resources.

What all this finally means is that there is no honest way to avoid advocating the need for massive redistributions of wealth and power internationally to
challenge the inequalities and irrationalities of an international capitalist system
operating under the aegis of an ever more blatantly imperial American state. This
will depend on a fresh mobilization of social forces, including western working classes who come to recognize how their own implication in globalization,
ranging from how their pension funds are invested to their participation in mass
consumerism, undermines their own welfare and security. Nothing less than
a massive shift in social power within each country would have to be effected
through this mobilization, allowing for the development of popular capacities to
transform states everywhere so as to genuinely democratize them and thereby
enhance the efficacy of new solidaristic international strategies to confront and
transcend capitalist globalization.

GLOBALIZATION AND THE STATE

Leo Panitch

Alice never could quite make out, in thinking it over afterwards, how it was that they began: all she remembers is, that they were running hand in hand, and the Queen went so fast that it was all she could do to keep up with her: and still the Queen kept crying 'Faster! Faster!', though she had no breath left to say so.

The most curious part of the thing was, that the trees and the other things round them never changed their places at all: however fast they went, they never seemed to pass anything ...

'Well, in *our* country,' said Alice, still panting a little, 'you'd generally get to somewhere else – if you ran for a long time as we've been doing.'

'A slow sort of country!' said the Queen. 'Now, *here*, you see, it takes all the running *you* can do, to keep in the same place. If you want to get somewhere else, you must run at least twice at fast as that!'

– Lewis Carroll, *Through the Looking Glass*

I. INTRODUCTION

Think of the Red Queen's Garden as capitalism. The relentless search for markets and profits brings about faster and faster changes in production and space, industry and commerce, occupation and locale, with profound effects on the

This essay was first published in *Between Globalism and Nationalism, The Socialist Register 1994*

organization of classes and states. It is through this ferocious process of extension and change that capitalism preserves itself, remains capitalism, stays the same
system. This paradox, or rather this dialectic, can only properly be grasped if we
understand that the 'bourgeoisie cannot exist without constantly revolutionizing
the instruments of production, and thereby relations of production, and with
them the whole relations of society'.[1] This was not an understanding merely
appropriate to what happened to the world in the first half of the nineteenth
century: it is no less appropriate to understanding what has happened over the
second half of the twentieth, and to what is taking place in the world today.

Now think of Alice, frantically running alongside the Red Queen, as the labour movement, or the social movements, or the broadly defined 'Left'. For all
the running they have made in this century, for all the mobilization and reform,
even the moments of revolution and national liberation, the world today is most
certainly still very much capitalist, indeed it would seem ever more so. Of course,
this does not mean the world is unchanged from what it was, and this is partly
due to the effect of those who have contested and thereby either insulated themselves against or modified the vast transformations wrought by the bourgeoisie.
But the institutions of the Left, not least the once powerful Communist and
Social Democratic parties, increasingly could not even keep pace and lost more
and more initiative to the forces of capitalist change. Their original ambition to
get somewhere else, to a social order beyond capitalism – that is, to socialism,
however conceived – more or less gradually gave way to attempts at adaptation
and accommodation to the dynamics of capitalist change. Yet the only result has
been that they became more and more ineffective in their attempts to tame the
market, and the social forces they had once mobilized and spoken for have become more than ever the victims of ruthless capitalist change.

It has become quite commonplace to recognize that some fundamental rethinking is required by the Left. But all too often such rethinking is still cast in
terms of grabbing hold of the bourgeoisie's hand and trying to run faster and
faster to match the pace of changes set by contemporary capitalism. This involves
a fundamental strategic misconception. If effective forms of movement ever are
to re-emerge on the Left, they will have to be less about keeping up with or
adapting to capitalist change, but rather more about developing the capacity to
mobilize more broadly and effectively against the logic of competitiveness and
profit in order eventually to get somewhere else, that is, to an egalitarian, cooperative and democratic social order beyond capitalism. To run, even twice as fast,
on capitalism's terms will not in fact lead somewhere else at all.

These considerations are especially germane in light of the challenge posed by
what has come to be known as 'globalization'. The apparent subjection of even
advanced capitalist social formations in recent decades to the competitive logics
and exigencies of production, trade and finance undertaken on a world scale has
entailed, as Robert Cox contends, 'subordination of domestic economies to the

perceived exigencies of a global economy. States willy nilly became more effectively accountable to a *nebuleuse* personified as the global economy; and they were constrained to mystify this external accountability in the eyes and ears of their own publics through the new vocabulary of globalisation, interdependence, and competitiveness'.[2] Notably, for Cox, as for David Gordon, globalization reflects less the establishment of a stable new international regime of capital accumulation than an aspect of the decay of the old 'social structure of accumulation'[3]; as Cox puts it, the tendency to globalization is 'never complete', and there is 'nothing inevitable' about its continuation. 'Any attempt to depict it must not be taken teleologically, as an advanced stage towards the inevitable completion of a latent structure. Rather it should be taken dialectically, as the description of tendencies that, as they become revealed, may arouse oppositions that could strive to confound and reverse them'. [4]

Most accounts of globalization, however, see the process as irreversible, and in this perspective the predominant strategic response becomes one which invariably tends to see the strategies, practices and institutions of the Left as perhaps having been appropriate to an earlier 'national' stage of capitalism but as having now been rendered outmoded and outdated by globalization. Just like Alice before she stepped through the looking glass, it is as though the Left used to be able to get somewhere else by running on the terrain of the nation state, but now that capital had escaped the nation state, the Left will have to learn to run with the bourgeoisie across the terrain of the globe. This approach has recently been well represented by David Held, for instance, for whom globalization implies a distinctively new 'international order involving the emergence of a global economic system which stretches beyond the control of a single state (even of dominant states); the expansion of networks of transnational linkages and communications over which particular states have little influence; the enormous growth in international organization which can limit the scope for action of the most powerful states; the development of a global military order ... which can reduce the range of policies available to governments and their citizens'. Since this new global order has apparently escaped the control of democratic institutions located at the national level, Held concludes that this means that 'democracy has to become a transnational affair'. Strategic priority must be given to 'the key groups, agencies, associations and organizations of international civil society', extending their capacity as agencies for democratic control through an appropriate recasting of the territorial boundaries of systems of accountability, representation and regulation, fortified by entrenched transnational bills of social, economic and civil rights.[5]

While characterizations of globalization as a qualitative new phase of capitalism such as these depart sharply from those who have understood capitalism as a 'world system' from its inception, in terms of the implications of globalization for the institutional capacity and strategic focus of the Left, the dilemma is precisely the same one as posed long ago by world system theorists. Thus Wallerstein:

While the multiple political organizational expressions of the world bourgeoisie – controlling as they did de facto most state structures – could navigate with relative ease the waters of murky geographical identity, it was precisely the world's workers' movements that felt obliged to create national, that is, state-wide, structures, whose clear boundaries would define and limit organisational efforts. If one wants to conquer state power, one has to create organizations geared to this objective. Thus, while the world bourgeoisie has, when all is said and done always organised in relationship to the world economy … the proletarian forces – despite their internationalist rhetoric – have been far more nationalist than they claimed or their ideology permitted … these movements are caught in a dilemma. They can reinforce their state power, with the advantage of holding on to a foothold in the interstate system, but they face the risk of making the detour the journey, in Hobsbawm's phrase. Or they can move to organise transnationally, at the great risk of losing any firm base, and at the risk of internecine struggle, but it may be that power is only truly available at the world level.[6]

Even those less inclined to reduce the tradition of socialist internationalism to mere rhetoric, nevertheless still see the prime cause of the weakness of the Left today in terms of internationalism having 'changed sides', as Perry Anderson recently put it: 'The new reality is a massive asymmetry between the international mobility and organization of capital, and the dispersal and segmentation of labour that has no historical precedent. The globalization of capitalism has not drawn the resistances to it together, but scattered and outflanked them … The age continues to see nationalisms exploding like firecrackers across much of the world, not least where communism once stood. But the future belongs to the set of forces that are overtaking the nation- state. So far, they have been captured or driven by capital – as in the past fifty years, internationalism has changed sides. So long as the Left fails to win back the initiative here, the current system will be secure'.[7]

There are a number of problems with this way of approaching the Left's strategic dilemmas in the face of globalization. The premise that globalization is a process whereby capital limits, escapes or overtakes the nation state may be misleading in two senses. First, there is often an overestimation of the extent to which nation states were capable of controlling capital in an earlier era; it is as if the Left's mode of practice was adequate in relation to the nation state and thus encourages a similar mode to be adopted at the global level: the problem is just one of running faster on the new terrain. But even for those not given to such illusions, there is a tendency to ignore the extent to which today's globalization both is authored by states and is primarily about reorganizing, rather than by-passing, states; it promotes, in this sense, a false dichotomy between national and international struggles and diverts attention from the Left's need to develop its own strategies for transforming the state, even as a means of developing an appropriate international strategy.

II. THE INTERNATIONALIZATION OF THE STATE

Any attempt to reassess Left strategies in the context of globalization must begin with the understanding that although the nature of state intervention has changed considerably, the role of the state has not necessarily been diminished. Far from witnessing a by-passing of the state by a global capitalism, what we see are very active states and highly politicized sets of capitalist classes hard at work to secure what Stephen Gill in his essay in *The Socialist Register 1992* (primarily focusing on the European Union but pointing to much broader tendencies of this kind) aptly termed a 'new constitutionalism for disciplinary neo-liberalism'.[8] In the past year alone, we have witnessed, not only with the GATT at the world level but also with the North American Free Trade Agreement (to be examined in some detail later in this essay) at the regional level, states as the authors of a regime which defines and guarantees, through international treaties with constitutional effect, the global and domestic rights of capital.

This process may be understood in a manner quite analogous to the emergence of the so-called laissez-faire state during the rise of industrial capitalism, which involved a very active state to see through the separation of polity from economy and guarantee legally and politically the rights of contract and property. We may recall, with Corrigan and Sayer, the long 'revolution in government' in England that stretched from 1740 to 1850: 'we should understand … what later became celebrated and dominant as "political economy" to be simultaneously the dis-covery of economy (and "the economy" argued for as a self-sufficient "private" realm governed by the laws of the market) and a politicization of a moral code (entailing specific forms of "policing") which makes that possible'.[9] Similarly, as regards the emergence of the modern corporation in the United States through the nineteenth century, Alan Wolfe showed that this could not properly be un-derstood as 'a triumph of laissez-faire. Laws could be changed only if the bodies that passed them were controlled; this meant that in order to take the corporation out of the public sphere and place it in the private one, the industrialists had to enter the public sphere themselves. Ironically, a political battle had to be fought in order to place an important – in the nineteenth century perhaps the most important – institution outside of politics, one had to have power in the state in order to make it impotent. Few clearer examples exist of how the struggle over legal parameters cannot be accepted as a given but becomes part of the activity of the state itself …'.[10] We are living through something like this in our own time: capitalist globalization is a process which also takes place in, through, and under the aegis of states; it is encoded by them and in important respects even authored by them; and it involves a shift in power relations within states that often means the centralization and concentration of state powers as the necessary condition of and accompaniment to global market discipline.

It must be said that most contributions to understanding the role of the state amidst the contemporary process of globalization have lagged behind the process itself, and on the whole remained quite thin, as least in comparison with two key contributions which were made on the subject two decades ago. In 1971 Robin Murray offered a seminal contribution to what he termed 'the territorial dialectics of capitalism' to the end of developing 'a framework which would allow a more substantial approach to the problem of the effects of an internationalization of capital on existing political institutions'.[11] The importance of his contribution was that, far from conceiving this as a process which could be understood in terms of capital 'escaping' the state, Murray demonstrated to the contrary that as capital expanded territorially one of the key problems it had to confront was how to try to ensure that state economic functions might continue to be performed. At issue was the structural role of the capitalist state in relation to 'what may most aptly be called economic *res publica*, those economic matters which are public, external to individual private capitals'. This included guaranteeing property and contract; standardizing currency, weights and measure; ensuring the availability of key inputs of labour, land, finance, technology and infrastructure; general macroeconomic orchestration; regulation of conditions of work, consumption and external diseconomies such as pollution; and provision of ideological, educational and communications conditions of production and trade. And alongside the performance of these *intranational* functions there stood the function of *international* management of external relations pertaining to any or all of these dimensions. Any capital which extended itself beyond the territorial boundaries of a state which had heretofore performed these functions had to either take these functions on themselves or have them performed by some other public authority. Historically this was often accomplished through colonialism and then neo-colonialism. In the contemporary era, and especially as regards the advanced capitalist states, it has primarily been a matter of 'states already performing or being willing to perform the functions of their own accord', so that foreign capital came to be serviced on the same basis as domestic capital.

To speak in terms of functions is not necessarily improperly 'functionalist' insofar as the range of structures that might undertake their performance, and the conditions which might mean their non-performance, are explicitly problematized. Murray explicitly did this, including by addressing the possibility that 'the contradictions of the international system will be such as to prevent their fulfilment at all'. Yet Murray saw no reason why, despite the major increase in the internationalization of trade, investment and finance capital in the 1950s and 1960s, the performance of both intranational and international state functions could not continue to be contained within the system of nation states. Especially as regards 'the *intranational* performance of public economic functions for extended capital', Murray stressed the positive advantages to capital in being able to play off one nation state against another: 'Thus, even where there is extensive territorial non-coincidence between domestic states and their extended capitals, this does not imply that the system of atomistic nation states is outdated. The [notion] ... that "multinational corporations and nations are therefore fundamentally incompatible with each other" is not necessarily true'.[12]

On the other hand, Murray discerned the contradictions entailed in a process which was exposing exchange rates and national monetary systems to an international money market, easing the process of international speculation and opening sources of credit outside the control of national authorities: 'There is accordingly a tendency for the process of internationalization to increase the potential economic instability in the world economy at the same time as decreasing the power of national governments to control economic activity within their own borders'. Attempts by states to correct balance of payments deficits in the context of this economic instability led to the adoption of policies which 'further weaken the national capital and increase the domination of foreign capital within the national economy'. Murray concluded from this that, precisely because capital was always a political opportunist which would take support from whatever public authority it could, '... existing states often suffered a decrease in their powers as a result of internationalization ... [yet] weaker states in a period of internationalization come to suit neither the interests of their own besieged capital nor of the foreign investor'.[13] As if recognizing the unresolved ambiguities in his approach over whether the territorial dialectics of capital extended or diminished the role of the state, Murray ended his article by calling for an 'elaboration of the connections between not only states, but the states and their capitals'.

Three years later, in a brilliantly original analysis, Nicos Poulantzas took up exactly where Murray had left off by explicitly problematizing the notion of states and 'their' capitals, and insisting that 'common formulations of the problem such as "what can – or cannot – the state do in the face of the great multinational firms", "how far has the state lost powers in the face of these international giants?" are fundamentally incorrect'.[14]

Poulantzas's immediate concern was with understanding the dominant role that American capital had come to play in Europe, including the process whereby European states 'take responsibility for the interests of the dominant capital'. This not only involved granting concessions and subventions to American capital of the same type as it granted to indigenous capital, but also acting as a 'staging post' by supporting American capital in its further extension outside Europe. This could 'go so far as to help American capital circumvent the American state itself (the anti-trust legislation, for example). The international reproduction of capital under the domination of American capital is supported by various national states, each state attempting in its own way to latch onto one or other aspect of this process'. This did not mean (in contrast to Murray) that the state policies weakened national capital, but rather that its industrial policies increasingly were concerned with promoting 'the concentration and international expansion of their own indigenous capital' by linking it with the international reproduction of American capital.[15]

The concentration of power by transnational capital did not take power away from the state; rather, 'the state intervenes precisely in this very concentration':

> The current internationalization of capital neither suppresses or by-passes nation states, either in the direction of a peaceful integration of capitals 'above' the state level (since every process of internationalization is effected under the dominance of the capital of a given country), or in the direction of their extinction by an American super-state, as if American capital purely and simply directed the other imperialist bourgeoisies. This internationalization, on the other hand, deeply affects the politics and institutional forms of these states by including them in a system of interconnections which is in no way confined to the play of external and mu-tual pressures between juxtaposed states and capitals. These states themselves take charge of the interest of the dominant imperialist capital in its development within the 'national' social formation, i.e. in its complex relation of internalization to the domestic bourgeoisie that it dominates. This system of interconnections does not encourage the constitution of effective supra-national or super-state institutional forms of agencies; this would be the case if what was involved was internationaliza-tion within a framework of externally juxtaposed states and capitals. These states themselves take charge of the interests of the dominant imperialist capital in its complex relation of internationalization to the domestic bourgeoisie.[16]

Transnational capital's interpenetration with domestic bourgeoisies may have rendered the notion of a national bourgeoisie increasingly arcane, but even an internal bourgeoisie 'implicated by multiple ties of dependence in the interna-tional division of labour and in the international concentration of capital' still maintained its own economic foundation and base of capital accumulation at home and abroad, as well as exhibited specific political and ideological features with autonomous effects on the state. Nor was this struggle one in which only dominant classes and fractions were at play: '... while the struggles of the popular masses are more than ever developing in concrete conjunctures determined on a world basis ... it is still the national form that prevails in these struggles, how-ever international they are in their essence. This is due for one thing to uneven development and the concrete specificity of each social formation; these features are of the very essence of capitalism, contrary to the belief upheld by the various ideologies of "globalisation"'.[17]

Poulantzas's unsurpassed contribution was to remind us that the internationali-zation of the state was a development which could not 'be reduced to a simple contradiction of a mechanistic kind between the base (internationalization of production) and a superstructural cover (national state) which no longer cor-responds to it'. Nor could the state be reduced to 'a mere tool or instrument of the dominant classes to be manipulated at will, so that every step that capital took towards internationalization would automatically induce a parallel "super-nationalization" of states'. If the focus of attention was put, rather, on relations and struggles among social forces, we would see that these did not shift to some hyperspace beyond the state. Rather, global class interpenetrations and contradictions needed to be understood in the context of specificities of the nation state's continuing central role in organizing, sanctioning and legitimizing class domination within capitalism.

III. THE ANTINOMIES OF ROBERT COX

It was only with Robert Cox's *Production, Power and World Order* in 1987 that a full-scale study of the internationalization of the state appeared which was founded on a historical materialist understanding of the role of 'social forces in the making of history' (the book's sub-title) rather than a false counterposition between globalizing capital and the power of states. The impact of Cox's book in challenging the dominant realist approach to the study of international relations has been comparable to the impact of Miliband's *The State in Capitalist Society* challenge to the pluralist approach to the study of comparative politics almost twenty years earlier. Writing over a decade later than Murray and Poulantzas, moreover, Cox was in a better position to analyze the changing modalities of the internationalization of the state induced by the new era of economic instability and crisis since the mid-1970s.

Cox's approach, like Murray's, is grounded in his understanding of the 'indispensable functions' the state has to perform in a capitalist society, from guaranteeing property and contracts to dismantling obstructions to markets to ensuring the soundness of money. Thus, 'the specialization of functions and centralization of state power' of the nineteenth century liberal state, which appeared 'to contradict the principle of abstinence from intervention', actually involved 'no contradiction, since to allow the market mechanism to function without disturbance required the sanction of coercive force, and to ensure this force was not to be used in particular interests but to defend the system as a whole required the creation of a specialized state apparatus'.[18] A recent critique of the Coxian approach by Peter Burnham for allegedly failing to recognize that 'the state meets the interests of capital-in-general by enforcing the discipline of the market through the rule of law and the rule of money', is in this sense entirely misplaced.[19] Cox is concerned, however, to go beyond this: '… in order to comprehend the real historical world it is necessary to consider distinctive *forms of state* … [and] the characteristics of their historic blocs, i.e., the configuration of social forces upon which state power ultimately rests. A particular configuration of social forces defines in practice the limits or parameters of state purposes, and the modus operandi of state action, defines, in other words, the *raison d'état* for a particular state'. Within these parameters, the state exercised power and choice in the organization and development of production and classes, although its actions 'in these matters are, in turn, conditioned by the manner in which the world order impinges upon the state'.[20]

It is in the specific context of the rise and fall of the hegemonic world order of

Pax Americana that Cox situates the internationalization of the state. Under the decisive shift in 'relative economic-productive powers' in favour of the United States and its 'unquestioned leadership' outside the Soviet sphere after 1945, the 'putting into place of the new order involved the transformation of state structures' from those which had existed in the pre-war non-hegemonic system of nationalist/welfare states. That the new order entailed *a transformation, not a diminution, of the state* – a reorganization of the state's structure and role in its external and internal aspects – is the decisive point. Within the framework of interstate agreements forged at Bretton Woods – and under the continued surveillance, incentives and sanctions of new international financial institutions (the IMF and World Bank) which 'behaved as accessories to U.S. policy' – *Pax Americana* 'was held in place by a configuration of different forms of state whose common feature was the role each played in adjusting national economic policies to the dynamics of the world economy'. The process of establishing and internalizing a 'notion of international obligation' to the world economy constitutes, for Cox, 'the meaning given to the term *internationalizing of the state*':

> *First*, there is a process of interstate consensus formation regarding the needs or requirements of the world economy that takes place within a common ideological framework (i.e., common criteria of interpretation of economic events and common goals anchored in the idea of an open world economy). *Second*, participation in this consensus formation is hierarchically structured. *Third*, the internal structures of states are adjusted so that each can best transform the global consensus into national policy and practice, taking account of the specific kinds of obstacles likely to arise in countries occupying the different hierarchically arranged positions in the world economy.[21]

It will be noted that whereas Poulantzas proceeded from *within* ('states themselves take charge of the interests of the dominant imperialist capital in its development within the "national" social formation'), Cox proceeds from the *outside-in*, beginning with international consensus formation and attendant agreements and obligations to which internal state structures are then adjusted. To be sure, Cox is careful to say that this 'was not necessarily a power structure with lines of force running exclusively top-down, nor was it one in which the bargaining agents were whole nation states'. Bureaucratic fragments of states engaged in a process of bargaining, with the hegemonic power structure 'tacitly taken into account', and, 'through ideological osmosis, internalized in the thinking of participants'.[22] Whereas in the interwar era, the state's political accountability was solely turned inward so that the state acted as a *buffer* protecting the domestic economies from external forces, the internationalization of the state after 1945 involves establishing a compromise between the international and domestic obligations of states. The state now takes the form of a *mediator* between the externally established policy priorities and the internal social forces to which it also still remains accountable. 'The centre of gravity shifted from national economies to the world economy, but states were recognised as having a responsibility to both'.[23]

The state was not less 'powerful' in terms of controlling the national economy than before the war. State intervention, as Cox points out, had proved incapable of pulling the economy out of the 1930s Depression; before the war no less than after the war, the state was primarily reactive, lacking 'the ability to conceive and carry through an organization of production and distribution that would replace the market. It could tinker or "fine tune"; it could not design'.[24] Rather than a loss of power, the internationalization of the state after 1945 reflected a shift in power inside the state, entailing 'a restructuring of the hierarchy of state apparatuses'. In appearance there was 'virtually nothing' to signal this change in structure; rather the goals pursued and the uses to which the structures were put changed. Agencies with direct links to the 'client groups of national economy', such as ministries of labour and industry and institutions of tripartite corporatism that had developed in the inter-war era, were not displaced. Indeed they, and the social forces attached to them, remained 'relatively privileged' and even 'preeminent'. But they were subordinated to prime ministerial and presidential offices, foreign offices, treasuries and central banks in such a way that they became 'instruments of policy transmitted though the world-economy linked central agencies'. [25]

A new stage in the internationalization of the state has arisen, however, in the wake of the crisis in the post-war order that emerged from 1968-75, a crisis which has led to the further expansion of 'the breadth and depth of the global economy', even while undermining American hegemony. The internationalizing of production and finance that grew through the 1950s and 1960s under the umbrella of *Pax Americana*, together with domestic inflationary pressures, industrial militancy and declining profits under conditions of full employment, engendered this crisis; the Bretton Woods exchange rates arrangement was abandoned, and the limits of the domestic fine-tuning capacity of tripartism were severely tested. Although Cox thus sees the crisis as having been generated as much by domestic contradictions as international ones, he nevertheless once again portrays the reconstruction of the state in the new era from the outside-in. A 'new doctrine' redefining the role of states 'was prepared by a collective effort of ideological revision undertaken through various unofficial agencies – the Trilateral Commission, the Bilderberg conferences, the Club of Rome, and other prestigious forums – and then endorsed through more official agencies like the OECD'.[26] This doctrine, virtually identical as Cox portrays it to the governing philosophy of what he calls the Thatcher-Reagan hyperliberal state form ('the fullest, most uncompromising instance of a liberal state'[27]), attacked the post-war compromise in both senses of the term: the domestic compromise which tied in labour and welfare interests; and the international compromise of mediating between national interests and the global order. Inside the state, there is a further shift in power away from those agencies most closely tied to domestic social forces and towards those which are in closest touch with the transnational process of consensus formation. As summarized by Cox in his essay in *The Socialist Register 1992*:

> There is, in effect, no explicit political or authority structure for the global economy. There is, nevertheless, something that remains to be deciphered, something that could be described by the French word 'nebuleuse' or by the notion of 'governance without government'.
>
> There is a transnational process of consensus formation among the official caretakers of the global economy. This process generates consensual guidelines, underpinned by the ideology of globalisation, that are transmitted into the policy-making channels of national governments and big corporations ... The structural impact on national governments of this centralisation of influence over policy can be called the internationalising of the state. Its common feature is to convert the state into an agency for adjusting national economic practices and policies to the perceived exigencies of the global economy. The state becomes a transmission belt from the global to the national economy, where heretofore it had acted as the bulwark defending domestic welfare from external disturbances. Power within the state becomes concentrated in those agencies in closest touch with the global economy – the offices of presidents and prime ministers, treasuries, central banks. The agencies that are more closely tied with domestic clients – ministries of industries, labour ministries, etc, – become subordinated. This phenomenon, which has become so salient since the crisis of the post-war order, needs much more study.[28]

It will be recalled that Cox had identified this same shift in power as the constitutive element in the reconstruction of the state in the Bretton Woods era. Although he does not make this explicit, it appears that now the corporatist and welfarist state apparatuses and the social forces allied with them lose the 'preeminent' and 'relatively privileged' position they had previously retained. But since they had already been substantively rendered 'secondary' even in the post-1945 era,[29] the substantive change he has in mind in the post-1975 era appears to have to do with the role of the already dominant state apparatuses of treasuries, central banks, prime minister's offices, etc. They seem less and less to be in a *bargaining* relationship with the forces representing the global economy, and more and more their agents.

The limits of the 'outside-in' orientation of Cox's approach to the internationalization of the state become revealed here. The notion of the state becoming a 'transmission belt from the global to the national economy' is not only too formal in its distinction between global and national economy, but also too 'top-down' in its expression of power relations.[30] It would appear that in his 1992 essay Cox conflated some aspects of the internationalization of the state going on since 1945 with developments that have taken place since the crisis of the mid-1970s. We seem to move directly from the state as a *buffer* (or now 'a bulwark') to that of it being a *transmission belt*, skipping over the post-war stage of the state as a *mediator* between the global and the national, with accountability going both ways. But even if this was an understandable telescoping of his theorization for the purposes of a brief essay, a framework that traces the internationalization of the state as a process that takes us from *buffer* to *mediator* to *transmission belt* in relation to global capital is perhaps too brittle.

I would argue instead that the role of states remains one not only of internalizing but also of mediating adherence to the untrammelled logic of international capitalist competition within its own domain, even if only to ensure that it can effectively meet its commitments to act globally by policing the new world order on the local terrain. It is in terms of the difficulty of such mediation that Cox's own insights on 'the tendency toward limited democracy' as a means of limiting popular domestic pressures on the state can, in fact, best be appreciated. What needs to be investigated is whether the important shifts in the hierarchy of state apparatuses really are those which bring to the fore those most involved with the international 'caretakers of the global economy', or whether a more general process is at work, determined more from within the state itself, whereby even those agencies without such direct international links, but which nevertheless directly facilitate capital accumulation and articulate a competitiveness ideology, are the ones that gain status, while those which fostered social welfare and articulated a class harmony orientation lose status. Whether that loss of status is considerable, or even permanent, however, partly depends on the transformations which these latter agencies are today going through in terms of being made, or making themselves, more attuned to the exigencies of global competitiveness and fiscal restraint. Ministries of labour, health and welfare are perhaps not so much being subordinated as themselves being restructured.

As for the structure of power at the international level, a 'nebuleuse' or a 'governance without government' is not well captured through the notion of a 'global centralisation of influence over policy' and the 'transmission belts' which emanate from them. Indeed, in an insightful passage in *Production Power and World Order* Cox himself traced the 'decline of centralized management characteristic of the world economy of Pax Americana' so that the world economy increasingly was better represented as 'a system than as an institution'. Whereas in the 1960s he identified a set of institutions with the U.S. Treasury at the apex and its policy criteria being internationalized through the IMF, World Bank and other such agencies, 'during the 1970s, private transnational banks assumed such an important role that the top management structure could no longer be convincingly represented exclusively in terms of state and interstate institutions'. The key development here was that 'private international credit expanded for lack of any agreement on how the official intergovernmental structures in the system could be reformed. The impasse on reform was the consequence of stalemate between the United States and the European countries on the future role of the dollar ...

In the absence of agreement on management by official institutions, dollar hegemony shifted to the financial market, that is to say, to the very largely unmanaged dollar itself ... Authority weakened at the apex of the international financial
system. Crisis did not produce effective centralization. U.S. power was too great
to be brought under any externally imposed discipline but was no longer great
enough to shape the rules of a consensual order'.[31] Cox does not see this problem as having been resolved by the early 1990s. Indeed, he stresses in his 1992
essay the 'parlously fragile condition' of international finance in a context where
not even the G-7 governments have been able to 'devise any effectively secure
scheme of regulation'.

It becomes particularly clear here that there is an unresolved antinomy in Cox.
On the one hand, there is one image of an increasingly centralized supranational
management structure, founded on ideological consensus among the elites that
populate transnational institutions and forums. He claims that the disintegration
of the norms of post-war hegemonic order led to an intensification among the
advanced capitalist countries of 'the practice of policy harmonization [which]
became correspondingly more important to the maintenance of consensus. The
habit of policy harmonization had been institutionalized during the preceding
two decades and was, if anything, reinforced in the absence of clear norms.
Ideology had to substitute for legal obligation'.[32] Is it this that transmits and links
hyperliberal policy from country to country? On the other hand, there is another image of a unregulated system of international finance – which appears to
be unregulated, moreover, in good part because of an inability to forge policy
consensus at an interstate level.[33] Is it this system of international finance that in-
ternationalizes the state, making accountable national policy makers of whatever
ideological orientation?

The antinomies in the Coxian framework, as the emphasis shifts back and forth
from social force to ideology to institution to system, has led one recent critic,
looking for a more orthodox and neater pattern of determinations, to throw up
his hands in frustration at an approach which

> ... in its frantic attempt to escape the twin evils of 'economism' and idealism of-
> fers little more than a version of Weberian pluralism oriented to the study of the
> international order ... Variables which comprise a social order – the economy, the
> polity, the civil society – are given no overall structure but rather each has a real
> autonomy which preclude overdetermination ... This factor approach is reflected
> in Cox's analysis to the effect that in the interaction between material capabilities,
> ideas and institutions no determinism exists, and relationships are reciprocal. The
> question of lines of force is an historical one to be answered by a study of the par-
> ticular case. However laudable in theory, the true consequence of this position is to
> produce a pluralist empiricism which lacks the power to explain either the systemic
> connection between values, social relations and institutions or the extent to which
> the historical appearance of capital as a social relation transforms the social order in

such a way that all relations are subsumed under the capital relation as the basis for valorisation.[34]

If the charge of a certain empiricism is perhaps not entirely off the mark, the general level at which Burnham demands primacy to be given to 'the capital relation' is hardly any answer. Indeed, Cox would readily grant determination at this level but then ask: so what? We have already seen that Burnham's critique of the Coxian approach for allegedly failing to recognize that 'the state meets the interests of capital-in-general by enforcing the discipline of the market through the rule of law and the rule of money', is entirely misplaced. Cox explicitly recognizes this, as we have seen, as regards both the liberal state of the mid-nineteenth century and the hyperliberal state of the late twentieth century; but what he wants to know is *what disciplines the state to do this* – and what makes it do it again in another form in another historical conjuncture? The role of the state is not best conceived as something given by the capital relation once and for all; but neither is it best conceived in terms of a transmission belt from the global economy to the national economy.

The role of each state is still determined by struggles among social forces always located within each social formation. Even though these social forces are also, to recall Poulantzas, 'implicated by multiple tiers of dependence in an international division of labour and in the international concentration of capital' and although the struggles may be seen as 'more than ever developing in conjunctures determined on a world basis', the specific national form still prevails in these struggles due to uneven development and the specificity of each social formation. (Is it really to international finance that governments in London or Ottawa are accountable when they prepare their budgets? Or are they accountable to international finance because they are accountable to the City of London or to Bay Street?) It is precisely in light of domestic as well as international concerns about the continuing salience of popular struggles at the level of the nation state that we need to locate current attempts at constitutionalizing neoliberalism. The internationalization of the state in the 1990s appears to be taking the form, in the continuing absence of the ideological consensus or capacity to bring about a transnational regulation of capital markets, of formal interstate treaties designed to legally enforce upon future governments general adherence to the discipline of the capital market. This arises out of a growing fear on the part of both domestic and transnational capitalists, as the crisis continues, that *ideology cannot continue to substitute for legal obligation* in the internationalization of the state.

IV. FORCED TO BE FREE: THE CASE OF NORTH AMERICAN FREE TRADE

The North America Free Trade Agreement which came into effect on January 1, 1994 most certainly fits the bill of constitutionalizing neoliberalism. Far more important than the reduction in tariffs, as President Clinton himself repeatedly intoned in the fevered run-up to the congressional vote on NAFTA in November, were the guarantees it provided for American investment in Mexico. As Ian Robinson has put it in one the best analyses of the deal, international trade agreements like NAFTA not only 'prohibit discrimination between national and foreign owned corporations [but also] create new corporate private property rights, possessed by both national and foreign investors ... It will function as an economic constitution, setting the basic rules governing the private property rights that all governments must respect and the types of economic policies that all governments must eschew'.[35]

NAFTA's Investment chapter proscribes attempts by governments to establish performance requirements on foreign TNCs (excepting in the Auto sector) and defines investor rights which are protected under the agreement very broadly to include not only majority shareholders but minority interests, portfolio investment and real property held by any company incorporated in a NAFTA country regardless of the country of origin. The Monopolies and State Enterprises chapter requires public enterprises not only to operate 'solely in accordance with commercial considerations' and to refrain from using 'anticompetitive practices' such as 'the discriminatory provision of a monopoly good or service, cross-subsidization or predatory conduct' (all of which is the bread and butter of TNCs themselves), but also requires public enterprises to minimize or eliminate any nullification or impairment of benefits' that investors, broadly defined as above, might reasonably expect to receive under NAFTA. The Intellectual Property Rights chapter, which grants up to 20 year copyright protection to a vast array of trademarks, patents, semiconductor and industrial designs, trade secrets, satellite signals, etc., goes furthest of all to 'extend existing property rights by quasi-constitutionally protecting them against future democratic governments with the threat of trade sanctions ... even though the effect of these rights is to restrict rather than enhance the free flow of ideas across national boundaries ...'.[36]

Taken together, these various provisions have the effect of redesigning the Mexican and Canadian states' relations to capital to fit the mould made in the American metropole by establishing and guaranteeing state defence of 'new private property rights that go well beyond those recognised in Canadian and Mexican law, if not that of the United States'.[37] What is particularly important to stress, however, is that *this is not something imposed on the Canadian and Mexican states by American capital and state as external to the latter; rather it reflects the role adopted by the Mexican and Canadian states in representing the interests of their bourgeoisies and bureaucracies as these are already penetrated by American capital and administration.* As John H. Bryan, Jr., President of Sara Lee Corp. put it, the 'most important reason to vote for NAFTA is to lock in [Mexico's] reforms'.[38] This was all the more pressing insofar as there was a widespread awareness among North American elites (long before the Chiapas revolt on the day NAFTA came into effect) of popular discontent with the hyperliberal policies Mexico had adopted over the past decade, and a concern that any eventual opening up of Mexico's limited democracy might endanger the re-election of a PRI government. Shortly before the passage of the Agreement, an article in the Toronto *Globe and Mail's Report on Business* quoted Alvaro Cepeda Neri of Mexico City's *La Journada* as saying: 'The booty of privatisation has made multimillionaires of 13 families, while the rest of the population – about 80 million Mexicans – has been subjected to the same gradual impoverishment as though they had suffered through a war'.[39]

But the Mexican state was not only acting in terms of the interests of its domestic bourgeoisie, nor even just concerned with providing further security guarantees to American capital in Mexico. It was also, in Poulantzas's terms, 'taking responsibility for the interests of the dominant capital' by endorsing NAFTA as an exemplary 'staging post' for a renewed American imperialism throughout Latin America, as well as a model for a similar constitutionalizing of neoliberalism on a global scale. The Chairman of Saloman Inc. did not mince his words when he said that the defeat of NAFTA 'would be a slap in the face to all leaders in the Western Hemisphere who have chosen the capitalist road over government-controlled economies'.[40] Indeed, if, as the Foreign Affairs Committee Chairman in the House of Representatives, Lee Hamilton, put it, 'the question is U.S. leadership in the world', it is notable that the greatest threat to NAFTA came from the opposition within the United States itself. The side deals on the environment and labour undertaken by Clinton were designed to allow for the necessary compromises within the American social formation: this succeeded to the extent that this divided the environmental movement; if the labour side deal failed to do the same, it was because, not surprisingly, it did not go as far as the environmental side deal and did not allow Canadian or American groups affected by NAFTA to challenge the non-enforcement of Mexican labour laws.

As regards the economic woes of the heartland of the empire, it is clear that the direct impact of NAFTA can only be minuscule. As Lester Thurow pointed out, a worst case scenario would entail the loss of 480,000 American jobs over the next five years; the best case would see the addition of 170,000 jobs:

> The small stream of jobs produced or lost by NAFTA will not be noticed in a sea of 130 million American workers … With a gross domestic product (GDP) only 4 to 5 percent of the United States, Mexico will not be an economic locomotive for America … From 1973 to 1992 the per capita American GDP after correcting for inflation rose 27 percent. Yet over the same period average wages for the bottom 60 percent of male workers fell 20 percent in real terms … Earnings prospects are collapsing for the bottom two-thirds of the work force … After suffering two decades of falling real wages it is not surprising that Ross Perot can appeal to millions of Americans who lash out at the Mexicans in their frustration … America is now a First World economy with a large, growing Third World economy in its midst.[41]

The Canadian experience under NAFTA's predecessor, the U.S.-Canada Free Trade Agreement (FTA), which served as the first staging-post for hemispheric free trade and even for the Tokyo Round of GATT, certainly demonstrates that the constitutionalizing of neoliberalism exacerbates rather than contains the tendencies of the new global capitalism to generate successive social as well as economic crises. The most recent study of Canadian employment trends since the inauguration of the FTA not surprisingly begins with a quotation from a currently popular Leonard Cohen song: 'I have seen the future, brother; it is murder':

> Official unemployment rose from 7.5% to 11.3% from December 1988 to August 1993. The ranks of the jobless swelled by 576,000, bringing the total to 1.6 million. Adding those who dropped out of the work force, the unemployment level rose to 2 million, doubling from 7.5% to 14%. If we include involuntary part-time workers which amounts to hidden unemployment, the 'real' unemployment rate is currently at 20% of the work force ... Free trade supporters, though admitting that jobs have been lost in the low wage/low skill sectors of the economy, claim that the FTA is assisting the high-tech sectors, which comprise the emerging new economy of the 21st century, to grow and create high value added permanent jobs. The record of the first four years does not bear this out ... It is clear that despite positive signs in a few subsectors [only four – pharmaceuticals, computer services, accounting services and management consultant services – to a total of 28,000 new jobs], the job creation numbers are minuscule. There is no sign of an expanding knowledge economy (either in manufacturing or services) to absorb the 434,000 workers displaced from the old and new manufacturing/resource economy, the 111,000 construction workers and the 104,000 workers displaced from the private sector, old and new, service economy due to restructuring and recession. The public service sectors – education, health and social services, and government administration – absorbed 148,000 workers, but, given, the extreme financial stress that these sectors are currently experiencing and the disinclination to change policy direction, even partial absorption by public sectors is not likely to continue in the future. The future is indeed bleak.[42]

It was a mark of how deep the lines of American imperialism ran in Canada that every issue, from social policy to defence to Quebec's status in Canada was interpreted during the course of the 1988 federal election through the prism of the pros and cons of the FTA. All sides of the debate took the position that the free trade agreement was a historic departure, an epochal turning point for Canada. Either it would finally free Canadian business from the fetters of tariffs and regulation, expose it fully to the rigour of competition, lay open a vast continental market for exports and investment. Or it would mean the end of Canada as we have known it for 121 years, shifting our economic axis southward, imposing the rule of business, destroying the welfare state, undermining Canadian culture, subverting national sovereignty. Both views were misleading. The outcome of the free trade election marked not a new chapter, but rather the punctuation mark on a very long historical sentence of economic and cultural integration with American capitalism.

Canada's particular status as a rich dependency in the American Empire rested on the fact that like the United States, and partly due to its geographic and cultural proximity to the United States, the development of capitalism in Canada was predicated on a class structure which facilitated capitalist industrialization.[43] A high wage proletariat and a prosperous class of small farmers drew American capital to Canada not only in search of resources, and not at all in search of cheap labour, but to sell to a market distinctly similar to the American. The national tariff designed to integrate an east-west economy and protect Canadian industry from competition from the south (and the flight of Canadian workers to the south) had the paradoxical effect of inducing the first American TNCs to jump the tariff barrier and sell to Canada's (and sometimes through Canada to the British Empire's) mass market. They were welcomed with open arms by the state as good corporate citizens, and funded by Canada's substantial and powerful financial capitalists. Through the course of the first half of the twentieth century, Canada moved from formal colonial status as a privileged white Dominion in the old British empire to a formally independent, but in reality quite a dependent status in a new kind of imperialism amidst a degree of direct foreign (American) ownership unparalleled anywhere on the globe.

Yet this status was still a privileged one, and Canadians shared in the spoils that went with American hegemony in the post-war order. Any dependent country has a degree of autonomy: this is especially true of a rich one with a substantial industrial proletariat not as easily subjected to the same pressures as American workers to accede to imperial demands of unswerving loyalty in a Cold War and therefore more open to socialist political ideas and mobilization. Canada's welfare state, however poor a cousin to those in northern Europe, eventually came to surpass what the New Deal had inaugurated in the U.S. This gave Canada a badge of civility compared with American society. Some public corporations and regulatory bodies took on the additional role of protecting what residual autonomy Canadian economy and culture could retain. But in doing this, they did not so much challenge the fact of, as negotiate the scope of, Canada's dependency.

From this perspective, we can see that the free trade treaty of 1988 was designed not to inaugurate but rather to constitutionalize, formalize and extend Canada's dependence on the U.S. in a world now marked by economic instability amidst rampant financial speculation and strong trade rivalries. Far from wanting to prove their entrepreneurial virility by taking the risk of becoming globally competitive, Canadian domestic capital sought to minimize the risk that Americans, when in protectionist mood, might treat them, their exports and investments, as merely 'foreign'. In turn, the Canadian government promised to give up those weak devices it had heretofore retained as a means of negotiating the scope of our dependency. Margaret Atwood (like Cox, following Antonio Gramsci) used a very Canadian metaphor to describe what the Mulroney government had done in entering into the FTA: the beaver was noted in medieval bestiaries for biting off its own testicles when frightened and offering them to its pursuer.

Even so, the free trade agreement failed to remove all restraints on American protectionism. Many opponents of the FTA pointed this out, implying they might be content with the deal if it promised even fuller integration. But what most opponents were really objecting to was the whole dependent path of Canadian development: they wanted to avoid a punctuation mark being put at the end of our long sentence of dependence. To defeat the deal would be to leave open the possibility of a 'nevertheless' or a 'however' – which might yet be written at some point in the future. They were encouraged by the emergence of a visible strain of anti-Americanism, even of anti-imperialism. An indigenous cultural community had long been straining to define Canadian identity in the face of dependence. The labour movement, once a strong if subordinate sponsor of continentalism, had also experienced a shift towards Canadianization as the American labour movement proved ever weaker and more abject in the face of economic instability. And considerable domestic ecology, peace, and feminist movements had emerged, often with socialists in leadership positions, and with greater salience in relation to Canadian governments than such movements had in the United States.

The anti-free trade forces were encouraged as well by the fact that the Canadian electorate showed no great enthusiasm for the Reagan-Thatcher hyperliberal state model. Just as the 1980s began, Canadians had opted for a Liberal platform which promised to install a 'fair tax' system rather than supply-side economics, and to foster a Canadian capitalist class with distinctive national goals and ambitions through the National Energy Programme and a strengthened Foreign Investment Review Agency. It had indeed been in reaction to all this, as well as to cries for protectionism in the U.S. Congress, that the business community launched free trade and pursued it with such remarkable unanimity. When the NEP was established, Canadian capitalists, no less than American ones, were determined, not only to get rid of it at the first opportunity, but to disable permanently such interventions by the state. They feared that popular pressures were pushing the state to become, not the hand-maiden to business it had usually been, but a countervailing power to it. Not just fear was at play here, but also greed: some elements of Canadian business had become full players on a continental plane while others harboured ambitions that they too might reap substantial profits if Canada embraced its continental destiny. This demonstrated that the point had long passed when business in Canada was interested in 're-claiming' the Canadian economy.

The continuing political predominance of business, despite the mood of the electorate and the volubility of progressive forces, was seen when opposition from a unified capitalist class destroyed the tax reforms advanced in the 1981 Budget, and when the Liberal government responded to the recession of 1981-2 by removing the right to strike from some one million of the three million organized workers in Canada. Yet the ideological impact of hyperliberalism still remained limited. In 1984 even the Conservatives sensed that they could not get elected on a Thatcher-Reagan platform. Mulroney ran a typically Canadian brokerage campaign promising everything to everybody, and declaring the welfare state a sacred trust. This did not make it a sacred trust, of course, given the powerful business pressures to which the government was beholden. But it emboldened people to defend the welfare state as soon as the Tories tried to undo it.

The decision to go for the free trade agreement, under considerable pressure from the Business Council on National Issues (a powerful lobby which grouped together the most powerful domestic and American corporations), thus took on a double purpose: to make permanent the dominance of business by formalizing continental integration in the face of American protectionism and Canadian economic nationalism; and to introduce Reaganomics by the back door of the free market ethos and provisions of the free trade deal. A popular coalition, funded by the labour movement and led by the leadership of the above-mentioned 'new social movements', marshalled against the FTA with remarkable fervour and determination to force the free trade election of 1988. But it must be admitted that this coalition, and much less the opposition parties, never really made clear what their alternative really was. The experience with the 1980-84 Liberal Government showed that a policy for more economic independence and social justice could not rely on the cooperation of business. Yet the anti-free trade coalition were afraid to spell out the conclusion that the alternative had to involve fundamental challenges to capital's power and radically democratizing the state. They were afraid to do so because the Canadian people had been so little prepared for such a departure, with the NDP's (Canada's social democratic party) failure in this respect particularly glaring.

Alongside a trenchant critique of the details and implications of the FTA, the anti-free trade coalition took a different tack. And it proved a shrewd one. They chose to mythologize the Canadian state as if it had always been a repository of Canadian independence and social justice. This was myth indeed. But nationalisms are built on myths, and this one became uncontested in the election with remarkable ideological consequences. The small badge of civility which a welfare state lends to Canadian social life in comparison with the American laid the basis for Canadian national identity to be defined in the 1988 election in almost Scandinavian terms, where pride in the welfare state was rather more justified. In this context, the outcome of the free trade election was, despite the narrow victory by the Tories, and the subsequent introduction of the FTA, rather ambiguous. Certainly, the victory of the business forces confirmed the historical trend toward continental integration. An exclamation mark had been added to

Canada's historical sentence of dependence.

Paradoxically, the election also confirmed the absence of an ideological man-date to carry through Reaganomics in Canada. The Tories and the business community accepted the anti-free trade forces definition of patriotism as at least involving a defence of the welfare state. The freedom to trade and invest by business was bought at the ideological cost of pledging allegiance to medicare and other social programmes. In so far as the popular coalition forged during the campaign against free trade set the terms of the debate, and forced their oppo-nents to adopt a defence of the welfare state as a central element in the definition of 'Canadianism', they provided a strong ideological basis for defensive struggles. The seeds of the destruction of the Conservative Party, reduced in the subse-quent 1993 election to only two seats in the House of Commons, were sown amidst the ambiguity of their 1988 victory on free trade. The challenge for the Left remained to enlarge the framework of struggle. A defence of the welfare state promises only stalemate so long as the power and mobility of capital remains untouched. In the context of Canada's reinforced dependency amidst global eco-nomic instability and financial speculation, a clear alternative to free trade and unbridled capitalist competition still remains to be articulated.

V. A PROGRESSIVE COMPETITIVE ALTERNATIVE?

There are those who ... believe that we can take on the challenge of competitive-ness *and* retain our socialist values; indeed they believe that competitiveness will create the very economic success essential to sustaining social programs. They are mistaken. In the first place they are wrong because, in the particular case of Canada, there is no capitalist class with the interest or capacity to develop a strong industrial base ... But they are more than just mistaken. The framework for competitiveness they invite us to accept is ultimately dangerous ... Once it is accepted, its hidden aspects ... such as attacks on social programs – quickly reassert themselves. Once we decide to play on the terrain of competitiveness, we cannot then step back without paying a serious price. Having legitimated the importance of being competitive (when we should have been mobilising to defend our social values), we would be extremely vulnerable to the determined attacks that will inevitably come in the name of 'global realities' ... The competitive model ultimately asks how the *corporate sector* can be strengthened. Our perspective asserts that it is the very strength of that sector that limits our freedom and belittles the meaning of 'community'.
– Gindin and Robertson, Canadian Auto Workers (CAW)[44]

The global recession of the 1990s is testimony to the economic failure of glo-bal hyperliberalism. Far from state policies having no effect, global trade com-petition among states has ushered in 'an unstable vicious circle of "competitive austerity"' whereby the cumulative effect of each state's policies is immense in the misery it causes. As Greg Albo summarizes this: 'each country reduces do-mestic demand and adopts an export-oriented strategy of dumping its surplus production, for which there are fewer consumers in its national economy given the decrease in workers' living standards and productivity gains all going to the capitalists, in the world market. This has created a global demand crisis and the growth of surplus capacity across the business cycle'.[45] Unfortunately, however, the programme for a more progressive form of competitiveness which has been advanced by most mainstream parties of the centre-left does not constitute much of an alternative. For a considerable period through the 1970s and well into the mid-1980s, a large portion of the Left refused to acknowledge that the crisis of the Keynesian/welfare state was a structural one, pertaining to the very nature of capitalism and the contradictions it generates in our time. Their response to the crisis, clearly visible in the Canadian free trade debate, was to point to relatively low unemployment levels in Sweden as evidence of the continuing viability of tripartite corporatism in sustaining the keynesian/welfare state.[46] This involved, however, ignoring or downplaying the very contradictions and conflicts that were undermining even the Swedish model, and eventually this naive stance was displaced by an attempt to emulate those countries which were most successful in the export-led competitive race. But rather than allow bourgeois economists calling the tune with their neo-liberal logic of deregulation, free markets, privatization and austerity to dictate the terms of the race, a 'progressive competitiveness' strategy is advanced by intellectuals on the Left (from social democratic to left-liberal to a good many erstwhile marxists) whereby labour and the state are urged to take the initiative and seize the hand of business in making the running towards competitive success.

At the core of the strategy, still largely inspired by a different facet of Swedish corporatism, is to support and guide both workers and capitalists towards high-tech/high-value-added/high wage production. The key to this is public policy promoting the widespread training of a highly skilled, highly flexible and highly motivated labour force, and encouraging enterprises to take full advantage of recent technological developments in microelectronics, to the end of producing high quality commodities at high productivity levels through flexible production methods. Equally founded on an acceptance of the irreversibility of globalization, but convinced that its connection with hyperliberalism is only a matter of the ideological colouration of politicians too closely attached to bourgeois economists, this approach still wants to give strategic priority to the state. Once shorn of an ideology of free markets as the premise of state policy in the process of globalization, the 'progressive competitiveness' strategy expects the state to be able to sustain a substantial social wage if it explicitly connects welfare and education to the public promotion of flexible production and technological innovation in those particular sectors which can 'win' in a global export-led competitive race. Relative prosperity (clearly based on an extension of the advantages of relative over absolute surplus-value extraction) would fall to those states which can guide capital and labour to adopt this 'smart' competitiveness strategy. With all its emphasis on training, this is indeed a strategy which is precisely about *learning* how to run twice as fast amidst globalization.

That such a strategy is both chimerical and dangerous is, in fact, already demonstrated by the experience in North America both by the Clinton Democratic administration and the Ontario NDP government elected in 1990. It presents a programme of vast economic readjustment for both labour and capital, with blithe disregard for how, in the interim, the logic of competitive austerity could be avoided; it presumes that mass unemployment is primarily a problem of skills adjustment to technological change rather than one aspect of a crisis of overproduction; it fosters an illusion of a rate of employment growth in high tech sectors sufficient to offset the rate of unemployment growth in other sectors; it either even more unrealistically assumes a rate of growth of world markets massive enough to accommodate all those adopting this strategy, or it blithely ignores the issues associated with exporting unemployment to those who don't succeed at this strategy under conditions of limited demand (and with the attendant consequence this would have for sustaining demand); it ignores the reality that capital can also adapt leading technologies in low wage economies, and the competitive pressures on capital in this context to push down wages even in high tech sectors and limit the costs to it of the social wage and adjustment policies so central to the whole strategy's progressive logic in the first place. It is hardly surprising that Albo in this context comes to the conclusion that even 'the progressive competitiveness strategy will be forced to accept, as most social democratic parties have been willing to do, the same "competitive austerity" as neo-liberalism ... as a cold necessity of present economic conditions'.[47]

Robert Cox, who terms this strategy 'state capitalist', and sees it as the only possible medium-term alternative to the hyperliberal form of state, makes it quite clear that it 'is, in effect, grounded in an acceptance of the world market as the ultimate determinant of development':

> The state capitalist form involves a dualism between, on the one hand, a competitively efficient world-market-oriented sector and, on the other, a protected welfare sector. The success of the former must provide resources for the latter; the sense of solidarity implicit in the latter would provide the drive and legitimacy for the former ... In its most radical form, state capitalism beckons toward an internal socialism sustained by capitalist success in world-market competition. This would be a socialism dependent on capitalist development, i.e. on success in the production of exchange values. But, so its proponents argue, it would be less vulnerable to external destabilization than attempts at socialist self-reliance were in weak countries ...[48]

Cox sees this option ('with or without its socialist colouration') as largely limited to late industrializing countries (such as France, Japan, Germany, Brazil, South Korea) with strong institutional and ideological traditions of 'close coordination between the state and private capital in the pursuit of common goals'. He is well aware that this type of state capitalism, while incorporating that portion of the working class attached to the world-market-oriented sector or employed in the welfare services sector, would nevertheless exclude many people ('disproportionately the young, women, immigrant or minority groups, and the unemployed') who would remain in a passive relationship to the welfare services and without influence in policy making. Amidst anomic explosions of violence from these groups, Cox expects that the state capitalist alternative's 'historic bloc would be thin' and that this might entail the kind of repression and insulation from democratic pressures which would particularly make illusory the prospects the state capitalist strategy holds out for an 'internal socialism'. Still, as of 1992, Cox took the position that state capitalist strategies in Japan and Europe constituted 'the only possible counterweights to total globalization at the level of states'. He held out particular hope that the European Community, where the 'unresolved issue over the social charter indicates a stalemate in the conflict over the future nature of the nation state and of the regional authority' might yet bring to the fore 'a capitalism more rooted in social policy and more balanced development', one reflecting the continuing influence of social democratic and older conservative traditions. Given the limited medium-term options of those on the Left who are looking for an alternative that would go beyond choosing between rival forms of capitalism, Cox urges them to look positively upon 'the ideological space that is opened by this confrontation of hyper-liberalism and state capitalist or corporatist forms of development'.[49]

Yet what is the evidence of such a confrontation? Cox exhibits here an unfortunate tendency to turn juxtaposed ideal-types, constructed for the purposes of analytic clarity, into real-world confrontations for which there is all too little evidence. The institutional and ideological structures that Cox points to as the basis for a state capitalist 'progressive competitiveness' alternative to hyperliberal globalization are in fact being subsumed as subsidiary sponsors of globalization in a manner quite analogous to the way Cox saw tripartite institutions of national economic planning as having become subsidiary elements in adjusting domestic economies to the world economy in the post-war order.

Both in Europe and in North America, ministries of labour (and the tripartite forums and agencies they sponsor) as well as ministries of welfare and education, are being restructured to conform with the principles of global competitiveness, but their capacity to retain their links to the social forces they represent in the state rests on their ability to tailor this reconstruction along the lines of 'progressive competitiveness' principles. In this way, key social groups that would otherwise become dangerously marginalized as a result of the state's sponsorship of global competitiveness may become attached to it by the appeal a progressive competitiveness strategy makes, especially through the ideology and practice of training, to incorporating working people who are unemployed and on welfare (or who soon might be) as well as the leaders of the unions, social agencies and other organizations who speak for them. Insofar as they are successful in this, moreover, ministries of welfare, education, labour, regional development, etc., may prevent their further loss of status in the hierarchy of state apparatuses and even recapture some of their previously foregone status. Insofar as it undertakes no greater challenge to the structure of the state or to the logic of global competitiveness than that of insisting that more, rather than less, state economic orchestration can be a more effective, and at the same time a more humane, handmaiden to competition, the 'progressive competitiveness' strategy ends up being not an alternative to, but a subsidiary element in, the process of neo-liberal capitalist restructuring and globalization.

The 'stalemate' over the European Social Charter sustains this interpretation. In North America, the most-oft cited guarantee that the progressive competitiveness strategy will not coalesce with the logic of competitive austerity is the European Community's Social Charter. It is pointed to as a model for other international agreements which would constitutionalize a high level of labour rights, social standards and corporate codes of conduct. On this basis, Robinson argues: 'If globalization can mean more than one thing … then the irreversibility of globalization no longer necessarily leads to neo-conservative economic and social policy prescriptions. In this light, national competitiveness, too, can mean more than one thing, depending upon whether it is achieved by cutting labour and environmental costs to TNCs, or promoting technological innovation and reducing the social, political, and environmental externalities associated with largely unregulated global market competition'.[50] This approach almost always involves vastly inflating the salience and significance of the European Social Charter, or, where its weakness is acknowledged (as Robinson does) fails to inquire whether the reason 'the most powerful labour movements in the world have made only very limited progress towards an adequate EC social dimension' is because of its incompatibility with even the 'progressive competitiveness' strategy of global competitiveness. The trenchant critique made by Robinson of NAFTA's side deals as a cosmetic means of buying off domestic opposition is not apparently seen by him, and so many others, as entailing a deeper lesson regarding such incompatibility.

Alain Lipietz has recently provided a chilling account of how the moderate EEC social democrats 'set up a Europe of traders and capital', hoping that a social dimension would follow, but failing to understand that they had already 'thrown away their trump cards by signing the Single Act of 1985':

> A single market for capital and goods without common fiscal, social and ecological policies could not fail to set off a downward competition between member states, each needing to bring its trade into balance. To deal with the threat of 'social dumping', Jacques Delors counted on a push *after the event* by unions in peripheral and social democratic countries to impose common statutory or contractual bases throughout the community. This has not happened, despite the (half-hearted)

protestations of the European parliament ... attempts to harmonise VAT failed ... [and] lack of harmonization on capital taxation is much more serious ... Even more serious was the surrender over social Europe. In September 1989, The European Commission proposed an insipid Social Charter ... In December 1991, at Maastricht ... legislative power in Europe was handed over to coordination by national governments; a state apparatus on auto-pilot. Social Europe was once more sacrificed, and reduced to a 'zero-Charter', with Britain opting out ... In essence, as it is presently emerging, Europe will be unified only for the sake of capital, to allow it to escape from state control; that is, from the tax authorities and from social legislation.[51]

It is, of course, not really an escape from state control. Lipietz's account would make no sense if it were. The governments of Europe are not trying to assert a control over capital at the nation state level while at the same time trying to foreswear control at the regional level. The states, including the social democratic-led ones, as Lipietz avers, are the political authors of the Europe of traders and capitalists. Of course, they reflect capital's domination in each social formation in doing so, but it must also be said that the notion that this capital is ready to sustain, as the basis of regional trade rivalries, a rival state capitalist form 'rooted in social policy and territorially balanced development' is belied by all the facts before us. Indeed, Cox may have been closer to the mark when he suggested in 1987 that the decline of American hegemony and the competitive pressures in the world system were acting on all states in such a way as to encourage an 'emulative uniformity'.[52] But his expectation at that time that this might involve common 'adoption of similar forms of state-capitalist development geared to an offensive strategy in world markets and sustained by corporatist organization of society and economy' only rings true if we see state capitalism, as we have suggested, not as an alternative to hyperliberalism but rather a subsidiary element sustaining competitive austerity, even in Europe. As Albo notes: 'it is not the Anglo-American countries who are converting to the Swedish or German models but Germany and Sweden who are integrating the "Anglo-American model" ...'.[53]

Even if American hegemony in international institutions has declined somewhat the continued direct imbrication of American capital in Europe as a powerful social force with which the European bourgeoisies remain interpenetrated still induces an 'emulative uniformity'. Poulantzas may have been wrong in his estimation in 1974 that each of the European bourgeoisies were too enmeshed in a structure of dependence on American capitalists to allow for a major extension of intra-regional cooperation in Europe. But he was not wrong in insisting that American capital must not be seen as standing outside Europe rather than a strong presence within it. Indeed, part of the reason for the failure of a 'Social Europe' has also to do with the mobilization of American firms in Europe against it from the early 1980s on.[54] The multidimensional spread of direct foreign investment, with mutual interpenetration among European, Japanese and American capitals reinforces this tendency for emulative uniformity.[55]

VI. CONCLUSIONS: 'IT AIN'T OVER 'TIL ITS OVER'[56]

It would indeed appear that there is no way of honestly posing an alternative to neo-liberal globalization that avoids the central issue of the political source of capitalist power, globally and locally: the state's guarantee of control of the major means of production, distribution, communication and exchange by private, inherently undemocratic banks and corporations. It is inconceivable that there can be any exit from today's crisis without a planned reorientation and redistribution of resources and production on a massive scale. Yet how can this even be conceived as feasible, let alone made a basis for political mobilization?

This essay has suggested that those who want to install a 'transnational democracy' in the wake of the nation state allegedly having been by-passed by globalization simply misunderstand what the internationalization of the state really is all about. Not only is the world still very much composed of states, but insofar as there is any effective democracy at all in relation to the power of capitalists and bureaucrats, it is still embedded in political structures which are national or subnational in scope. Those who advance the nebulous case for an 'international civil society' to match the 'nebuleuse' that is global capitalist governance usually fail to appreciate that capitalism has not escaped the state but rather that the state has, as always, been a fundamental constitutive element in the very process of extension of capitalism in our time.

Sol Picciotto, who himself wants to give strategic priority to 'international popular organisation' as the best way forward, is nevertheless careful to warn against 'naive illusions that social power exists quite independently of the state', and calls for 'more sophisticated analyses of the contradictions of the state and the ways they can be exploited to build the strength of popular movements, while remaining aware that the national state is only a part of the overall structure of power in a global capitalist society'.[57] The international constitutionalization of neoliberalism has taken place through the agency of states, and there is no prospect whatsoever of getting to a *somewhere else*, inspired by a vision of an egalitarian, democratic and cooperative world order beyond global competitiveness, that does not entail a fundamental struggle with domestic as well as global capitalists over the transformation of the state. Indeed, the contemporary era of the globalization of capital may have finally rendered the distinction between national and foreign capital more or less irrelevant as a strategic marker for the Left. The two centuries-old search for a cross-class 'producer' alliance between labour and national capital as an alternative to class struggle has taken shape in recent years in the form of the progressive competitiveness strategy, but its weaknesses have been very quickly revealed in the context of the globalization of capital.

It is necessary to try to reorient strategic discussions on the Left towards the transformation of the state rather than towards transcending the state or trying to fashion a progressive competitive state. At the most general level this means envisaging a state whose functions are not tied to guaranteeing the economic *res publica* for capitalism. We have seen how the internationalization of the state entails a turning of the material and ideological capacities of states to more immediate and direct use, in terms of both intranational and international dimensions, to global capital. The first requirement of strategic clarification on the Left must be the recognition that it must seek the transformation of the material and ideological capacities of states so that they can serve to realize popular, egalitarian and democratic goals and purposes. This does *not* mean attempting to take the state as it is presently organized and structured and trying to impose controls over capital with these inappropriate instruments. Nor does it mean trying to coordinate such controls internationally while resting on the same state structures. The point must be to restructure the hierarchy of state apparatuses and reorganize their *modus operandi* so as to develop radically different material and ideological capacities.

'One of the principal tasks of the capitalist state', David Harvey notes, 'is to locate power in the spaces which the bourgeoisie controls, and disempower those spaces which the oppositional movements have the greatest potential to command'.[58] The Left must take this lesson out of the book of capital to the end of relocating power to the benefit of progressive social forces. The same might be said about the important role the state can play in the distribution of time as an aspect of power. Radical proposals coming forward on the Left today for a statutory reduction in the working day to as little as four hours are not only directed at coping with the appalling maldistribution of employment in contemporary capitalism, but, as Mandel and Gorz both stress, are designed to establish the conditions for the extension and deepening of democracy by providing the time for extensive involvement in community and workplace decision making.[59]

To emphasize the continuing importance of struggles to transform the state does not mean that territorial boundaries within which claims to state sovereignty are embedded ought to be seen as immutable. One of the important insights of Poulantzas was to point to the regional disarticulations that resulted from the extended reproduction of international capital within the framework of existing nation states. The integration of national with international capital upsets the old bases for national capital's unity; and at the same time regional discontents with state policies which are increasingly articulated with the needs of the global economy have provided fertile ground for a resurgence of old nationalisms with a separatist purpose. Right-wing nationalisms, and the parochialisms and intolerances they both reflect and engender, must be combated on every front. But it is not always necessary for the Left to oppose the break-up of an existing state, just as it is not wise to dismiss out of hand attempts at international rearticulation of sovereignties through the creation of regional federations. The question is only whether the locus of power is thereby shifted to those spaces wherein democratic and inclusive movements which are oppositional to capital can expand their space and powers through a reorganization of sovereignties.

For instance, while left-internationalists usually shake their heads in dismay at the apparent stupidity of Quebec leaving the Canadian federation at the very moment when France should be joining a federal Europe, it is by no means necessarily the case that the existing Canadian federal state lays a firmer foundation for democratic challenges to capital than would close and amicable cooperation between an independent Quebec and a restructured Canadian state. Indeed more might be expected from two nation states each of whose *raison d'état* was expressly more egalitarian and democratic in purpose rather than binational and territorial (*Ad Mare Usque Ad Mare*, it has often been pointed out on the Canadian Left, does not quite match *Liberty, Equality and Fraternity* as an expression of *raison d'état*.) Nor should it be necessarily thought that a federal Europe must be one that necessarily extends democratic powers rather than disperses them more thinly in relation to a greater centralization of state powers oriented to fulfilling capital's *res publica* on a continental terrain. Moreover, a federal state composed of the *existing* states of Europe is one that continues to rest on the *modus operandi* of these states. As every Canadian knows, capitalist forces are as capable of playing off the units of a federation against one another and against the centre, as they are of doing so with sovereign nation states; indeed the process may be more easily obscured behind an interminable debate over the division of constitutional powers.

Alain Lipietz, while taking as 'a starting point that the struggles and social compromises are still settled at the level of the old-established nations of Europe', would like to see social and political unification as quickly as possible insofar as this would be democratically structured so as to overcome the terrible condition of competitive austerity. But he admits that while it 'is better to have a Europe which is progressive (in the alternative sense of the word) than a France, a Sweden, etc, which are progressive in isolation … the present dilemma does not lie here. We are asked to choose between a Europe of *possibly* alternative states, and a united Europe which is liberal-productivist. My response is that if this is the choice, the first solution is better …'. He admits that in the short term it is unrealistic to expect a united Europe to be based on anything other than 'liberal-productivism'. But it is no less unrealistic to expect that this will change in the future without a prior change in the configuration of social forces and restructuring of state apparatuses in the member countries.[60]

A 'possibly alternative state' to those sponsoring globalization amidst competitive austerity today would have to be based on a shift towards a more inwardly oriented economy rather than one driven by external trade considerations. This in turn would have to mean greater emphasis being placed on a radical redistribution of productive resources, income and working time than on conventional economic growth. This could only be democratically grounded, as Albo puts it, insofar as 'production and services [were] more *centred* on local and national needs where the most legitimate democratic collectivities reside'. Democratically elected economic planning bodies at the 'micro-regional' level, invested with the statutory responsibility for engineering a return to full employment in their communities and funded through direct access to a portion of the surplus that presently is the prerogative of the private financial system to allocate, should be the first priority in a programme for an alternative state.

This alternative could not be realized without at least some trade controls and certainly not without quite extensive controls over the flow of capital. (Indeed, it is improbable that such capital controls can be realized without bringing the financial system within the public domain and radically reorganizing it in terms of both its structure and function. This used to be known, when the Left was still innocent about its terminology, as the 'nationalization' of the banks). Of course, this would necessarily require interstate cooperation to install managed trade (rather than autarky) and to make capital controls effective. Have we then gone through this exercise only to come full circle – right back to the internationalization of the state? Certainly not. International agreements and treaties between states will most certainly be required, but they will have the opposite purpose to the constitutionalizing of neoliberalism: they will be explicitly designed to permit states to effect democratic control over capital within their domain and to facilitate the realization of alternative economic strategies.

The feasibility of this alternative scenario rests entirely on conditions that still remain to be established. It is all too easy to predict the immense pressure and exertion of naked power that would emanate from international capital and dominant states to a country that was even near the point of embarking on such a strategic alternative; all too easy (and, of course, intentionally or unintentionally demobilizing) because what it ignores are the prior material and political conditions that would bring the possibility of change onto the historical agenda. Some of these are material in the economic-technical sense of the term. Thus, even the technical feasibility of short-term capital controls is an open question today. Yet the instability of the world financial system is such that we are likely to see the 'discovery' of means of control and regulation, whether before or after an international financial collapse. But it is, above all, the political conditions that need to be created. The impact of domestic and external resistance is unpredictable in abstraction from the character, strength and effectiveness of the social forces that will mobilize within states and put the alternative on the agenda. Cox is extremely insightful on this when he insists at the end of *Production, Power and World Order* that once 'a historical movement gets underway, it is shaped by the material possibilities of the society in which it arises and by resistance to its course as much as by the … goals of its supporters'. Yet this is why, he insists, that 'critical awareness of the potentiality for change … concentrates on the possibilities of launching a social movement rather than on what that movement might achieve

… In the minds of those who opt for change, the solution will most likely be seen as lying not in the enactment of a specific policy program as in the building of new means of collective action informed by a new understanding of society and polity.'[61]

This will happen within states or it will not happen at all, but it will not happen in one state alone while the rest of the world goes on running with the bourgeoisie around the globe. Alternatives arise within international political time: the movement-building struggles arise in conjunctures which are, as Poulantzas understood, more than ever determined on a world basis. Movements in one country have always been informed and inspired by movements abroad; all the more so will this prove to be the case as opposition builds to the evils globalization is visiting on peoples right around the globe, increasingly also including the developed capitalist countries. There is no need to conjure up out of this an 'international civil society' to install a 'transnational democracy'. Rather we are likely to witness a series of movements arising that will be exemplary for one another, even though national specificities will continue to prevail. It is to be hoped, of course, that these movements will as far as possible be solidaristic with one another, even though international solidarity movements cannot be taken for alternatives, rather than as critical supplements, to the struggles that must take place on the terrain of each state.

There is a stifling tendency on the Left today to draw facile lessons from previous failures of attempts to escape from the logic of globalization. The limits faced by the Alternative Economic Strategy in Britain in the mid-1970s and the French Socialist programme at the beginning of the 1980s are particular favourites employed to 'prove' that capital has the unchallengeable power to escape the state. But was there even the political will in these cases, let alone the movement or the material conditions, to try to escape the control of capital? (François Mitterand had learned to 'speak socialist', in the immortally cynical words of Gaston Defferre, but what failed in 1981–82 was primarily an attempt at a Keynesian reflation at a very inopportune moment rather than the far more radical assault on capitalism that had been envisaged in the 'Programme Commune'. And while U.S. Secretary of State William Rodgers harboured 'cosmic' fears in 1976 that Tony Benn might precipitate a policy decision by Britain to turn its back on the IMF which might in turn lead to the whole liberal financial system falling apart, Rodgers quickly found he could count on the support of the rest of the Labour Cabinet let alone the Treasury and the Bank of England and the MI5.[62])

It is time the Left stopped reading its own faulty memory of such past moments into all potential futures. It would seem that the last word, like the first, belongs to Lewis Carroll's *Through the Looking Glass*:

'That's the effect of living backwards', the Queen said kindly;
'it always makes one a little giddy at first —'

'Living backwards!' Alice repeated in great astonishment.'
I never heard of such a thing!'

'—but there's one great advantage in it, that one's
memory works both ways.'

'I'm sure *mine* only works one way,' Alice remarked.
'I can't remember things before they happen.'

'It's a poor sort of memory that only works backwards,'
the Queen remarked.

NOTES

1 'Manifesto of the Communist Party', in Karl Marx, *The Revolutions of 1848: Political Writings, Volume I*, D. Fernbach, ed., London 1974, p. 70.

2 Robert Cox, 'Global Perestroika', in R. Miliband and L. Panitch eds., *New World Order? The Socialist Register 1992*, p. 27.

3 David Gordon, 'The Global Economy: New Edifice or Crumbling Foundations?', *New Left Review* 168, March/April, 1988.

4 Robert Cox, *Production, Power and World Order*, New York, 1987, pp. 253, 258.

5 David Held, 'Democracy: From City-states to a Cosmopolitan Order?', *Political Studies*, XL, Special Issue, 1992, pp. 32-4.

6 Immanuel Wallerstein, *The politics of the world-economy*, Cambridge, 1984, pp. 10-11.

7 Perry Anderson, *A Zone of Engagement*, London 1992, pp. 366-7.

8 Stephen Gill, 'The Emerging World Order and European Change', in Miliband and Panitch, eds., *New World Order?* London 1992.

9 Philip Corrigan and Derek Sayer, *The Great Arch: English State Formation as Cultural Revolution*, Oxford 1985, p.105.

10 Alan Wolfe, *The Limits of Legitimacy*, New York 1977, p. 22.

11 Robin Murray, 'The Internationalization of Capital and the Nation State', *New Left Review* 67, May/June 1971, pp. 84-108.

12 Ibid., p. 102, citing *Monthly Review* of November 1969, p. 12.

13 Ibid., p.109.

14 Nicos Poulantzas, *Classes in Contemporary Capitalism*, London 1974, pp.70-88.

15 Ibid., p. 73.

16 Ibid.

17 Ibid., p. 78.

18 Cox, *Production, Power and World Order*, op.cit., (henceforth *PPWO*), pp. 132-3.

19 Peter Burnham, 'Neo-Gramscian hegemony and the international order', *Capital and Class* 45, Autumn, 1991, p. 90.

20 *PPWO*, pp. 105-6.

21 *PPWO*, p. 254.

22 *PPWO*, pp. 256-9.

23 *PPWO*, pp. 254-5.

24 *PPWO*, p. 189.

25 *PPWO*, pp. 214, 220-1, 228, 266, 281.

26 *PPWO*, pp. 259, 282-3.

27 *PPWO*, p. 289.

28 Cox, 'Global Perestroika', *op. cit.*, pp. 30-1.

29 See *PPWO*, p. 266 and p. 283.

30 See *PPWO*, p. 259, for an earlier use of this term.

31 *PPWO*, pp. 300-3.

32 *PPWO*, p. 259, emphasis added.

33 To be sure, Cox sees even this system to some extent in ideological and institutional terms: 'The capital markets in question cannot realistically be thought of as nonpolitical. They are not cast in the classical model of an infinity of buyers and sellers of money; rather they are composed of a limited number of oligopolists whose consensus can be ascertained by a few telephone calls and whose individual judgements are based on a balancing of financial risk-taking and prudence, of political pressures and personal prejudices.' *PPWO*, p. 301.

34 Peter Burnham, 'Neo-Gramscian hegemony and the international order', *Op. cit.*, pp. 77-8.

35 Ian Robinson, *North American Free Trade As If Democracy Mattered*, Canadian Centre for Policy Alternatives, Ottawa, 1993. Two other excellent analyses are: Christian Deblock and Michele Rioux, 'NAFTA: The Dangers of Regionalism', *Studies in Political Economy* 41, Summer 1993, pp. 7-44; and Ricardo Grinspun and Robert Kreklewich, 'Consolidating Neoliberal Reforms: "Free Trade" as a Consolidating Framework', forthcoming in *Studies in Political Economy* 43, Spring 1994.

36 Ibid., p. 2.

37 Ibid., p. 20.

38 *Business Week*, November 22, 1993, p. 34.

39 *The Globe and Mail Report On Business*, Toronto, November 1, 1993.

40 *Business Week*, November 22, 1993, p. 35.

41 Lester Thurow, 'An American Common Market', *The Guardian Weekly / The Washington Post*, November 21, 1993.

42 Bruce Campbell (with Andrew Jackson), *'Free Trade': Destroyer of Jobs. An Examination of Canadian Jobs Loss Under the FTA and NAFTA*, Canadian Centre for Policy Alternatives, Ottawa 1993, pp. 1-6.

43 See my 'Dependency and Class in Canadian Political Economy', *Studies in Political Economy* 6, Autumn 1981.

44 Sam Gindin and David Robertson, 'Alternatives to Competitiveness', in D. Drache, ed., *Getting on Track: Social Democratic Strategies for Ontario*, Montreal, 1992, pp. 32-3, 39.

45 Greg Albo, '"Competitive Austerity" and the Impasse of Capitalist Employment Policy', *The Socialist Register 1994*.

46 See the critique of this position in my *Working Class Politics in Crisis*, London 1986, esp. chs. 4-6; and in my 'The Tripartite Experience', in K. Banting, ed., *The State and*

Economic Interests, Toronto 1986.

47 Albo, *op. cit.*

48 Cox, *PPWO*, pp. 292-4.

49 See Cox, 'Global Perestroika', *op. cit.*, esp. pp. 31 and 41; and *PPWO*, esp. pp. 292 and 297-8.

50 Robinson, *op. cit.*, p. 44.

51 Alain Lipietz, *Towards a New Economic Order*, Oxford 1992, pp. 156-9.

52 Cox, *PPWO*, pp. 298-9.

53 Albo, *op. cit.*

54 See John Lambert, 'Europe: The Nation-State Dies Hard', *Capital and Class*, 43, Spring 1991, esp. p.16. For a somewhat different appreciation of Poulantzas's contribution to that offered here, see Sam Pooley, 'The State Rules, O.K.? The Continuing Political Economy of Nation States', in the same volume.

55 See Cox, *PPWO*, p. 360; and Harry Magdoff, 'Globalization – To What End?', *The Socialist Register 1992*, pp. 44-75.

56 With apologies to Yogi Berra.

57 Sol Picciotto, 'The Internationalisation of the State', *Capital and Class* 43, Spring 1991 p. 60.

58 David Harvey, *The Condition of Postmodernity*, Oxford 1989, p. 237.

59 Ernest Mandel, *Power and Money*, London 1992, esp. p. 202; and Andre Gorz, *Critique of Economic Reason*, London 1989, p. 159.

60 Lipietz, *op. cit.*, p. 135.

61 Cox, *PPWO*, pp. 394-5.

62 See Daniel Singer, *Is Socialism Doomed?*, Oxford 1988; Leo Panitch, 'Socialist Renewal and the Problem of the Labour Party', *The Socialist Register 1988*; and Panitch and Miliband, 'The New World Order and the Socialist Agenda', *The Socialist Register 1992* (esp. fn. 24)

CAPITALISM AND THE NATION STATE IN THE DOG DAYS OF THE TWENTIETH CENTURY

Manfred Bienefeld

INTRODUCTION

With global capitalism triumphant, the idea that humanity must ultimately choose between socialism or barbarism would seem preposterous if working people's historic gains were not being reversed, if political extremism was not flourishing, if economic and social polarization were not growing, if nations and societies were not disintegrating, if ethnic, religious and imperialist wars were not proliferating and if lean and mean ideologies were not diluting compassion and destroying the meaning of responsible citizenship. As it is, it is not so surprising that some people claim to be able to hear the faint hoofbeats of barbarism in the stillness of the early dawn.

The hegemonic ideology counters such hysteria by endlessly repeating its dog-eared promises of progress and efficiency, but careful observers note that, as they lose credibility, these promises are being steadily diluted. Gone is the dream of the leisure society, and that of full employment, that of a regular, secure job and that of a compassionate society. Is there an end to this? And where does barbarism begin?

A new realism is changing the terms of our debates. The ghost of Malthus stalks the land declaring human progress a delusion, asserting the iron law of poverty, defining the crisis of the developing world as a problem of 'surplus population'. The ghost of Hitler beckons with dreams of pure ethnic or religious states, promising

This essay was first published in *Between Globalism and Nationalism, The Socialist Register 1994* desperate people some ground on which to make a stand against the faceless forces destroying their lives. And in the belly of the beast, the ghost of Reagan poisons the political process with its insidious appeals to a crass individualism that teaches people to hate taxes and politics and to put their trust in personal wealth, however obtained.

And now some influential mainstream voices claim to have heard the hoofbeats at close range and have declared barbarism imminent and inevitable, allegedly driven by 'exogenous' factors, like population growth, resource scarcity (sic) and 'differences among civilizations'.[1] Taking the social and political disintegration that attends globalization as a given, they announce barbarism's arrival and tell people they must accept it. Once again, it seems that 'there is no alternative'! And if globalization continues unchecked, they may be right.

Samuel P. Huntington forecasts a future full of bloody 'culture wars' spawned by 'differences among civilizations' which he claims to be 'not only real' but 'basic'.[2] This crude and ultimately racist assertion obviously need not be true since history is full of examples of cultural assimilation and coexistence. But it is actually coming true as globalization forces weak, indebted and disempowered nations to accept policies that radically expose them to fierce competitive pressures from an unstable and volatile global economy. Under these conditions they are often unable to maintain the delicate political balances on which social cohesion, political stability and cultural coexistence so often depend.

More recently Robert Kaplan has delivered a similar message, inviting us to think about the 'extremely unpleasant' possibility that the world faces 'an epoch of themeless juxtapositions, in which the classificatory grid of nation-states is going to be replaced by a jagged-glass pattern of city-states, shanty-states, nebulous and anarchic regionalisms'. Today's West Africa is said to be the picture of this future, showing

> what war, borders, and ethnic politics will be like a few decades hence … West Africa is becoming *the* symbol of worldwide demographic, environmental and societal stress, in which criminal anarchy emerges as the real 'strategic' danger. Disease, overpopulation, unprovoked crime, scarcity of resources, refugee migrations, the increasing erosion of nation-states and international borders, and the empowerment of private armies, security firms, and international drug cartels are now most tellingly documented through a West African prism. … [It] provides an appropriate introduction to the issues … that will soon confront our civilization. … it is a microcosm of what is occurring, albeit in a more tempered and gradual manner, throughout … much of the developing world; the withering away of central governments, the rise of tribal and regional domains, the unchecked spread of disease, and the growing pervasiveness of war.[3]

But Africa was not always like this, nor was its present plight inevitable. The comprehensive disaster that has befallen it was ushered in when its intransigent creditors imposed radical neoliberal policies on weak, indebted and distressed economies. It was their claim that these policies would lead to accelerated development,[4] but they actually led to a predictable disaster. Thus, in 1983, a reviewer of the World Bank's 'Berg Report' wrote that he regarded

> the document as a whole fundamentally wrong in its analysis; self-serving in its implicit allocation of responsibility for current problems; misleading in its broad policy prescriptions; and totally unrealistic both with respect to the social and political implications of its 'solutions' and with respect to its assumptions about real aid flows, price and market prospects for African exports and the robustness of Africa's struggling institutional structure.
>
> It is both arrogant and meaningless for the Bank to assert in that context that … the way forward lies through a greater concern with technical expertise and a greater reliance on the market. Such advice cannot be followed for any length of time under current circumstances because the social and political consequences … would be so dramatic that the policies would be devastated by the political whirlwinds which would be unleashed. As in the past these domestic political responses could then be blamed for the disasters which follow, rather than being seen as more or less direct consequences of the acceptance of the[se] externally designed policy prescriptions.[5]

By 1985, the World Bank complained that 'borrowers and lenders often fail to take account of the institutional, social, and political rigidities that restrict a country's capacity to adjust';[6] and by 1988, its Chief Economist for Africa lamented that 'we did not think that the human cost of these programs could be so great, and economic gains so slow in coming'.[7]

Neoliberalism was not the only cause of Africa's problems but its crude ideological prescriptions made many bad situations worse. Certainly the current turmoil was not the inevitable result of either government intervention in the economy, or the tribal or ethnic heterogeneity of many African states. The latter claim is especially pernicious in its implicit suggestion that only ethnically homogeneous states can be viable, a misconception based on the tautology that successful states eventually appear homogeneous. Moreover, it ignores the fact that ethnic homogeneity is an illusion, as illustrated by the fact that many Ethiopians used to think the Somalians lucky because they all came from the same tribe; until that country exploded into clan warfare.

This does not mean that culture or history do not matter; only that the trajectory of history is not genetically defined; and that material circumstances have a powerful bearing on the scope for cultural coexistence or merger. That scope is reduced when nations lose their sovereign power to mediate potential internal conflicts and to manage the competitive process in ways that are sensitive to domestic social and political circumstances. The resulting risks are even higher in the case of technologically and administratively weak, or politically and culturally divided, societies like those of Africa. Which is why the imposition of these policies was so indefensible there, and why it is now so distressing to see the perpetrators blame the victims.

Lest anyone doubt the ability of neoliberal policies to produce disastrous results when applied radically and insensitively to inappropriate situations, they need only look at Eastern Europe. Here these policies have decimated living standards and undermined institutions, social cohesion and political stability. As a result, the growth rates of secessionist movements, civil wars, ethnic conflicts, racism and fascism has been rivalled only by those of crime, poverty, prostitution and the Warsaw stock market index.[8] And amidst this carnage the IMF and the US government insist that these policies must be sustained or intensified, even as they profess their deep commitment to democracy. But,

> by demanding draconian economic changes, by giving full unconditional support to the Yeltsin team and by ostracizing the previous Parliament – thereby contributing to the collapse of the political centre – the Clinton Administration (along with the international financial institutions) has contributed to the Zhirinovsky phenomenon. … Ironically, what the West predicted would happen without Yeltsin – that is, the rise of a nationalist-Communist movement – has happened because of him. … The boosters of shock therapy should be chastened by what they have wrought. In the future they must pay more attention to the virtues of stability and consensus.[9]

Of course, the market extremists will deny responsibility and blame some allegedly exogenous factors (like corruption or the lack of entrepreneurship) for these failures, apparently unaware that policies must be designed for the real world, not for the text book models.[10]

It should be a sobering thought that the same institutions that are 'managing' these developments in Africa and Eastern Europe are using the same logic and the same policy prescriptions to push globalization in the rest of the world. Their performance in these regions can leave no doubt in anyone's mind as to their commitment to these policies and their determination not to be deflected from them by mere political opposition or by some 'transitional' costs, no matter how high, how general or how permanent.

That is why the prophets of barbarism must be taken seriously, but it is also why we must reject their phoney fatalism. So long as globalization continues to undermine the capacity of national governments to manage the competitive process in accordance with socially and politically derived limits and priorities, then West Africa and Eastern Europe may well afford us a glimpse of our future. But it will be so only if we allow it to be so; if we remain deaf to the cries of help from the societies presently being destroyed; or to the voices of those who still believe in the possibility of building stable, prosperous societies in which people can live in harmony with nature and with each other, while working in less stressful, more interesting jobs and devoting an increasing part of their lives to social and cultural pursuits. Technology has made this dream a possibility; politics must realize it.

This dream is all but universal, and it contains the essence of the socialist dream. Its realization must be the central focus of our political efforts to develop a plausible politics for the twenty first century. And our struggle must begin by rescuing the secular, territorial nation state from those who would abandon it and from those who would replace it with the disastrous notion of an ethnic or religious state. We must do so not because, once rescued, the nation state would necessarily allow us to achieve our goal, but because its loss would leave us in a barbaric global wilderness for a hundred years.

To those arguing that we must accept a barbaric future because there is no alternative, we reply that the prospect of barbarism will provide the stimulus needed to renew the struggle for democratic socialism, now as in the past.

POSITIVE PROMISES AND HEGEMONIC IDEOLOGIES

Meanwhile the mainstream continues to promise prosperity and welfare gains through globalization, while downsizing its promises in accordance with the harsh facts of economic life. But it is gradually losing its capacity to persuade a sceptical population that globalization serves their long term interests and this threat to its status as a hegemonic ideology has led to two responses: more rhetoric about measures to ameliorate the transitional costs responsible for this erosion of support; and a much heavier emphasis on the alleged irreversibility of the process. The message is now subtly altered to read: the process serves your interests, as well as possible, under difficult circumstances; transitional costs can, and will, be substantially ameliorated; and, in any event, 'there is no alternative'.

Given that what appears to be possible under these conditions does not include full employment, or protection of incomes, of the social wage or of working conditions, it is not surprising that this message is difficult to sell to a generation that has just lived through twenty-five years of that which is now said to be impossible, namely stable and dynamic growth with full employment, increasing income equality, increasing leisure, improved working conditions and social and political stability. To them these promises look more like threats.

But then, these promises were even further diluted in an even tougher and more realistic restatement of the positive promise of globalization in Robert Reich's *The Work of Nations*.[11] Since Reich's previous work had emphasized the important positive contributions made by national industrial policies in the past, and since he writes as a political liberal explicitly concerned with the welfare of America's working people, it comes as some surprise to find that he accepts globalization as the only option, even though he acknowledges that it threatens to undermine the living conditions of the majority of those people. So what is the promise held out by this vision of globalization? And how plausible are the arguments that lead to these conclusions?

Reich believes that globalization implies a peaceful, prosperous and dynamic future for the world economy as a whole, but warns that only a minority of America's working people are in a position to share in the resulting benefits. Meanwhile, the majority faces a long term decline in their standard of living, unless their skills can be substantially enhanced. The central challenge is, therefore, 'whether there is still enough concern about American society to elicit sacrifices' capable of financing the training that is the only way to 'help the majority regain the ground it has lost and fully participate in the new global economy'. Unfortunately, in the absence of any external threat to the US after the collapse of the Soviet Union, 'it is far from clear … whether it is possible to rediscover our identity, and our mutual responsibility' to the degree necessary.

Despite his explicit concern for the welfare of America's working people, and his appeals to the charitable instincts of America's skilled (comprador?) elite, Reich's argument provides that elite with the perfect rationale for a unilateral declaration of independence. By accepting that in a global world the legal, moral and material foundations of citizenship have become all but meaningless, he legitimizes and encourages the view that individuals have no self interested reasons to be concerned about the welfare of their fellow citizens; that a failure to fund the training on which the future welfare of the majority depends, would have no significant impact on its quality of life. No wonder that Reich ultimately has so little faith in his own appeals to that rich minority's charitable instincts. One can but agree that in a world as Reich presents it, the minority would be most unlikely to rise to the challenge that he poses.

Reich's analysis is based on four indefensible premises. Globalization is inevitable and irreversible; a globalized world would provide the rich minority with a steadily improving quality of life; a world of five billion individuals would be dynamic and efficient; and America's (and the world's) working majorities could be rescued from impoverishment by increased training. These false premises engender complacency among an elite that actually has a lot to lose from unchecked globalization, and false hopes among a working majority whose economic decline is not going to be arrested by some training funded through the charitable (or waning patriotic) instincts of the fortunate few. Let us examine these premises more closely.

IRREVERSIBILITY, INEVITABILITY AND THE REAL WORLD

Reich's conclusion that globalization must be accepted as a *fait accompli* in the policy process must be, and is, primarily based on its assumed irreversibility. It cannot be based on any positive benefits, since these accrue only to a minority, while the majority is threatened with an open ended, permanent decline in its standard of living. Moreover, this decline could only be averted if the skilled minority were prepared to finance the upgrading of their skills out of compassion, or a vestigial sense of social responsibility which Reich considers no more than a remote possibility, since that minority is said to be divesting itself rapidly of the responsibilities of citizenship. On these terms, no responsible union leader, or citizen, could consider accepting globalization on its merits, which is why Reich has to base his case for its acceptance on the claim that there is no choice; that globalization is inevitable and irreversible.

To emphasize this fact he begins with a graphic description of a world in which alternative 'national' policies have become more or less inconceivable. In this world a nation's citizens are no longer 'bound together ... by a common economic fate' and

> As almost every factor of production – money, technology, factories, and equipment – moves effortlessly across borders, the very idea of an American economy is becoming meaningless, as are the notions of an American corporation, American capital, American products, and American technology.

In response, America can only try 'to increase the potential value of what its citizens can add to the global economy, by enhancing their skills and capacities and by improving their means of linking those skills and capacities to the world market'. Only then could it alter the fact that, at present, only 'a small portion of America's workers' are able to seize the opportunities presented by globalization, while 'the majority of Americans (are) losing out in global competition'. Unfortunately, such an initiative is not very likely 'when the very idea of an American economy is becoming meaningless', and since things may get a lot worse yet. Indeed, with the collapse of its traditional 'enemy' in Eastern Europe, America may face more dramatic political disintegration.

> America may simply explode into a microcosm of the entire world. It will contain some of the world's richest people and some of the world's poorest, speaking innumerable languages, owing many allegiances, celebrating many different ideals. These individuals will be efficiently connected to the rest of the globe – both economically and culturally – but not necessarily to one another. Our collective identity will fade. There will be no national purpose, and no pretence of one.

Reich can only accept this disastrous vision of the future because his belief in the irreversibility of globalization appears to be absolutely unconditional, and because he appears to believe that such an America could remain dynamic, efficient and stable enough to provide the skilled elite (his 'symbolic analysts') with a steadily improving quality of life. The former assumption is illogical and untenable, as argued below; the latter is unlikely to prove justified, as the following two sections will show.

The irreversibility of globalization cannot be treated as unconditional since both the erosion, and the restoration, of national sovereignty is necessarily a matter of degree. Hence, when extreme consequences threaten, the demand for policy reversals at the margin can and will become overwhelming. The limits of the politically possible will alter. People will demand consideration even of policies that may initially be difficult to implement, remembering that short term pain can be justified by long term gain. In this process, things deemed impossible yesterday, will emerge as feasible options today. Who could have imagined the New Deal in 1929? And who would have thought that in 1992 *The Economist* would call for a restoration of some international capital controls, or that in the same year, a regular correspondent of the *Financial Times* would argue that the 'nationalisation of the banks' was now the only way to deal with Britain's financial woes?[12] Unfortunately Reich quite inexplicably chooses not to explore or discuss such possibilities but merely declares the 'old nationalist policies' off limits and irrelevant. This is a shame, and a worry.

The worry turns to confusion, or consternation, when Reich reveals, much later in the book, that he also believes that any attempt to reverse globalization would be necessarily bad. Thus, whatever the circumstances he warns that nations must,

> eschew trade barriers ... as well as obstacles to the movement of money and ideas across borders ... [because these] ... would only serve to reduce the capacity of each nation's work force to enjoy the fruits of investments made in them.[13]

But if this is true, then why is America's majority now threatened with a pervasive decline in a standard of living that was sustained over many years and at a time when profits were higher, labour less well trained, the economy more protected and productivity lower? And how does he reconcile this claim with his earlier work showing that the nationalist policies he now decries were not detrimental to welfare or efficiency? And why the earlier emphasis on irreversibility? Ultimately one suspects that it is Reich's commitment to globalization itself that has become unconditional, though for reasons that remain unclear.

The irreversibility of globalization becomes important for its proponents only when its inherent desirability is in doubt. At that point the argument for globalization must come to depend on the stick, rather than the carrot. It must now be accepted, however reluctantly, because there is no alternative. But this demobilizing conclusion follows only if the process is driven by some exogenous factor, like technical change. The implication would be quite different if the driving force turned out to be primarily political, taking the form of rules and regulations of institutions designed to produce and protect the globalization process because it serves certain specific interests at the majority's expense. In this case the claim that these policies were irreversible would cease to be demobilizing and would turn into a rallying cry for those who recognize that the interests of the majority require a reversal of those political choices.

So is globalization technologically driven? The claim is most common and most plausible in the case of financial deregulation where the proliferation of electronic media has, indeed, created formidable problems for national regulators. However, even here, the evidence shows the claim to be clearly indefensible. In fact, financial deregulation was, and is, primarily politically driven.

The claim that financial regulation has become impossible for technical reasons is obviously untenable. First, because many of the world's most successful economies were slow to liberalize their financial markets and still regulate them extensively today.[14] Second, because where there is the political will, as with the laundering of drug money, regulation is deemed feasible, even though it may be difficult. Third, when the World Bank advises countries to liberalize financial markets slowly, in order to minimize the risk of speculative destabilization, it implicitly confirms that such regulation is currently occurring and implies that it is possible in future.[15] And, finally, the fact that almost everyone accepts global financial regulation as both necessary and feasible, implies the feasibility of national regulation, both because global regulation is far more difficult and because it would, in any case, require regulators to monitor transactions at some sub-global (or national?) level in order to be feasible.

The inescapable conclusion is that financial liberalization is politically driven, and that technology has been both a means and an excuse. The incentive was the opportunity to make enormous fortunes by creating mountains of credit – and debt – 'in a wonderful country called Offshore … where there were no rules at all, because there was no country'.[16] And those fortunes continue to grow, despite the global economy's sluggish performance. In fact, 1993 was a bumper year for the folks in finance, as

> Goldman, Sachs offered bonuses of at least $5 million each to its 160 partners … the top hedge funds reaped profits of hundreds of millions of dollars, and a fund's manager gets the lion's share of that … even the not so top dogs made out like bandits (so that) hundreds of investment bankers who aren't partners will clear the million dollar bonus hurdle … and even junior investment bankers, five years out of business school will take home bonuses of $250,000.[17]

And all this in a country where 'real average wages have declined by 18% between 1972 and 1990',[18] where unemployment remains persistently high, where poverty is on the rise, where urban decay has reached unimaginable levels and where the casualization of labour is rampant. The real question is not whether this pattern of development is reversible, but how long it can last?

To be sure, for the moment these 'deregulated financial markets' have given those who control the flows of international finance a 'stranglehold … on government monetary policy',[19] and a veto power over attempts to reregulate finance. But before those same people start talking about irreversibility and 'the end of history', they might reflect on the fact that it is the real economy that ultimately gives money its value. With electronic money you can't even light a fire to keep warm.

In the final analysis, financial regulation depends on the political will to enforce adequate sanctions, so that, given the risk of discovery, the majority of people will observe the law. The fact that such laws can always be technically evaded (by some, for a time) is not an argument against them or their enforcement, any more than the existence of unsolved murders constitutes an argument against the homicide laws. In fact, the biggest obstacle to the enforcement of financial regulations today, is not the computer or the fax machine, but the poisonous individualism of the eighties which has undermined people's willingness to observe the law by corroding the ethical and ideological foundations on which law enforcement, taxation and the ability to justify social investment ultimately rest. But such fashions change. People are not born with such venal views, and throughout history, popular uprisings have persuaded many a surprised ruling class to suddenly rediscover its sense of social responsibility when it thought it no longer needed one.

The alleged irreversibility of globalization will be increasingly challenged as more people experience its costs and recognize that these are not due to minor or temporary disturbances afflicting a small minority, but are part of an open ended and long term challenge to the majority's quality of life. Once that majority also understands that the obstacles standing in the way of a reversal of these trends are not immutable historical laws or technological inevitabilities, but political choices imposed on them by a venal and short sighted minority, the time will be ripe for change.

In the meantime, it is worth noting that the global elite itself clearly does not believe in irreversibility. Otherwise it would not be so actively creating new international institutions and agreements to threaten any country contemplating a reversal on any front with collective retaliation. And the range of policy instruments being made subject to retaliation in this way is constantly being extended by agreements like the Canada-US Free Trade Agreement (CUFTA), the North American Free Trade Agreement (NAFTA) and the Uruguay Round of the GATT, which are all much more than trade agreements. They are explicit attempts to roll back national sovereignty.

Thus, the new GATT agreement has so narrowed the range of policy options available to governments in the developing world that a critic, writing before the final agreement was signed, described its potential impact as follows:

> The powers and position of TNCs would be enhanced, the sovereign space of countries would be reduced and the process of transnationalisation of the world economy (and of the Third World) would be carried forward to an extent where it would not be easily reversible. It will divide the world between the 'knowledge-rich' and 'knowledge-poor', with the latter permanently blocked from acquiring the knowledge and capacity to be rich. ... In economic and social terms, Third World countries and their peoples could be said to be on the point of being rolled back to the colonial era.[20]

Some take comfort in the thought that countries generally only enter such agreements voluntarily, but this is to ignore the fact that what appears to be voluntary, is often tinged with more than a hint of blackmail and coercion.[21]

Moreover, those governments frequently do not represent the national interest in any real sense. In fact, governments dominated by international capital often seek to enter such agreements to protect their interests from domestic political challenges.

Canada's experience provides a particularly explicit example of this. Thus, when its Mulroney government broke an explicit election promise by announcing its intention to seek a Free Trade Agreement with the United States, the Minister for International Trade told a reporter that 'the main reason' why Canada needed such an agreement was 'to ensure that no future Canadian government could ever return to those bad old nationalist policies of the past'![22] It is a sad comment on Canada's democracy that this treasonable and utterly undemocratic statement did not lead to the Minister's, let alone the Government's, resignation.

In such a world, collective security takes on a whole new meaning, as the national fractions of a global elite seek multilateral protection from other domestic political forces, be they Chiapas Indians, Moscow conservatives or persistent social democrats. But, as these elites sit ensconced in their rich ghettoes, behind their electric fences and their security guards, their actions speak louder than their words. And these show clearly that they know it is not so.

Globalization is not inevitable and certainly not irreversible. Moreover, the main obstacles to its reversal are the institutional and legal barriers erected by international capital to extend its power and to protect its interests. This means that something can be done. And, eventually, something will be done. We can only hope that when countries finally begin to push for reversals at the margin, those who are now holding the world to ransom do not make good on their threats to respond with massive retaliation. And if they do, we must hope that the world's intellectuals have not been so mystified and suborned that they blame the ensuing disaster on those who dared to begin the reversal of a process that was always bound to lead to disaster.

WHAT FUTURE AWAITS THE 'FORTUNATE FEW'?

The second premise of Reich's argument is that globalization promises the skilled minority a wonderful future of health, wealth and happiness in a stable, dynamic and efficient world. Even though Reich points out that 'the peace of mind potentially offered by platoons of security guards, state-of-the-art alarm systems, and a multitude of prisons is limited',[23] there is no doubt that he presents their future as a beguiling and seductive one. Globalization will serve their long term interests and they are quite rational, from a self interested point of view, to be preparing to 'complete their secession from the union'. Moreover, by doing so, they will not significantly impair their quality of life.

But this vision is based on a narrow, materialistic definition of the quality of life, an extremely individualistic view of the world and a naive view of the political process. In fact, the mismatch between this vision and the actual future is likely to be even greater than that between today's Los Angeles, and the 1994 Los Angeles that people imagined in the fifties.

The truth is that in an ever more fragmented, volatile and competitive world this minority's gains will be shallow and precarious. Material gains will be offset by other losses, like increased personal and economic insecurity, more fragmented and transitory family and community relationships and an increasing incapacity to protect spiritual, ethical or environmental standards from erosion by the forces of competition. In fact, it is doubtful whether such a society could prevent competitive pressures from pushing people systematically beyond the limits of the law in the desperate struggle for economic survival. Corporate competition would come to resemble the world of organized crime, where people have to take responsibility for their own security and for the enforcement of contracts and the law, as each actor defines them.

Life will become extremely uncertain, even for the fortunate few. Their skills will be constantly threatened by technical change, by competition and by changing patterns of corporate control over assets (physical and financial), the knowledge and the media outlets, needed for the minority to exercise its skills. In short, the markets for those skills will become ever more unstable and oligopolistic. The Russia of the nineties may be the model for this future; a future that will be truly barbaric, as law enforcement is 'privatized', economic security is abolished and trust is all but eliminated. In such a world, even the elite's quality of life would be desperately low by any reasonable definition.

The 'Malibu forever' future that Reich promises the global elite is thus a delusion. In the fiercely individualistic and competitive world that he envisages, society will lose its capacity to manage the resulting centrifugal forces. Efficiency will eventually take a back seat to survival, and technology will lose its lustre and even its value. In a chaotic and barbaric world a computer cannot do much to raise efficiency. Indeed, for most of the people trapped in such a nightmare, it will be just another useless thing you cannot eat.

These issues are politically important because it is not unreasonable to think that, given a clearer appreciation of the future that actually awaits them, many members of the global elite would be willing to sacrifice some personal income in return for the chance to live in diverse, peaceful communities able to satisfy the basic human need for 'both affection, generated in small groups, and respect, gained by activities that are consonant with community values and that respond to shared concerns'.[24] Unfortunately, such choices are now being unwittingly foreclosed in the insane scramble for a socially destructive form of efficiency that is being enforced by today's unregulated competitive markets. People must be freed from the misapprehension that increased wealth necessarily means increased choice and, hence, increased happiness. We need to give more thought to the choices foreclosed in the process of attaining that wealth. Too often our political choices are pre-empted by hostages that have been given to fortune in the process of creating irrational economic obligations.

As Stephen Marglin has reminded us,

> We torture language when we say our young people 'choose' to join one or another of the authoritarian or destructive cults that abound. Many of them seem to be searching, however desperately, for the community and family that our single-minded attention to GNP has helped to destroy. In short, rather than expanding the domain of choice uniformly, growth expands choice in some dimensions but restricts it in others.[25]

And globalization is foreclosing choices as it shapes the choices of the future. Even if the global elite could continue to enjoy an ever rising aggregate income, it would have to endure its good fortune in a grim world ravaged by crime, social polarization, political instability, the intensification of work, personal isolation and pervasive economic insecurity. No doubt people would adjust to such a life and they might even come to love it, given the alternative of life among the dispossessed. But that does not mean they would have chosen it had they been given a genuine choice. At the end of the day, what they get may not be what they would have wanted, had they made their choices before the options were decimated. That is why time is of the essence.

INSTABILITY AND INEFFICIENCY IN A GLOBALIZED WORLD

But the news for the global elite and others is even worse than this, since an unregulated global economy is unlikely to remain dynamic and efficient, so that not even the promise of higher aggregate material incomes is likely to be fulfilled. Although most mainstream economists insist on claiming that further economic liberalization will always tend to increase both efficiency and total output, those claims are based more on ideology and bad theory, than on history or science.

Most neoliberals do not appear to realize just how much is implied by their injunction that even a minimalist state must be responsible 'only' for contract enforcement. This is not simply a matter of drafting some laws, paying a police force and hiring some prosecutors. It requires the creation of a society in which the vast majority of people are prepared to obey the law voluntarily, settle most of their differences without recourse to the law, or to violence; pay their taxes because they are 'the price of civilisation';[26] restrain their search for immediate personal advantage in line with ethical standards; and ultimately define their self interest as members of society, not as pure individuals.

Reich clearly values people's sense of social responsibility but fails to realize that, in its absence, contract enforcement at reasonable cost becomes impossible. And with it goes the promise of efficiency, prosperity and stable growth, on which the stable prosperity of the skilled minority also depends.

Nor can the contract enforcement function be delegated upwards to the global level as is suggested when people propose global regulation of an area like finance.

This is to confuse a political task with a technical one. Such regulation has to be embedded in a political process capable of writing rules with enough legitimacy to allow them to be enforced at reasonable cost and with a minimum of coercion. It is because globalization is not creating such a framework, that the word does not describe a positive process of global construction, but a negative process of national disintegration. Moreover, effective international regulation will only become possible when stable and cohesive nation states, broadly representative of their people, cooperate to establish and enforce mutually agreeable rules at an international level. In the same way as those nation states should be based on smaller, viable communities through which people could exercise their responsibilities as citizens and define themselves as social beings.

The issue of contract enforcement is but one of the ways in which social and political conditions are critically important determinants of economic efficiency. Competition cannot lead to true and sustained efficiency unless it is embedded in a social and political matrix that is capable of restraining the struggle for economic efficiency sufficiently, to allow society to make genuine choices trading off economic efficiency against other objectives like environmental protection, social cohesion, political stability or the ability to maintain full employment. But such choices can only be made within political entities with sufficient sovereignty to enforce them, and a sufficiently open and democratic political process to legitimize them. Such entities are termed 'generic nation states' for the purposes of this discussion and they are an essential prerequisite for the efficient functioning of markets.

More broadly, economic theory itself understands quite clearly that the consequences of the deregulation of markets can range from increased efficiency and growth to chronic instability and even crisis, depending on the place, the extent and the context of the deregulation. And the process of globalization has tended to push deregulation too far, too fast almost everywhere, partly because the debt crises have increased the leverage of those who created them and who benefit from globalization, and partly because the destruction of the sovereign powers of nations makes it more difficult to restrain the resulting pressures in accordance with local circumstances. As a result, it becomes more and more difficult to make good policy in any sphere as globalization increases the distance between the policy process and the real world. The result is a reminder that 'the quality of information on which all investment decisions must rely tends to deteriorate with distance'.[27]

Globalization has made national economic management far more difficult, but it has not created a global economy. Indeed, even in finance, where this process has probably gone furthest, outside of a few commodity markets, it remains true that 'there are only limited examples of truly global financial services, markets or products'. Moreover, even the trend has not been uniformly in the direction of more global operations, as indicated in a February 1993 issue of the *AMEX Bank Review*, which reported 'an observed retreat of financial firms away from global expansion, returning to national/local bases' and then explained this 'observed withdrawal of financial firms from their global ambitions [as] more a reflection of the over capacities in certain markets'.[28] Those global markets that do exist are largely unregulated and this has tended to make them relatively volatile, unpredictable and irrational. They have performed poorly by almost any standard; they are partly responsible for the global economy's present inability to return to steady growth; and they are substantially responsible for the disaster that befell so many developing economies in the eighties; and there is every reason to think that they will generate similar, or larger, problems in the future. Certainly the record of the recent past lends little support to the claim that globalization will foster dynamic economic growth. In fact, fifteen years of aggressive neoliberal deregulation have produced the most disappointing economic performance since the war.

That unregulated markets should have performed so badly should not have come as a surprise. Even someone like Frank Hahn, writing from a neoclassical perspective, warned in 1982 that the neoliberal 'advocates say much more than even pure theory allows them to say, and infinitely more than the applicability of that theory permits'.[29] In particular, they fail to take adequate account of the dangers posed by the inherent instability of the investment function, whose dependence on highly subjective expectations can potentially lead it to generate large and extremely wasteful deviations from an economically efficient growth path. That is why so many successful countries used various non-economic mechanisms to manage their economies at the national level. His argument is worth citing at some length.

> If the invisible hand is to operate there must be sufficient opportunities for intertemporal and contingent intertemporal trade. In fact there are not enough of these opportunities. The lack of contingent markets means that the market economy is associated with more uncertainty than pure theory allows. The lack of intertemporal markets means that great weight must rest on market expectations. The Rational Expectations hypothesis substitutes an internal and psychic hand for the market. Each individual somehow has learned how the invisible [hand] would have performed if it had been given markets within which to perform. If it is agreed that this is not of high descriptive merit, there is, in fact, no obvious mechanism by which intertemporal decisions can be co-ordinated. This was Keynes's view. I have yet to see it refuted. The French drew the conclusion that they at least required indicative planning. The Japanese have for a long time employed non-market institutions to supplement private investment decisions. In Germany, the banks seem to act as market substitutes. In Britain, where politicians now follow gurus rather than arguments we are all set to rely on the invisible hand doing a job which, in practice, it will not and cannot do.[30]

Five years later, a paper by Professors Dornbusch and Frankel showed that exchange rates had become far more volatile since their deregulation in the seventies, and that the proportion of those fluctuations that could be explained by changes in the underlying economic fundamentals − i.e. relative inflation rates, productivity growth, costs of production − was 'close to zero'![31] These fluctuations were thus irrational, costly and distorting.

Another study, assessing the performance of deregulated international exchange rate markets, led Paul Krugman to a rather forthright and blunt conclusion that stands in sharp contrast to the repeated claims that deregulation of these markets would yield substantial benefits and pose no speculative risks.

> At this point, belief in the efficiency of the foreign exchange market is a matter of pure faith; there is not a shred of positive evidence that the market is efficient, and ... similar results obtain for other asset markets ... that is, both the bond and the stock market. ... The bottom line is that there is no positive evidence in favour of efficient markets, and if anything a presumption from the data that [these] markets are not efficient. ... The important conclusion ... is that we are freed from Friedman's ... argument ... that an efficient market could not exhibit destabilizing speculation. ... Now we know that in fact no evidence supports this hypothesis – that it is one maintained purely on faith.[32]

This is a devastating conclusion for those, including Reich, who confidently assert that globalization will yield efficiency gains, and that tampering with it must yield commensurate losses. In their more candid moments, the World Bank and the IMF also acknowledge the ambiguity of the impact of deregulation. Thus the Bank has described the seventies lending spree, that created the devastating debt crisis of the eighties, as evidence 'that competitive financial markets ... can still make mistakes', having already pointed out that deregulated financial markets frequently 'tend towards instability and fraud'.[33]

The IMF, too, has discovered a downside to its financial policy prescriptions. Thus it has warned that financial liberalization 'may ... result in destabilizing and inefficient capital market speculation';[34] and that the economic recovery of the early nineties has been so slow and hesitant because the collapse of earlier speculative booms had led to 'wealth losses and financial sector repercussions associated with asset price declines [that] have restrained consumption and investment'.[35] The same point was made rather more forthrightly in 1991 by a senior US banking official who declared that 'the borrowing binge of the past decade is the key reason why lending is tight'.[36]

The problems to which these statements refer are not minor ones. The human, social and economic losses imposed on much of the developing world by the debt crisis of the eighties were enormous, as are the costs of the delayed recovery of the early nineties. Moreover, the mechanisms that produced both these problems and the $5 million annual bonuses for the partners at Goldman, Sachs remain in place and are presently stimulating new speculative asset inflations whose costs will come due in a few years time. Undoubtedly they will again be paid for by the poor and the middle classes of the world through wage reductions, cuts in social services and taxes to fund public bailouts of the same speculators who caused the problem in the first place, who already have several million dollar bonuses to console them and whose losses are, in fact, merely paper losses reflecting irrational and unwarranted speculative gains.

Only a Gilbert and Sullivan opera could do justice to this global shell game. Until it is written, some passages from a recent IMF report on *International Financial Markets* will serve. Referring to recent difficulties encountered by banks in various industrial countries, the report says,

> A crucial question to ask … is why after a long postwar period of stability have banking problems become so widespread and occurred with such frequency? What is it that induces banks in different countries to abandon – seemingly periodically – the principles of sound banking? Although no single answer can do full justice … at least one common thread running through many recent banking crises merits attention. That thread is the recognition that the competitive pressures unleashed by financial liberalization do not merely increase efficiency: they also carry risks, as banks and other institutions alter their behaviour to ward off institutional downsizing.
>
> Faced with a potential downsizing of their operations, many banks responded to this new, less hospitable environment by increasing the riskiness of their portfolios.
>
> In the end, the increased risks taken by banks were often exposed and turned into losses by a significant shift in economic conditions. … Where these risks were not adequately protected … the losses subsequently spilled over into the public domain.[37]

A rough translation of this tortured language would begin by recalling the warning delivered to the Canadian government by the Chairman of Sun Life Assurance, who warned that 'a very liberal regulatory regime is an invitation to get yourself into trouble'.[38] The 'trouble' in question results from the speculative bubbles often created by the credit expansion that is made possible by deregulation. Participation in these binges is all but obligatory since fund managers who fail to participate will generally be unemployed long before their caution is vindicated. After all, to most people, $5 million in the hand makes the number of birds in the bush academic.

Ironically, the cautious fund manager who did not participate in such a process would not even turn out to be right from his institution's, or profit maximizing client's, point of view, even though he would be right from the economy's point of view, since such boom/bust cycles are highly undesirable and wasteful; distort prices and misallocate capital; redistribute income in a highly regressive manner; and bankrupt many otherwise viable and desirable businesses. But from a narrow institutional perspective he would have missed out on a 'glorious' opportunity to cash in on the run up of the boom and, if he'd been clever enough to bet on the subsequent fall in the futures markets, he could have made big money in both directions. George Soros, now famous for making one billion dollars in ten days speculating against the British pound, explained it all in his book *The Alchemy of Money.*

> Commercial banks … seek to maximize their profits within the framework of existing

regulations and they cannot afford to pay too much attention to the systemic effects of their activities. A commercial banker who refuses to go after what seems like a profitable business is liable to be pushed aside, and even if a bank decided to abstain there are many others anxious to take its place. Thus, even those who realized that the international lending boom was unsound found themselves obliged to participate or lose their places.

There is an important lesson here: participants are not in a position to prevent a boom from developing even if they recognize that it is bound to lead to a bust. That is true of all boom/bust sequences. Abstaining altogether is neither possible nor advisable. For instance, in my analysis of mortgage trusts I clearly predicted a bad end, yet my advice was to buy now because the shares would have to rise substantially before they crashed.[39]

To be fair to Soros, he wrote all this as a warning, making it clear that he considered these events to be wasteful, destructive and inherently undesirable. Indeed, he even identified and advocated the only solution that is available to deal with such problems when he said:

> The lesson to be learned is that financial markets need to be supervised. Only some kind of intervention, be it legislative, regulatory, or a gentle hint from a central bank, can prevent boom/bust sequences from getting out of hand.[40]

Unfortunately, globalization makes this more difficult by undermining the national capacity to regulate these processes. As a result, boom/bust cycles proliferate and expand, leaving Mr. Soros to make more billions in 1993 as one of the most successful hedge fund managers on Wall Street. It was not as if he hadn't warned us.

And the gyrations continue. Asian property and stock market shares are the current favourites. The results will be the same, only more so. And their costs will come on top of those still being borne from the previous cycles. These things don't come cheap, as the IMF reminds us.

> When such banking and financial crises occur, their resolution can be costly. For example it has been estimated that the saving and loan crisis on the Unites States carried a $180 billion price tag for the tax payer (equivalent to over 3 percent of GDP).[41]

No wonder governments everywhere have to cut social services and curb their profligate spending on education and unemployment insurance. No wonder social democracy is on the run. Somebody has to pay for those $5 million dollar bonuses!

Eventually these bills will become unpayable. Once wages have been slashed to the bone, unemployment insurance abolished and education privatized, the bailouts will have to stop, especially since, by then, public sector revenues will also have collapsed as the real economy falters under the weight of accumulating debt, the burden of unemployment and the reality of weak consumer spending. Then there will be a financial crash, maybe a depression and if we are unlucky, a war. And soon economists will start preaching the benefits of globalization again. Or maybe not?

The possibility of another depression has even been raised in the pages of *The Economist* which published a special section on international finance that began by noting that, in the eighties, the world economy had undergone a 'decisive change' in which 'many of the boundaries between national financial markets (had been) dissolved'. The results were said to be disturbing, since 'the trend towards financial integration ... makes exchange rates ever more volatile, harder to control, more disruptive of economic policy-making and ever more of a nuisance to companies that trade and invest across borders'. In fact, 'financial dread' was said to be 'the mood of the moment', including dread of another depression.

> The changes in international finance of recent years have not made ... a crisis any less likely. In some ways, quite the reverse. ... Just as the new international dimension of finance has added to some risks that may help to start a crisis – greater instability in currencies, faster transmission of economic disturbances across borders, new opportunities for leverage, increased susceptibility to the illusion of liquidity and so on – so it has also weakened (or anyway complicated) the traditional remedies of economic policy. In the new world of finance, the seas are rougher and the life-rafts flimsier.[42]

The bottom line is that unregulated markets are dangerously unstable and ultimately economically inefficient. At the same time, their social and political consequences are both deeply undesirable and ultimately unsustainable. In Karl Polanyi's words 'such an institution could not exist for any length of time without annihilating the human and natural substance of society'.[43] And globalization is nothing but a renewed attempt to create such an impossibility. There can be no such thing as one single global economy, since there is – and there could be – no meaningful global political process to manage that market. And without such management, that market could not function either efficiently or effectively. That is why

> it was not simply 'capitalist production' which historically demonstrated its relative superiority in the competitive struggle. It was 'capitalism, as organised in an effective, modern nation state', which must claim this distinction. The qualification is most important.[44]

For all of these reasons, Reich's naively optimistic prognosis for America's (and the globe's) fortunate minorities misses the mark. Even this group has many reasons to be concerned about the future if globalization continues on its present course. It must be persuaded by argument and by the threat of political opposition to accept a political compromise through which it can regain its social and political legitimacy, in return for agreeing to recreate sovereign political spaces within which capital, labour, and other constituencies can bargain and in which the resulting agreements can be enforced; in which the political process can establish social, political, ethical and environmental priorities and trade them off against efficiency; and in which full employment can be pursued as an overriding priority. In the early post-war era, capital was persuaded to accept such an agenda due to the realism inspired by the disaster of the twenties, the depression, the war and the communist threat. We can only hope that, this time, a similar result can be achieved with less costly and terrible inducements. The first step is to disabuse the fortunate few of the notion that all is well for them. It is not.

WHY IS THE TRAINING SOLUTION SO POPULAR WHEN IT CAN'T WORK?

This brings us to the fourth and last pillar of Reich's liberal version of the neoconservative defence of globalization, namely the claim that the majority of America's working people, who are threatened by globalization, can be 'saved' by training schemes financed by the fortunate few. This claim is crucial, since no ideology could hope to remain hegemonic by promising the majority of the population steady immiserization, on top of the chronic economic insecurity and the social disintegration people are already being asked to accept as an inevitable part of this lean and mean world. Unfortunately the promise that training will – or even could – protect the threatened majorities in the world from a pervasive decline in their standards of living is totally implausible.

The training gospel has three features that explain its enormous popularity in circles otherwise adamantly opposed to government intervention in the economy. It is vague enough that it can be supported by almost everyone; it implicitly places the blame for their plight on the victims; and, if successful in increasing their supply, it will actually reduce the 'privileges' enjoyed by the few workers still able to command a high wage. Let us explore each of these features in turn.

Why the broad appeal? Training is a motherhood issue because it sounds positive but has so little content that it is compatible with any political position. A commitment to training need not lead to any action, partly because it is difficult to tell whether it has done so. This is because every country is already training people on a large scale; no one knows what sort of training is actually needed in a globalizing world; any training initiatives will remain subject to the existing fiscal constraints; and the success or failure of such training schemes is difficult to establish since no one can be expected to forecast the detailed skills required. The market establishes success or failure *ex post*. Hence this commitment need not and often does not lead to significant action or expenditure. At the same time, the issue can be used to undermine some remaining bastions of opposition to the rollback of the welfare state. As a result, adoption of the training myth can actually lead to 'less than nothing' as far as working people are concerned.

For example, the issue can be, and is being, used to undermine the principle of unemployment insurance. If skills are the central problem, then the state can limit its responsibility to the provision of some training, however flimsy or irrelevant, and then wash its hands of the unemployed. This represents an abdication of a fundamental social and moral responsibility, in a world in which access to productive assets and opportunities is increasingly restricted by highly concentrated and oligopolistic property rights. And the training myth makes it easier for the state to slide out from under this obligation by diverting unemployment insurance funds to training schemes that would have been created in any case. In addition, the focus on training can also provide a good platform from which to intensify an attack on working conditions more generally. Slogans like the need for 'permanent retraining' or for 'lifetime learning' can easily be used to describe and justify a world of casualized labour in which workers are paid what it takes to get them to the factory gate each day, hoping that the straw boss will give them the nod. This is the ultimate logic of the fully deregulated labour market now being touted as the next big policy issue by the international financial institutions.[45] And finally, the training issue provides a good basis from which to push education even further into a purely instrumentalist path, leaving ideas like education for its own sake, for socialization or for citizenship, to fall by the wayside. More choices foreclosed!

The second feature that makes the emphasis on training so attractive to many is that it makes the individual responsible for his or her plight. To reject this argument is not to reject the idea of personal responsibility, or to deny the value of training. It is to question the implicit removal of responsibility from an economic system in which unregulated markets are undermining the social fabric, misallocating resources, reducing efficiency on any reasonable definition and destroying people's access to work under conditions compatible with broader social and ethical objectives.

The idea that it is the deficient skills of the unemployed that are the cause of their problem also implies that training could restore full employment – in good jobs! But, this claim really cannot be taken seriously. Since millions of highly trained people are unemployed today, the argument must assume that someone, somewhere knows a different kind of training that would alter this outcome, at an acceptable cost and within an acceptable time frame. But this is simply foolishness, even though there is no shortage of snake oil peddlers claiming to have solutions among the ranks of the management gurus and the 'Training for Success' entrepreneurs.

The third reason for the popularity of the training panacea in right wing circles is the fact that the good jobs now held by Reich's skilled minority, command high wages because of their relative scarcity. If training initiatives had a significant impact on the supply of those skills, this would tend to reduce those wages – or 'privileges'. Although it would also raise the standard of living of some members of the marginalized majority, the ultimate result would be to increase the proportion of working people in the marginalized group, so long as labour remained in surplus at the global level. This is because in a competitive economy with surplus labour, the wage is determined by labour's supply price, irrespective of its average productivity.

Ultimately, the threat to the majority of the world's working people will only be lifted with the arrival, or the achievement, of global full employment and that is not imminent or likely in the absence of a global political mechanism to make it happen. Until then, globalization will continue to depress the direct wage, the social wage and the living conditions of most working people, and this process will intensify if access to productive assets, including information and knowledge, is placed even more firmly in the hands of large corporate entities that have no explicit social responsibilities and that cannot be influenced through democratic political processes.[46] In such a world, the main impact of training will be to reduce the size of the 'fortunate minority' and increase the size of the 'declining majority'.

To solve the employment problem, capital and capitalists must once again be embedded in a system in which the pursuit of profit is undertaken within clearly defined social and political constraints, including the need to construct jobs and careers in ways that accommodate the needs of individuals as people, and the needs of communities as social and cultural entities. In the absence of such conditions, full employment will either remain an unattainable mirage, or be achieved at such a desperately low level of wages and under such deplorable social and working conditions that it will be self-defeating and ultimately even inefficient.

Of course, training could improve the position of specific groups, like Reich's American majority, or maybe Canada's workers, since it is possible for a society to capture a larger share of the good jobs that remain in a slowly growing, 'downsizing' world. However, such success will be largely (though not entirely) at someone else's expense, and can therefore be expected to lead to increasing conflict. Moreover, success in that struggle is most likely to be achieved by countries able to maintain a high degree of social cohesion and political stability, precisely because efficiency is increasingly a social phenomenon, depending on reliable human relations, social stability, good communications and low costs of law enforcement or environmental clean ups. Ironically, countries that have achieved success on such a basis, are currently being pressed to alter their policies by countries that have been less successful economically, but that have more power. In this way, inferior policies (both economically and socially) are displacing superior ones. In fact a Toronto based consultant recently reported a conversation in which a former US trade negotiator is said to have acknowledged that, in his opinion, Japan's industrial policies have been very successful but, since the US could not emulate these successfully, the Japanese would have to be persuaded, or forced, to abandon them. Whether true or not, the report illustrates some of the dangers, and the potential irrationality, one should expect when intense economic rivalry occurs in an unregulated world.

Finally, training must not be treated as a 'cargo cult'.[47] To be effective, it must always be accompanied by other initiatives and by investment in infrastructure, industry and technology. In fact, a recent comprehensive study of this issue concluded that success is likely only when 'investment in vocational education [occurs] … in those skills relevant to rapidly growing industries, and, more generally, in industrially dynamic economies'.[48] The same was true if education was to have an impact on poverty:

> to reduce poverty, the public sector has to invest in education, to plan balanced growth, and to manage an incomes policy that 'lifts all boats'.[49]

Of course, the training mystique, like the promise of prosperity, is rapidly losing credibility as growing armies of retrained people wait for the illusory good jobs. Thus Canada, which has strongly encouraged students to study science and engineering for many years, has just been told that

> because of the slow economy, cost reductions and corporate efforts to improve productivity, there will be little or no growth in R&D employment [in Canada] over the next five years. … [since] the current aim of the corporation is to achieve higher productivity with the same or already diminished number of employees.[50]

To assess the training argument in the face of such evidence, one cannot just 'take everything as given' and tell the frustrated graduates they must make the best of an uncertain world. One needs to acknowledge that the training argument was used to sell a very risky policy to people who feared just such an outcome. Those who claimed that other good jobs would come along, now have a responsibility to justify those claims, not so that we can gloat at their discomfort, but so that people will be a little less gullible the next time around.

Ultimately the claim that training would protect the majority never had a chance because it was both politically and analytically wrong. It was politically wrong, because the promised training effort never had a chance of materializing, because financial constraints were bound to get in the way of good intentions;[51] since the fortunate few were never likely to fund those promises on a charitable basis (as Reich had anticipated); and since many politicians never had any intention of keeping those promises.[52] It was analytically wrong because even if a big training effort had been funded, it would not have solved the problem. In fact, even of the relatively few people that were trained for high skill jobs in Canada, only a very few got even close to a well paying, secure job. This suggests that training would not have solved the problem even had there been much more of it.

PROTECTIONISM: THE GREAT TABOO OF THE POSTMODERN AGE

For all these reasons, even Reich's sober reassessment of globalization's promise is far too sanguine. Irreversibility is a threat, not a promise; the global elite's future is not assured; and the majority's immiserization will not soon be arrested. Barbarism beckons unless the mindless destruction of the social fabric and of existing political identities is halted, but this cannot begin until the discussion of protectionism can be rescued from the realm of religious fanaticism and returned to that of rational discourse. It has become the great taboo of the age. Economists regularly frighten the children, and each other, with gruesome tales of the ravages inflicted by this unspeakable evil: in the thirties, in the developing world and, especially, in their economic models. As with all irrational taboos, the foundation of this repressed hysteria is pure ideology. The true believers espouse it as a matter of faith, while those whose interests it serves, worship it as the basis of their power.

The endlessly repeated claim is that protectionism, in all its various forms, would reduce welfare, destroy efficiency and increase conflict. That is the message that reaches the people after the complex underlying debates have been simplified for public consumption by the media, the respectable experts and the great institutions, established to pronounce on such matters – and to promote globalization. To hear them say it, one would think the truth about these matters had been unambiguously established. Thus, the Managing Director of the IMF told the world at the end of the disastrous eighties that:

> There is at the present time a kind of silent revolution in the world. More and more countries recognize that there are good policies and there are bad policies ... that removing all structural impediments to growth is the only way to progress.[53]

Such blanket assertions cannot begin to be supported by the empirical evidence, by history or even by neoclassical theory. What support they do have stems almost entirely from models constructed on the assumption that economic liberalization increases efficiency, growth and welfare; models based on a theory that defines optimal outcomes as 'outcomes produced by perfectly competitive markets'. When economists abandon this tautology and address the real world, blanket condemnations of protection, or of national intervention, turn out to be utterly untenable.

In fact, the case for positive industrial strategies, using a variety of protective devices to build a strong national industrial and technological base is both historically and theoretically strong. At a minimum, this is because many economies do not possess the internal conditions needed to respond positively and constructively to an intensification of international competition. This means that 'when the first-best policies are either unavailable or damaging on other dimensions, a proindustry trade regime has a second-best role to play'.[54]

The theoretical case for a proactive industrial policy has a long history,[55] and was confirmed once again by the experience of the East Asian NICs,[56] leading one authority to remark that the typically applied rule of thumb in evaluating infant industry protection – learning periods of about five years and a maximum effective protection of 10-20 per cent optimally administered through subsidies rather than tariff or import controls – would seem to be much too conservative, judging at least from the historical experience of South Korea and Taiwan.[57]

These insights have also been reflected in the so-called 'new trade theory', which showed that, even within a neoclassical framework, a number of interventionist policies in trade and industry can be expected to enhance efficiency and strengthen the relative competitive position of the instigating economy, once oligopoly, imperfect information flows, externalities and learning effects are taken into account.[58] However, by undermining the general case for economic liberalization, this argument opened a Pandora's Box of possibilities and reminded everyone how little economists had to contribute to policy discussions in an imperfect, disequilibrium world.

Many economists must therefore have been relieved when these open-ended policy conclusions were generally reversed, once the threat of trade (or other?) retaliation was taken into account. Retaliation usually tended to negate both the advantages to the instigating country and the potential efficiency gains. On this basis, the consensus in favour of market deregulation and non-intervention could be restored, though with some notable exceptions.[59] Indeed, the case now appeared even stronger because it could claim to have taken full account of real world imperfections.

But there is all the difference in the world between a defence that rests on the intrinsic merits of non-intervention, and one based on the threat of retaliation. The latter is essentially a coercive argument and, moreover, applies only to individual economies making policy choices within a particular international trade regime, which determines the likelihood and the extent of retaliation. In such a case, the threat of retaliation has to be factored into any decision under those conditions, but it does not have to be accepted as immutable. Trade regimes are subject to change in time.

For a discussion of the merits of particular international trade regimes, the fact that a wide range of interventionist, national policies can be dynamically efficient has far reaching implications, however. If global efficiency and welfare are to be maximized, the trade regime should give its member states enough sovereign power to make use of such policies, and protect them against unwarranted retaliation for doing so. That is what the early Bretton Woods agreement attempted to do, with its explicit provision for capital controls and for temporary trade restrictions (when 'material damage' was inflicted on an economy). And it was this feature of the agreement that allowed member states to sustain full employment, and to implement national political compromises on issues like income distribution, working conditions and social conditions. This in turn contributed to the fact that the period during which these rules prevailed was the most stable, egalitarian and successful period of economic growth in history. There is no reason why the world could not do as well in the future, if it restored the necessary conditions of national sovereignty. Unfortunately, the international trade regime is currently being pushed in exactly the opposite direction from that required.

As for the historical evidence regarding protection, the two most common generalizations are that the depression of the thirties conclusively demonstrated the evils of nationalism and protection, and that the great success of the early post-war period illustrates the desirability of trade liberalization. But neither of these claims is persuasive.

Polanyi's interpretation of the depression is dramatically different and far more persuasive. It argues that the terrible events of the thirties were the painful and ultimately inevitable result of the excessive economic liberalization of the twenties, which had produced ever greater economic, social and political turmoil. The resulting contradictions eventually triggered political upheavals in which societies reasserted control over their economies in a variety of ways, ranging from those of the Fascists to the New Deal and to Sweden's early social democracy.[60]

This argument is far more plausible than that which claims that, after decades of success and prosperity, governments suddenly abandoned free trade in favour of protectionism for no material reason, and then added insult to injury by massively deflating their economies in the midst of a recession. In fact, Polanyi's account brilliantly documents the world's long desperate struggle, under the leadership of the League of Nations, to use neoliberal policies to resolve the persistent contradictions afflicting the world economy; the fact that the intensity and the persistence of these efforts merely exacerbated the economic imbalances, the political tensions and the social dislocation until these eventually led to painful and sometimes barbaric policy reversals.

Polanyi's account of the twenties ought to sound eerily familiar to students of today's crisis. The problems that had accumulated and that eventually had to be resolved, included: an explosion of unserviceable debt that eventually induced economic stagnation, low investment and rising unemployment; extreme economic instability, leading to speculative boom/bust cycles that misallocated resources, fuelled economic insecurity and destroyed otherwise viable assets and skills; and a dramatic increase in income inequality, which undermined the moral and political legitimacy of political and economic systems.

The converse claim that the extended economic boom of the post-war period can be ascribed to economic liberalization was always less well founded and has been further discredited by the deplorable economic, social and political results associated with accelerated economic deregulation over the past two decades. Indeed, these have recently persuaded even *The Economist* to call for the restoration of some national controls over capital,[61] recalling an earlier assessment that had appeared in *The Financial Times* in the wake of the 1987 stock market crash. This had echoed Polanyi's earlier assessment of the depression, by suggesting that there might now be an urgent need to reassess the merits of the process of deregulation and globalization.

> The post-war economic system was designed by people who had endured the chaos of the 1930s. They may have erred too far on the side of controls and constraints on markets – *although it is at least arguable that the 'golden era' of trade expansion was possible only because the regime governing capital flows was so illiberal* [emphasis added].
>
> It now seems increasingly clear, however, that the reaction against government intervention and managed markets in the 1970s and early 1980s went too far. There was a pervasive retreat from responsibility.[62]

By now that retreat from responsibility has gone very much further; the difficulties standing in the way of its restoration have grown; but so has the recognition that there is a problem and that it requires a solution. That will provide the basis of the political response that is needed. And that political response can only occur within sovereign political spaces, within which a democratic process can define and implement the kind of social and ethical framework that is required if markets are to serve societies, rather than destroying them.

TOWARDS A POSITIVE NATIONALISM

So far this paper has argued that globalization is essentially a destructive process, creating a world that will not be stable, efficient or socially desirable. As it gradually destroys the capacity of nation states to manage economic processes to some broad social purpose, it does not, and cannot, replace these capacities at a global level. As a result the competitive process will become increasingly unstable and destructive, threatening social cohesion, political stability and human welfare. Even economic efficiency, the one thing the process was supposed to deliver with certainty, is increasingly undermined by instability, uncertainty, speculation, persistent excess capacity and the stifling presence of unserviceable mountains of debt. And there is no reason to believe that this process is about to stabilize. In fact, the opposite is more likely, as contradictions grow more severe and as governments further lose their ability to deal with domestic fiscal problems and external obligations in ways that can be reconciled either with their social responsibilities or with the need for internal political stability.

The current situation is made more dangerous because the international financial institutions have clearly decided that the way out of this impasse is to further accelerate the deregulation of markets, focusing especially on the deregulation of labour markets. This is likely to have particularly explosive social and political consequences. It is nothing short of incredible that they are advocating the US labour market model for Europe, thereby revealing the full extent of their inability to distinguish between socially destructive and socially desirable sources of efficiency. Together with their demonstrated willingness to accept unlimited social, human and economic costs as the price of transition in Eastern Europe, no one can doubt their open ended commitment to the ideology of the market. Although, within that paradigm, they would prefer to see welfare conditions improve, this is a secondary concern which must be addressed within the framework of 'sound economic policies'. They do not entertain the thought that, in an unregulated world, it is those 'sound policies' that create the 'facts of economic life' within which welfare services, labour laws, social services and progressive income taxes have to be progressively dismantled, because 'efficiency' demands it.

The solution to this crisis will not, therefore, come from those international institutions, as some optimists believe. And this is not only because of their blinkered ideological approach, but also because they are not embedded in a political process that could make their policies truly sensitive to local circumstances, or that could lend those policies the legitimacy they need to be effectively implementable. 'Generic nation states' have been defined as the political entities that must fulfil those tasks. But what are their prospects? Is their resurgence a real possibility, or is it a functionalist dream? And if their revival is possible, is it likely to take a positive or desirable form? The answers to these questions are far from clear.

The need for such states arises from the fact that unregulated markets are not viable, not efficient and not socially desirable. That is why the link between nation state and market has been so very close from the outset; why both emerged more or less simultaneously in history. Mercantilism was the economic ideology of the monarchical state, but its limitations were exposed with the accelerated growth of rationalism and commerce in the eighteenth century. This new world demanded a new way of defining the link between the individual and society, as the divine right of hereditary status and the absolute teaching of the church lost their power to induce people to internalize the rules and values of the social order. A new basis had to be found for providing people with the possibility of defining themselves as members of 'a society', as social beings. And this vacuum was filled intellectually by theories ranging from Rousseau's social contract, in which the object was achieved almost entirely through positive inducement (the carrot), to the Hobbesian state, reluctantly accepted as a necessary evil (the stick). In practice, the void was filled by nationalism, a term that first came into use in the middle of the eighteenth century and that dominated the landscape by its end. As compared to the monarchical state, the nation was an egalitarian, populist concept, and those who brought it into use tended to equate 'nation' with 'people'.

It was the 1750s ... that saw new intellectual distinctions being made between the monarchical state (the government) and the nation. In 1755 an obscure (French) cleric named G.F. Coyer, condemning his more sophisticated contemporaries, began to preach that no love was so pure as that felt for the nation, and that this embraced both the state and all orders of society. 'Amidst the growth of French cultural nationalism ... a new political attitude, a "new patriotism", ... was coming into existence, pairing together king and the whole French people as the proper objects of patriotic feeling'.

These inchoate beginnings appear to have culminated in the concept of 'nationalism' only after the French Revolution had brought these beliefs to power – and to grief – in a major nation.[63]

Ever since, the nation state has been an essential mechanism for the management of increasingly complex societies and economies. Some regard it as the root of all evil; others as a means through which humanity can aspire to the highest ideals of selfless devotion to society. And both may be right, since nationalism has probably approximated both judgments at some time or other. The truth is that the political content of this political entity is undefined, and must remain so. It is, after all, one of the purposes and attractions of national sovereignty to enable societies to make choices that allow them to be different; to live by different cultural or social norms; to set different priorities between efficiency and other social objectives.

But why, at the dawn of the twenty-first century, should we pin our hopes of rescuing the social vision with which we began on the nation state? Has this particular political and ideological solution to the problem of reconciling our individuality with our essence as social beings, not been overtaken by history? And do we not know that the nation state has historically been merely a vehicle for capital to enforce the logic of the market, while covering its tracks with fine sounding phrases about social responsibility and patriotism?

These fundamental questions have to be incorporated into the discussion of the 'generic nation state'. The question that is posed by history, is: In what form can we realistically hope, at the end of the twentieth century, to redefine and reconstruct political entities that would allow us to manage the increasingly destructive and irrational forces of global competition, while providing individuals with the capacity to define themselves as social beings and while containing the risk of conflict between such political entities? The 'generic nation state' is defined as any political entity that performs the first two of these functions. The answer to the third then has to be defined in terms of some positive model of international cooperation, that will protect the sovereignty of those generic states and discourage predatory behaviour through collective security provisions.

This paper cannot hope to deal adequately with these enormous issues. It will merely reflect on some of the difficulties that will be encountered as we prepare to meet the challenge of globalization. Three questions will be addressed: Why nation states? What are the prospects for a restoration of national sovereignty? And, what are the prospects for a restoration of a positive, humane nationalism?

The focus on nation states derives primarily from a pragmatism born of a total inability to conceive, let alone construct, a meaningful political process at the global level. The truth is that Trotsky and the international socialists were always right, analytically, but their message was always politically useless. In fact, it tended to lead either to paralysis or to a Warrenite[64] acceptance of globalization as a positive process developing the forces of production and the conditions for socialism. Well, we are there now. The forces of production have been developed to a level that unquestionably makes it possible to provide all people with a comfortable material existence with only a moderate expenditure of effort by each person. But where are the conditions for socialism? As we address the question of how to bring those forces of production under social control, we must begin somewhere, and it cannot be the world. Not only would this be utterly impractical, it would imply and require a degree of centralization in political discussion and organization that would be extremely dangerous, and very difficult to reconcile with the diversity that is surely one of our objectives. In short, just as global financial regulation can only be built on effective national regulatory systems, so the global management of the competitive process, or of a socialist economy, must be built on sub-global units, namely 'generic nation states'.

The emphasis on 'generic' nation states makes the point that these need not be the existing nations, as bequeathed by history; that it is possible for these to be either larger, supranational entities (like Europe), or smaller, sub-national ones (like Catalonia). However, this does not mean that such changes should, or could, be considered lightly. They are always fraught with enormous dangers and will almost always be positively retrograde when they lead to a demand for ethnically defined states, on the spurious grounds that only such states are legitimate or viable. The current proliferation of such demands reflects the growing instability and economic insecurity that has been spawned by globalization and the growing inability of existing, territorial states to manage the regional or ethnic divisions within their borders. But the creation of ethnic splinter states will not solve these problems and will generally create new and even bigger ones. After all these little states will still have the global market to contend with. Indeed, the resurgence of the ethnic state must be regarded as a major step in the direction of barbarism. Once the rights of citizenship depend on our ethnic genealogy, we will all end up living in apartheid South Africa.

The future must lie in restoring the sovereignty of existing territorial states, within which such ideals as equality, non-racism and an unqualified acceptance of a sense of social responsibility are, at least, conceivable and realistic objectives. That sovereignty must then be used to create the political space that is needed to restore the gentler, more humane societies that people clearly want, and that they know to be possible. On such secure foundations, such nations can then gradually seek to unite with others in larger regional political entities (such as Europe), once a sufficiently coherent political process allows the conditions for democratic legitimacy to be established at that higher level. The power to manage the centrifugal forces of competition will ideally reside at these higher levels, embedded in a regional political process. And the space thereby created for social and cultural diversity can be used to give more power to lower levels of government and administration, and to the organizations of civil society. The principle of subsidiarity is a useful way of thinking about this process of devolution, although its real impact will naturally depend on the way it is actually defined in practice.[65]

But even if a focus on the nation state could be defended, is it a feasible or realistic objective today? No doubt much conspires against it. Indeed, most of this paper has shown that globalization has substantially undermined the material base of the nation state and has erected serious institutional obstacles to block any attempt to reverse this process. However, it has also shown that those developments are not inherently irreversible, and that the growing conflict between the demands of an increasingly unstable and illegitimate economic system and gradually disintegrating social systems, are presently transforming the political landscape and shifting the limits of the politically possible. It is in this context that it is vitally important to channel people's anger in a positive and constructive direction, rather than allowing it to sweep them away on the rising tide of fascism, monarchism, religious fundamentalism or ethnic nationalism.

Of course, the fate of recent social democratic governments shows clearly just how difficult it is to realize any alternative vision, no matter how moderate, in the world as presently constructed. But these failures must merely lead to a redoubling of our efforts, secure in the knowledge that the disastrous consequences of the present policies will continue to swell the ranks of the politically disaffected and will continue to intensify and legitimate the search for an alternative. After all, who would have thought that, in 1992, one would find a long time correspondent of the *Financial Times* of London considering the nationalization of the banks as a serious policy option for Britain?

> The latest analysis from the invaluable Professor Tim Congdon ... which examines the current state of British banks, savings institutions and insurance companies ... describes a catastrophe waiting to happen. ... This crisis of the financial intermediaries rules out any domestic recovery for years, even assuming that it can be contained. Congdon puts the earliest date at the late 1990s. That could be optimistic. The private sector's boot-straps are broken. ... There is one tried and proved remedy: bank nationalisation.[66]

In short, people are seriously discussing policy choices that would have been deemed unthinkable only a few years ago. This does not mean that they are now on the side of the people. They may want to nationalize the banks in order to bail out the speculators with public money. But the change is significant because it means that new political coalitions can emerge, new possibilities are arising. Moreover, through links between similar coalitions in different nations, one can begin to discuss the shape of a new set of international institutions, that must one day be constructed to secure and protect national sovereignty in a context where those states are encouraged and advised to use their sovereign powers to pursue domestic full employment growth, as an overriding priority, and to reconcile their other objectives and their trading relationships with that commitment.

Such initiatives may not succeed immediately, since the obstacles now standing in their way are formidable. But the struggle must continue, because the current process is not viable and, unless the explosive political forces that are now being generated by it can be channelled in a positive direction, barbarism may become the only option. Let us remember that it is not the option people would choose. And that if they appear to choose it at some stage, it will be because they have been given the choice only when it was no longer a choice, but a *fait accompli*.

And so we come to the final question: What chance of a positive, constructive nationalism? Again, there can be no doubt that the odds are long. The post-war world demonstrated that it is possible for nations to provide a context within which working people can strike bargains with capital that can transform their lives, allowing them to live a better, more secure life, working in more pleasant working conditions for higher wages and in relatively stable communities. Historically these gains were enormous, though enormous problems also remained. But it represented a historic achievement, and there was no reason, in principle, why that process could not have continued, if those political entities had retained sufficient control of their economies to allow those national bargaining processes to continue. But once capital slipped out from under these arrangements, it soon undermined them through the forces of unregulated international competition. The rest, as they say, is history.

Now some would argue, with some reason, that it is not possible to manage capital. That the dissolution of that post-war phase of stable, widespread prosperity was inevitable and that social democrats never seem to learn. They make a very important point that needs to be addressed when we discuss the kinds of controls that should, can and need to be exercised over the competitive process in order to ensure that it can serve our social objectives. Here, another version of the principle of subsidiarity might again be helpful: allow as much freedom for decentralized decision making in the market, as is compatible with the objective of a dynamic, stable economy capable of functioning within socially and politically defined constraints reflecting social, political, cultural, ethical and environmental objectives. No doubt that question will never be answered definitively, but then, only a fool would expect it to be. Bertrand Russell once said: 'Education is a process of becoming confused at a higher level'. To which we need only add that: 'History is the ultimate process of education'.

NOTES

1   S.P. Huntington, 'The Clash of Civilizations' *Foreign Affairs*, Summer 1993.

2   S.P. Huntington, 'The Clash of Civilizations' *Foreign Affairs*, Summer 1993. It is surely appropriate that this prediction of inevitable culture wars should emanate from the same mind that coined the phrase 'forced draft urbanisation' to describe the flood of refugees created by U.S. bombing and defoliation campaigns at the height of the Vietnam war. Since urbanization was universally associated with 'development', he described this displacement of rural people as an unexpected benefit of those campaigns.

3   R.D. Kaplan, 'The Coming Anarchy', *Atlantic Monthly*, February 1994, pp. 46 and 48. All of the following quotations are from this article.

4   World Bank, *Accelerated Development in sub-Saharan Africa: an Agenda for Action*, World Bank: Washington D.C., 1981; also known as 'The Berg Report', after its chief author Elliot Berg.

5   M.A. Bienefeld, 'Efficiency, Expertise, the NICs and the Accelerated Development Report', *IDS Bulletin*, 14:1, Institute of Development Studies: Sussex UK, 1983, pp. 18 and 22.

6   World Bank, *World Development Report 1985*, World Bank: Washington D.C., 1985, p. 2.

7   Cited in *The Toronto Globe and Mail*, 22 June 1988.

8   This rose by over 700 percent in 1993 and was, therefore, termed the most successful stock market in some of the financial press. No doubt this was meant to be whimsical. The 'market' trades in the shares of seven firms, and is a particularly crass example of a speculatively driven, destabilizing and irrational phenomenon.

9   Editorial *The Nation*, 3/10 January, 1994, p. 3/4.

10 The World Bank has actually described the policy prescriptions which it imposed on its clients during the first decade of its policy lending, as 'text book' policies which took inadequate account of local social and economic realities. World Bank, *Adjustment Lending: An Evaluation of Ten Years of Experience*, Washington, D.C.: World Bank, 1988, p. 66.

11 The arguments presented in Reich's book attracted special attention because the author was a leading liberal democrat, who has since become Secretary of Labour in an administration that garnered much electoral support by voicing 'grave, but unspecified' reservations about NAFTA, and then proceeded to make its passage an overriding policy priority, achieving its Congressional victory on the basis of a Republican majority voting with Democratic minority. R.B. Reich, *The Work of Nations*, New York: Vintage Books, 1992. The quotations which follow all come from pages 3 to 8, or 321 to 323.

12 Laurence Harris, *The (London) Financial Times*, October, 1992.

13 Reich, op.cit., p. 312.

14 This has been especially true of Japan and South Korea. Thus a special report on 'offshore banking in Asia', in the *Far Eastern Economic Review*, described the rapid expansion of this phenomenon in each of seven Asian countries and then concluded with a report on Japan which declared that in Japan such flows were still almost completely under the control of the government authorities. Typically, the Review then proceeded to denounce the 'anachronistic bureaucratic culture' that was clearly impeding progress in Japan. This despite the fact that the section had begun by announcing that the entire offshore phenomenon was primarily driven by the desire to avoid taxation! *Far Eastern Economic Review*.

15 Obviously if one can deregulate slowly, then the degree of regulation is a matter of policy choice, not a technological given. These issues are more extensively discussed in M.A. Bienefeld, 'Financial Deregulation: Disarming the Nation State', *Studies in Political Economy*, No. 37, Spring 1992.

16 A. Smith, *The Roaring Eighties*, Toronto: Summit Books, 1988, p. 19.

17 Amey Stone, 'Sorry, This Year your bonus is only ... $5 million', *Business Week*, 17

January 1994, p. 27.

18 A. Donner, 'Canada's Economic and Industrial Outlook', Speaking Notes (mimeo), January 1994.

19 J. Toporowski, 'Why the World needs a Financial Crash', *The (London) Financial Times*, February 1986, p. 21.

20 C. Raghavan, *Recolonization: GATT, the Uruguay Round and the Third World*, London: Zed Books, 1990, p. 45.

21 CUFTA, NAFTA and the Uruguay Round were all negotiated against the background of the implicit or explicit threat of trade sanctions. The fact that these threats were usually not 'official' threats made by the negotiating parties does not preclude their effectiveness.

22 Pat Carney as cited in *The Toronto Globe and Mail*.

23 Reich, op.cit., p. 302.

24 A. Etzioni, *An Immodest Agenda: Rebuilding America Before the 21st Century*, Toronto: McGraw-Hill, 1983, p. 33.

25 S. Marglin, 'The Wealth of Nations', in *The New York Review*, XXXI:12, July 19, 1984, pp. 41-44. (A review of I.M.D. Little, *Economic Development: Theory, Policy, and International Relations*, New York: Basic Books, 1984).

26 This felicitous phrase was coined by one of FDR's advisors and is a useful antidote to the fecklessly selfish messages emanating from the revolting tax revolts of the neoliberal age.

27 Economic Council of Canada, *A New Frontier: Globalization and Canada's Financial Markets*, Ottawa, 1989, p. 25.

28 AMEX Bank Review, *Globalisation, Regional Blocs and Local Finance*, 20:2, 22 February 1993.

29 F. Hahn, 'Reflections on the Invisible Hand', *Lloyd's Bank Review*, No. 142, April 1982, p. 20.

30 Ibid., p. 12.

31 R. Dornbusch and J. Frankel, 'The Flexible Exchange Rate system: Experience and Alternatives', Paper presented to the International Economic Association Basle Round Table conference on *Survival and Growth in a Polycentric Economy*, October 1987.

32 P. Krugman, 'The Case for Stabilizing Exchange Rates', *The Oxford Review of Economic Policy*, 15:3, Autumn 1989, pp. 65-66.

33 World Bank, *World Development Report 1989*, World Bank: Washington D.C., p. 4.

34 IMF, *Staff Studies for the World Economic Outlook*, Washington D.C.: IMF, August 1989, pp. 8-9.

35 IMF, *World Economic Outlook*, IMF: Washington D.C., October 1993, p. 10.

36 *The Toronto Globe and Mail*, 8 October 1991, p. B6.

37 IMF, *International Financial Markets: Part II. Systemic Issues in International Finance*, IMF: Washington D.C., pp. 2/3.

38 John McNeil, Chairman of Sun Life Assurance Co. of Canada as cited in K. Dougherty, 'Open war feared in finance reform', *The (Toronto) Financial Post*, 13 November 1990.

39 G. Soros, *The Alchemy of Finance*, Toronto: Simon and Shuster, 1987, p. 100.

40 Ibid., p. 101.

41 IMF, *International Financial Markets: Part II. Systemic Issues in International Finance*, IMF: Washington D.C., p. 2.

42 'Peaceful Co-existence' in 'World Economy: Survey' section, *The Economist*, 19th september 1992, p. 46.

43 K. Polanyi, *The Great Transformation*, Boston: Beacon Press, 1944, p. 3.

44 M.A. Bienefeld, 'The International Context for National Development Strategies: Constraints and Opportunities in a Changing World', in M.A. Bienefeld and M. Godfrey, eds., *The Struggle for Development*, Toronto: Wiley, 1982, p. 31.

45 IMF, *World Economic Outlook*, ch.4.

46 For a fuller discussion of this issue see: M.A. Bienefeld, 'Basic Needs in the Competitive Economy', *IDS Bulletin*, Sussex (England): Institute of Development Studies (University of Sussex), 9:4, June 1978; and M.A. Bienefeld, 'The International Context for National Development Strategies: Constraints and Opportunities in a Changing World', in M.A. Bienefeld and M. Godfrey, eds., *The Struggle for Development*, Toronto: Wiley, 1982.

47 The term stems from several documented instances in which residents of some remote Pacific islands responded to the cessation of air traffic at the end of WWII by clearing 'runways' in the bush, hoping that this would bring back the planes on which they had come to depend for many things.

48 W.H. Haddad, M. Carnoy et al., 'Education and Development: Evidence for New Priorities', *World Bank Discussion Paper No. 95*, Washington D.C.: World Bank, 1990, p. 49.

49 Ibid., p. 15.

50 P. Hadekel, 'Future bleak for R&D students,' *The Ottawa Citizen*, 24 December 1993, p. F1. The article summarizes the findings of a survey of the research and development spending plans of 160 companies, undertaken by the Conference Board of Canada.

51 The mainstream would argue that these financial constraints would have been worse without their liberalization policies. However, this claim is generally no more than a pure tautology, reflecting their unshakeable, but indefensible, faith in the idea that freely functioning markets yield optimal results. The neoclassical theory of the second best shows that this faith is utterly misplaced when applied to the real world. It shows that even if one accepts all of the restrictive and unreal assumptions of that theory, it is impossible to say anything about how the removal of some market imperfections will affect a world with many such imperfections. The result may be an increase or a decrease in both welfare and efficiency. In the real world, on the other hand, we have seen that leading neoclassical theorists, the World Bank, the IMF and The Economist all accept that it is likely that the liberalization of the global economy – and especially that of global financial markets – has led to unnecessary instability, excessively high risk taking, inordinately high interest rates, an extensive misallocation of resources reflected in a stifling burden of uncollectible debt and unwarranted and unethical shifts in income distribution.

52 Maybe the most crass example of this process was the promise of 'special compensation' for Canadians who stood to lose their jobs as a result of the CUFTA. This was much advertised and promised and played a significant role in calming people's fears. Then, immediately after the agreement was signed, the government announced that it could not keep this promise because it was impossible to tell which people lost their jobs as result of the agreement, and which lost their jobs for other reasons. The case is noteworthy because it is so obvious that the government was fully aware of this diffi- culty from the outset, and because it did not feel the need to mince words or to allow

a decent interval to elapse before telling people they had been had.

53 IMF, *IMF Survey*, 18 October 1989, p. 290.

54 D. Rodrik, 'Conceptual Issues in the Design of Trade Policy for Industrialization', *World Development*, 20:3, 1992, p. 312.

55 F. List and R.G. Harris, *Trade, Industrial Policy and International Competition*, Toronto: UofT Press, 1985.

56 R. Wade, *Governing the Market*, Stanford University Press, 1992.

57 H.D. Evans, *Comparative Advantage and Growth: Trade and Development in Theory and Practice*, London: Harvester Wheatsheaf, 1989, p. 309.

58 P. Krugman, 'Scale Economies, Product Differentiation, and the Pattern of Trade', *American Economic Review*, Vol. 70, 1980, pp. 950-59.

59 Some neoclassical economists did not share this view and concluded that, even after accepting the risks of retaliation, there was still a case to be made for 'targeted, firm specific intervention' designed to strengthen specific, high value added parts of the manufacturing sector. In Canada this view was eloquently and forcefully presented by Professor Richard Harris in a study written for the *Royal Commission on the Economic Union and Development Prospects* ('the McDonald Commission'). However, the Commissioners, in their wisdom, summarily dismissed this argument without refuting any of its central propositions. See R.G. Harris, *Trade, Industrial Policy and International Competition*, Toronto: UofT Press, 1985.

60 For a fuller discussion of this argument and of its relevance to the current crisis, see M.A. Bienefeld, 'The Lessons of History and the Developing World', *Monthly Review*, 41:3, July-August 1989.

61 'Peaceful Co-existence' in 'World Economy: Survey' section, *The Economist*, 19th september 1992, p. 46.

62 M. Prowse, 'The message of the markets', *The (British) Financial Times*, 24th October 1987, p. Weekend FT 1.

63 G. Newman, *The Rise of English Nationalism*, London: St. Martin's Press, 1987, pp. 162-163.

64 Bill Warren *Imperialism: Pioneer of Capitalism*, London: Verso, 1981.

65 Subsidiarity is defined as a principle which states that, given certain defined objectives, power should remain at the most decentralized level that is compatible with their successful achievement.

66 L. Harris, 'Time to nationalise private sector debt', *The (London) Financial Times*, 19th October 1992, p. 23.

IN DEFENCE OF CAPITAL CONTROLS

James Crotty and Gerald Epstein

I. INTRODUCTION

The story of the rise and fall of the Golden Age of modern capitalism is an oft told tale. But for all its familiarity, it is easy to forget that the Golden Age was, among other things, an era of effective national economic regulation. It was the age of the 'social contract'[1] or capital-labour 'accord' (however loaded in capital's favour these arrangements might have been) under which the Keynesian state, with the acquiescence of capital, was to pursue full employment and build a stronger social safety network. Golden Age central banks fixed exchange rates and determined interest rates with only sporadic interference from a relatively small class of financial speculators. Such state regulation was made possible by the emaciated condition of the domestic rentier class, capital controls on international financial flows, and the as yet quite limited size and power of multinational corporations (MNCs).

The limited extent of globalization was hardly the only important determinant of the Golden Age, nor even its most important condition of existence. But the acceleration of the process of globalization of finance and capital investment and the increase in the openness of trade that took place as the Golden Age evolved does seem to have been an essential element in the dynamics of its demise. The continuation of the globalization process over the past two decades has created tenacious impediments to the restoration of a regime of sustained full employment and real wage growth.

In this essay we will argue that a set of policies to gain more control over the

This essay was first published in *Are There Alternatives? The Socialist Register 1996* international flow of money and, perhaps, goods is an essential component of any serious package of progressive structural reforms designed to achieve sustained full employment and greater equality of income and wealth. In making this argument we are in a minority, but we are not alone. Indeed, in recent years there has been renewed support for capital controls, even among policy makers and mainstream economists.

Several factors help explain this growing interest. First, speculative attacks against the EMS in 1992 drove Great Britain and Italy out of the exchange rate mechanism, generated enormous macroeconomic problems for Sweden, Spain and other countries, and forced a widening of the bands for countries that remained. A number of respected mainstream economists have wondered whether capital controls may be necessary to bring about the transition to European Monetary Union.[2] Second, the recent Mexican disaster frightened even committed neoliberals. In this sensitive environment, the International Monetary Fund, in a move that made headlines and generated a critical editorial in the *Wall Street Journal*, cautiously argued for the occasional desirability of controls on inward capital flows to developing economies.[3] Finally, the continuation of devastatingly high unemployment in Europe and wage stagnation and increased inequality in the US has led to renewed interest in capital controls among progressives as a way of allowing countries to use macroeconomic policy to promote full employment. The surprise best selling book by *The Guardian*'s Will Hutton, *The State We're In*, calls for capital controls as a way of promoting full employment. Other respected progressive academics who have recently supported controls as part of a restructuring program include Juliet Schor, Fred Block, and Andrew Glyn.[4]

However, even proponents of controls remain ambivalent about their feasibility. Is it possible to control capital when billions of dollars can move across cyberspace in a nanosecond? Can the international cooperation that may be required to control capital ever really occur? And, maybe globalization and the constraints that it imposes aren't all that important? For example, Andrew Glyn, one of the economists on the left who has written most often and most perceptively and supportively on the economics of capital controls recently seemed to shift gears, arguing that the primary impediment to full employment at present lies in the fact that labour has failed to support a binding incomes policy that commits working people to non-inflationary wage and benefit demands at full employment.[5] He believes that the costs, tensions and pressures of sustained full employment, magnified as they are in the current environment, should be 'explicitly counted and willingly shouldered by the mass of wage and salary earners'.[6] The problems of globalization complicate the issue to be sure, according to Glyn, but constraints on international mobility are not an essential element in its solution.

We share Glyn's belief in the need to constitute a new set of domestic political arrangements that will commit labour, capital and the state to egalitarian full-employment policies. The problem is this: *in the absence of the enactment, or at least the credible threat of enactment, of capital controls and trade restraints, what lever-age can labour and the citizenry possibly use to force capitalists to even bargain seriously over these issues, never mind to persuade them to agree to any new political understanding other than one that delivers the total and complete surrender of all progressive social and economic values?* There are a depressingly large number of costly adjustments that the working class would have to 'willingly shoulder' in such a new domestic deal as Glyn now advocates. The US, for example, suffers not just from excessive average unemployment, but from urban decay, public infrastructural disinvest-ment, a health care system that is not viable in the longer run, an emaciated social safety network, a growing underclass of low-paid, under-employed workers, and so forth. Is the working class to voluntarily agree to pay all the costs involved in solving these problems? Under existing political conditions, it is certainly clear that the economic elites will refuse to do so. And are engorged rentier incomes to be guaranteed in this new deal along with adequate corporate profits? The point is that *world elites have no incentive at present to jettison their current economic and political agendas.* Capital controls or their threat are the means to create such an incentive.

Discussions among economists about the pros and cons of capital controls usually take place in a fairly narrow context. Would this or that control help country X maintain a moderately lower interest rate or a somewhat lower rate of unemployment? Given the problems of evasion, or the propensity of controls to induce or worsen corruption, or the inefficiencies assumed to follow any inter-ference with market incentives, the case for controls is normally rejected more or less out of hand. We want to consider capital controls in a much broader context. We are concerned with the current and future implications for the quality of life of the majority of the world's people of the continued development and perfec-tion of the neoliberal global economic regime. Sustained high unemployment is now taken for granted across Europe and in most of the world. Inequality is on the rise everywhere. The US, though celebrated for its less-than-very-high unemployment rate, is suffering from secularly falling real wages, rising poverty rates, massive urban decay, and rising racial tensions. Its social safety net, miserly by developed country standards, is being torn to shreds by an arrogant and ig-norant Congress whose only accountability is to wealth and power. Of course, these problems cannot be contained within the economic sphere. Deep fissures in the social fabric are appearing everywhere, and the body politic is not im-mune to the poisons this regime is spreading around the world. Racial hatred, immigrant bashing, and neofascism have made their reappearance on the global political scene.

In this context, the key question is not whether this control or that is on bal-ance cost effective. Rather, we need to consider whether or not capital controls can help alter the current configuration of class economic and political *power* in order to facilitate the creation of new political commitments in support of full employment macropolicy, public investment, credit allocation and income redistribution. There are three ways in which capital controls can be helpful in this regard. First, such controls directly restrict the ability of rentiers and MNCs to threaten labour and the political majority by running away. Freedom to 'run' is one of the main sources of capitalist political power in the current neoliberal regime. Second, controls can facilitate the attainment of full employment, at least in the short to intermediate run, thereby strengthening labour's bargaining power. Third, the imposition of moderate controls and the *threat* to implement comprehensive controls (on trade and the movement of real and money capital) and more powerful state economic intervention in general may be the only way to get capital to consider supporting more progressive institutional arrangements, inducing them into negotiations toward a political 'new deal' in the belief that only in this way can they protect themselves against the possible emergence of an overtly anti-rentier or even anti-capitalist regime or, alternatively, the development of political and social chaos.

Fortunately, the political feasibility of capital controls may be greater than is commonly believed. The current system of capital mobility, however profitable in the short run, is not operating in the long run interests of many of those capitalists engaged in producing goods and services. It is primarily the global rentier class that consistently benefits from the current system of capital mobility.[7] While it is true that the rentier class has gained tremendously in size as well as economic and political power in the post-war period, their assets still constitute a small fraction of total capitalist wealth. Hence, the constitution of a coalition of interests between labour and fractions of industrial and commercial capital against the parasitic interests of rentiers might be attainable under the right conditions.

As for economic feasibility, the case is even stronger. Economists do not doubt that capital can be controlled. The only issue is at what cost. Neoliberal economists assume that the current economic system is operating virtually without flaws; thus any costs associated with interference in the system is automatically considered to be too high a price to pay. We agree that the costs of imposing controls must be compared with the costs of not imposing them. However, contrary to the dominant view, it seems clear to us that the costs of maintaining the current neoliberal regime are absolutely astronomical. Any reasonable estimate of the efficiency costs to the nation of a system of capital controls must pale in comparison with the costs of doing nothing. As we shall see in Part IV of this essay, there is a broad range of controls that are possible; and capital flight can be frustrated not only by international cooperation among states, but also by appropriate sequencing and vigorous enforcement of various controls by particular governments.

II. FROM THE GOLDEN AGE TO THE RESURGENCE OF
THE GLOBAL RENTIER CLASS

We offer here a brief and selective chronology of events leading to the birth
and death of capitalism's Golden Age in the 1950s and 1960s[8] and then to the
construction of a global neoliberal regime in order to draw attention to five key
points. First, the systems of capital controls and credit allocation put in place after
the war helped make the Golden Age possible. Second, the unravelling of these
controls contributed substantially to the Golden Age's subsequent demise. Third,
the alliance between industrial and financial capital that emerged in this period,
as well as increased competition among nations for shares of the enlarging international financial market, were central to the dynamics of its demise. Fourth, the
current neoliberal regime was created by global economic elites to facilitate their
victory in a one-sided class war waged against working people around the world.
Fifth, this regime has given capital such power over labour and society that no
attempt to create a new progressive domestic policy coalition is likely to succeed
unless accompanied by a direct assault on the foundations of that regime through
capital and perhaps trade controls.

By the beginning of the twentieth century, a globalized economy had become
a reality. London, New York and Parisian bankers could move money to the far
corners of the globe in no time at all, financing trade, public works, and speculation of vast proportions.[9] The free movement of money – anywhere, anytime
– was the keystone of a liberal society and the basis for the accumulation of un-
told wealth by rentiers like Morgan, Rothschild, and Aldrich. Then came the
calamities which destroyed the liberal order: the two World Wars and the Great
Depression.[10] If the Great Depression and War brought about an enormous re-
shuffling of national fortunes, it also dramatically reshuffled the pecking order of
ideologies and classes. The sacred economic ideas of the day – the gold standard,
independent central banks, and free international capital mobility – had all come
to be seen as purveyors of calamity rather than pillars of stability. John Maynard
Keynes was only the best known of many economists who discredited the idea
that free international capital mobility and unregulated private finance were the
sine qua non of economic progress.[11] Indeed, in many parts of the capitalist world,
no group bore more blame for the economic crisis than the rentier class and its
allies, the central bankers. Among the early casualties of the depression was the
independent power of many central banks, including the Federal Reserve and
the Bank of England, both of which were brought under the direct control of
their governments in the 1930s.[12]

The planning undertaken by governments to more effectively wage the Second
World War hastened the maturation of a political process already in motion: the
institution of financial controls and economic planning in much of the advanced
capitalist world. When Harry Dexter White for the US and John Maynard Keynes
for England met to begin negotiations to construct the post-war economic order,

there were two things on which they agreed. Controls over international capital movements would be necessary to achieve economic prosperity in the post war world; and such controls would be most effective if countries developed comprehensive national regulation of all foreign exchange transactions and cooperated with each other in enforcement of these regulations.[13] They wrote provisions which protected countries' rights to institute comprehensive controls into early drafts of the Bretton Woods Agreement; these provisions survived more or less intact. Keynes proposed voluntary international cooperation in his drafts, while White argued that such cooperation should be mandatory. In his 1942 draft, for example, White proposed that governments be required 'a) not to accept or permit deposits or investments from any member country except with permission of the government of that country, and b) to make available to the governments of any member country at its request all property in form of deposits, investments, securities of the nationals of that member country'.[14]

The early proposals of Keynes and White met with fierce opposition from New York bankers. Mandatory controls would interfere with the profitable business of accepting flight capital, as the New York bankers had done in the 1930s. And bankers opposed capital controls because they knew they would be used to support significant government intervention in post war domestic economies. They eventually succeeded in removing the mandatory aspects of international controls enforcement. The 1943 version of White's draft stated that countries had to cooperate in enforcing controls 'only if the IMF had recommended it'.[15] In addition, countries were no longer required to repatriate flight capital at the request of the originating government, only to provide information about it. There was virtually nothing concerning nations' obligations to help each other enforce controls included in the 1944 Joint Statement. In the end, though, the Bretton Woods Agreement did reject the sanctity of unregulated private capital flows and the liberal, open, financial order with which it is associated.

It should be noted that one reason the New York bankers were not even more effective in striking controls from the Bretton Woods agreements was that industrial capitalists in the US and elsewhere rejected free capital mobility. In particular, those industrialists – largely from capital-intensive and high tech sectors – who had provided Roosevelt with crucial business support in the 1930s strongly supported effective capital controls.[16] In other important countries (such as Japan, Germany, France and Italy) both financial and industrial interests agreed on the need for controls.

Indeed, at the start of the post-war period virtually all the countries in the world, with the important exception of the US, had extensive capital controls on outflows, inflows or both. For many countries such controls were seen as necessary to protect modest foreign exchange reserves in the face of strong import demand and tempting financial investment opportunities in the US. But for others, controls facilitated the creation and allocation of credit and the regulation of trade that were important parts of government directed national development plans. Countries, such as Germany, for whom controls seemed an unfortunate necessity rather than an essential element of economic planning, began to remove their controls early in the post-war period. But virtually all such countries eventually reinstated controls in some form.[17] The German Government 'while opposed to capital controls in principle, also resorted to them in practice'.[18] A coalition of bankers and industrialists committed to an export-led development strategy saw capital controls as essential for the maintenance of a stabilized and undervalued Mark. The German government therefore reimposed controls on inflows again from 1960 to 1969, in 1971 and even in the early 1980s.

Japan, on the other hand, was more ideologically committed to the use of controls as part of its industrial development strategy. Its Foreign Exchange and Trade Control Law of 1949 brought 'formal prohibitions on capital transactions and restrictive licensing for financial institutions engaged in international business. There were also informal controls, such as administrative guidance of the foreign exchange positions of Japanese banks'.[19] Capital and exchange controls allowed Japan to keep the cost of credit low, to channel credit to desired uses, and to stabilize the Yen at an undervalued level to promote exports. These policies were, as in Germany, the reflection of a coalition of interests between industry and finance. In France as well, a strong alliance between the state, finance and industry supported controls as part of an overall industrialization strategy. The French had used controls since 1915; in 1966 their post-war system of controls was significantly strengthened, when a new law gave the government the right to control all foreign exchange transactions between France and the rest of the world, oversee the liquidation of foreign funds in France and French funds abroad, and prescribe conditions for the repatriation of all income earned abroad. Among the developing countries, South Korea used highly restrictive capital controls most effectively.[20] Controls on both outflows and inflows were a necessary adjunct to the industrial and credit allocation policies which made South Korea one of the first developing country 'economic miracles' in the post-war period.[21] Of course, controls were misused in some countries. But the point is that they played an essential role in creating virtually all of the great post-war secular booms.

In sum, the creation and reproduction of the Golden Age was facilitated by several key conditions. First, the rentier class was weak. Some economies were flush with liquidity after the war years, real interest rates were modest, and capital accumulation was primarily financed by the flood of internal funds created by growth and a consistently high rate of profit. This was an age in which the interests and needs of real capital accumulation dominated those of financial capital. Second, capital controls helped keep finance primarily national while domestic financial regulations and credit controls channelled funds to priority domestic uses. Both aspects were important: domestic rentiers had little power over the accumulation process and capital controls prevented them from augmenting their power by threatening to 'run away' if interest rates and inflation rates did not suit them. Largely because of controls, the overall flow of private cross border finance was quite low in the 1950s and early 1960s. Rentiers thus had yet to gain veto power over macropolicy. Third, though the dislocations and uneven destruction wrought by the war meant that trade had to be of some significance, it was less important than it was to later become, while direct investment across borders was inconsequential. Firms thus were forced to rely primarily on strong rates of growth of domestic aggregate demand for their own expansion and profit. Industrialists as a group were unable to resolve their cost problems by national policies of high unemployment without destroying the main markets for their own goods. And with political commitments made by capital to labour during the war to cement their allegiance to the war effort still in effect, conditions were ripe for the creation and maintenance of the political and economic arrangements that led to full employment and rising social wages across Europe and, to a somewhat lesser extent, in the US.

Unfortunately, the history of the post-war financial order is one that culminates in the ultimate triumph of rentiers and MNCs and the restoration of an open global financial and economic system. A major contributing factor to this victory was that as important segments of business became more international in orientation they joined the bankers in their support of a more financially open global economy. Thus united, they became too politically powerful for most governments to successfully oppose.

In our view, the contradictions and strains that brought the Golden Age to its demise in the late 1960s and early 1970s were primarily domestic. The economic and political power of the working classes in the advanced countries was invigorated by sustained full employment and a rising social wage. This period saw an eruption of strikes, militant demands for better wages and working conditions, and a push by labour for more democratic control of the labour process. These challenges to capital created the cost side of the squeeze on the profit rate characteristic of this period. At the same time, industrial capital was trying to undercut labour's power by shifting production to non-union sites either at home or abroad; foreign investment and its threat became increasingly important weapons in this conflict. Meanwhile, citizens around the developed world demanded a more generous social wage, creating strains on the public purse.[22]

Of course this is also the initial period of the resurgence of the global rentier class. The modern global rentier class evolved through an increase in the size and power of rentier interests in many advanced capitalist countries combined with increased openness of world financial markets. As it became larger, the rentier class began to form coalitions with segments of industrial and commercial capital, in some cases as the result of the creation of huge financial/industrial conglomerates, a veritable merging of rentier and industrial interests under one corporate roof.

The clearest early signpost of this new unity occurred in the 1960s in the context of the implementation of a capital controls program in the US and the associated rise of the Eurodollar market. When the US government set up its voluntary capital controls program in the 1960s, it tolerated and even promoted the Eurodollar market in London in order to prevent the subversion of the program by large US banks and multinational corporations. The Eurodollar market allowed both big banks and multinational industry to gain access to deposits and loans abroad without immediately hurting the US balance of payments. The push by British Banks and the British Government to restore London as a world financial centre, with a deregulated international financial market unhindered by capital controls, finally let the globalization genie out of the bottle.

The US had become decidedly hostile to international capital controls by the early 1970s. When the declining US trade position precipitated a run on the dollar and threatened the collapse of the Bretton Woods system, European and Japanese governments proposed extensive cooperative capital controls to help maintain the fixed exchange rate mechanism. The US government vetoed their proposal.[23] Without the support of the US, the attempt to maintain international regulation of the emerging global rentier class was doomed to failure. By the middle 1980s virtually all advanced countries were in the process of loosening or even eliminating controls. Their general demise was the result of a combination of internal and external political pressures, the precise mix of which varied from country to country. Much of the external pressure emanated from the US As noted, the US had encouraged the development of the Eurocurrency markets in London in the 1960s. Euromarkets then became the site of the freest international capital market since the 1920s; this created pressure on other countries to dismantle their own capital controls so that their financial institutions could more successfully compete in the emerging global marketplace. In the 1970s, the US succeeded in changing the language of the IMF bylaws, for the first time giving the IMF the power to force countries to reduce or even eliminate capital controls. Finally, in the late 1970s and 1980s, the US directly pressured a number of countries, Japan among others, to open their capital markets. Germany played a similar role within the EMS. Nevertheless, in most cases the primary cause of the demise of capital controls was probably domestic. Domestic industry and finance, having become more globalized and more outward oriented, eventually became more unified in their opposition to controls. They had also lost much of their commitment to the social contracts that originally made capital controls attractive to them. The accumulation of these international and domestic pressures to remove controls eventually overcame certain resistance among OECD governments.

Symptoms of the death of the Golden Age were easy to spot. Real wage growth slowed everywhere; in the US it vanished. Average industrial and commercial profit rates declined markedly. But the rentier class continued to expand in size as well as in its propensity to cross borders. The central events in this process of expansion revolved around the creation of an ocean of petrodollars recycled by the exploding Eurodollar market to the Third World. Petrodollar recycling represented a new evolution for global rentiers since loans to developing countries had previously been modest in amount, and came primarily from governments and international lending agencies, not private financial institutions. The second OPEC price increase in 1978-79 accelerated this process. Inflation spiked again. Exchange rates instability skyrocketed. The Europeans tried to delink from the US dollar and form their own exchange rate system in an attempt to insulate themselves from this chaos. Capital controls in much of Europe were temporarily reintroduced.

In political terms, the 1970s can perhaps be best understood as a time of distributional struggle among and between classes over who would bear the costs of slower growth, rising rent extraction by oil producers, and increased economic instability and insecurity. The decade saw no clear cut winner. The rentier classes in particular fared poorly. Inflation adjusted equity prices dropped rapidly over the decade; indeed share prices divided by money wages fell dramatically all across the OECD. Meanwhile, inflation at times rose above nominal interest rates in the late 1970s, giving rentiers negative real rates of return. By 1980 the economic elites in the developed world were seething with anger at their failure to win this distributional struggle. If the 1970s was their decade of discontent, the 1980s was to be their decade of revenge.

A run on the US dollar in 1979 kicked off the decisive phase of capital's war against labour and the social contract. US Federal Reserve Chairman Volcker proceeded to implement his attack on inflation and the US working class, precipitating the Third World debt crisis. Super-tight US monetary policy, along with like-minded policies implemented elsewhere in the OECD, raised world real interest rates, helping create a global recession. The global recession created an environment that permitted European elites, who were not in a political position to simply tear up the social contract, to violate it with some impunity. European unemployment rates, which had increased from about 3% to about 6% between 1973 and 1980, levitated to above 10% by the mid-eighties, never to return to their 1970s, let alone their 1960s, levels.

Thus, by the early 1980s all the pieces needed to implement the new political agenda of the more unified elites were in place. Rentiers wanted the devolution of all regulatory controls on the movement of money – within the country and across borders. They wanted inflation smashed quickly. Finally, they wanted low taxes on rentier income and on the rich. The agenda of industrial capital was generally consistent with rentier interests; only questions of the depth and length of the desired recession separated them. To raise profits and create greater managerial autonomy, they wanted to complete the job started in the 1970s and break the economic and political power of labour. They sought lower real wages and more freedom to organize work and workers as they saw fit; the weakening or even destruction of unions and the reduction of the social safety net were necessary conditions for achieving this result. They also wanted to loosen the government regulatory apparatus and cut business taxes even further. In the decade or so to follow, US rentiers and industrialists got almost all of what they wanted; their European counterparts had to settle for less.

The 1980s also saw the accelerated expansion of a deregulated financial sector swollen by high real interest rates, rapidly rising debt to income ratios in the business, household and government sectors, and speculatively driven financial asset prices. Since there had been no increase in world saving, the sustained secular rise in indebtedness, along with the rentier-dictated anti-inflation mania of central banks, kept constant upward pressure on real interest rates. The relation of the financial sector to the nonfinancial sector thus had changed dramatically from the hey-day of the Golden Age. The financial sector now absorbed a vastly increased share of the income flows generated in the real sector which it used primarily to fund its own self-expansion. Finance had become a parasite on and impediment to real sector growth.

Of course, governments everywhere became increasingly dependent on the rentier class. The post-1973 slowdown in economic growth reduced the rate of increase of tax revenues and raised demands for higher spending. Serious budget deficits first arose after 1973; they increased (relative to GDP) in the 1980s. Cuts in taxes on business and the rich further weakened the fiscal position of the state. Finally, the record high real interest rates of the period raised the cost of servicing the ever rising stock of government debt. Throughout the developed and the developing worlds, governments became burdened with their heaviest debts since WW II. With rentiers now inclined to boycott bonds issued by governments that tolerate inflation or run deficits that are considered irresponsibly large, raising their interest payments and punishing their exchange rates, fiscal as well as monetary policy had fallen under rentier dominance.[24]

The political-economic strategies implemented by capital in the 1980s were astonishingly successful in settling the distributional struggle in capital's favour in the US and in much of the Third World, and reasonably successful in the rest of the OECD. Looking at the US, we can say that the elites have substantially destroyed the old social contract. Meanwhile, the economies of the Second and Third Worlds have become increasingly open to First World exploitation. Indeed, with the acceleration of globalization, with the increasing allegiance to neoliberal policies and ideology, with further privatization, and with legally binding treaties such as GATT and NAFTA, the very concept of nationalist economic policies is beginning to seem hopelessly naive.

The central point that needs recognition is how integral the process of globalization has been to the unfolding of this story. The proximate cause of the end of the Golden Age was the collapse of US international financial hegemony and of global financial stability brought on by a run on the US dollar in the early 1970s. And the proximate cause of the onset of global monetarist terror in the 1980s was the run on the dollar in 1979 that brought Volcker to power. The policies adopted in the 1980s then produced the speculative booms and financial fragility that further enlarged and empowered the rentier class. Indeed, the general environment of uncertainty that followed the Golden Age was fuelled by waves of global hot money flooding into and then out of different countries, dramatically raising exchange rate instability. This ocean of hot money has grown ever wider and deeper as financial sectors inflate, technological and organizational innovation accelerates, and, most importantly, the ability and the desire of governments to control these flows erodes. Unless and until we restore some reasonable degree of societal control over the 'freedom' to move goods, jobs and, especially, money across borders at will, attempts to implement full employment macropolicies or to write domestic new deals will be doomed to failure.

III. CAPITAL CONTROLS AS PREREQUISITES FOR PROGRESSIVE MACROPOLICY

The crucial question in this context is whether capital controls (and perhaps also trade management) are necessary conditions for the implementation of full employment and egalitarian economic policies. There are actually two important sub-questions involved here. First, do unregulated investment, trade, and financial capital flows make the implementation of a long term or sustained policy of full employment difficult if not impossible? Second, do they significantly weaken labour's ability to force capital to agree to a new, progressive, egalitarian domestic economic regime? We believe that the answer to both questions is yes, and that, therefore, capital controls are an essential precondition for the reconstruction of a regime of sustained full employment and reduced inequality. Obviously, some countries face less binding external constraints on the implementation of progressive domestic economic policies than do others. But, in our opinion, capital controls would enhance the ability of a progressive political alliance in *any* country to successfully pursue sustained full employment and a more progressive income distribution.

How do trade openness and unregulated real and financial capital flows impede the ability of government to pursue high wage, high employment, egalitarian policies? To answer this question it is first necessary to ask how extensive capital mobility really is. On the one hand, the quantity of two-way short-term flows (so called gross mobility) has increased dramatically, and is now at astronomical levels. These are the movements of capital that most observers have in mind when discussing the 'hyper-mobility' of capital. On the other, the net transfer of long term capital from one country to another is still at a lower level relative to the size of economies than it was at the turn of the century. But things are changing. With the rise of neoliberal ideology, the increased power of the global rentier class and the strengthening of international protections for foreign investment embodied in NAFTA, agreements of the EU, and other international legal arrangements promoted by the IMF, World Bank and other institutions, the pace of long term and net capital flows is dramatically accelerating. If the current pace continues, the level of international capital mobility even on a long term and net basis is certain to eventually increase substantially over the early twentieth century peaks. In sum, short term international mobility is already extensive; and if current trends continue, long term mobility will continue its dramatic rise as well.[25] In this context, let us consider the following issues.

Direct investment

Changes in technology and the prying open of Second and Third World economies to unrestricted foreign investment have made it easier for multinationals to invest anywhere and to produce an increasing variety of goods and services using a broader spectrum of relatively low cost foreign labour skills. While still modest relative to domestic investment in the advanced countries, foreign direct investment is not insignificant and is growing fast. Foreign investment can have two deleterious effects on the domestic economy: it can substitute for, and thus reduce, domestic investment; and it can affect the relative bargaining power of labour and capital in the negotiations that determine wages and working conditions, primarily in those industries experiencing capital outflow, but in related industries as well.

There are arguments on both sides of the question as to whether foreign investment by domestic corporations is a complement to or substitute for domestic investment by these same companies. But taking into account the increasingly wide range of labour skills available to advanced country MNCs abroad at a fraction of the cost of domestic workers, as well as the frequent absence of unions, environmental restrictions, health and safety regulations, taxes, and so forth in less developed countries, it seems reasonable to conclude that foreign investment in the advanced countries is on balance a substitute for domestic investment.[26]

Under virtually anyone's theory of wage determination, the loss of capital and technology in the domestic economy caused by foreign direct investment should lower productivity and therefore the real wage, at least in the short run. The magnitude of this effect should not be large, however, because the proportion of the potential domestic capital stock that has run away is not large. But if one accepts, as we do, the more realistic view that the division of the national product among the factors of production is mediated by a complex set of institutions and practices that determine the relative power of the contending parties, it is not at all clear that the effect on wages of runaway capital is minor. How many companies have to run away, leaving behind unemployed and underemployed workers and depressed communities and regions, in order to lend credibility to the threat by other companies to do the same? In an environment of substantial secular unemployment such as we have lived through in the past 15 years, even partial credibility can frighten workers into making major concessions. Until we find a reliable way to measure the growth of such threat-credibility, we will have no way of knowing for certain what we believe to be the case: that foreign direct investment has had a major effect on wage behaviour in the advanced countries in recent years.

Trade and financial capital flows

Consider the situation confronting a nation that wants to implement a macropolicy designed to achieve sustained full employment. Assume this nation is completely open to trade and to real and financial cross border investment flows, and that trade is a significant component of GDP. The trade-related impediments to a full employment macropolicy in such an open, trade-dependent nation are many and complex. Here we simply list four. First, increased income growth will induce a rise in imports that will lessen the impact of a given degree of policy stimulus on GDP (or will lower the policy 'multiplier'). Second, the rising trade deficit will, other things equal, precipitate a fall in the nation's exchange rate that, in current speculative currency markets, could be of substantial magnitude. Third, the fall in the exchange rate will cause a deterioration in the real terms of trade – the quantity of imports earned by a given volume of exports. If traded goods and services are a large percentage of GDP, this could lead to a large reduction in real wages and in the national income. Fourth, this surge in imports itself will cause competitive downward pressure on domestic real wages. As we shall see, these trade-related problems will interact with financial capital flows to sabotage the full employment policies that spawned them.

Those who do not believe that globalization is a major cause of the deterioration in economic performance over the past twenty years often point out that while dependence on trade did increase substantially since the 1960s, its rise has not been all that dramatic, and that while direct investment did increase by dramatic proportions, it remains small in absolute terms. However, no one can deny that financial capital flows have increased dramatically and have reached unprecedented relative and absolute levels. The daily turnover in the foreign exchange market, which was about $15 billion in 1973 and about $60 billion in 1983 is now approximately $1.3 trillion, an amount perhaps sixty times the volume needed to finance trade, one that dwarfs the less than one trillion dollars available to the governments of the advanced countries for exchange rate stabilization purposes.[27]

What impediments to our hypothetical full employment macropolicy might today's global rentier class cause? The primary problems are that the fall in the exchange rate caused by the higher trade deficit and lower interest rate associated with this policy will be *larger*, will take place *sooner*, and will be *more uncertain* or unpredictable in size. The term 'rational expectations' is an oxymoron in the world in which we live. We can 'predict' the future only through guesses, hunches, rules of thumb, and social conventions. And perhaps no important world market is more subject to the speculative instability and fundamental uncertainty endemic in the real world than the current global money market. Any significant movement of an exchange rate in either direction can start a stampede into or out of any currency in this market; herd behaviour is the norm.[28] Thus, as our new full employment policy – with its reliance on low interest rates and its promise of higher inflation and larger trade deficits – begins to be implemented, global rentiers will jump ship, touching off an exchange rate decline which could turn into a free fall. Knowing that they don't know how fast or how deep the drop will be, even investors who are not hostile to the longer term objectives of the host government may quite sensibly decide to play it safe by shifting their funds elsewhere, perhaps with the intention of returning when the exchange rate pressure has subsided.

These problems are greatest, of course, for small, trade-dependent developing countries. But even large countries will suffer when rentiers decide to run away from their currencies. The central bank may be forced to defend the exchange rate through high interest rates, striking a blow to domestic investment. Financial instability may rise as higher interest rates undermine the stability of banks dependent on short term deposits to fund their investment in long term loans and bonds purchased earlier when rates were low. Higher interest rates may transform a difficult fiscal deficit into a fiscal nightmare: the government will pay much higher rates to finance its deficits and turnover its debt. Heavily indebted industrial and commercial corporations are subject to the same kinds of financial shock; greater financial fragility in this case means less capital investment. In short, substantial capital flight can generate tight constraints on policy. Unfortunately, vast inflows of capital can eventually prove to be almost as damaging. The crisis in Mexico in 1994–95 is a case in point.[29]

The main point is that the problems caused by the decline of the exchange rate are magnified and quickened. In essence, the problems which the new expansionary policy might have generated only slowly and in concert with its benefits, are now magnified and appear *before the benefits have a chance to even be experienced*. It is easy to see why the objectives of the new policy might be impossible to attain under these conditions. It is easy to see how public support for the policy could easily evaporate in this environment. It is also easy to see, given the logic of this scenario, why even well meaning governments – an endangered species – would shy away from anything resembling a policy of sustained full employment. With central banks universally opposed to such policies and rentiers ready to severely punish any government which tries one, it is easy to understand why the majority of the world's population has had to suffer the consequence of secularly high unemployment for the past two decades.

The virtual elimination of full employment macropolicies is not the only serious problem caused by financial aspects of globalization. The existence of this ocean of hot money, subject as it is to fads and fashions, has helped create enormous actual as well as potential instability in exchange rates. This rise in exchange rate uncertainty potentially affects the decisions of all economic agents influenced by international prices and quantities; a group that grows apace with globalization. That is to say, the evolution of the global rentier class has substantially increased the deleterious impact of uncertainty on economic performance. Nowhere is this more important than in reducing the pace and changing the composition of capital investment spending. The current era is thus one in which productive accumulation is being strangled by financial capital – through debt burdens, high interest rates, fickle short-term finance, heightened uncertainty, and restraints on expansionary macropolicy. Freedom to cross borders at will has substantially enhanced the ability of the rentier class to enrich itself while impoverishing society.

IV. WHAT IS TO BE DONE?

We have no doubt that existing impediments to the implementation of effective capital controls are many and are powerful. The main general problem is this: the most efficient potential solutions to our current economic problems are global in character, but there are no obvious democratic political mechanisms at hand through which to design and implement global institutional change of the kind we need. Such mechanisms as we do have are national or regional in character.

To see the potential superiority of global solutions, suppose that *all* governments decided to cooperatively pursue full employment through larger budget deficits and lower interest rates. Under such global cooperation no country need confront serious problems from rising trade deficits, or capital flight, or currency devaluation. Thus, the need for capital or trade controls would be substantially diminished. If this need did arise, cooperative agreements to enforce capital controls would make them much more efficient and harder to evade. Keynes was surely on the right track when he based Britain's 1940s proposals for a new international order on the concept of an international central bank empowered to expand the world's credit supply to accommodate and sustain global economic expansion. The bank was to assist countries that develop balance of payments problems through faster than average growth, and penalize surplus countries, forcing them to grow faster.

Clearly then, the most effective method for creating global full employment is cooperative macropolicy expansion, cooperative capital controls, an international central bank in the Keynes mode, and an international Social Charter enumerating and enforcing minimum wages and working conditions, minimum social and economic rights, and appropriate environmental standards. Unfortunately, current prospects for attaining such comprehensive global agreements are dim. Governments everywhere are beholden to national and global economic elites who are either quite content with the status-quo or who want to push the neoliberal agenda even further. Cross border labour and citizen alliances are developing, but they have not evolved to the point where they could have a serious impact on global economic policy. 'The focus on nation states derives primarily from a pragmatism born of a total inability to conceive, let alone construct, a meaningful political process at the global level'.[30]

Thus, the best political prospects for major change exist at the national or regional levels, but here is where the economic impediments to the implementation of effective controls are greatest. Comprehensive controls in a single nation, if they remain in place for a long period of time, become increasingly difficult and costly to administer and, under the intentionally leaky enforcement procedures that normally prevail, increasingly easy for the economic elite to evade.[31] The smaller (and more politically isolated) the country and the tighter its integration in and dependence on world markets, the harder the problem becomes. It is especially hard for a small, globally dependent country to unilaterally implement powerful comprehensive capital controls designed to thwart all the forces that will rebel against permanent, egalitarian full employment policies.

This is not to say that it cannot be done. If the government's economic planning mechanism is comprehensive and coherent and if the controls' enforcement mechanisms are powerful and vigorously, even ruthlessly, enforced, then the successful use of long term controls by smaller countries is possible – as South Korea and Taiwan, among others, have demonstrated. Nevertheless, the political units best able to unilaterally adopt a program of capital controls in pursuit of expansionary egalitarian policies and the eventual achievement of a new social contract are relatively large countries (especially those, such as the US and Japan, that are not excessively dependent on trade), and appropriate regional alliances, such as the EU.

Let us assume that, with the possible exceptions discussed below, it is most reasonable to consider the possibility of controls for the case of large nations or appropriate alliances. What set of capital and/or trade and/or direct investment controls would best facilitate the achievement of a new progressive full employment program? The first thing to realize is that the answer to this question is contingent on all those things that influence the relative power and the political perceptions of the main economic classes; freedom of capital to cross borders is just one determinant of capitalist class power. *Any* combination of domestic economic policies and cross border controls that can bring industrial and rentier capital to political negotiations willing to accept a progressive social contract, or that can help unite labour and segments of industrial capital against rentier intransigence is satisfactory. In the best of circumstances moderate controls might suffice. Under more common, less propitious circumstances, it might take relatively strong capital controls accompanied by a believable threat that the refusal of capital to cooperate in bargaining will result in the rigorous control of trade, investment and financial flows and a generally more interventionist state.

There is no single policy with respect to controls that is optimal in all countries under all circumstances. Nevertheless, we present below a sample list of feasible national or regional capital controls to emphasize that, under the right conditions, including controls in any strategy designed to produce sustained full employment is a pragmatic political act. The claim that strong controls are not technically feasible or economically sustainable is, we will show, simply inconsistent with the facts. We cannot over-emphasize the point that the primary impediments to the successful use of capital controls are *political*, not technical. It is not support for capital controls, but the contrary belief that progressive economic restructuring can be achieved without at least the threat of such controls that is utopian.

V. CAPITAL CONTROLS AND INTERNATIONAL COOPERATION

What not to do

The first task facing those who want to reign in the domestic political power of MNCs and global rentiers is to stop any further liberalization of the rules governing international capital mobility. At regional as well as global levels, moves are afoot to further reduce the ability of nations to control international capital mobility. This is especially true with regard to foreign direct investment. For example, the United States is proposing an extension of the North American Free Trade Agreement to Chile and other countries in the Caribbean and Latin America. This so-called 'Free Trade' agreement is primarily an agreement to reduce the ability of communities to regulate, restrict or control foreign companies which invest there. This will only serve to diminish national policy autonomy. For its part, while the EU will eventually continue negotiations for its enlargement, the rules governing the outflow of direct foreign investment to lower wage areas must be carefully monitored and shaped so as not to further enhance capital's bargaining position.

At the global level, negotiations are continuing for an agreement on the international protection of foreign investment within the framework of the World Trade Organization. These protections, if ratified, would dramatically reduce the ability of national democratic forces to establish restrictions on foreign investment. These attempts must be resisted. Finally, we should continue to oppose conditionality requirements imposed by the IMF and World Bank which trade access to credit in return for limitations on the ability of nations to restrict capital mobility. But we should not stop here: a good offence is the best defence.

Stand-by controls on capital flight

Instead of using international institutions to promote capital mobility, they should be used to limit destructive capital flight. A system of international stand-by controls on capital flight could be negotiated that required countries to return capital that crossed borders in violation of any nation's laws.[32] Such stand-by controls would be especially helpful to the enforcement efforts of smaller, poorer countries. While small countries can and do implement capital controls, the costs of unilateral enforcement can be high, especially if the country is very dependent on imports, exports or foreign investment. There is ample precedent for such agreements. As discussed earlier, Keynes and White saw such international cooperation as a key to any sensible international financial regime, and they tried to write such cooperation into the Bretton Woods Agreements.

International cooperation in monitoring and controlling the movement of funds is already occurring, and the tightening of such controls seems virtually inevitable. Already, law enforcement officials from around the world are desperately seeking better mechanisms to restrict the laundering of drug money. For example, Switzerland has reduced its bank secrecy laws as applied to drug related and other illicit financial movements partly as a result of pressure from the US. Efforts to reduce tax evasion by multinational corporations is another pressure point; many governments have an interest in seeking international cooperation to better identify and control the international movement of corporate funds. What is needed, then, is an extension of these ongoing efforts at international co-operation on the restriction of financial flows to include mandatory cooperation in support of national capital controls – as originally proposed by Harry Dexter White.

An internationally coordinated transactions tax

Another globally coordinated measure which has received wide discussion among academics and some international organizations is the so-called Tobin Tax, named after Nobel Laureate economist James Tobin.[33] The Tobin Tax is a small percentage tax on all foreign exchange transactions. It is designed to discourage excessive short term speculation without discouraging longer-term, presumably more efficient flows of capital and uses of foreign exchange.

The tax would work like this. Say the rate of tax is 0.5 per cent on all foreign exchange transactions, both when buying and when selling foreign exchange. An investor who buys $1 million in foreign exchange, invests it in a foreign bank for 1 month, and then sells it again (and does this every month), will pay (0.005) X 12 X 2 X $1 million or a total of $120,000 in tax (or a tax rate of 12% per year). If she buys and holds only for one day, and she does this every day, she will pay tax at the rate of 365% per year. Only a very large expected profit on speculative dealings could justify such foreign exchange churning. On the other hand, if she buys and holds a 1 year bond, she will pay a tax of 1% or $10,000 on a million dollar investment.

Tobin points out that such a tax would have to be levied globally or at least in all major financial sectors. Otherwise, foreign exchange transactions would simply move to an untaxed locale. Implementing such a coordinated international tax would be relatively easy. Any of the international financial institutions, such as the IMF, BIS, or WTO could implement and enforce the tax with the help of local authorities. The international coordination of financial regulation is widening and deepening in any case. Moreover, there are relatively few technical obstacles to such a tax, since the same computer technology that facilitates capital flows could be used to monitor and tax them.

However, there are serious limitations to the Tobin Tax as a mechanism for dealing with the disruptions created by contemporary international capital mobility. A small tax would not discourage massive speculation based on the expectation of a one shot, immanent, large devaluation, as in the recent British or Mexican cases. Indeed, mainstream advocates of the tax see this as an advantage: they do not want to discourage speculation against what they see as unsustainable or ill-advised policies.

Implementing an internationally coordinated Tobin Tax would be a major step forward and we strongly endorse it. But it would not be sufficient to qualitatively alter the domestic political class balance of power. While such a tax might allow for a temporarily lower interest rate in one country undertaking an expansionary policy, it would not protect countries implementing longer term policies which dramatically differ from the international lowest common denominator. Deeper and broader controls would likely be necessary to bring about the results we require. And these deeper controls are, in the present environment, likely to be implemented only at the national or regional levels.

VI. CAPITAL CONTROLS AT THE NATIONAL OR REGIONAL LEVELS

Controls on direct foreign investment

Consider first controls on foreign direct investment. There is a wide range of experience with constraints on the activities of MNCs. With respect to inflows, many countries have restricted the purchase of domestic companies by foreigners anywhere in the economy (South Korea) or in certain sectors (oil, Mexico). Other countries have allowed only the purchase of minority shares in companies, or in companies of particular sectors (the media, US). With respect to outflows, countries have placed general restrictions on foreign direct investment (South Korea), or have controlled particular investments (for example, the sale of sensitive high technology production processes to potential enemies). The general considerations outlined above apply here: the point is to get sufficient control over capital to create a qualitative change in the domestic political balance of class power.

Restrictions on bank lending to non-residents

A widely discussed measure which would discourage shorter-term flows is based on the recognition that speculators must first obtain a currency before they can sell it. Non-resident speculators often borrow domestic currency from financial institutions for future resale. To reduce the incentive for such speculation, countries or regions could place a tax on lending to non-residents, or a requirement that a portion of all such loans be put into a non-interest bearing account.[34] In the case of a deposit requirement, the size of the requirement could be proportional to the size of the loan. Because speculators receive no interest on these deposits, they function as a tax. The higher the interest rate, the higher the interest foregone, and thus the higher the tax rate. Hence, the higher the interest rate differential between home and abroad (and therefore the greater the incentive for speculation), the higher the rate of the tax.

These controls could eventually become quite leaky. Residents may begin to borrow from domestic banks in order to lend the money to non-residents, thereby circumventing controls. Advocates of such controls, therefore, see these policies as being effective only in the short term. For longer term controls on capital, stronger medicine is clearly required.

Using the tax system to reduce capital mobility

Perhaps the easiest and most efficient way to reduce destructive capital mobility is to use a well developed, politically accepted institution which all advanced industrial countries rely on: the tax system. The great advantage of reliance on the tax system where feasible is that it involves no new bureaucracy and, at least in the advanced countries, is reasonably cost effective.

Consider first the imposition of a 'Keynes' tax – a tax on the sale of any financial asset held for less than a target length of time, say one or two years.[35] The Keynes tax is a natural complement to the Tobin tax because before large sums of 'hot' money can flee the country, they must first be harvested through the sale of assets or by borrowing. Taxing the sale of the asset and taxing the foreign exchange transaction should have the same qualitative effect on the profitability of flight. And a Keynes tax can be applied unilaterally. Of course, since it penalizes domestic financial market 'churning', a Keynes tax would also have a salutary effect on the stability of domestic financial markets. Similar results could be obtained through changes in the provisions of the capital gains tax: penalty rates (relative to ordinary income) applied to the sale of assets held for less than the target period could be very effective.

The tax system can also be used directly as a type of capital control by treating differentially income generated from foreign and domestic financial investment. For example, until 1995 the tax treatment of gains and losses on the foreign and domestic securities held by the very powerful Japanese insurance industry were set so as to severely limit the incentive to invest abroad. These tax laws were quite effective in achieving their desired results. Institutions such as pension funds and insurance companies hold large and rapidly rising shares of advanced country domestic financial wealth, and they are trading securities across national borders at an increasing rate. By taxing the gains from cross border investments at a penalty rate and by discriminating against the deductibility of cross border losses, governments could substantially reduce the propensity of money to move into and out of the country.

Another way to see the point that the tax systems can be used to control capital mobility is to note that in some cases tax systems already promote capital outflows. In the United States, for example, tax rules that govern multinational corporations' transactions (such as transfer pricing, deferral of tax payments and deductibility of taxes paid in foreign jurisdictions) have had the effect of promoting outward foreign direct investment. These rules could be changed to discourage such outflows.

Focusing on the tax system makes it clear that enforcing international capital controls need be no harder (and no easier) than imposing taxes. Taxes, like capital controls, are, to some degree, evaded. It costs money and takes effort to collect taxes as it does to control capital mobility. But where there is a will to collect taxes, they are collected; it would simply take a change in the tax law to extend this mechanism to reducing international capital mobility.

Dual exchange rates

Dual (or multiple) exchange rates can substitute for or reinforce the tax proposals discussed earlier.[36] A major problem with capital flight, as noted above, is that it can significantly lower the exchange rate, greatly increase the cost of imports, and thereby substantially lower the standard of living. The destructive effects of capital flight could be reduced if their impact on the cost of imports could be attenuated or eliminated.

That is what dual exchange rates attempt to do. Separate exchange rates are established for trade and capital transactions. The government stabilizes the rate used for trade, but allows the rate used for capital transactions to float. In this system, even if capital flight greatly depreciated the value of the exchange rate, businesses would be able to obtain foreign exchange from the government at the old rate in order to import products. Hence, the attempt by speculators to sell domestic currency need not increase the cost of imports. Such dual exchange rates have been widely used, particularly in developing countries. In 1975, three industrial countries used dual exchange rates, and 22 developing countries did so. By 1990, only one industrial country (South Africa) used them, but the number of developing countries using them increased to 34.[37] Andrew Glyn has recently proposed using them in Great Britain.[38]

A difficulty with dual rates is that people try to evade them by buying the cheaper currency from the government, then using it to purchase financial assets abroad. Hence, a strong enforcement mechanism may be required to reduce the likelihood that the country will run out of foreign exchange because of illegal capital flight. Eventually the government may find that it needs to implement quantitative controls.

Quantitative restrictions

The most commonly used capital controls are quantitative in nature. There have been a dazzling array of controls used by different countries at different times. In 1975, 17 industrial countries and 85 developing countries had some types of quantitative restrictions on payments for capital transactions on the books. By 1990, 11 industrial countries and 109 developing countries had them.[39] Of course, having them on the books and strongly enforcing them may be two different things. In the 1992 ERM crisis, for example, Ireland and Portugal implemented strong capital controls simply by enforcing and strengthening controls that were already law. To give the reader an idea of current practice, we list some examples of controls that have been used recently.[40]

In Ireland in 1992: (1) all credits to non–resident Irish pound-denominated accounts in excess of 250,000 pounds had to be reported to the Central Bank unless the credit was trade-related; (2) residents were not allowed to make financial loans in Irish pounds for periods of less than one year to non–residents without the permission of the Central Bank; (3) foreign currency accounts were available to residents but with restrictions: for example, deposits made with funds converted from Irish pounds had to be held for at least three months; (4) forward foreign exchange transactions in Irish pounds for speculative purposes were prohibited – minimum maturity requirements of 21 days were imposed; and (5) as the crisis developed, the law was strengthened so that all currency swaps required central bank approval.[41] In Portugal during the same crisis, all short term local currency lending to non–residents was prohibited.

More comprehensive quantitative controls have also been used. These could be held out as a threat to bring capital to the bargaining table if milder controls don't suffice. For example, in Argentina, in April 1982, (as in many countries in the early post-war years) all sales of foreign exchange were prohibited except for imports and for principle repayments and interest payments on foreign loans. In Mexico in the summer of 1982, all foreign exchange transactions were made subject to control, with the Banco de Mexico (and its designated agents) being the only authorized foreign exchange supplier. A 5,000 peso limit was imposed on imports and exports of domestic currency and limits were placed on the amount of foreign currency that could be taken out of Mexico by each person. Issuance of payments and other transactions in pesos abroad by Mexican credit institutions was prohibited. Profit and royalty remittances associated with foreign direct investment in Mexico were limited to 15 per cent of equity subject to foreign exchange availability.[42] And the list goes on.

As these examples suggest, there is a whole panoply of quantitative controls which can and have been used. These range from controlling a select set of transactions to controlling all uses of foreign exchange, including trade. There is no shortage of examples and experiences to either adopt or to use as a threat.

V. CONCLUSION

Two questions immediately come to mind when assessing the case for capital controls. First, even if they worked would they be a good thing? Second, will they work, for how long and at what cost?

Even if one dismisses the notion that unfettered free market capitalism delivers the goods, one may still raise objections to capital controls. First, won't they reduce the flows of capital to poorer countries that badly need them?[43] The best answer is that private capital markets are currently doing a poor job of transferring useful capital to most poor countries. In fact, the net flow of capital to poorer countries is much smaller than is commonly realized. There are substantial two-way flows, but little net transfer of funds; and much of what does flow is short term and unstable.[44] The citizens of Mexico as a whole did not benefit from the huge flow of mutual fund money that went their way.[45] What is needed is a much better public mechanism of capital transfers to poorer countries, not more unstable two-way flows.

Second, won't controls drive financial business away from a country's financial centre and cost income, revenue and jobs? This threat is often highly exaggerated. Andrew Glyn argues that the City of London's dealings in sterling (as opposed to other business), actually brings in very little revenue to the U.K. He notes that 'The City's contribution to the balance of payments is indeed "invisible' in more ways than one".[46] But even if this financial business is lost, that may not be such a bad thing. Many financial sector jobs in the US and other financial centres are not by most accounts socially productive.[47] These clerks and MBA's could be much better used elsewhere in the economy. Indeed, that is one point in favour of capital controls: they can facilitate policies that will achieve a more socially rational use of physical and human resources.

There is evidence based on statistical analysis and case studies that suggests that capital controls can be effective, at least in the short to medium term. Marston shows that capital controls on outflows were effective in keeping domestic interest rates in Britain, France, and Germany below international levels in the 1960s and 1970s, before they were dismantled.[48] Grilli and Milesi-Ferretti, in a study of 61 developed and developing economies, find that countries with exchange and capital controls tend to have lower inflation adjusted interest rates than those that don't.[49] Epstein and Schor report econometric work indicating that in the 1970s and early 1980s countries with capital controls tended to have lower unemployment rates.[50] Manuel Pastor and James Boyce and Lyuba Zarsky both report econometric studies which suggest that capital controls reduced capital flight in the 1980s in a number of developing countries.[51] Most of these studies refer to controls on outward flows. The International Monetary Fund report on the experience of many countries with inward capital controls during the last five years or so found that such controls have been effective in stabilizing exchange rates and interest rates.[52]

The strongest and most convincing evidence that relatively strict capital controls are not only technically feasible, but can be used successfully as a crucial component of a national interventionist strategy to achieve long term growth and stability has already been presented. The so-called 'economic miracles' of late twentieth century capitalism – including Japan, South Korea, Germany and Sweden – all used capital controls in conjunction with a whole set of interventionist policies to achieve decades-long prosperity. These cases provide compelling evidence that controls, when implemented properly and embedded in a coherent national economic plan, can work brilliantly. Of course, progressive economists have no desire to simply replicate the Japanese and South Korean development experiences. The design and implementation of an effective long term interventionist growth plan requires a prior political 'contract' or agreement that forces all major class strata to accept the roles and responsibilities given to them in the plan. In both Japan and South Korea, this political commitment was imposed by force on the weaker classes by the stronger. Japan smashed labour's political power in the late 1940s (with the help of US occupation forces) while Korea 'still enforces tough anti-strike laws that go back to the years of military rule'.[53] We hope to see the enactment and/or threat of controls used to help democratically create the political preconditions required for the constitution of an effective and progressive economic program. Unless and until working people can substantially reduce the economic and political power of rentiers and globally oriented industrialists, no such progressive economic program will be possible. Capital controls can help solve this *political* problem. Whatever their other flaws, the experience of the 'economic miracle' countries demonstrates conclusively that there are no economic or technical impediments to the successful use of controls.

But haven't things changed? Aren't Japan, Korea and the other 'success stories' dismantling their controls? To some extent, they are. But, as we have stressed, the primary reasons are *political, not economic or technical.* An extremely interesting study by Daniele Checchi suggests one reason why even countries that have used controls effectively are retreating from them to some degree.[54] In a careful econometric analysis he found that in two out of three countries he studied (that is, in Great Britain and Japan, but not in Australia) more intensive use of capital controls was associated with a higher labour share of income. Hence, capital controls, possibly by contributing to lower unemployment and more rapid economic growth, may have enhanced labour's power vis-à-vis industrial capital and rentiers.

The evidence reviewed here supports our thesis that capital controls are technically feasible, and that even comprehensive controls can be maintained for long periods of time with very positive effects on economic performance. Thus, as we see it, it is a mistake for the debate about controls on the left to continue to focus on their technical feasibility. That is not really in dispute even on the right: as *The*

Economist put it recently, those 'who demand that the trend of global integration be halted and reversed, are frightening precisely because, *given the will, governments could do it*'.[55] Indeed, as we noted at the beginning of this essay, it is not at all clear that even if progressives fail to support capital controls they will stay off the political agenda. It is virtually inevitable that another financial earthquake such as global rentiers recently experienced in Mexico will erupt in the future, perhaps next time in the more dangerous form of a financial meltdown in a major country. One of these events is likely to trigger a demand for the reinstitution of controls by rentiers and industrialists. The left had best come to grips with the question of controls before they are unilaterally imposed on us by our political enemies.

It is often argued that the implementation of capital controls by a progressive government is self-defeating because capital will flee the country as soon as the policy is given serious political attention, before the controls can be implemented. There is some validity to this argument, but it applies as well to *any* serious policy proposal (such as low interest rates, higher taxes on the rich or tighter financial market regulation) perceived to be against the interests of rentiers. Should we abandon support of all progressive policies out of fear of such retribution? In any case, several considerations suggest that the problem may be manageable. If capital controls are part of a sensible, believable overall plan to raise the rate of economic growth and reduce economic uncertainty over the longer run, some holders of longer term real and financial assets might not see flight as their most profitable option. More important, the *sequence* in which various controls are introduced can affect the degree of severity of the problem. Suppose relatively moderate Keynes and Tobin taxes are introduced first. If more powerful controls are contemplated thereafter, they can be preceded by a substantial rise in the magnitude of these taxes. In the same vein, taxes on some transactions involved in the flight of capital can be applied retroactively, again limiting the gain from flight. And it is possible to enact *standby controls* in conditions where there is no immediate plan for their implementation. At some future time when more comprehensive controls are considered, the standby controls can be used without prior notice to prevent anticipatory capital flight. That is, under proper sequencing, the cost of flight can be raised just as the incentive to flee goes up.

In sum, these problems are indeed serious, but not in principle insurmountable. What remains most relevant is the potential contribution of capital controls to the economic success of a progressive full employment policy regime and their ability to change the political power of the contending classes.

Politically, the real question is whether it is likely to be possible for a democratically constituted majority coalition to wrest effective control over government economic policy in all its dimensions from rentiers and industrialists in the absence of controls or, at bare minimum, the credible threat of their implementation. That is, can the veto power over economic policy currently held by an increasingly powerful, arrogant and pitiless capitalist class be broken by working people without the use of controls? Is Andrew Glyn correct that the most effective way to solve the severe problems of the current conjuncture is for the working class to unilaterally agree to pay any and all costs that arrogant capital might demand for its permission to move the economy closer to full employment?

Our answers to these questions are clear. We believe it will not be possible to restore the political and economic position of working people to anything resembling their Golden Age status (never mind improving on it) unless we can successfully challenge the domestic political power of capital. Since one of the crucial pillars of capitalist power is the unrestricted freedom of rentiers and MNCs to roam the world in search of economic profit and political dominance, constraints on this freedom in the form of capital and trade controls are a necessary precondition for the creation of a more favourable class power balance. Without a substantial structural rise in the power of labour relative to capital, the hoped for constitution of a 'new deal' committing capital, labour and the state to the pursuit of sustained full employment, greater economic equality and a more adequate social welfare system may turn out to be nothing more than a dream. And if that turns out to be the case, if the neoliberal regime continues to deepen and strengthen, the cost to humanity may prove to be incalculable.

NOTES

We are grateful to Leo Panitch and Ilene Grabel for helpful comments on an earlier draft.

1   The term 'social contract' is used in this essay in a metaphorical rather than a literal sense. It refers to the multiplicity of laws, formal agreements, and informal arrangements, conventions and practices through which capital, labour and the state, or various segments thereof, coordinated their actions in pursuit of agreed upon economic objectives. When in the course of this essay we argue in favour of the use of controls over international economic flows as a means to force capital to 'negotiate' a progressive new 'social contract' or a 'New Deal' with labour and the citizenry, we do not mean to limit our political vision to some grand national convocation of labour, capital and the state. A new 'social contract', should one eventuate, is more likely to evolve from a wide range of economic and political agreements negotiated at various private and public sites.

2   See, for example, Barry Eichengreen, James Tobin and Charles Wyplosz, 'Two Cases for Sand in the Wheels of International Finance', *Economic Journal*, 105 (January), 1995, and the references there.

3   International Monetary Fund, *International Capital Markets; Developments, Prospects, and Policy Issues*, Washington: IMF, 1995. However, the report maintained the IMF's strong opposition to controls on outflows.

4   See also the excellent collection of articles in Jonathan Michie and John Grieve Smith, eds., *Managing the Global Economy*, Oxford: Oxford University Press, 1995, especially the chapters by Akyuz, Cornford and Kelly.

5   Andrew Glyn, 'Social Democracy and Full Employment', *New Left Review*, 211, 1995.

6   Ibid., p.55.

7   By global rentier class we mean national rentiers with an interest in the free flow of capital across borders. While such rentiers do not, strictly speaking, constitute a class, they do have important economic and political interests in common. Moreover, these common interests are institutionally represented by the World Bank, the IMF, and most of the central banks of the world.

8   For other discussions of the rise and fall of the Golden Age and the Bretton Woods System, see Fred L. Block, *The Origins of International Economic Disorder*, Berkeley: University of California Press, 1977, and Stephen A. Marglin and Juliet B. Schor, eds., *The Golden Age of Capitalism*, Oxford: Clarendon Press, 1990.

9   Robert Zevin, 'Are World Financial Markets More Open? If so, why and with what effects?', in Tariq Banuri and Juliet B. Schor, eds., *Financial Openness and National Autonomy*, Oxford: Oxford University Press, 1992.

10 Eric Hobsbawm, *The Age of Extremes*, New York: Pantheon, 1994.

11 James Crotty, 'On Keynes and Capital Flight', *Journal of Economic Literature*, Vol. 21, 1983.

12 Gerald A. Epstein and Juliet B. Schor, 'The Structural Determinants and Economic Effects of Capital Controls in the OECD', in Banuri and Schor, eds., *Financial Openness and National Autonomy*.

13 The discussion here draws very heavily on C. Randall Henning, *Currencies and Politics in the United States, Germany and Japan*, Washington: Institute for International Economics, 1994; John B. Goodman and Louis Pauly, 'The Obsolescence of Capital Controls? Economic Management in an Age of Global Markets', *World Politics*, Vol. 46 (October), 1993; and especially Eric Helleiner, *States and the Reemergence of Global Finance*, Ithaca: Cornell University Press, 1994.

14 Quoted in Helleiner, *States and the Reemergence of Global Finance*, p. 38.

15 Ibid., p. 47.

16 Thomas Ferguson, 'From Normalcy to New Deal: Industrial Structure, Party Competition, and American Public Policy in the Great Depression', *Industrial Organization*, Vol. 38, 1984.

17 Goodman and Pauly, 'The Obsolescence of Capital Controls?'.

18 Henning, *Currencies and Politics*, p. 314.

19 Henning, *Currencies and Politics*, p. 314; Donald J. Mathieson and Liliana Rojas-Suarez, *Liberalization of the Capital Account; Experience and Issues*, International Monetary Fund Occasional Paper 103, Washington, D.C.: International Monetary Fund, March, 1993, p. 9.

20 Jessica Gordon Nembhard, *Capital Control, Financial Regulation and Industrial Policy in South Korea and Brazil*, Westport, Ct: Praeger Publishers, 1996.

21 Alice Amsden, *Asia's Next Giant*, Oxford: Oxford University Press, 1989.

22 Samuel Bowles, David Gordon and Thomas Weisskopf, *After the Wasteland*, Armonk, New York: M.E. Sharpe, 1990.

23 Helleiner, *States and the Reemergence of Global Finance*.

24 A growing proportion of this increasing pool of public debt is held by non-resident rentiers. And government bonds held by foreigners have a much higher rate of turnover

than bonds held domestically. Thus, 'the opinions of international bondholders have become increasingly important in countries with big public-sector debts. In recent years bond markets have passed votes of no confidence [in the fiscal policy of] several heavily indebted governments, including those of Canada, Italy and Sweden'. Moreover, 'when the global capital market dislikes an economic policy it moves fast' (*The Economist*, 7 October 1995).

25 See Gerald A. Epstein, 'International Financial Integration and Full Employment Monetary Policy', *Review of Political Economy*, Vol. 7, No. 2, 1995, and Gerald A. Epstein and Herbert Gintis, 'International Capital Markets and the Limits of National Economic Policy', in Banuri and Schor, eds. *Financial Openness and National Autonomy*, and the references cited there.

26 James Burke, 'The Effects of Foreign Direct Investment on Investment, Employment and Wages In the United States', mimeo, University of Massachusetts, Amherst, 1996; Martin Feldstein, 'Foreign Direct Investment and National Investment', NBER Paper, 1994. A recent *Wall Street Journal* article on the transfer of technology and high skilled jobs from the US to China by the Boeing Corporation noted that the cost to Boeing of equivalent labour in China and the US was $120 and $3,530 per month respectively (10 October 1995, p.1).

27 *The Economist*, 7 October 1995. Glyn ('Social Democracy and Full Employment', p. 48) reports that daily turnover is 'four times the total gross central bank intervention during the 1992 ERM crisis ($270 billion)'.

28 James Crotty, 'Are Keynesian Uncertainty and Macrotheory Compatible? Conventional Decision Making, Institutional Structures, and Conditional Stability in Keynesian Macromodels', in Robert Pollin and Gary Dymski, eds., *New Perspectives in Monetary Macroeconomics*, Ann Arbor: University of Michigan Press, 1994.

29 Ilene Grabel, 'Marketing the Third World: The Contradictions of Portfolio Investment in the Global Economy', mimeo, Graduate School of International Studies, University of Denver, 1995. Colin Danby, 'Constructing a Crisis: Mexican Financial Liberalization, 1989-1994', paper presented to the Eastern Economic Association, March, 1995. International Monetary Fund, *International Capital Markets; Developments, Prospects, and Policy Issues*, Washington: IMF, 1995.

30 Manfred Bienefeld, 'Capitalism and the Nation State in the Dog Days of the Twentieth Century', in this volume, p. 72, p. 122.

31 Since small country governments are often tightly controlled by economic elites, it is not surprising that they normally permit themselves modes of evasion of their own capital controls. Controls are not in principle unenforceable. Consider for example the case of South Korea, where 'violations of prohibitions on overseas capital transfers were punishable by a minimum sentence of ten years in prison and a maximum sentence of death' (Ilene Grabel, 'Marketing the Third World', pp. 28-9). Since the Korean government was serious about enforcement, its controls were quite effective for decades.

32 Fred Block, 'Remaking Our Economy; New Strategies for Structural Reform', *Dissent Magazine*, Spring 1993, pp. 170-1.

33 James Tobin, 'A Proposal for International Monetary Reform', *Eastern Economic Journal*, 4, 1978; James Tobin, 'A Tax on International Currency Transactions', in United Nations, *Human Development Report*, 1994.

34 Barry Eichengreen, James Tobin and Charles Wyplosz, 'Two Cases for Sand in the Wheels of International Finance', *Economic Journal*, 105 (January), 1995.

35 See Dean Baker, Robert Pollin, and Marc Schaberg, 'The Case for a Securities Transaction Tax: Taxing the Big Casino', Washington, DC: Economic Policy Institute, mimeo, 1995. As Baker, Pollin and Schaberg note in their Table 1, numerous industrialized countries have financial transactions taxes, including the US, which has a 0.0004% tax on stock sales. As discussed above, since domestic currency can also be borrowed and then sold abroad, deposit requirements or taxes on borrowing may also be required to get maximum effectiveness from the Keynes tax. But since a large portion of the run away funds will come from the sale of domestic financial assets, the Keynes tax should be reasonably effective even on its own.

36 R. Dornbusch, *Exchange Rates and Inflation*, Cambridge, Ma.: MIT Press, 1989; Glyn, 'Social Democracy and Full Employment'.

37 Mathieson and Rojas-Suarez, *Liberalization of the Capital Account*, p. 5.

38 Andrew Glyn, 'Market dual: jobs vs. currency', *New Economy*, 1994.

39 The total number of countries included in the sample increased from 128 in 1975 to 153 in 1990 (Mathieson and Rojas-Suarez, *Liberalization of the Capital Account*, p. 5, Table 1).

40 IMF, *International Capital Markets*, ch. 5.

41 Ibid., p. 104.

42 Ibid., p. 106.

43 Fred Block, 'Remaking Our Economy; New Strategies for Structural Reform', *Dissent Magazine*, Spring 1993.

44 Block, 'Remaking Our Economy'; Epstein, 'International Financial Integration and Full Employment Monetary Policy'; Epstein and Schor, 'The Structural Determinants and Economic Effects of Capital Controls in the OECD', in Banuri and Schor, eds., *Financial Openness and National Autonomy*.

45 Colin Danby, 'Constructing a Crisis'; Grabel, 'Marketing the Third World'.

46 Glyn, 'Market dual', p. 196.

47 See James Crotty and Don Goldstein, 'Do US Financial Markets Allocate Credit Efficiently?', in Gary Dymski, Gerald Epstein and Robert Pollin, eds., *Transforming the US Financial System*, Armonk, NY: M.E. Sharpe, on the allocational inefficiency of US financial markets. Robert Fitch ('Explaining New York City's Aberrant Economy', *New Left Review*, 207, 1994) has vividly described how reliance on global and domestic banking, real estate and insurance has helped bring the city of New York to its knees.

48 Richard C. Marston, *International Financial Integration; A study of interest differentials between the major industrial countries*, Cambridge: Cambridge University Press, 1995.

49 Vittorio Grilli and Gian Maria Milesi-Ferretti, 'Economic Effects and Structural Determinants of Capital Controls', IMF Staff Papers, 1996.

50 Epstein and Schor, 'The Structural Determinants and Economic Effects of Capital Controls in the OECD', in Banuri and Schor, eds., *Financial Openness and National Autonomy*.

51 Manuel Pastor, Jr., 'Capital Flight from Latin America', *World Development*, Vol. 18, No. 1, 1990. James Boyce and Lyuba Zarsky, 'Capital Flight from the Philippines, 1962-1986', *The Journal of Philippine Development*, Vol. 15, No. 2, 1988.

52 IMF, *International Capital Markets*.

53 Shigeto Tsuru, *Japan's Capitalism: Creative Defeat and Beyond*, Cambridge: Cambridge University Press, 1993; *Wall Street Journal*, 20 October, 1995, p. A9A.

54 Daniele Checchi, 'Capital Controls and Distribution of Income: Empirical Evidence for Great Britain, Japan and Australia', *Weltwirtschaftliches Archiv*, 128, 1992.

55 *The Economist*, 7 October 1995, p.16, emphasis added.

A WORLD MARKET OF OPPORTUNITIES?
CAPITALIST OBSTACLES AND LEFT ECONOMIC POLICY

Gregory Albo

As Ralph Miliband observed in his last book, *Socialism for a Sceptical Age*, the socialist project for a radical social order of equality has rested on two central propositions: capitalism constitutes a massive obstacle to resolving a range of social evils and injustices; a socialist alternative makes possible a resolution of these offences and inequities.[1] The pessimism that infuses the Left at the end of the century is founded, in the first instance, in the re-assessment of capitalist market processes as more efficient in meeting human needs than previously conceded and, moreover, capable of extensive institutional variation so as to allow egalitarian policy outcomes without confronting capitalist social power. Economic efficiency can be combined with social equity.

It is further argued that socialist economic policy is, in any case, no longer capable – if it ever was – of advancing solutions to the injustices of capitalist markets (let alone of offering a plausible alternative social order). This political qua policy impotence is due, in large measure, to the formation of a world economy that provides an overwhelming external constraint to policies that are inconsistent with the *irreversible* processes of globalization. The crisis years after 1974 have ceded, moreover, to an era of *restabilized* capitalism, ascendant and embraced in all corners of the world. So even if there is a margin of manoeuvrability for national economic policies, as Paul Hirst and Grahame Thompson assert (to cite a much noted recent example), this is merely a question of further building 'extra-market institutions' to manage the new conjuncture as capitalist markets

This essay was first published in *Ruthless Criticism of All That Exists, The Socialist Register 1997*.

have proven their greater inherent efficiency and dynamism.[2] If there are *injustices* still residing in capitalism, and even New Labour concedes there are, these are best resolved by measures that work with rather than against markets. Egalitarian policy measures should thus only seek to equalize market opportunities through widening the 'stakes' in capitalist enterprises via employee share ownership plans, self-employment initiatives, life-long training accounts, and the like.[3] To uphold socialist propositions in the face of the prevailing political consensus is, as Miliband himself recognized of the predictable charge, 'to demonstrate a lamentable lack of realism'.[4]

In the advanced capitalist countries, this broad disillusionment with Left economic policy is deeply entwined with the last two decades of social democratic setback and retreat followed by further openings to the disciplines of neoliberalism and the world economy. The electorally most successful case of social democratic governance over this period, the example of Australian Labour, has only offered, in the brilliant analysis of John Wiseman, a 'kinder road to hell' of cutbacks and austerity in its efforts to recast itself as an 'East Asian capitalism'.[5] Labour's defeat at the polls in 1996 promises to veer Australia down the even more treacherous path of neoliberal austerity in a desperate effort to maintain a faltering external competitiveness. The postwar social democratic strongholds of Austria and Sweden have their governments extensively scaling back their welfare states, disposing state enterprises and adopting the neoliberal policy stance of economic openness and flexible labour markets. With the external sector bursting from capital outflows and unemployment at pan-European levels, it cannot seriously be maintained, as so many on the Left still attempted to do even during its 1980s break-up, that the Swedish model is still alive and prospering.[6] A similar story could be told of the Rhineland Model of Germany, which has all of Sweden's problems and others. Its 'concertation capitalism' has witnessed over the last year increasingly ferocious efforts by employers to scale back employee benefits and involvement. Ever alert to new opportunities to proclaim that the legacy of reform is being cast aside, New Labour's Tony Blair, on a visit to Wall Street in April 1996, drew the lessons from these experiences that a social democratic Britain 'must be competitive internationally to help attract international business investment. I am a passionate free trader and unashamed anti-protectionist'.[7]

The divergent economic trajectories after 1974 that first seemed to characterize social democratic governments like Sweden's and technologically-ascendant countries like Germany's now only seem to be alternate routes converging in neoliberalism. Indeed, the varied experiences of the 'previously existing socialisms' of Eastern Europe and the anti-imperialist nationalisms of the Third World also appear to represent no more than circuitous and calamitous routes to ending up on the same capitalist road. The world economy in the 1990s accommodates, it seems, only one model of development: export-oriented production based on flexible labour markets, lower real and social wages, less environmental regulation and freer trade. Neoliberal economic strategies are proposed for political and economic conditions as vastly different as those faced by the new ANC government in South Africa, the Olive Tree centre-Left coalition and transitional economies like the Czech Republic or Hungary.

These concessions to the imperatives of the law of value in the world market – 'we are powerless, there is no alternative' – has been met with a mixture of rejoicing and submission. The leading neoliberal periodical, *The Economist*, has exulted in the transformation so that today – without even a hint of reflexive irony – the central political 'challenge is to help the global capital market to become more effective in encouraging good behaviour [by governments]'.[8] The 'shock therapy' strategy for integration into the world economy is simply, as its foremost strategist, Jeffrey Sachs puts it, the most efficient means to gain the 'organizational methods and financial capital needed to overcome the dismal economic legacy of the past forty years'.[9]

The Left has met these developments with far more resignation but with the same sense of inevitability. A stalwart American Liberal such as Robert Reich baldly concludes that 'as almost every factor of production ... moves effortlessly across borders, the very idea of an American economy is becoming meaningless'.[10] Fritz Scharpf, a leading strategist of the German SDP, voices what is often assumed on the Left that 'unlike the situation of the first three postwar decades, there is now no economically plausible Keynesian strategy that would permit the full realisation of social democratic goals within a national context without violating the functional imperatives of a capitalist economy'.[11] Social democracy must rethink its traditional aspirations to accommodate the new imperatives of global capitalism to maintain, at least, 'socialism in one class'. The only egalitarian policy that it is possible to pursue in the context of internationally mobile capital – and Scharpf is more ambitious than most – is one that redistributes income and jobs among workers as 'growth rates are inadequate and because the distributive claims that capital is able to realize have increased'.[12]

Yet, to make any sense of these formulations, a further set of premises must be held. The present geographical expansion of accumulation must be seen, for instance, as an *irreversible* process that reflects economic dynamism and stability supplanting instability and crisis. It must be argued additionally that any specific *constraints* to economic *stability* can be overcome by policies that further expand global market opportunities.[13] Neoliberals argue for free trade and the deregulation of labour markets as the means to surpass the constraint of limited markets; social democrats opt for policies to train an insufficiently skilled workforce to overcome market constraints on labour adjustment. Within these confines economic policy disputes do indeed go 'beyond Left and Right', as Anthony Giddens phrases it; they are limited to the issue of which specific constraint should be acted upon and the relative speed of flexible adjustment of market processes.[14] But no one disputes that flexible adjustment of markets will occur to allow the harvest of globalization to be reaped.

A final premise is that capitalist globalization represents an historically *progressive* development such that traditional socialist economic objectives, on grounds of political necessity and economic soundness, must be rejected as hopelessly flawed. There is no political need for the Left to put forward policies that encroach upon capitalist social property relations beyond that of a 'stakeholders' capitalism'.[15] Indeed, the principal struggle for socialists today, as writers from as diverse methodological backgrounds as Andrew Gamble and John Roemer have advised, should be limited to the Pareto-optimal distribution of 'ownership rights' between workers and capitalists in internationally competitive enterprises.[16]

There is good reason, however, to at least qualify, perhaps even to reject, each of these premises about internationalization. This essay will, first, briefly re-call the instabilities that still reside at the centre of the world economy and the limitations of neoliberal adjustment measures. It will then question the claims made by social democratic economic policy advocates that only *specific constraints* need to be overcome to re-establish stability, concluding that Miliband's first proposition on the obstacles that capitalism poses *as a system* cannot be relinquished. Finally, an outline of emerging alternative principles for socialist economic policy to confront these obstacles and constraints will be presented. Rather than a world economy being a new opportunity, contemporary internationalization of markets is a contradictory 'space of flows' between the 'spaces of places of production' that are constituted by the specific territorially-embedded conflictual social property relations of capitalism.[17] The economic programme of the Left cannot, following Miliband's second proposition, put to the side questions of market disengagement and the democratic organizational forms that will permit the *transition* to a more fundamentally egalitarian and co-operative economy.

I. NEOLIBERALISM AND IMBALANCES IN THE WORLD ECONOMY

The neoliberal claim that market exchanges always tend to arrive at equilibrium depends upon a number of highly abstract assumptions; they are embedded in deductive models which, however rigorous, are set outside of concrete time and space. The neoliberal position begins from the proposition that overcoming the constraint of *limited markets* is central to resolving unemployment and trade imbalances. Capitalism is an economic system best understood as a process of free individual exchange operating in competitive markets. According to individual behavioural preferences, *individual* economic agents save, innovate and form firms to purchase labour; others prefer leisure, consumption and sell their labour. In accord with the famous law of Say, all demand is effective demand; and if prices are not constrained flexible adjustment in competitive markets will ensure that all needs are satisfied and all markets clear. Unemployment is the 'mutual' and 'voluntary' product of limitations of local labour market flexibility and the global competitiveness of firms. The role of trade in expanding market opportunities and re-allocating resources on the basis of Ricardian comparative advantage – that is, specialization in production where relative cost advantage is highest produces shared output gains for trading nations – depends on free trade in commodities and financial liberalization which ensures that 'savings are directed to the most productive investments without regard for national boundaries'.[18] Globalization is, in other words, capitalism surpassing the limited market constraint on the division of labour: it is a market of expanding opportunities.

There are many angles from which to address strong objections to this idealized view of market processes always balancing. An unemployed worker willing to work for a lower real wage, for example, does not itself lead to a job offer – at least not without resistance from existing employees whose jobs he may take away or whose wages may be cut. From the firm's perspective, given the incompleteness of market information, a low wage offer often signals lower labour quality and hence a less employable candidate. Such lack of flexible prices in the real world raises, of course, the traditional Keynesian argument that decreasing real wages in rigid labour markets not only fails to increase employment, but it also takes demand out of the system causing a further increase in the jobless. This is not to say that wage-cutting does not occur as unemployment levels rise, but that quantity adjustments are as important as price movements so that market-clearing is unlikely to be smooth and instabilities may be compounded. The trends claimed to have caused the real wage rigidity – demographic bulge, welfare and unemployment insurance rates, trade unionization – have been reversed and inflation has fallen to some of its lowest levels in over half a century. As David Gordon acidly noted, it is more accurate to speak of a 'rising natural rate of unemployment' with no acceptable neoliberal explanation, except the preposterous notion of an exogenous shift in the preference functions of individuals toward more unemployment.[19]

The existence of unemployment, whether from wage rigidities or information asymmetries, poses a serious problem for free trade policy. For comparative advantage to hold each country is *assumed* to have full employment and to be producing on their production possibility frontier, that factors of production are completely mobile internally and subject to perfect competition, that monetary fluctuations do not occur and trade is balanced. None of these, of course, are real world assumptions. Predictions from free trade theory, such as output and employment smoothly expanding in new export sectors, or no country consistently running surpluses or deficits, have only the most brittle historical foundation: they are only assertions that in the long run it will all work out.[20] The case for protectionism, or at least for the regulation of trade, is on stronger theoretical grounds purely in terms of employment considerations alone. Even granting all the assumptions necessary for static gains from trade, trade balance depends upon processes of adjustment occurring in actual societies and through history: workers everywhere must have the capacity to raise wages and rates of technical progress must equalize over time or else competitive advantage and trade surplus will become cumulative, raising structural trade imbalances and problems of employment in deficit countries. The deficit country with strong trade unions and high money wages will be forced to adjust, but not the surplus country with weak unions and low wages. It is always difficult to impose appreciation or expenditure increases on surplus countries, as the U.S.-Japan trade rivalry over the last decade indicates. There is instead a tendency for competing countries to match devaluation and austerity to avoid large losses. Indeed, this becomes an imperative as economies become more open. In other words, trade liberalization, especially in a climate of uncertainty and unemployment, tends to reproduce the same effects as protection: everybody attempts to export unemployment but now through competitive austerity which limits domestic demand for imports and improves the price of exports.

While international exchanges have grown tremendously, vastly outstripping the growth of the real economy, the argument that global markets 'provide healthy discipline which in the long term will encourage better economic policies and performance'[21] cannot be sustained in the face of growing evidence of unevenness and instability rather than equalization and equilibration. Economic openness as measured by dependence on exports has increased from under 30 percent in 1950 to almost 40 percent by 1994 in the six largest OECD countries, with trade volumes in the U.S. alone doubling since the early 1970s. Structural trade imbalances have become a key feature of the world economy. The Third World debt crisis remains unresolved: total debt levels have continued to rise, and debt servicing in terms of GDP remains where it was when the debt crisis began in the early 1980s. As important for global imbalances, the structural current account deficit that the U.S. has been running since the early 1980s has made it the largest debtor in history. In contrast, Asia and Japan in particular have been running current surpluses. The clearest measure of the problem is that financial flows, in all forms increasing exponentially over and above trade volumes, have assumed ever greater salience in any calculation of global economic activity. International banking, for example, at the peak of the boom in the 1960s accounted at about 1 percent of GDP of market economies while it now measures more than 20 percent. Foreign exchange transactions are exceeding $1 trillion U.S. *daily* reflecting an explosion in speculation in global equity, bond and currency markets. Financial movements of this order are completely out of any rational balance when trade volumes are only $3.5 trillion *yearly*. These trends certainly indicate a growth in interdependence of production zones through economic flows, but are as much symptoms of disarray, instability and stagnation as of dynamism.

As the economic crisis developed from the 1970s into the 1980s, the advanced capitalist countries turned to policies of disinflation.[22] International trade became a competitive battle for market share and unit labour costs in a futile effort to maintain domestic employment. The mounting trade deficits of many countries – which floating exchange rates were promised to stabilize but failed miserably – were added to fiscal deficits arising from slow growth. As Paul Sweezy has argued, the financing of these deficits meant that international credit markets boomed but increasingly apart, and often directly at odds, from developments in the real economy.[23] Yet rather than stabilize aggregate demand or the external sector, by the mid-80s all the advanced countries had begun to adopt supply-side policies of cutting wages and welfare, adding competitive capacity and financial liberalization. Third World countries went through a similar process of structural adjustment as import-substitution industrialization policies were abandoned for export ones to pay off credits. In other words, all countries were putting more resources into the external sector while cutting domestic demand. This could only increase volatility in the international market and the capacity of interdependent financial markets to swiftly transfer any economic instability across the world economy. In the 1990s most Latin American and African economies continue to be extremely depressed. All economies in Eastern Europe remain well below the pre-shock therapy output peaks of the 1980s. Stagnant growth and wage depression encompass all the advanced countries, including Northern Europe and Japan. Yet even more resources are being re-deployed to the external sector at the same time as austerity policies dominate wage-setting and government economic strategies.

We should be extremely careful to avoid attempting to explain every recent turn – from the collapse of state plans in India to unemployment in Paris to the lack of a universal health plan in the U.S. – to the forces of globalization. It is difficult not to record, however, that a stable alternative for capitalist expansion is far from being achieved. Yet the imperatives of the world economy compel that this unstable process be kept going. Nobody is willing to break ranks first, which is understandable in light of the sanctions that would be viciously meted out by global markets. But this is not warrant to engage in the pretence that imbalances are being overcome, that neoliberal polices are theoretically coherent, that globalization is irreversible or that labour market adjustment is producing socially just outcomes.

II. OPEN-ECONOMY SOCIAL DEMOCRACY

The problems associated with market adjustment to imbalances of trade or unemployment has a lot to do with the fact that economic processes occur in real historical time rather than the timeless space of neoliberal equilibrium models. In discussing the future of the international payments system after the war, Keynes charged that 'to suppose that there exists some smoothly functioning automatic mechanism of adjustment that preserves equilibrium if only we trust to methods of laissez-fare is a doctrinaire delusion which disregards the lessons of historical experience without having behind it the support of sound theory'.[24] In the real world, capitalist techniques and workers' wage demands do not alter instantly with excess labour supply; currency devaluation does not necessarily produce expenditure-switching to domestic industry or export demand: in the Keynesian view, relative price adjustments to restore equilibrium take time to work themselves out in a world of uncertainty.

According to social democratic economic policy, the temporal processes of adjustment signify that the market needs to be governed by managing the *specific* constraints impeding capitalism from reaching the full employment volumes of output that is to the benefit of all, capitalists and workers.[25] This is the central – and ultimately conservative – message of Keynes' *General Theory*: 'if effective demand is deficient, not only is the public scandal of wasted resources intolerable, but the individual enterpriser who seeks to bring these resources into action is operating with the odds loaded against him'.[26] In the postwar period this meant that capitalists had to support a 'national bargain' over taxes and investment, and workers had to endorse public consumption and to set nominal wages so as to control inflation to maintain external balance and a positive sum game of high profits, high employment and rising incomes.[27] Within the capitalist bloc, the Bretton Woods system emphasis on national adjustment helped, as did the low trade volumes and partial controls over capital mobility left over from the era of depression and war. Temporary import controls, wage restraint through incomes policies or realignment of pegged currencies was enough to restore adequate payments balance. It was thought – in perhaps the most egregious of bourgeois modernism's faith in progress through quantity – that with the release of the constraint on demand growth could be endless (and that planetary ecology could take care of itself). The distributional relations necessary for high employment, however, have not been so easily found since the 1970s. Slow growth and declining productivity has meant that capitalists have been less willing to accept the old Keynesian 'national bargain' between the social classes. In order to restore profits, high unemployment rather than incomes policy has kept wage claims in check. Internationalization of production, too, has strengthened the leverage of capitalists to bargain, especially as the various GATT rounds lowered trade tariffs, and low wage production zones such as Korea and Brazil gained technological capacity and foreign investment. All this added to the competitive export pressures already internal to the advanced capitalist bloc. The social democratic experience of Sweden is telling: although developing the foremost 'social market' and raising its relative competitive position, Sweden has had an 'employer offensive' for over a decade to lower real wages, cut taxes and allow unemployment to rise. Direct investment by Swedish capitalists abroad has increased from below 1 percent of GDP in 1982 to above 6 percent by 1990, and it continues to rise.[28] Andrew Glyn now notes that 'Sweden has joined the rush towards stabilisation and explicit anti-egalitarianism as the route to economic recovery'.[29] Nowhere does the old social democratic positive-sum national compromise within a con-straint-freed capitalism still hold.

As a consequence, the social democratic 'rethink' of economic policy for an alternative to neoliberalism has had to address three options. First, an attempt could be made to counter internationalization by controlling capital mobility, by protecting domestic producers and employment by controls over the traded sec-tor and by building alternative planning mechanisms all the way from the local to the international spheres. Second, national stabilization policies could try to maintain the welfare state, establish a competitive exchange rate to insulate do-mestic compromises and redistribute a more slowly growing output and income so as to keep unemployment down (although in consequence likely allowing national competitiveness to fall relative to less egalitarian countries willing to lower unit labour costs more directly). Finally, the challenge of the world market could be met head-on by attempting to raise national competitiveness relative to competitors through improving workplace productivity by involving highly-skilled workers, by adopting new production techniques and by developing new products for export.

The first option is closest to traditional socialist orientations (although it could vary tremendously in methods and ends) and would entail confronting the dis-embedded processes of the world market. It would, no doubt, alarm domestic and foreign capitalists, the consequences of which in a global market could be massively disruptive for individual states accepting the challenge. In the eyes of social democratic policy-makers (at least since the defeat of the Left inside social democratic parties in the early 1980s), this has never really been an option. Social democratic policy had already come to accept internationalization of economic flows over the postwar period and this has been a parameter that social demo-cratic leaders have not wanted to breach, above all because they know that capi-talists would actively oppose it. The second strategy is closest to postwar social democracy, and it once was plausible for countries with large and solidaristic un-ions. But such 'shared austerity' is entirely defensive in posture and increasingly difficult to sustain as external pressures increase and relative economic decline takes hold. There is, in any respect, little fondness any longer amongst capitalists for such a strategy as it keeps in check their market power relative to workers and closes off the option of higher unemployment for external competitiveness. The third option of forming an 'open-economy social democracy' amounts to a more offensive strategy, which, through the promises of increased productiv-ity and output, would possibly re-found the positive-sum compromise between the social classes.[30] This strategy has special appeal because it suggests that there is something 'activist' social democratic governments can do to protect the 'na-tional interest'. If markets are imperfect historical processes, labour adjustment, trade flows and international specialization cannot be left to the working out of comparative advantage through free trade: states can and must help 'shape advantage' to improve labour market performance, trade balance and competitiveness.[31] Some workers and some capitalists might, under the right conditions, even favour this third strategy of launching a 'stakeholders' capitalism'.

The case for a social democratic economic policy of national competitiveness has, moreover, a basis in the theoretical critique being advanced against the pure Ricardian trade theory of neoliberalism. One aspect comes from within the confines of general equilibrium theory itself.[32] That is, if imperfect competition and economies of scale are introduced into international trade models, then 'extra profit' can be gained as price will exceed marginal cost. In these cases, it cannot be ruled out that state intervention into industry may improve economic welfare and domestic output. In industries with technological spillovers to other sectors or that may earn technological rents by protecting their initial product development the case is even somewhat stronger. New industries, for example, often require protection before they can face import competition. Historical precedence and increasing returns to scale can 'lock-in' market share before rivals gain a chance to develop. In this way, the technically superior BETA recorders lost out in the capitalist marketplace to the less capable VHS in the early 1980s. The earlier QWERTY typewriter case and the massive aerospace complex around Seattle are other oft-cited examples. It is possible, in other words, to have a 'strategic trade policy' to get new products developed and into markets as quickly as possible to maximize the profit-shift between countries. Thus even within general equilibrium theory states can 'logically' adopt protective tariffs and industrial policies that depart from free markets and comparative advantage: the ideologically contentious question is whether or not they are politically successful in choosing industrial winners.[33] For liberals, like Paul Krugman, the answer is no and the case for free trade stands.[34] For social democrats, like Robert Kuttner, the answer is yes and the German and East Asian experiences suggest an alternative approach.[35]

The social democratic case for shaped advantage can be bolstered once the general equilibrium model of individual agent market exchanges is let go, and alliances of competing states and firms are explicitly allowed to shape the 'path-dependency' of economic outcomes. That is, 'history matters' to economics. If the income elasticities of various commodities diverge through time, for example, as the early dependency theory critique of Raul Prebisch argued for primary commodities relative to manufactured goods, price divergence and growth polarization may well occur.[36] For countries locked into the production and trade of declining commodities, initial competitive advantage becomes an obstacle to future competitive viability. Shaped advantage can also be invoked to explain something about more general processes of economic decline and ascendancy that has historically shifted the places of states in the world economic hierarchy. Countries losing technological capacity, it is argued, can suffer the economic misfortunes vividly depicted by Britain's fall in world standing. In this case, every attempt at demand expansion by a 'weak' country to raise output 'to catch-up' ends in an economic policy 'stop' to avert a looming balance of payments crisis as high demand sucks in imports. A vicious cycle of stop-go keeps investment in check over the historical long-run because sustained high investment requires stable growth. But depreciation does not correct the underlying productivity differences and thus the reason for the imbalances. As a result, competitiveness increasingly comes to depend upon low cost production or continual competitive devaluations as new technical capacity is blocked from being built. In contrast, technologically ascendant competitors can continue to keep investment high in new techniques as this only adds to output capacity thereby enhancing the payments position and competitive advantage over the long-run.

This conception of 'cumulative causation', in which trade volumes and export and import propensities impact upon aggregate demand, unemployment and competitiveness, becomes more critical the more that states have large open sectors.[37] Competitive performance holds the potential for competitive advantage (or disadvantage) and higher levels of employment (or unemployment). In a liberalized world trading system, the competitive pressures to achieve advantage intensify as technical development and product specialization spread in a continual process of imitation and innovation, of 'catching-up', 'forging-ahead' and 'falling behind'. The implications of this point – so central to the programmatic designs of national competitiveness and the project of 'stakeholders' capitalism' – need to be underlined. In this view, trade occurs not based on 'differential endowments' of the factors of production, but rather on the basis of 'country-specific conditions of technological learning and accumulation'.[38] The conditions that define national (or regional) competitiveness can be summarized as the input efficiencies derived from product quality, workplace 'trust' between workers and employers, 'learning-by-doing' and research effort. As technological change is a continual process of building up technical skills capacity and entrepreneurship, a 'Schumpeterian technological dynamism' needs to be nourished as an overarching societal policy objective.[39] In open economies, therefore, economic growth and unemployment levels are increasingly dependent upon world market share and export capacity derived from relative competitive advantage in the world hierarchy of competing nations. The social democratic redistributional agenda of the 'mixed economy' is thus succeeded by the 'mixed enterprise economy' of 'stakeholders' capitalism' that is at the core of open-economy social democracy. It is also what lies behind the conclusion, stated here by the British centre-Left Institute for Public Policy Research but held across social democratic parties, that 'globalisation offers more opportunities than threats for British business, people and government'.[40]

There are several competing social democratic positions – though to some extent they complement each other – on how shaped advantage can be supplemented to meet also the internal balance of employment (while keeping unit labour costs competitive for external balance). The 'progressive competitiveness' strategy, most closely allied to the views of shaped advantage, emphasizes the demand-side *external* constraint produced by internationalization. Social demo-cratic employment policy should, therefore, concern itself with the growth of productive capacities (or effective supply) so as to keep unit labour costs low by productivity gains rather than low wages. Productive capacities are, according to Wolfgang Streeck, productivity enhancing collective goods such as training, research and development and workplace trust that encourage flexible adjust-ment of production and labour supply to externally set demand conditions.[41] The problem, however, is that the market fails to provide an adequate supply of these collective goods and creates needless conflicts over the need for joint govern-ance between capital and labour in their production. Yet, in fact, they form the national basis of competitiveness in high-waged high value-added economies. Training policies should, therefore, be the central component of a jobs and wel-fare strategy, while relationships of 'trust' and co-operation should be fostered within enterprises through works councils and other forms of 'associative de-mocracy'. A strategy of effective supply can contribute, Joel Rogers and Streeck insist, to the 'restoration of competitiveness in western capitalism ... [and] can establish a new bargain between equity and efficiency'.[42]

Another variant of the social democratic strategy is that of 'shared austerity'. It stresses that the *internal* constraint of distribution relations is critical. Incomes pol-icy has a role to play in spreading work through wage restraint and keeping unit labour costs down for exports. For Andrea Boltho, the highly centralized collec-tive bargaining institutions of the corporatist countries 'lead to a much greater responsiveness of real wages to unfavourable shocks ... [lessening] their destruc-tive effect on unemployment'.[43] Thus the control of inflation for export position and the struggle to spread work falls on corporatist labour market institutions. These institutions also provide the basis, according to Glyn, for the solidaristic income and tax policies that allow 'employment-spreading' of capitalist sector work and income and the financing of public sector employment. 'In a context of weak private demand and slow productivity growth, maintaining full employ-ment required severe restraint on workers' pay and consumption to keep exports competitive, investment profitable and the budget under control. Where social democracy was capable of mobilizing such support, full employment was sustain-able'. Glyn argues that in today's world the key issue is not economic openness, but rather the need to re-establish these mechanisms 'for regulating conflicting claims over distribution and control'.[44] But given that the key distributional compromise today excludes the capitalist class, high employment depends upon the collective capacity of trade unions (supported by social democratic parties) to impose restraint on their members – 'shared austerity in one class'.

A third position, the 'international Keynesian' perspective, maintains that removing the demand constraint of an open-economy simply requires the *political will* to re-establish expansionary policies at the supranational level where leakages to exports and capital outflows would be irrelevant and where competitive firms could realize the additional output for export. This was the view of many on the Labour Left, seeking to maintain and expand on postwar gains, in response to the sharp upturn in unemployment in the 1970s and neoliberal governments in the 1980s.[45] And more bluntly recently stated by David Held: 'government economic policy must to a large degree be compatible with the regional and global movements of capital, unless a national government wishes to risk serious dislocation between its policy objectives and the flows of the wider international economy'.[46] International co-ordination of economic policy is, therefore, required to re-establish the basis for adequate effective demand conditions for higher growth and lower unemployment that are now beyond the capacity of any single state. A 'cosmopolitan democracy' imposed on global governance structures, of the kind favoured by Held, would be one means to legitimate the rules of international economic co-ordination.

All these views avoid the neoliberal illusions that free trade and deregulation of labour markets will resolve trade and employment balances. There is an understanding here of the processes of cumulative causation, of the interaction between internal and external imbalances, of actual contemporary trade patterns and the comparative cost advantage of various competitive capitals, the differentiation of development amongst regions, and of the variable means by which employment may be spread. Unfortunately (but all too common among progressive economists), as Leo Panitch has pointed out, there is little analysis of why social democratic governments have instead gone so far to accommodate neoliberalism.[47] The answer may lie, as he suggests, in the *inadequacy* of the strategy of shaped advantage. For the fact is that it fails to adequately account for the mechanisms of the constraints on governments and thus the obstacles capitalism poses to stabilizing the imbalances resident in the world market.

First, let us consider the treatment of the growing reserve army of unemployed.[48] Unemployment is regarded as the result of the rate of accumulation generated by competitive capacity and demand conditions. Employment must then be a constant coefficient of average labour required per unit of output. Shaped advantage to improve competitive capacity, however, will lower this coefficient through labour-saving technological change (the basic form of technical change within capitalism). If work-hours and employment ratios are left constant despite technical advance, there must be an increase in total income and total employment hours demanded to compensate for the labour-saving per unit of output otherwise unemployment will increase. This 'knife-edge' balance was difficult to maintain in even the conditions of the 'golden age'.[49] But when the strategy must be implemented in our actual historical time and with the expectation that external trade will increase relative to domestic output, it becomes fanciful to imagine that this balance can be achieved.

Indeed, growth in trade will need to exceed the growth rate of output, which must itself exceed the combined growth rates of productivity and employment to absorb the many forms of the reserves of unemployed. Moreover, as technological change continues through time (notably in the traded goods sector whose advantage is being shaped), the growth of trade must continue at an accelerating rate to generate a given volume of employment and hours of work. In a stable world economy with a co-ordinated international macroeconomic policy it is extremely dubious that this would all work out; in a capitalism that generates differentiated competitive capacities and that is exhibiting the trade asymmetries and currency instability that exist today, it is quite impossible to envision. Shaped trade advantage to improve external competitiveness in the hope that trade growth will overcome internal obstacles to high employment is no substitute for national and local employment policies to constrain the capitalist market.[50]

Apart from the problem of unemployment, a second fundamental problem is an equally dubious assumption that shaped advantage offers a solution to the external imbalances that derive from the uneven development of competitive capacities within capitalism. Indeed, the reliance on market adjustment may well compound global external imbalances by the competitive imperatives of shaped advantage in the present world configuration. Let us further consider the obstacles capitalism presents just on the basis of developing the theme of uneven competitive capacities as it relates to individual country strategies. At the conceptual level, a trade surplus has its presupposition in unit labour costs and hence export prices that are internationally competitive. Countries of successful export-led growth can sustain high investment without fear of a balance of payments crisis. The trade surplus is expected, moreover, to have positive effects on national income and employment. If the profit from full capacity utilization is reinvested in new technological capacity, and exchange rates do a poor job of equilibrating trade balance through appreciation, then economic growth and competitiveness will be maintained through decline in unit labour costs from productivity advance in surplus countries.[51] The point is, however, that *the opposite will be the case for deficit countries which will have listless investment and faltering technological capacity.* This seems to explain in good part the consistency of countries in structural current account deficit and declining competitive capacity such as Britain and the U.S., in relation to countries such as Germany and Japan that have been relatively in constant surplus. In other words, uneven development and trade imbalances can be expected to persist as one of the normal obstacles capitalism presents to alignment of market-friendly development trajectories.[52]

For individual technologically laggard countries, then, the problem is to rupture the vicious circle of stagnation before it perpetuates chronic relative decline or the potential falling per capita incomes of absolute peripheralization. The strategy of shaped advantage proposes to convert the institutional structures and social relations that have fostered a particular model of development over time into a new development model of national (or regional) competitiveness. Strengthening competitive capacity will require, for example, a shift in existing resources out of present usage (and they may still be at maximum usage even if relatively uncompetitive) or mobilization if unemployment exists or plant is lay-ing idle. This investment shift would, then, entail a 'collective' decision either to lower wages, to reduce public consumption or to tax the financial and produc-tive sectors to raise capital. The investment in new capacity, moreover, would have to be planned and investment banks of considerable size and dynamism established to push through the industrial policy programme. All of this requires a great degree of non-market co-ordination and political mobilization. This raises all the well-known problems of attempting to graft one economic model (or set of technologies) from one institutional context to another: the existing social relations and geographies of production provide an enormous obstacle to mobi-lization into new production sectors and work relations.[53]

This is what we can call the 'capitalist reformer's dilemma': market-led proc-esses will tend to reinforce the existing patterns that are judged to be inadequate, but state-led projects will run up against embedded market power and institu-tionalized rules of co-ordination of economic policy yet require the co-operation of the actors that command these resources. There may thus be no co-operative political foundation for the project of shaped advantage from the capitalist classes internal to declining societies or within the capacities of the existing state appara-tuses. The foundation may be as weak on the workers' side: it will involve union leaderships in taking on the corporatist agenda of external competitiveness at the expense of traditional collective bargaining and social demands. If the strategy is vigorously pursued to its final logic in national competitiveness, it is more likely to split than unite workers in rising sectors from those in declining sectors (over subsidies, adjustment policies, exchange rates) and those in the private from the public sector (over competitive tax rates, comparable pay levels, commodifica-tion).[54] There is, at the level of the structural logic of collective action, no 'com-mon interest' in national competitiveness that does not have to confront the institutionally and geographically embedded social property relations of power. From the vantage point of the capitalist reformer's dilemma, shaped advantage is simply unfeasible.

The relative decline in competitive capacity in existing plant will, therefore, tend to push these countries to put their wage structures into competition to lower unit labour costs to resolve trade imbalances. As the Anglo–American cases of the U.S., Britain and Canada have demonstrated over the last decade, it is quite possible to restore relative competitive capacity in certain sectors, or even across countries as a whole, on the basis of devaluing labour and intensifying work-hours, although the damage to the welfare of the working population may be enormous. Given the potential basis for competitiveness in devalued wages, the ruling bloc may quite logically – and quite consciously with Labour and Socialist Party Governments as in New Zealand and Spain – prefer the option of raising the rate of exploitation by undermining workers' rights and thus actively – and not merely passively – oppose moving in the direction of industrial planning. This strategy is not blind irrational logic which a better policy mix would change, as social democratic theorists often claim, but an accumulative logic within the system itself.

Putting wages into competition and opposing policies of shaped advantage may, moreover, be a quite logical response even in countries that would appear to have the foremost institutionalized conditions for opposing low wage strategies. Hypothetically, it is possible to envision external competitiveness being shaped on the foundation of the 'high institutional pre-requisites' of a stakeholders' capitalism of shaped advantage (although quite clearly not all countries can do so in an unregulated world market). This conceptualization would posit a 'world indifference curve' between the external competitiveness of diverse (national) economic models differentially internalizing environmental costs and involving highly-skilled workers.[55] The 'competitiveness indifference curves' depicts a static equivalence from the standpoint of capitalists between the strategies of environmental dumping and cheap flexible labour versus environmental cost internalization and expensive skilled workers. On a static basis alone it is quite unclear why capitalists would choose the latter model *except* for a minority of workers to operate key production positions where skill and stability are required when undertaking the former involves fewer costs. Nor does the flexible model prevent firms from undergoing continual innovation in product and technique (as the 'drive system' of exploitative work-hours applied to American software engineers proves all too well).

The only way to avoid this conclusion is to fall back on technologically determinist claims that the flexible specialization of new technologies (or that of Japanization or Kalmarianism) uniquely leads to skills upgrading across the labour force.[56] This is not an empirically plausible argument: capitalists in even technologically leading countries are just as likely to forward policies for devaluing labour and limiting the skills upgrading of workers to as narrow a stratum as feasible. The foreclosure of the cheap labour option to competitiveness depends upon strong and mobilized unions actively opposing – rather than co-operating with – capitalists in the pursuit of national competitiveness. To accept national competitiveness as the objective of economic policy as proposed by the policy of shaped advantage is, in fact, to undermine the structural capacity of workers to oppose cheap labour strategies when capitalists propose this, as they inevitably do, on the very basis of national competitiveness. And it is to sacrifice the long-time egalitarian project of building up workers' independent productive capabilities apart from the logic of the capitalist enterprise. Capitalism provides a blockage to shaped advantage producing egalitarian outcomes in technologically ascendant countries too.

Beyond the drawbacks at the level of individual countries, there are even greater contradictions for social democratic economic policies of shaped advantage at the level of the system as a whole. This third fundamental problem can be seen, first, by simply moving from one country to a second trading partner whose only objective is maintaining payments balance so as to avoid a deterioration in internal economic conditions. To the extent that shaped advantage relies on export-led growth at the expense of internal demand, trading partners must leave their economies open while the country shaping advantage improves its competitive position. An immediate problem arises: if the partner whose market is to be penetrated responds with austerity or protectionism (or even the potentially more disruptive shaped advantage policies of their own) to preserve their payments position, any trade and employment gains are wiped out.[57] There may be internal efficiency gains from industrial rationalization, but how they affect employment and output will be determined by both countries' internal policies as the payments position will simply balance. Whatever output and employment gains occur if overall trade volumes increase, given payments in balance, depends upon an assessment of static gains from trade against the loss of macroeconomic control from opening the economy. The extent to which economies have gained from trade has always been a historical minefield (given that trade shares and output gains have a complex interaction and not a uniform correlation). The macroeconomic loss of control may be small initially but everyone except neoliberals would concede that it can cumulatively build so as to be damaging. Managed trade such as voluntary export restrictions provides a partial solution to the problems arising between two trading partners shaping advantage, although this is less generalizable to the international economy as a whole. But trade controls of even this sort lead to a broader range of planning than is implied by shaped advantage.

If a single trading partner encounters obstacles for shaped advantage, a world of many – if not all – countries seeking to shape advantage for national competitiveness poses enormous hurdles for social democratic economic policy. There is a basic compositional fallacy of aggregation underlying a strategy of shaping advantage for national competitiveness: all countries cannot be export-oriented to solve their individual employment imbalances. The world market as an opportunity to increase output and employment may work if virtually no one else follows. But the more countries that adopt a strategy of shaped advantage, the less likely this is to be the case – in other words, a positive game for some can become a negative-sum game for all. The reasoning is straightforward. For individual country strategies, there is every incentive for national competitiveness over unit labour costs to spread from productivity gains to austerity *even* in technologically leading countries as trade imbalances persist. Technological laggards must compete on lower wages to reduce unit costs or face a deteriorating trade deficit (especially as surplus countries may not increase aggregate demand). The sluggish conditions for realization, while capacity to produce more output is increasing from productivity advance, makes it imperative that technological leaders eventually follow or lose their surpluses and employment. The pole of structural competitiveness will keep being pushed higher as economic openness increases so that all regions – from Johannesburg to Delhi to Manchester to Montreal – must keep up with the pace being set by productivity advance in Frankfurt and Tokyo and by low wage manufactures exporters in Shanghai and Nogales.

This is, more or less, the configuration that the world economy is now locked into.[58] The increased congruence and depth of business cycles since the economic clampdown and oil crisis of 1971-73, particularly the Volcker shock of 1981-82, the stock market deflation of 1987 and the 1991-92 U.S. Budget slowdown, illustrate the demand-side precariousness that is now embedded and successively leaving unemployment at higher levels over the cycle. Every time the U.S. moves to remedy its structural imbalances by deflating or devaluation (which blocks export strategies elsewhere), the rest of the capitalist countries must respond or face massive upset (of which Japan, in its own way, is now a victim). But then it becomes quite unclear – and no one has an answer to it – how the credit-money being advanced to the U.S. will be paid for by eventual U.S. payments surpluses. So the world economy moves sideways; and even the technologically advanced countries with an explicit policy of shaping advantage like Japan and Germany begin to feel the sting of 'competitive austerity' through spreading informalization and increased exploitation.

In countries with a more egalitarian policy legacy such as Sweden, the 'shared austerity' strategy of using incomes policies to spread work and keep unit labour costs low will be increasingly invoked as traditional competitive devaluations are now ruled out by capital mobility, responses by trading partners and capitalists less willing to make national bargains over income distribution. This strategy, however, might well worsen the international demand problem too by reducing purchasing power and throwing more exports into a world market less capable of absorbing them. And this external impact will feed back through a neoliberal world to make more 'advanced' compromises on work conditions and wages consistent with external competitiveness difficult to sustain (especially as competitive devaluations become more difficult to undertake as increased openness favours currency stability and capital outflows). Internally, in a world hostile to alternative development models, employers will become increasingly opposed to centralized bargaining and more openly politicized to break with the 'egalitarian model'.[59] But 'shared austerity in one class' will also become politically unstable as it reaches the limit of the organizational capacity of unions to continually demand restraint for national competitiveness, especially in a context where the class distribution of income is becoming more unequal.[60]

The North American bloc of countries, in contrast, explicitly adopt a strategy of devaluing labour and informalization so as to combine both high levels of productivity, intensive resource exploitation and relatively cheap labour. At the moment, they are rewarded by climbing the ranks of the world competitiveness charts, while peripheral economies that are severely indebted like Ghana, or that depend upon exploiting environmentally endangered resources like Newfoundland, eventually buckle and collapse from the exhaustion of a never-ending competitive spiral. Thus external competitiveness increasingly turns to those societies that combine cheap labour with improving technological capacity and externalization of environmental costs. But even in Korea this does not appear to be enough. In justifying the passage of repressive trade union laws that weaken job security in secret session in the middle of the night, Korean President Kim Young-Sam responded: 'The stark reality facing us today is that without the labour reforms, workers will get neither the income nor jobs in the face of cut-throat global economic competition'.[61]

There is still a fourth fundamental obstacle to shaped advantage strategies if we add the real world condition of massive capital mobility. Here the problem is more indirect but equally damaging to the assumption that globalization is irreversible. Shaped advantage requires long-term planning horizons and thus what social democrats like to call 'patient capital'. Yet financial capital in a global market is increasingly driven by short-term demands for profit and liquidity against risk. In contrast to the wisdom of the financial press for investors, for borrowers international diversification of financial portfolios makes any degree of risk (which increases with the period of investment) and profit for a specific country less acceptable as there are more options to combine less risk and more profit. This will produce pressure toward a world interest rate the more that net capital flows grow relative to trade balances and thus a reference rate of return for capital advanced will be formed irrespective of specific conditions for accumulation.[62] In purely static terms, then, global financial markets pose an obstacle to industrial policy. If there is instability, this increases risk and creates dynamic uncertainties which means that financial capital will be even less willing to be tied to the long-term investments necessary to increase capacity in export industries. Moreover, speculative runs stemming from either systematic trade imbalances or alternative political projects, such as with Mexico at the end of 1994 or France in the early 1980s, can rapidly destabilize any industrial plans.

Capital mobility and floating exchange rates in a world economy thus raise the old Keynesian problem of the mismatch of time horizons of industrial and financial capital to a new level. The 'Tobin Tax' proposals 'to throw sand into the wheels of financial capital' by a tax on international capital transfers might slow some of these processes at the margin.[63] But it neither can prevent new speculative instruments from emerging nor address the source of the problem in the increasing autonomy of the circuits of credit money from the real economy. We face a situation where rentier interests determine national development models and can veto them through the currency convertibility of capital flight. The obstacles this poses to shaped advantage in fact makes the traditional socialist argument that democratizing financial capital and 're-embedding' international financial flows are necessary conditions for political alternatives *more economically sound and politically necessary than ever.*

The international Keynesianism forwarded by some social democrats as the means to regulate the imbalances of a global economy do not resolve either the trade or capital mobility problems. To call for democratized structures of international governance simply begs the question: 'to do what?' At the national and regional levels, it is already known from postwar experience that the capital allocation for industrial plans required extensive constraints on capital mobility. More democratic international institutions of themselves only imply a greater political legitimacy to the global economic space formed by internationalized capital movements. Any other agenda pursued by these agencies would require a break from the consensus that globalization is irreversible and the capitalist market essentially efficient that forms the basis for the social democratic policy of shaped advantage.

Similarly, international Keynesianism must assume that world market imbalances only stem from a specific problem of adequate demand. Yet global demand stimulation to reduce unused capacity would likely only compound the trade imbalances already evident in a situation of differentiated competitive capacity. It will do nothing to clear these imbalances. Neither will it reverse unemployment in economically declining regions that lack industrial capacity (or who have lost an earlier advantage in natural resources, as with the competitive assault on the Atlantic fishery).[64] Nor will it reverse the cheap labour strategies adopted in, say, southern U.S. states like Alabama. Moreover, the capitalist market imperatives to compete prevent the co-operation necessary for international reflation. How do you compel co-operation when it is always possible to do better in terms of trade balance and employment by cheating, through import restraints, cheap currency or austerity, before your competitor does? The lack of symmetry in adjustment processes, uneven development and the export fallacy of shaped advantage all raise capitalist obstacles that only stronger forms of international co-ordination than mere international reflation, or vague calls for democratic international governance, could meet.

The key obstacles confronting the social democratic case for shaped advantage stem from the differentiating processes produced by competitive capitalists in a world market. The objective of equalization of relative competitiveness and output levels lies behind the project of national competitiveness. But this objective runs up against the capitalist reformer's dilemma. It is not the state that guides economic enterprises (even ones with stakeholders' rights), allocates investment and, most plainly, controls balance of payments flows in a competitive world market. These all depend upon the actions of profit-seeking capitalists who may or may not identify their particular interest with the 'national interest' of a stakeholders' capitalism in external competitiveness. In any respect, the national interest is defined by the state in relationship to the structural attributes of the various blocks of capital resident in the national formation and their historical models of development. Canadian capitalists, for instance, have favoured large capital inflows to prop up their domestic investment levels and thus have typically not been pre-occupied about the composition of exports or a chronic current account deficit. British capitalists have typically exported long-term capital and allowed a weak payments situation to be covered by short-term borrowing (a pattern that only modestly shifted under Thatcherism). Each state has accommodated rather than challenged the relative competitive weakness and economic decline that these different processes have entailed. The balance of payments as a constraint of competitive capacity (as registered in the flow of accounts) is always relative to particular class strategies and the institutional arrangements and economic structures that inscribe these strategies. The embedded social relations stand in the way of all attempts by individual states to import models of national competitiveness developed through different historical processes and class relations.

The strategy of shaped advantage suggests all economic actors can adopt outward-oriented trade and industrial strategies while ignoring the contradictions that such actions pose for capitalism as a whole. Some advocates of shaped advantage, such as Robert Kuttner and Susan Strange, have argued for managed trade to maintain balance between states to avoid generating competitive austerity.[65] But trade management only makes the case that the capitalist obstacles which prompt a strategy of shaped advantage can not really be resolved by it: they require international regimes that plan trade and control capital mobility. What is altogether contestable, however, is an open-economy social democracy that begins from the premise that 'states are not like markets: they are communities of fate which tie together actors who share certain common interests in the success or failure of their national economies'.[66] Such tenuous arguments as Hirst and Thompson advance can hardly be said to constitute an adequate defence of the notion that the world market constitutes an opportunity for social development that is historically progressive so as to make socialist economic policies inappropriate and irrelevant. But even the strongest case for social democratic economic policy for national competitiveness must rest on indefensible assumptions that globalization is irreversible, that market imperatives require the global economy be maintained as it is, and that, even if the planet is ravaged by endless economic growth, there is no other way to sustain employment.

III. SOCIALIST ALTERNATIVES AND DIVERSITY OF DEVELOPMENT

Capitalist economic policy is usually narrowed to the choice-theoretic definition of the most efficient use of scarce resources as determined by self-interested individual agents. *Socialist economic policy may be defined as the development of demo-cratic capacities for control of the transformation of economic structures towards egalitarian ecologically-sustainable reproduction.* In capitalist economies, this is primarily the is-sue of market disengagement and control strategies. In socialist economies, this is primarily the issues of democratic planning and co-ordination. Yet the only thing that obliges us to conclude that there is no alternative to pursuit of international competitiveness is the *a priori* (and unexamined) assumption that existing social property relations – and hence the structural political power sustained by these relations – are sacrosanct.[67] Even *The Economist* seems to concede the point. They admit that the 'powerless state' in the global economy is a 'myth' in that govern-ments have 'about as many economic powers as they ever had'.[68] It is in this sense that the notion that the nation-state acted as an institutional container of social power and regulator of economic activity before globalization, and that it is no longer capable of doing so today, is fundamentally misleading. The processes of world market formation together with the 'international constitutionalization of neoliberalism has taken place through the agency of states'.[69]

This does not mean that the imperatives of competition in a world market have not lessened the autonomous agency of individual capitalists or states. The NAFTA, Maastricht, and the WTO agreements all have restricted the capacity of nation-states (or regions) to follow their own national (or local) development models. It does mean, however, that the limits on state policy are to a significant extent self-imposed. The world market certainly places limits on state policy, but there is no obligation to accept these imperatives.[70] If we are prepared to question the social property and power relations of capitalism that impose world market imperatives – a proposition that should lie at the centre of socialist economic policy – the scope for state action and the range of alternatives increases.

Globalization has to be considered not just as an economic regime but as a sys-tem of social relations, rooted in the specifically capitalist form of social power, which is concentrated in private capital and the nation-state.[71] Globalization basically means that the market – now the world 'space of flows' or exchanges – has become increasingly universal as an economic regulator. As the scope of the market widens, the scope of democratic power narrows: whatever is controlled by the market is not subject to democratic accountability. The more universal the market becomes as an economic regulator, the more democracy is confined to certain purely 'formal' rights, at best the right to elect the political ruling class. And this right becomes less and less important, as the political disrepute of parlia-ments testifies, as the domain of political action is taken over by market impera-tives. So the more internationalized capitalism becomes, the less possible it is for socialists just to tinker with economic policies to improve equity or firm-level competitiveness. The more internationalized the economy the less possible it is for socialist economic policy to avoid political contestation over the social property relations of capitalism.

An alternative to globalization, then, is as much a question of democracy in opposition to the imperatives of the market as it is of alternative development models. The opposite to globalization is democracy, not only in the crucial sense of civil liberties and the right to vote, but also in the no less crucial sense of the capacity to debate collectively as social equals about societal organization and production, and to develop self-management capacities in workplaces and communities. Democracy in this sense is both a form of political organization and an alternative to the market as an economic regulator.[72]

The geographic expansion of production prompts, then, challenging questions for socialists about the spaces and scales for both economic activity and democracy. (I say for socialists, but it is hard to conceive how anyone genuinely committed to democracy can seriously avoid these questions.) The alternative logic to the imperatives of a global capitalist market suggests a dual, and somewhat paradoxical, strategy: expanding the scale of democracy while reducing the scale of production.[73] Expanding the scale of democracy certainly entails changing the governance and policy structures of international agencies and fora, but also of extending the basis for democratic administration and self-management nationally and locally. Let us be clear here. Expanding the scale of democracy along these dimensions in any meaningful sense will entail a challenge to the social property relations of capitalism. To make collective decisions implies some democratic capacity, backed by the coercive sanctions of the state, to direct capital allocation and thus to establish control over the economic surplus. The point is to enhance, with material supports, the capacities of democratic movements (which will vary tremendously according to the class relations and struggles in specific places), at every level, from local organizations to communities up to the nation-state and beyond, to challenge the power of capital.

Reducing the scale of production means shifting towards more inward-oriented economic strategies, but also forming new economic relations of co-operation and control internationally. The logic of the capitalist market creates a need for large-scale production, an obsession with quantity and size, to which all other considerations – of quality, of social need, of bio-regionalism, of negative externalities, of local democracy – are subordinated. The general objective of socialist policy should be to devalue scale of production as the central economic objective by putting other social considerations before quantity and size. Of course, the massive material inequalities between nations mean that the general principle of reducing the scale of production will vary between developed and developing countries.[74] Certain major industrial sectors necessary to produce adequate levels of welfare will obviously need to be put in place. Scale economies will also be important in some sectors to achieve the most efficient plant size in terms of reducing inputs and environmentally damaging outputs. But the reduction of scale should remain the general guiding principle, in keeping with the socialist conviction that production should above all meet basic needs, foster self-man-agement capacities and adopt more labour-intensive techniques when capital-in-tensive ones, like clear-cut foresting or chemicalized agriculture, have crippling environmental consequences. The desperate levels of economic insecurity, the volume of contamination and resource use, and degradation of local ecologies in the developed countries has surely made clear that economic growth cannot be equated with human welfare in any simple manner.[75]

There are two corollary propositions that would seem to follow from this strategic orientation for socialist economic policy. First, it implies taking a strong stand in favour of the institutional structures at the level of the world economy that favour alternative development models. There is a sound basis to this ap-proach. The postwar period displayed a variety of models of economic develop-ment, in the diversity of Fordism in the North, import-substitution industriali-zation the South, and the various 'socialist experiments'.[76] Even the attempt to impose a neoliberal homogeneity of development confirms this: there is now a diversity of disasters across the North, the East and the South. The concept of inward strategies is, to a degree, a notional orientation as all economic strategies will necessarily have a vibrant open component and in all cases the world config-uration will need to be accounted for. But, as Ajit Singh has argued, openness is a multi-dimensional concept that can apply variously to trade, capital movements, migration and culture and between times and places. International economic relations should not be a uniform market compulsion, but always encompass a 'strategic degree of involvement' in external exchanges.[77] In this view, balance of payments is still an accounting measure of the 'space of flows' of money and com-modities internationally (although necessarily disaggregated to account for the distributional interests of social classes) and a constraint indicative of productive capacities in specific 'spaces of production'. But payments balance also represents, however indirectly, the articulation between diverse economic models and thus the social relations of production between specific places of production. It is im-possible for socialists to put forward alternatives unless it is insisted that there are variable ways of organizing economic and ecological relations, and of managing the external relations between diverse models. The objective of such a solidaristic international economic policy can be summed up like this: the maximization of the capacity of different national collectivities democratically to choose alternate development paths subject to the limitation that the chosen path does not impose externalities (such as environmental damage or structural payments surpluses or deficits) on other countries. This objective can only be realized through re-em-bedding financial capital and production relations in democratically organized national and local economic spaces sustained through international solidarity and fora of democratic co-operation.[78]

Second, full employment has come to mean a level of unemployment associ-ated with stable prices even within social democratic employment policy. But this mixes up labour and product market performance and contains nothing of the traditional demands of the Left that employment be related to production for need and not for exchange. As Joan Robinson once noted, it would be 'preferable to take a simple-minded definition, and to say that there is "full employment" when no one is unemployed'.[79] Better still would be a definition that incorporated the measure of adequate labour market performance. Full employment might then be seen in relation to the maximization of voluntary participation of the adult population in socially-useful paid work at full-time hours for solidaristic wages.

This strategic orientation for a socialist economic policy for market disengagement allows us to put some order around a set of economic principles that have been emerging out of the Left and Green movements. These principles should be envisioned as transitional (they neither represent socialism nor even the model-building of recent years) in the sense of 'structural reforms' that initiate democratic modes of regulation against market imperatives.[80] For both substantive reasons, as well as to maximize support today for socialist economic policy, they should be conceived as a strategy to move in the direction of full employment and alternate development models which encompasses aspects of the following.[81]

(1) *Inward-oriented economic strategies will be necessary to allow a diversity of development paths and employment stability.* Economic policies have been geared to cost-cutting, fostering capital mobility and common treatment without regard to the integration of national economies or local production. Governments have poured an inordinate amount of resources into the export sector, although these efforts have not dented unemployment (and probably could not, even in the absence of stagnation). Yet, it is an absolute falsehood that freer trade will necessarily lead to an expansion of employment and income. There are all sorts of conditions, such as infant industries, mass unemployment or research market failures, that make the theoretical case for protective devices such as quotas and tariffs for positive industrial strategies. There is an equally strong theoretical – not to speak of moral – case against free trade in goods produced in absolutely appalling labour conditions.

The Left debate about trade and protectionism has often been, therefore, specious and hopelessly contradictory. Free trade is recognized as a neoliberal project, but rejection of it is shied away from as an affront to internationalism. It is feared that protection of domestic workers will come at the expense of workers abroad. Yet, it should not be a question of being for or against trade: this is a conjunctural strategic issue related to stability and egalitarian outcome. World trade in its present form is massively imbalanced, unstable and coercive in its regulatory impact on national economies; the consequence is increased social polarization of income and work. At stake, then, is a wider principle: the active pursuit of alternative development paths for full employment requires that the open sector not restrict domestic priorities, and that *the international system support rather than undermine these options.*[82] The export orientation of all economic strategies is neither sustainable nor desirable; it will have to be replaced by a strategy of inward development (which is essential to any egalitarian economic strategy). This is partly what the early Bretton Woods system permitted through temporary trade restrictions to allow full employment policies.

This casts a quite different light on what should be expected of trade. It means, for example, that trade would have to come under regulation to allow different orientations on local production, environmental standards, restrictions on child labour, and so on, without sanction from 'worst-practice' production models. In other words, divergent economic models imply a degree of tariff protection and control over the open sector. It has proven impossible, moreover, for surplus countries to inflate enough, or deficit countries to deflate enough, to restore payments balance without further job losses. A single global market, with no common labour or ecological standards, will inevitably bargain down from the fear of competitive losses in conditions of competitive austerity. Of course, if the use of tariffs and quotas in support of employment, or to resolve payments imbalances, is to be minimized a degree of international co-ordination and planning of trade is required. None of these measures imply closing the economy from trade as economies of scale, diversified consumption, and transfer of new products and processes remain important. However, they quite clearly imply planning the open sector in the national context with international regulation and co-ordination required for the clearing of balances and the reinforcement of long-term diverse development trajectories.

(2) *Financial capital must be subjected to democratic controls on debt payment and capital mobility.* It seems quite clear from the histories of the interwar period and the post-1974 experience that the external constraint on national economic policy less imposes itself from outside than grows out of the internal contradictions of domestic accumulation and the actions of the national state. A phase of material expansion, as Giovanni Arrighi and Elmar Altvater contend, ends in a phase of internationalization as products seek markets and capitalists seek higher returns in financial flows.[83] A series of problems arises: financial assets are increasingly oriented to short-term returns because of stagnant output; debts cannot be serviced; national economies are increasingly vulnerable to currency movements as central bank reserves are dwarfed by financial flows.

International debts, with virtually all countries becoming more indebted, pose a special difficulty. Settling them requires a net surplus of exports: everything goes into competitive and export capacity with the hope of paying debts plus interest. But other countries adopting the same approach of expanding exports and lessening import demands generates weaker employment conditions all around. Because of weaker demand, meeting debt and interest payments requires further squeezing of the public sector and workers' living standards. It is impossible, then, to redistribute work at solidaristic wages and to continue to transfer massive funds to financial interests. Finding an alternative way out of the debt crisis is essential to the expansion of employment and alternative development. The debt burden can only be alleviated by either a controlled inflation leading to negative or minimal real rates of interest or a rescheduling of payments that accomplishes the same thing. Anything else simply temporally displaces an inevitable default into the future while running down resources and capacities in the present. A hierarchy of credit and capital controls – a credit regime – also needs to be drawn up and implemented to constrain the power of financial capital over national development. Such measures might range from: micro banks; more democratic control over national banks and credit allocation to enforce planning; short term taxes on speculative turnover in currency, bond and equity markets; quantitative capital controls; and restructured international agencies that regulate credit repayment and long term capital flows. Macroeconomic stability will be wishful thinking without financial controls.[84]

3) *Macroeconomic balance requires not only aggregate demand management, but also new forms of investment planning and collective bargaining norms.* It is one thing to say that there is a capitalist employment crisis and quite another to say that releasing the aggregate demand restraint to increase output will necessarily lead to employment expansion. This misses the point that capitalist development means increased output but with increased surplus labour (and an indeterminate effect on workers' incomes). An appalling dimension of capitalism, and neoliberal employment policy, is that the costs of the system's need for flexibility are borne by workers while the benefits are reaped by capitalists. This is as unacceptable today as it has ever been. Macroeconomic stability should translate into employment stability through firm level job security but also a social guarantee of re-training and new job creation in local communities facing industrial restructuring. Such macroeconomic balance will have to entail new mechanisms of control over market forces: national and sectoral planning councils; planning agreements over investment flows and technology strategies; regional and local development boards; and public ownership of core sectors (including financial industries).

Macroeconomic balance means something quite beyond control of demand volatility of the Keynesian kind. There are distributional imbalances between the social classes, public and private goods, present consumption and future sustainability. On ecological, anti-globalization and equity grounds a redistributional macroeconomic balance makes eminently more sense than one of unrestrained growth.

For effective demand to be restored, the break that has been put on productivity-sharing with workers to the end of cost-cutting needs to be revoked. But egalitarian employment also requires more than this. Increased production requires consumers for the output and the income for this should certainly go to workers. Yet output increases have to become more ecologically constrained. So reductions in work-time, which are the most effective means to increase employment historically, should be strongly pushed. A trade union bargaining norm of an 'annual free-time factor' should, in solidarity with the unemployed, have precedence over an 'annual wage improvement' in sharing out productivity increases (allocated to favour additional employment and the poorest workers). Any decline in employment will also depend upon the form the expansion takes. Capitalist sector jobs are governed by the logic of profitability; non-capitalist sector jobs (in the state and collective organizations) are governed by the logic of redistribution. The decline in capitalist sector employment in the manufacturing sector is permanent. Employment growth should be tilted, therefore, toward sustainable community services which are more labour-intensive. The question really is not one of work to do: there is a serious lack of adequate public facilities from new classrooms to art galleries; there is a tremendous pent-up demand for affordable health care, housing and public transportation; and there is a great deal to be done in terms of environmental clean-up from the wreckage caused by industrialization and neoliberalism.

(4) *Reducing unemployment will entail both less work and a redistribution of work.* Postwar employment policies fought unemployment through faster growth of output and exports. Contemporary capitalist employment policies attempt, with little success, to do the same. If export-led strategies to increase employment in conditions of competitive austerity soon become a zero-sum (or negative) game of dumping job losses on other countries who will eventually respond in kind, national macroeconomic expansion will not be sufficient to lower unemployment. In the absence of measures to restrict population growth (and given the objective of not lowering the participation rate of adults in the economy), employment growth alone would require a significant level of expanded output. The increased capital-intensity of production suggests, moreover, that growth rates would have to consistently approach, or exceed, levels of the postwar boom to lower unemployment (at present average hours of work and labour force growth). This still would leave unaddressed unused labour stocks and productivity gains that even at modest levels would require significant growth. Yet levels of growth of the postwar period, with similar extensive growth bringing more land and resources into production, would be enormously costly to the natural environment. Growth-centred employment strategies must now be firmly rejected as both unviable in reducing unemployment and undesirable on ecological grounds.

An unexpected side-effect of globalization has been an increase in work-time as part of competitive austerity (time reduction initially stalling with the crisis in 1974 and now getting longer and more polarized).[85] Hours of work and intensity of work have increased even as workers' purchasing power has been cut. The movement to lower hours has typically required an international movement to impose an alternative logic on capitalism's tendencies to increase work intensity and hours. In a static sense, it is quite obvious that work, like income, is unequally distributed. But unlike income redistribution work redistribution has the positive consequence of producing free-time. A variety of measures are equalizing of work-time (especially if developed as universal standards): overtime limits and severe restrictions on 'double-dipping' by professionals; extending vacations and national holidays; and voluntary job-sharing plans by work-site. But to have a major impact on unemployment nothing will do except a sharp reduction in standard work-time with the clear objective of moving to an average annual volume of, say, 1500 hours of work with a 32 hour work-week (bringing the advanced industrial countries below current German levels). Existing plant might be worked harder (until fixed investment expands) through expanded shift work. But with slow output increases, the short term reduction in unemployment will require a shift in income (offset by productivity gains, less hours, lower unemployment claims and better public services) as well as work. So a strategy of less work must be implemented in as egalitarian a manner as possible (avoiding the folly of having only the public sector work shorter hours, which both ruins public goods and increases inequality). An expansion of output will then have the maximum impact on employment. A defensive struggle to spread work can form the basis of an offensive struggle for a different way of life.

(5) *A 'politics of time' should extend beyond setting standard hours to consider the allocation of work-time and free-time.* 'Work without end' has been the history of capitalism. Fordism added 'endless consumption' and the Keynesian conviction – check the old textbooks – that expanded output should always have precedence over reduced work-time for any labour time freed by productivity advance. Changing this orientation will raise questions of an existential order about work, employment and the self-management of time. This has a collective and a personal side. On the personal side, there is an obvious increase in discretion over free time. It is also possible to pursue more flexible patterns of work-time through flex-time, banked time, single seniority lists based on hours worked, and paid educational leaves that re-shape the control of time. There is an equally important collective side to lowering work-time. There is, for instance, more time, as both Andre Gorz and Ernest Mandel have argued, for collective decision-making in administrative and legislative activities.[86] The radical reduction in work-time, with greater worker control over the allocation of time, raises the concrete possibility of the long-standing goal of the socialist movement for a 'democratically controlled economy'.

(6) *Productivity gains in the labour process should be negotiated against the requalification of work.* The economic crisis also relates to the supply-side crisis of production (which in turn structures labour demand). The new technologies further restructure the supply-side by changes to the labour process and work-time. Competitive austerity, however, is compelling work speedup and job fragmentation of a Taylorist kind, even though this often involves sacrificing productivity gains that might occur from increased worker input into production. A positive restructuring – which would depend upon altering the balance of class relations on the shopfloor and in society – would entail exploiting the capacity of the new technologies to involve workers in production and the planned elimination of boring, repetitive jobs. The fight against Taylorism extends into the kind of training that is premised on preserving and expanding workers' skills. This means long-term, broad skills rather than short-term, specific ones; transferable skills over firm-specific skills; theoretical as well as practical knowledge; and skills that extend worker autonomy over the labour process. Thus formal qualifications, earned through institutional training or a mixture of formal training and on-the-job training, tend to allow workers more flexibility and control over their labour process. The requalification of work would extend broad skills of technical competency to all workers.

Employment and education have always been linked. Training plays a central role in industrial policy and thus aggregate and sectoral labour demand, in matching labour supply with skills demand, facilitating adjustment between jobs, and in improving skills in cyclical downturns. So training has to fit with other initiatives as it cannot create labour demand for imaginary jobs. But building workers' capacities and skills as a continual process has the positive benefit of providing an oversupply of high skills, which can make easier adjustment to demand and technology shifts. Increased worker participation in the labour process to increase productivity is undoubtedly a struggle waged on the terrain of the capitalists. Yet re-uniting conception and execution and re-building workers' capacities advances materially the possibility of worker self-management which any democratic socialism must be premised upon. Life-time education rather than narrowly conceived 'training' should really be the goal.

(7) *The requalification of work should be linked to quality production within a quality-intensive growth model.* It is not possible any more to simply lay to one side the quality of the growth process, issues of work process and product design, or production for social need. The failure of social democratic Keynesianism was possibly greatest here, in that it never developed state, community or worker planning capacities or offered a 'different way of life'. Keynesianism above all attempted to alleviate the capitalist unemployment problem by growth in the quantity of consumption goods and thereby the quantity of employment hours demanded. Yet it is now more necessary than ever to connect the skills, resources

and employment that go into the labour process to the ecological quality of the production process and the use-values which come out.

An alternative socialist policy might accentuate a number of positive trends that can be discerned. The requalification of work, for example, makes it feasible for unions to develop their own technology networks, popular plans for industry, and socially-useful products. As well, there is an element of the new technologies that does allow decentralized small-scale batch production or flexible specialization (although this cannot be generalized into an entire economic system as some wildly wrong theories did in the 1980s).[87] This allows for a whole range of customized instruments, clothing, housewares. Quality-intensive growth also speaks to the provision of public services. Here the problem is two-fold. The bureaucratic Fordist-style of the postwar public sector can also gain from diversified and quality production to overcome standardization and input-controlled production of public services. The quantitative restrictions of austerity have also seriously damaged the quality and range of public goods from such basics as clean streets to the more aesthetic of the variety of art available in public spaces. A socialist economic policy will foster, therefore, a quality-intensive growth model that encourages workers' skills and capacities, incorporates resource-saving and durable production techniques, and produces free time, collective services and quality products.

(8) *The decline in work-time allows the administrative time for workplace democracy.* An unexpected benefit from decreased work-time is that it allows for a democratic expansion of employment by freeing administrative and deliberative time for workplace and community planning of output and work. With work-time reduction and job security so central to an alternative, it is quite necessary and possible to put workplace planning agreements on the bargaining table. These include, most obviously, information on compensation, profits, trade and investment plans, but also should advance toward product design and long term workers' plans. Labour productivity gains not taken in increased output can be taken in increased time devoted to workers' control and environmental sustainability. Of course, capital will not yield such 'structural reforms' over democratic control without threat of capital strike. Capital would prefer to continue with Taylorism than risk worker self-management. But it is exactly this that makes the external regulation over capital flows so critical.

(9) *Local planning capacities will be central to sustaining diverse development and full employment.* Postwar Keynesianism concentrated on centralized aggregate demand management with little economic planning. It was recognized that employment planning and adjustment policies were a necessary supplement to demand management in tight labour markets. Yet this largely remained limited to forecasting occupational and labour force trends. It did not involve planning

resource usage and never even extended to implementing the postwar idea of a 'public works shelf' of projects to be taken up in downturns. The local component of planning was labour exchanges which served largely as a location for job listings and counselling, but which never did much in the way of identifying local job or skill needs. In many countries, even these most limited services provided by local employment centres have been allowed to run down under neoliberal policies. An alternative employment policy will, in contrast, have as a priority the development of local administrative capacities. There is a desperate need to formulate local labour plans that account for the existing labour stock and skills, but also forecast local labour force trends, skill shortages and job trends. This kind of knowledge cannot be found or developed centrally. Local labour markets, therefore, must become much more forward-looking and active planning units rather than the passive dispensers of dole payments or centres for the video display of job postings that they have become.

There is an added dimension to local planning. In the service sector, where most job growth will be, the challenge is to not only raise the quality of work and pay, but also to collectivize many service activities that are too expensively provided by private markets (daycare), or are not available at all because of underfunding (cleaner environment). It is impossible to envision these being done without planning of resource use and input from users and producers of the services. How does one go about providing library resources in a multi-cultural society from an office tower in Washington or Berlin? Decentralized popular planning should be central to a non-capitalist 'third sector', that is, self-managed community services (either newly formed or partly devolved from traditional state administration) such as cultural production, environmental clean-up, education and leisure. These activities will have to be planned, through local labour market boards, to determine socially-useful activities, community needs, and local skills. This reinforces the linkages between the expansion of employment and the formation of democratic capacities.

(10) *Socialist economic policy should encompass new forms of democratic administration.* Employment policy, the central focus of this discussion, is typically administered though traditional hierarchical bureaucracies of central offices of control, planning and funding and decentralized employment exchanges.[88] The exchanges grew in prominence with war mobilization and the subsequent adoption of unemployment insurance schemes. The exchanges embodied, in many ways, the worst aspects of postwar bureaucratic administration: poorly planned and ill-focused at the centre and rigid and remote in local communities. Where could it have possibly been said that the local employment centre was the key location for discussing and planning work in the community? Yet, in a democratic society where most of us spend a large portion of our adult lives working (or seeking work), this is exactly what they could and should be. It would be quite possible to es-

tablish a statutory labour market system structured through local, democratically accountable bodies. This could be encompassed within a national employment policy, with the local boards allowed a decentralization of decision-making and thus local communities a more active role in establishing production, employment and training priorities. Such democratically elected boards could serve as a 'space for the alternative' on a broad range of local issues: where workers' plans are linked to community economic development plans; where the improvement in the quality of jobs is actually taken on as a societal project; where workers and unions are specifically given resources and assistance to form employment plans; where community environmentalists and unions come together around health and safety and workplace pollution; and where communities are mandated to plan local needs and to provide socially-useful employment.

IV. CONCLUSION: CAPITALIST OBSTACLES, SOCIALIST IMPERATIVES

It is conventional wisdom that the internationalization of capitalist economies at the end of the twentieth century has created historical conditions that have vitiated traditional socialist economic objectives and, indeed, their policy means as well. This accounts, in part, both for the boldness with which neoliberal policies are being pursued and the appalling servile character of the latest revisionist turn of social democracy. I have argued, in contrast, that the internationalization of market processes has caused unmitigated disasters in many parts of the world as well as economic imbalances and social polarizations between and within countries that cannot be resolved by economic approaches that would intensify these processes. This is the case for both neoliberal and social democratic policies targeted at widening the economic space for internationalization. Widening the space for international governance of the market to match its global expansion, as the advocates on the Left for a 'cosmopolitan democracy' and the formation of an 'international civil society' argue, begs far more questions than it answers and depends upon an untenable view of market processes (even when accompanied by the laudable goal of 'throwing sand into the wheels' of global financial capital). Capitalist social relations remain a massive obstacle to social justice.

There are eventually only two options facing individual countries in the hyper-competitive conditions of structurally imbalanced and unmanaged internationalized capitalist markets – protectionism or austerity. In the current conjuncture, the neoliberal 'Washington Consensus' of the IMF, World Bank and the GATT-WTO has ruled out protectionism – and thus the 'beggaring-thy-neighbour' process of exporting unemployment of the 1930s – by lowering tariff and non-tariff barriers. The Consensus's constraints on protectionism, however, do not resolve the underlying pressures but only shifts them elsewhere (particularly as the WTO is as much a pact for private investment flows as a trade agreement). Thus the entire burden of adjustment has to fall on a continual process of technical rationalization (which is slow, costly and risky), intensification of work and environmental degradation. The demand-side effects of this defensive adjustment produce a spiral of 'competitive austerity' so that the pressure to rationalize and cut costs is ceaseless. Improving external balance and competitiveness in the 1990s takes the form of 'beggar-thy-working class' policies of expanding unemployment at home. Neither neoliberal free trade nor social democratic proposals of shaped advantage for national competitiveness provide an exit from this destructive form of capitalism. Nor would simply taming financial markets resolve it as this would only modify the temporal dimension of the asymmetries in the world economy and not their spatial underpinnings. This view retains, moreover, the misguided faith common amongst the new market socialists in the allocative efficiency of global markets in determining investment and research and development, as opposed to the allocative efficiency of democratic planning in determining where these expenditures might best meet social needs. This is an impossibly shallow view of consumer sovereignty and the sustainability of present distributional and consumption patterns.

These criticisms still leave, of course, the most difficult question: on what basis might a political challenge to these processes be mounted and socialist economic policies be forwarded? The social democratic proposal to forge a progressive competitiveness approach to internationalization, often put in terms of creating a 'stakeholders' capitalism', has been the pole of attraction for most Left political parties and intellectuals. But as a result of the contradictions analyzed here, nowhere is this strategy posed as a serious alternative to neoliberalism. It is the North American model of longer hours of work at income-splitting, insecure jobs and an impoverished public sector that is spreading. This is the case even in Sweden and Germany, which best combine the pre-conditions of strong labour movements brokering compromises with a national bourgeoisie traditionally committed to national competitiveness. Similarly the East Asian miracle economies, so commonly put forth as a progressive alternative to neoliberalism in even the usually most clear-headed socialist periodicals, only make the case that state intervention to support national industry is not always a failure in raising output levels. They are neither generalizable models because of the external constraint nor desirable ones on the egalitarian, democratic or ecological grounds of socialist politics.

I have argued in this essay, again in opposition to most current thinking on the Left, that socialist economic policy still provides a vital alternative to resolving these problems. This is not to declare that ready-made blueprints can be offered: it is to search for viable sets of strategic orientations and principles around which struggles in specific times and places might advance. The calls made in this context for re-territorialization of the 'spaces of production' and for constraints over the 'space of flows' of monetary and commodity exchanges at the world level should, then, hardly be controversial. To cite Miliband again: 'The fact of class struggle on an international scale inexorably points to the need for a socialist government to preserve as large a measure of independence as is possible ... socialists cannot accept a parallel political internationalization which, for the present and immediate future, is bound to place intolerable constraints on the purposes they seek to advance'.[89] The point of controversy more properly resides in two areas: at what political moment, to what extent and in what forms should sovereignties be sacrificed to democratized multi-national blocs and international agencies reinforcing the diverse autocentric, ecologically-sound development trajectories of its constituent members; and at what moments, to what extent and in what forms should internal democratic planning forums and modalities within states be encouraged to plan and control production and ecology? Working through these challenges requires political movements which are thoroughly international in their thinking, linkages and solidarities. But such movements can only arise if they are firmly rooted in their own local and national communities and ecologies in developing their democratic capacities and economic alternatives. The obstacle lies not in the impossibility of developing viable socialist economic policies for these movements to pursue as opportunities present themselves. Nor are the sentiments of a majority of the world's population North and South, who wish for a 'different way of life' from the competitive treadmill and despairs of capitalism at the end of the century, inhospitable to such policies. The obstacle is a minority class that draws its power and wealth from a historically specific form of production. There is a route forward if the market basis of this power is seen for what it is: contingent, imbalanced, exploitative and replaceable.

NOTES

A shorter version of this article appeared in *Monthly Review* in December 1996.

1   Ralph Miliband, *Socialism for a Sceptical Age* (Oxford: Polity Press, 1994), p.1.

2   P. Hirst and G. Thompson, *Globalisation in Question* (Oxford: Polity, 1996). They put it: 'The opposite of a globalized economy is thus not a nationally inward-looking one, but an open world market based on trading nations and regulated to a greater or lesser degree both by the public policies of nation states and by supra-national agencies'. The case is built around, inter alia, protection of investment flows, co-operative capitalists and faster growth. See: *Globalisation*, p.16.

3   See: David Miliband, ed., *Reinventing the Left* (Oxford: Polity, 1994); and N. Thompson, 'Supply Side Socialism', *New Left Review*, N. 216 (1996).

4   Ralph Miliband, *Socialism for a Sceptical Age*, p.2.

5   J. Wiseman, 'A Kinder Road to Hell? Labour and the Politics of Progressive Competitiveness in Australia', in L. Panitch, ed., *Socialist Register 1996: Are There Alternatives?* (London: Merlin, 1996).

6   Just at the time many Marxists were coming to praise and advocate the Swedish model as the way of the future, one of its main architects was decrying its end. See: R. Meidner, 'Why Did the Swedish Model Fail?', in R. Miliband and L. Panitch, eds., *Socialist Register 1993: Real Problems False Solutions* (London: Merlin, 1993).

7   'Labour Leader Seeks to Reassure NY Financiers', *Financial Times*, 11 April 1996. In his new year interview with the *Financial Times*, 16 January 1997, they reported that Blair 'really does believe the ideological battles over economics during the present century will be seen in the long sweep of history as an aberration'.

8   'The World Economy', *The Economist*, 7 October 1995, p.5.

9   Quoted in P. Gowan, 'Neo-Liberal Theory and Practice for Eastern Europe', *New Left Review*, N. 213 (1995), p.9.

10 R. Reich, *The Work of Nations* (New York: Knopf, 1991), p.9.

11 F. Scharpf, *Crisis and Choice in European Social Democracy* (Ithaca: Cornell University Press, 1991), p.274.

12 *Ibid.* Scharpf invokes 'socialism in one class' positively, if gloomily, as the necessary strategy for the present period. In contrast, Leo Panitch, in *Social Democracy and Industrial Militancy* (Cambridge: Cambridge University Press, 1976), p.244, notes the loss of the objective of taking anything away from capital.

13 I follow here E. Wood's distinction in conceptualizing capitalism between the market as opportunity 'always conducive to growth and the improvement of productive forces', and the market as imperative with 'its specific laws of motion which uniquely compel people to enter the market and compel producers to produce "efficiently" by raising labour productivity'. See: E. Wood, 'From Opportunity to Imperative: The History of the Market', *Monthly Review*, 46:3 (1994).

14 A. Giddens, *Beyond Left and Right: The Future of Radical Politics* (Cambridge: Polity Press, 1994).

15 The idea of stakeholding refers to some notion of inclusiveness and partnership in private enterprises, but the rhetoric of partnerships is easily applied by social democrats to state policy as well. There may or may not be some participation or property rights attached to the term. But it describes well the type of capitalism favoured by social democratic policies for national competitiveness.

16 J. Roemer, *A Future for Socialism* (Cambridge, Ma.: Harvard University Press, 1994); and A. Gamble and G. Kelly, 'The New Politics of Ownership', *New Left Review*, N.220 (1996). This view recalls Paul Samuelson's comment, in the midst of the 1950s 'end of ideology' phase, that as far as economic theory was concerned it was a matter of indifference if workers hired capitalists or capitalists hired workers. The mixed economy had made dispute over modes of production pointless. For the new market socialists, socialism is now a question of degrees of ownership mixes in a global marketplace.

17 'The coherence, such as it is, arises out of the conversion of temporal patterns into spatial restraints to accumulation. Surplus value must be produced and realized within a certain timespan. If time is needed to overcome space, surplus value must also be produced and realized within a certain geographical domain. ... It is production in particular locales that is always the ultimate source of [capitalist] power'. See: D. Harvey, *The Limits to Capital* (Oxford: Basil Blackwell, 1982), pp.416 and 423.

18 'The World Economy', *The Economist*, 7 October 1995, p.4. The Hecksher-Ohlin theorem adds that the basis of comparative advantage will be a country's relative abundance of factors of production. Floating exchange rates of currencies, moreover, will keep trade in balance by altering relative prices. Hence free trade is always to be preferred to national (or local) self-sufficiency. For accessible surveys of the relevant

literature and its critique see: D. Irwin, *Against the Tide: An Intellectual History of Free Trade* (Princeton: Princeton University Press, 1996); and R. Heilbroner and W. Milberg, *The Crisis of Vision in Modern Economic Thought* (Cambridge: Cambridge University Press, 1995).

19 D. Gordon, 'Six-Percent Unemployment Ain't Natural', *Social Research*, 54:2 (1987); and J. Michie and J. Grieve Smith, eds., *Unemployment in Europe* (London: Academic Press, 1994).

20 The most interesting case being Ricardo's own example of Portugal: S. Sideri, *Trade and Power: Informal Colonialism in Anglo-Portugese Relations* (Rotterdam: Rotterdam University Press, 1970). See also the critiques in: J. Friedan, 'Exchange Rate Politics: Contemporary Lessons from American History', *Review of International Political Economy*, 1:1 (1994); and M. Bienefeld, 'Capitalism and the Nation State in the Dog Days of the Twentieth Century', in this volume.

21 'The World Economy', *The Economist*, 7 October 1995, pp.4–5. *The Economist* goes so far as to argue that the outcomes of trade liberalization are efficient because they are the result of freer markets even when they 'give perverse signals'.

22 For a survey of the trends described here see: A. Glyn, et al., 'The Rise and Fall of the Golden Age', in S. Marglin and J. Schor, eds., *The Golden Age of Capitalism* (Oxford: Oxford University Press, 1990).

23 P. Sweezy, 'The Triumph of Financial Capital', *Monthly Review*, 46:2 (June 1994).

24 J.M. Keynes, *The Collected Writings: Activities 1941-46, Shaping the Postwar World, Bretton Woods and Reparations* (Cambridge: Cambridge University Press, 1980), pp.21-2.

25 By social democratic economic policy we mean the set of economic ideas and practices to compensate for specific market constraints and failures within capitalism. They are market controlling and *not* transitional strategies.

26 J.M. Keynes, *The General Theory of Employment, Interest and Money* (London: Macmillan, 1936), pp.380-1.

27 This national compromise had its parallels in the import-substitution industrialization strategies of the South and the command economies of Eastern Europe.

28 S. Wilks, 'Class Compromise and the International Economy: The Rise and Fall of Swedish Social Democracy', *Capital and Class*, N. 58 (1996), p.103.

29 'Growth and Equality since 1945: The Role of the State in OECD Economies', in C. Naastepad and S. Storm, eds., *The State and the Economic Process* (Cheltenham: Edward Elgar, 1996), p.96.

30 Ian Roxborough, for example, in looking at open-economy social democracy in Latin America argues that 'there is no question of attempting a complete reversal of all neoliberal reforms'. See: 'Neoliberalism in Latin America: Limits and Alternatives', *Third World Quarterly*, 13:3 (1992), p.432.

31 R. Kuttner, *The End of Laissez-Faire* (Philadelphia: University of Pennsylvania Press, 1991).

32 The relevant essays are accessible in P. Krugman, ed., *Strategic Trade Policy and the New International Economics* (Cambridge: MIT Press, 1986). For evaluations from Right and Left: M. Corden, 'Strategic Trade Policy', in D. Greenaway, et al., eds., *A Guide to Modern Economics* (London: Routledge, 1996); and M. Humbert, 'Strategic Industrial Policies in a Global Industrial System', *Review of International Political Economy*, 1:3

(1994). The new trade theory also explains empirical trade phenomena such as intra-industry trade and the extensive trade flows between developed economies, two facts poorly dealt with in the pure Ricardian case.

33   W. Ruigrok and R. van Tulder's *The Logic of International Restructuring* (London: Routledge, 1995), Ch.9, goes even further in arguing that virtually the entire Fortune 100 list of the world's largest non-financial corporations enjoyed key government support and trade protection. This is another example of just how ideological the theoretical defence of free trade is.

34   'Is Free Trade Passe?', *Journal of Economic Perspectives*, 1 (1987); and 'Does the New Trade Theory Require a New Trade Policy', *The World Economy*, 15 (1992).

35   Kuttner, *The End of Laissez-Faire*, Ch.4.

36   R. Prebisch, *The Economic Development of Latin America and Its Principal Problems* (New York: UN Economic Commission for Latin America, 1950). The assumption of shaped advantage is that the key issue is surplus trade in manufactured goods for high growth. But as students of Canada have long noted, there can be high growth with deficits in value-added trade. The real question becomes the form, quality and control of development, an assessment precluded by notions of national competitiveness. The classic argument remains: M. Watkins, 'A Staple Theory of Economic Growth', *Canadian Journal of Economics and Political Science*, 29 (1963).

37   The cumulative causation argument builds on the work of Nicholas Kaldor and Joan Robinson. The implications of the arguments today, however, have become skewed away from the need to control the open sector, as the Cambridge Economic Policy Group and the British Alternative Economic Strategy argued in the late 1970s in its case for import controls, toward primarily export promotion in high technology industry as globalization has blocked other options. There is some relation to the Marxian notion of absolute cost advantage as developed in different directions by dependency theory, especially in A.G. Frank, *Capitalism and Underdevelopment in Latin America* (New York: Monthly Review Press, 1967) and S. Amin, *Unequal Development* (New York: Monthly Review Press, 1976), and in value theory by G. Carchedi, *Frontiers of Political Economy* (London/New York: Verso, 1991) and A. Shaikh, 'Free Trade, Unemployment and Economic Policy', in J. Eatwell, ed., *Global Unemployment* (Armonk: M.E. Sharpe, 1996).

38   G. Dosi and L. Soete, 'Technical Change and International Trade', in D. Dosi, et al., eds., *Technical Change and Economic Theory* (London: Pinter, 1988), p. 419. Also see: G. Dosi, K. Pavitt and L. Soete, *The Economics of Technical Change and International Trade* (Hemel Hempstead: Harvester, 1990); and C. Freeman and L. Soete, *Work for All or Mass Unemployment?* (London: Pinter, 1994).

39   Thus the social democratic case for shaped advantage has particularly strong advocates in the economically declining powers of Britain, Canada and the U.S., as with popular writers like Will Hutton, James Laxer, Lester Thurow and Robert Reich.

40   Commission on Public Policy and British Business, *Promoting Prosperity: A Business Agenda for Britain* (London: IPPR, 1997), quoted in M. Wolf, 'Labour of Prosperity', *Financial Times*, 21 January 1997.

41   W. Streeck, *Social Institutions and Economic Performance* (London: Sage, 1992). For a wider assessment of these views see: G. Albo, 'Competitive Austerity and the Impasse of Capitalist Employment Policy', in R. Miliband and L. Panitch, eds.,

Socialist Register 1994: Between Globalism and Nationalism (London: Merlin, 1994); and P. Burkett and M. Hart-Landsberg, 'The Use and Abuse of Japan as a Progressive Model', in L. Panitch, ed., *Socialist Register 1996: Are There Alternatives?* (London: Merlin, 1996).

42 J. Rogers and W. Streeck, 'Productive Solidarities: Economic Strategy and Left Politics', in David Miliband, ed., *Reinventing the Left*, p.143. See also the critique of these views developed by Ash Amin, 'Beyond Associative Democracy', *New Political Economy*, 1:3 (1996).

43 'Western Europe's Economic Stagnation', *New Left Review*, N.201 (1993), p.73. Also see: R. Dore, R. Boyer and Z. Mars, eds., *The Return to Incomes Policies* (London: Pinter, 1994); T. Notermans, 'Social Democracy and External Constraints' (University of Oslo: ARENA Working Paper #15-95, 1995); Scharpf, *Crisis and Choice*; and J. Pekkarinen, M. Puhojola and R. Rowthorn, eds., *Social Corporatism: A Superior Economic System* (Oxford: Clarendon Press, 1992).

44 'Social Democracy and Full Employment', *New Left Review*, N.211 (1995), pp.54-5. This view, of course, is somewhat marginal to the actual policy orientation toward national competitiveness of social democratic parties today. In actual practice the solidarity is invoked by social democratic governments to impose real wage losses on workers via a consensus to lower unit labour costs and tax loads.

45 See, for instance, S. Holland, ed., *Out of Crisis* (Nottingham: Spokesman, 1983).

46 D. Held, *Democracy and the Global Order: From the Modern State to Cosmopolitan Governance* (Stanford: Stanford University Press, 1995), p.131.

47 'Globalisation and the State', in this volume.

48 See the arguments in J. Eatwell, ed., *Global Unemployment* (Armonck: M.E. Sharpe, 1996).

49 Thus Canada exhibited what I have termed a 'limping golden age' to describe growth conditions which were more extensive than the intensive growth of other Fordisms and also that exhibited a secularly growing unemployment level since the 1940s. See: G. Albo, *The Impasse of Capitalist Employment Policy? Canada's Unemployment Experience, 1956-74* (Ottawa: Carleton University Ph.D. Thesis, 1994).

50 See: R. Rowthorn and J. Wells, *Industrialization and Foreign Trade* (Cambridge: Cambridge University Press, 1987), pp.25-7.

51 Devaluation also loses some of its impact for deficit countries in that the increased complementarity of economies makes imports less price-sensitive. This is another consideration for the need to control the open sector and to reduce import elasticities.

52 See: A. Singh, 'Openness and the Market-Friendly Approach to Development: Learning the Right Lessons from the Development Experience', *World Development*, 22:12 (1994).

53 For a full development of this theme see the compelling arguments in: D. Coates, *The Question of UK Decline* (London: Harvester, 1994); J. Tomaney, 'A New Paradigm of Work Organization and Technology?', in A. Amin, ed., *Post-Fordism* (Oxford: Blackwell, 1994); and J. Price, 'Lean Production at Suzuki and Toyota', *Studies in Political Economy*, N.45 (1994).

54 This position has been best articulated by the most dynamic and successful union in North America: Canadian Auto Workers, *False Solutions, Growing Protests: Recapturing*

the Agenda (Toronto: CAW, 1996).

55 This formulation is offered by A. Lipietz, moving somewhat away from his earlier views, but its antecedents also lie in the position of R. Boyer on offensive and defensive forms of flexibility strategies. They are, of course, arguing for the more egalitarian outcome and do not gloss over some of the contradictions as do advocates of flexible specialization, diversified quality production and others. See: A. Lipietz, 'The New Core-Periphery Relations: The Contrasting Examples of Europe and America', in C. Naastepad and S. Storm, eds., *The State and the Economic Process* (Cheltenham: Edward Elgar, 1996); and R. Boyer and D. Drache, eds., *States Against Markets: The Limits of Globalization* (London: Routledge, 1996).

56 See especially M. Piore and C. Sabel, *The Second Industrial Divide* (New York: Basic Books, 1984). For a critique see the excellent J. Peck, *Work-Place: The Social Regulation of Labour Markets* (New York: Guilford, 1996).

57 D. Laussel and C. Montet, 'Strategic Trade Policies', in D. Greenaway and L. Winters, eds., *Surveys in International Trade* (Oxford: Blackwell, 1994); and M. Kitson and J. Michie, 'Conflict, Co-operation and Change: The Political Economy of Trade and Trade Policy', *Review of International Political Economy*, 2:4 (1995).

58 See: J. Robinson, 'The Need for a Reconsideration of the Theory of International Trade', *Collected Economic Papers, Vol. 4* (Oxford: Blackwell, 1973); and R. Guttman, *How Credit-Money Shapes the Economy* (Armonk: M.E. Sharpe, 1994), pp.345-6.

59 R. Mahon, 'Swedish Unions in New Times' (paper presented at the Annual Meetings of the APSA, Chicago, 1995).

60 In other words, the rate of return to capital is set by world market forces and wages must adjust, with corporatist institutions providing the best means to do so. This recalls Marx's old warning that 'wages are the dependent and not the independent variable' in terms of capital accumulation.

61 'Seoul Threatens to Expel Foreign Trade Union Groups', *Financial Times*, 14 January 1997.

62 E. Altvater, *The Future of the Market* (London: Verso, 1993), pp.83-4.

63 J. Tobin, 'A Proposal for International Monetary Reform', *Eastern Economic Journal*, 4 (1978); and B. Eichengreen, J. Tobin and C. Wyplosz, 'Two Cases for Sand in the Wheels of International Finance', *The Economic Journal*, 105 (Jan. 1995).

64 Thus the regional differentiation of competitive capacities must be compensated by regional planning agencies whose tasks are to do what other levels of government previously did, but with the loss of the main instruments to control development – currency controls and import controls.

65 Kuttner, *End of Laissez-Faire*, Chs.6-8; J. Stopford and S. Strange, eds., *Rival States, Rival Firms: Competition for World Market Shares* (Cambridge: Cambridge University Press, 1992); and R. Blecker, ed., *U.S. Trade Policy and Global Growth* (Armonk: M.E. Sharpe, 1996).

66 Hirst and Thompson, *Globalisation in Question*, p.146.

67 The point is that the 'capitalist reformer's dilemma' cannot be overcome within its own terms. As Mike Lebowitz argues, there is in fact a need for socialists to create a 'capitalists' dilemma': the penalty for refusing to compromise is a loss of control over financial and productive assets. See, for example, his 'Trade and Class: Labour Strategies in a World of Strong Capital', *Studies in Political Economy*, N.27 (1988).

68 'The Myth of the Powerless State', *The Economist* (October 7, 1995), p.16. They were, of course, warning of the dangers of state intervention.

69 L. Panitch, 'Globalisation and the State', in this volume, p.36; and S. Gill, 'Globalisation, Market Civilisation and Disciplinary Neoliberalism', *Millennium*, 24: 3 (1995).

70 As Elmar Altvater puts it: 'Successful adaptation to exogenous conditions has relatively little to do with the functioning of markets; on the contrary, it depends on the extent to which nations manage to control the operation of world market forces by political power'. See: *The Future of the Market* (London: Verso, 1993), p.81.

71 See: N. Poulantzas, *Classes in Contemporary Capitalism* (London: Verso, 1974).

72 See: E. Wood, *Democracy Against Capitalism: Renewing Historical Materialism* (Cambridge: Cambridge University Press, 1995), conclusion.

73 This is, of course, a theme from the ecological Left going back to the 1970s, but also now among some Marxists, notably in the important journal *Capitalism, Nature, Socialism* under the editorship of Jim O'Connor. This should not be confused with an autarkic strategy, but control of the external sector internationally and nationally for reasons of democratic diversity, ecology and equality.

74 Economies of scale here means increased output for a given amount of inputs through long production runs. Increasing returns to scale are conceptually possible from other forms of organizing production by combining flexibility, external organizational economies and specialization. Robin Murray's varied writings have made this point most forcefully in attempting to find the rational kernel in current debates about production. See, for instance, 'Ownership, Control and the Market', *New Left Review*, N.164 (1987).

75 B. Sutcliffe, 'Development after Ecology', in V. Bhaskar and A. Glyn, eds., *The North, The South and the Environment: Ecological Constraints and the Global Economy* (New York: St. Martin's Press, 1995).

76 The variability of capitalist development has, if anything, increased, now that the world configuration is no longer that of the classic age of imperialism. The flows of the world economy are no longer a one-sided necessity for capitalism in the North. How else to account for the four tigers of Asia, the relative economic decline and trade problems of the U.S., and the mobilization of national capitalists in numerous countries against inward-oriented economic policies? The study of imperialism today is about the *particular mechanisms* which allow a centre economy to advantageously control the local resources of a periphery, rather than a search for uniform laws. This definition encompasses relations of dependence between advanced capitalist states, as between Canada and the U.S. On the importance still of national models see: S. Berger and R. Dore, eds., *National Diversity and Global Capitalism* (Ithaca: Cornell University Press, 1996); and J. Zysman, 'The Myth of a "Global Economy": Enduring National Foundations and Emerging Regional Realities', *New Political Economy*, 1:2 (1996).

77 A. Singh, 'Industrial Policy in the Third World in the 1990s: Alternative Perspectives', in K. Cowling and R. Sugden, eds., *Current Issues in Industrial Economic Strategy* (Manchester: Manchester University Press, 1992). This is to say that differentiated competitive capacities do not always lead to cumulative competitive weakness; that external relations must be managed so as to not defeat other planning objectives; and

that internal class struggles are crucial to embedding a process for more autonomous and integrated economies. This point is being argued forcefully and lucidly by C. Leys, *The Rise and Fall of Development Theory* (London: James Currey, 1996) and M. Bienefeld, 'The New World Order: Echoes of a New Imperialism', *Third World Quarterly*, 15:1 (1994).

78 This would appear to be a strong version of Robert Cox's suggestion that 'the core institutions of a new multilateralism would have to reflect [civilisational] diversity. … a weak centre in a fragmented whole'. See: 'Civilisations in a World Political Economy', *New Political Economy*, 1:2 (1996), pp.153-4.

79 *Collected Economic Papers*, Vol. 1. (New York: Augustus M. Kelley, 1951), p.105.

80 A transitional socialist economic strategy 'between the demands of today's struggles and tomorrow's alternative society', as John Palmer has pointed out, 'remains a seriously under-theorized subject among Marxists'. Important recent surveys, however, have helped clarify some of the issues at hand for socialist economies. See: J. Palmer, 'Municipal Enterprise and Popular Planning', *New Left Review*, N.159 (1986), pp. 117 and 122; D. Elson, 'Market Socialism or Socialization of the Market', *New Left Review*, N. 172 (1988); and R. Blackburn, 'Fin de Siecle: Socialism after the Crash', *New Left Review*, N.185 (1991).

81 This draws upon material published in G. Albo, 'Canadian Unemployment and Socialist Employment Policy', in T. Dunk, S. McBride and R. Nelson, eds., *Socialist Studies Annual N. 11: The Training Trap* (Halifax: Fernwood, 1996).

82 Recent valuable surveys have developed further ideas on alternative trade regimes: J. Michie and J. Grieve Smith, eds., *Managing the Global Economy* (Oxford: Oxford University Press, 1995); M. Barratt Brown, *Models of Political Economy* (London: Penguin, 1995), Chs.17-19; and G. Epstein, J. Graham and J. Nembhard, eds., *Creating a New World Economy* (Philadelphia: Temple University Press, 1993).

83 G. Arrighi, *The Long Twentieth Century* (London: Verso, 1994), pp.230-8; and E. Altvater, 'Financial Crises on the Threshold of the 21st Century', in L. Panitch, ed., *Socialist Register 1997: Ruthless Criticism of all that Exists* (London: Merlin, 1997).

84 For relevant surveys, with the first closer to the views here, see: J. Crotty and G. Epstein, 'In Defence of Capital Controls', in this volume; and R. Pollin, 'Financial Structures and Egalitarian Economic Policy', *New Left Review*, N.214 (1995).

85 The views here follow A. Lipietz, *Towards a New Economic Order* (New York: Oxford, 1992); and G. Strange, 'Which Path to Paradise: Gorz and the Greens', *Capital and Class*, N. 59 (1996).

86 E. Mandel, *Power and Money* (London: Verso, 1992), p. 202; and A. Gorz, *A Critique of Economic Reason* (London: Verso, 1989), p.159.

87 See: C. Sabel, 'Flexible Specialization and the Re-emergence of Regional Economies', in P. Hirst and J. Zeitlin, eds., *Reversing Industrial Decline* (Oxford: Berg, 1989). This is a point on which Wolfgang Streeck's work cited above has been most insightful, but also see R. Mahon, 'From Fordism to ? New Technologies, Labour Markets and Unions', *Economic and Industrial Democracy*, 8 (1987).

88 This approach to administration draws upon: G. Albo, D. Langille and L. Panitch, eds., *A Different Kind of State? Popular Power and Democratic Administration* (Toronto: Oxford University Press, 1993).

89 *Socialism for a Sceptical Age*, pp.179-80.

TAKING GLOBALIZATION SERIOUSLY

Hugo Radice

I. INTRODUCTION

More than thirty years ago, the expansion of US corporations abroad through foreign direct investment was already giving rise to a substantial literature on the origins, behaviour and consequences of what were then usually called multinational corporations (MNCs).[1] The conventional social sciences responded quickly to these new developments. In international economics, a new sub-discipline arose on the economics of MNCs; in business and management studies, the new field was labelled 'international business'; while international relations and politics specialists created the field of 'international political economy', centred on the international politics of the evolving world economy. At the same time, the re-emergence of a more vigorous left from the deep-freeze of the Cold War was generating a body of radical scholarship, especially in the social sciences, which looked at the new phenomenon of MNCs in the framework of revitalized theories of accumulation and imperialism.[2]

Thus, while the term 'globalization' scarcely existed fifteen years ago and has enjoyed a meteoric rise as a focus for debate both in academia and in the world at large,[3] its central social institutions and processes – MNCs (now usually renamed TNCs), cross-border flows of foreign investments, technologies and tastes, governmental and intergovernmental policies towards these flows – have in fact been under intensive study for a long time. Indeed, many of the current debates around globalization, not least its effects upon the nation-state, are clearly prefigured in the 1960s and 1970s.[4] Some of the fiercest of these debates, for example about the real

This essay was first published in *Global Capitalism vs. Democracy, The Socialist Register 1999* extent and significance of globalization, were in fact being conducted with equal ferocity and on almost exactly the same lines more than twenty years previously.

So what has changed? Why has a hitherto rather distant and esoteric subject suddenly become such a hot intellectual property? The simple answer might be that Foreign Direct Investment (FDI) and other measurable activities have become much more important, and have therefore attracted more attention. But two other factors are also important. First, these activities have intrinsically posed important challenges to established orders, both in the 'real world' of politics and business, and in the theories of the social sciences, and hence those of us who argued for their significance faced a lot of scepticism and resistance. This sort of process is understood well enough in the sociology of knowledge, and it persists to this day.

Secondly, and more importantly, the practices of international business helped to undermine the ability of governments to manage their economies along the established post-war Keynesian lines, and thus contributed to creating the economic crises and the crises of economic policy of the 1970s and 1980s. Indeed, the leaders of international business and international finance have almost without exception lauded and supported the abandonment of welfare-state Keynesianism in favour of what we now call 'neoliberalism'. Since 1970, we have seen the shift from Keynesianism to monetarism; the breakdown of Bretton Woods; the Reagan/Thatcher assault on labour, the welfare state, and public ownership; and more recently the apparent resurgence of 'flexible', 'Anglo-Saxon' capitalism as against 'Eurosclerosis' and East Asian 'cronyism'. All these may be experienced, from a national perspective within each country, as victories of right over left, market over state, capital over labour; but it is the practices of international business, the core economics and politics of globalization, that has transmitted, reproduced and refined these shifts.

A decade of debate around the idea of 'globalization' is at last giving rise to a promising response which can challenge the swaggering triumph of neoliberalism. This essay reviews the debates within the framework of conventional international political economy, in which the central issue is the relationship between the global economy and the nation-state; suggests a critique of this framework, based on a less state-centred analysis of global capitalism; and, finally, briefly points to the political conclusions that flow from this critique.

II. THE GLOBALIZATION DEBATE IN INTERNATIONAL POLITICAL ECONOMY

What is globalization? Most commonly, it is defined as a process through which an increasing proportion of economic, social and cultural transactions take place directly or indirectly between parties in different countries;[5] the term is then synonymous with 'internationalization'. This sort of definition, used for example by Hirst and Thompson, presupposes an 'original condition', a starting-point for the process, in which the world is made up of distinct and self-sufficient national economies, each under the jurisdiction of an independent nation-state.[6] It leads to the hypotheses that if globalization proceeds 'far enough' it must lead to the replacement of an 'inter-national' world economy by a single integrated global economy; and that the globalization process confronts, threatens or undermines the nation-state.

This way of looking at globalization raises a number of methodological issues. First, the implicit 'national' starting-point makes no long-term historical sense, since 'international' transactions have been crucial to economic and political dynamics in many parts of the world since centuries before the development of industrial capitalism. Secondly, attempts to measure globalization in the above sense founder on the choice of measures, the availability of data and the time period considered. Such measures are also heavily dependent on the chances of political history and geography, so that international transactions are inevitably more significant for nations that are small, resource-poor, or subject to colonial or other forms of external domination. Thirdly, although a review of these measures quickly reveals enormous quantitative and qualitative differences in the way different nations are internationally integrated, and of course huge inequalities of condition as well, the model of globalization in itself abstracts from these differences and inequalities. Fourthly, as a starting-point for analyzing the dynamics of the world economy today, this approach falsely counterposes the global to the national, and thus paves the way to seeing the central political issue as one of 'globalization versus the (national) state'.

Nonetheless, a lot of the debates about the extent and significance of globalization take place within this framework. In particular, contributors such as Gordon, Hirst and Thompson, Ruigrok and van Tulder, Wade, Zysman and Weiss have argued that globalization has been greatly exaggerated.[7] Eight main conclusions arise from this sceptical literature. Taking these points in turn, but remaining within the same framework of analysis:

1. The extent of globalization

If we accept as meaningful measures such as trade/GDP or FDI/GDP, and accept the available data, then globalization may not have occurred between the 1890s and the 1990s, but it *has* occurred between the 1940s and the 1990s. The historical data suggest that since around 1970, the global character of capitalism (measured in these ways) has been substantively restored, after 40 years in which the industrial core – and to some extent other zones – was fragmented into more autonomous national economies. With regard to the core elements of trade, finance and direct investment, this is the conclusion reached in a thorough review of the empirical evidence by Perraton *et al.* which will not be repeated here.[8] It suggests that globalization, as a process of change through time, is very much a reality in recent times.

2. 'International' versus 'global'

The counterposition of these two models is abstract and artificial. Historically, the paths of 'national' economic development in *every* country over the last several centuries have been created – consciously or unconsciously, by individuals or states – in a global context. World markets in labour, finance and products have created or denied opportunities for structural transformation to national business leaders and other elite groups; world politics, diplomacy and warfare have shaped the capacities and policies of national governments to direct such transformations. National economies are better seen as zones of relatively deeper economic integration within a single, highly-differentiated world economy; and nation-states as interdependent political entities in a complex inter-state system. On the whole, economic and political interdependence appear to have increased since the 1940s, in line with trends in trade, finance and investment, but the 'system as a whole' has always been both national and global. This argument cannot be pursued further within a framework that automatically counterposes 'state' and 'market'.

3. Globalization or regionalization

There is a further pointless counterposition in the sceptical account, between globalization and regionalization. It is scarcely surprising that in the real world of transport and other distance costs – including those arising from cultural differences, protectionism, etc. – businesses will look first to neighbouring countries for markets, labour, capital, or production sites. Hence higher levels of trade, capital flows, etc., will be found between adjacent territories such as Canada and the USA. In the colonial era, trade and capital flows were less geographically regional simply because the political systems of colonialism were designed to reduce those 'distance costs' for the merchants and financiers of the colonial power (and greatly increase them, of course, for those of other powers). Quite why the recent pattern of regionalization should be considered as anything other than a concrete *form* of internationalization is not clear. Interestingly, the Japanese debates on globalization recognize that intra- and inter-regional trade and investment flows are intimately related.[9]

4. A 'triad' phenomenon?

It is undoubtedly the case that trade and investment flows are concentrated among the advanced industrial countries; again, this is hardly surprising, since they constitute the largest and richest markets in a world where most economic activity is now based on production for sale at a profit. At one level, this is a conclusion that only counts against the most extreme 'straw man' version of globalization as a homogenizing process, yielding equality of economic conditions between all nations. At another level, however, it is significantly misleading, in so far as it implies that globalization (however exaggerated or mythical overall) is somehow more of a reality in the OECD countries. On the contrary, it is as a result of ever-deeper international integration that what used to be called the Third World has become ever more fragmented and differentiated in the last thirty years. Without, of course, challenging the 'triad' for industrial supremacy, the so-called NICs have built substantial industrial capacities and won significant shares of global industrial exports. At the same time, the most impoverished regions of the world are 'marginalized' precisely through exclusion from the global economy. Finally, the financial crises that have struck so many non-OECD countries in the last twenty years, and indeed some 'weaker' OECD members such as Mexico (1994) and South Korea (1997-8), have their origins and their resolutions in the subordination of national financial systems to world capital and money markets.

5. Embeddedness – 'holding down the global'

Sceptics argue that the globalization myth centres on an image of hypermobile capital, or better, *vulture capital*, circulating high in the ethereal realm of global money, and descending to feast on the state treasuries and pay-packets of immobile governments and workers. They rightly point out that while this might apply to short-term or explicitly speculative capital movements – holdings of cash or short-dated bonds – the more significant and transformative capital movements involve putting down economic, social and political roots. Direct investments typically lead to the purchase and installation of fixed plant and equipment, the training and retraining of staff whose productivity depends on length of service and mutual loyalty, and the long-term nurturing of essential supporting relations with suppliers, customers and above all national and local governments and officials.[10] Such arguments can draw effectively both on transaction-costs economics, and on the 'embeddedness' literature, which usually refers back to Polányi[11] and lies at the heart of the modern comparative sociology of economic systems.

However, while the sceptics are right to reject a naive 'vulture capital' model, they tend to exaggerate the extent to which capital can be 'held down'. First, many of the investments that have most concerned analysts of globalization are precisely ones which require little in the way of sunk costs: not only the labour-intensive manufacturing, assembly and service work that forms the 'new international division of labour',[12] but also some of the most highly-skilled activities in R&D and finance, where human resources are highly mobile. Secondly, when investors do 'tie up' capital and thereby put it at risk, they demand 'incentives' which have the effect of off-loading that risk onto local taxpayers and workers: in a world where there is intense competition for inward investments, these demands are usually met.[13] Thirdly, 'embeddedness' is by no means exclusively a local or national phenomenon. A dense network of international institutions, both private and public, also 'embed' businesses operating across borders, while business practices, norms, standards and cultures are increasingly shaped and reproduced at a global level.[14]

6. The powers of national governments

In the ongoing debate in international political economy (IPE), this is the critical issue. There is little doubt that deeper international economic integration, and especially the globalization of finance, has reduced significantly the 'traditional' post-1945 capacity of national governments to manage 'their' economies by means of fiscal and monetary policies, labour and welfare legislation, and a variegated regulatory regime for business which included extensive public ownership. Thus for Robert Gilpin, by the 1980s, 'the fundamental question initially posed by late nineteenth-century Marxists and subsequently by Keynes regarding the ultimate compatibility of domestic welfare capitalism with a liberal international order once again came to the fore'.[15] However, the sceptics, from Warren to Gordon to Weiss, nonetheless argue about the extent and the reversibility of this loss of 'state capacity'.[16]

Broadly, there are three themes in this strand of scepticism. The first is related closely to the empirical arguments already reviewed on the extent of globalization: for example, Weiss surveys evidence that governments do have the power to sustain differences in fiscal and monetary policies,[17] while Helleiner argues that financial liberalization is in fact reversible.[18] A common theme is that policy changes which have been presented as the result of inexorable globalization have in fact been chosen, more or less freely, by governments, perhaps in response to special *domestic* interests, and these governments can equally well choose to restore the *status quo ante*.[19] Secondly, particular varieties of state, or of 'state-societal arrangements',[20] may be better equipped to resist the erosion of state capacity, or to refashion it around new zones of autonomy: thus Weiss cites the 'governed interdependence' between state and business in Japan as permitting the evolution of industrial policy rather than its abandonment.[21] Thirdly, it may be argued that in the context of supranational regionalization, traditional capacities could be recovered at a regional level, for example in the European Union,[22] although this would require a major advance in the degree of political integration.[23]

Many other writers, however, from Murray to Gill and Law to Drache continue to insist that there has been a real loss in the policy autonomy of national governments which cannot easily be recovered.[24] Empirically this view rests mainly on two points. Firstly, the changes from broadly Keynesian-welfare-statist policies to broadly 'neoliberal' policies have been so consistent through the past twenty years and all around the world that it is hard to see them as either contingent or the result of independent policy choices by national governments. If there are certain exceptions, or variations, this is scarcely surprising given the enormous and indeed growing inequalities of wealth and power, both private and public, in the world today; in any case, many of the exceptions cited by the sceptics are contested.[25] Secondly, the transformation of the IMF, the World Bank and the GATT/WTO from benign intergovernmental regulators to the global policemen of the free market represents a deep institutionalization of this trend; one which is buttressed by the proliferation of other forms of transnational regulation, both regional (NAFTA, EU) and global (OECD, BIS), whose institutions by and large sing to the same tune. Again, the fact that, for example, the OECD has been unable as yet to bring to fruition the Multilateral Agreement on Investment merely indicates that in a highly differentiated world capitalism the establishment of uniform norms is bound to be a difficult matter: twenty years ago, even the drafting of the Multilateral Agreement on Investment would have been unthinkable.

Within the conventional IPE framework, the debate on the continued existence of state capacities will continue to centre on the accretion of empirical evidence.[26] It certainly remains feasible to press for the restoration of regulatory public powers over private interests, both nationally and transnationally, if only because, as Hirst and Thompson in particular emphasize, the nation-state remains the primary locus of political legitimation.[27] However, the real need is to address the question of what it is that 'the state' is trying to do, and why.[28]

7. Globalization, capitalism and the 'Anglo-Saxon' model

An apparent implication of globalization is that it not only is intimately associated with neoliberal policies, but also is leading to the dominance of liberal or 'Anglo-Saxon' capitalism, and the gradual erosion or (as in the Soviet case) abrupt disappearance of all alternative economic systems. Proponents of globalization on the political right and in much of the business press make no secret of their objective: a universal 'free market' capitalism in which the state is 'rolled back' to the limited functions supposedly sanctioned by Adam Smith. In the 1990s, the 'Anglo-Saxons' have been on a roll: they can point to the collapse of the Soviet model, the 'sclerosis' of continental Europe and Japan, the renewed dynamism of liberalized Latin America, and most recently the 'East Asian crisis', as convincing evidence for their case. This is particularly galling for globalization sceptics, since many of them have either contributed to or drawn upon literatures which champion alternative models on the basis of their superior performance in earlier decades.

One line of response in the face of globalist triumphalism is to continue to argue, empirically or theoretically, the merits of more organized or 'trust-based' forms of capitalism. Thus for Carlin and Soskice, it is precisely because of its distinctive institutional structures that Germany has been able to weather the unprecedented strains of absorbing the former East Germany;[29] while Berggren and Nomura argue that despite some changes in Japanese business behaviour in the 1990s, its system too demonstrates remarkable resilience.[30] In more theoretical vein, both Chang and Lo convincingly draw on heterodox economics to press the case for forms of state intervention in industry;[31] while in the field of labour studies and human resource management, the debate on skill formation and productivity growth still goes against the neoliberals.[32] Secondly, if, as appears to be the case, Anglo-Saxon liberalism is closely associated with regressive tax and welfare policies, and a redistribution of income and wealth from rich to poor, this can be presented as an unacceptable price to be paid. Similar arguments, rooted in the traditional argument about the market's failure to deal with economic externalities and social costs, are advanced from an environmental standpoint. Thirdly, growing instability in the world economy can be blamed not on too much regulation, but rather on too little. Thus, Wade and Veneroso attribute responsibility for the East Asian financial crisis to both the deregulation of national financial systems, as in South Korea in the 1990s, and the absence of regulation which generated excessive lending to the region by American and European banks.[33]

On the face of it, the empirical evidence from the 1990s does on balance suggest a strengthening of the Anglo-Saxon model.[34] On the other hand, the fashion for identifying and contrasting competing models of capitalism, which was given a strong fillip by the collapse of the Soviet system, conceals important methodological weaknesses, many of them inherited from the Cold War comparisons of models of 'industrialism' or 'post-industrialism'. In addition, if we examine in more detail some of the key institutional components of the models, there is enormous variability within particular countries, both through time[35] and across sectors, which tends to undermine the emphasis in the comparative literature on the 'path-dependence' of national systems. Finally, it is not clear whether superior performance should be attributed to institutional differences, or whether the persistence of particular institutional patterns should be attributed to superior economic dynamism, or indeed to the possession of specific military, political or economic advantages that have no particular institutional shape.[36]

8. Building alternatives to neoliberal globalization

Whatever the long-term prospects for the Anglo-Saxon model of capitalism, the current political dominance of neoliberalism is only too apparent. But the sceptics argue that this can be challenged by mobilizing those interests that have suffered from this dominance, essentially around the reconstruction of a regulatory, interventionist state. If globalization, deregulation, privatization, etc., directly benefit particular groups of capitalists[37] or bureaucrats, then this can be reversed in the political arena by offering an alternative that is more attractive. Generally, the sceptics seek to update social democracy: what they offer is not a simple return to the postwar recipe of state intervention, welfarism, etc. – nowadays routinely caricatured, in Britain, at least, even by some supposed progressives, as 'tax-and-spend' policies – but a 'modernized' social democracy which accepts the basic economic and political structures of capitalism, but seeks to ameliorate the outcome for the disadvantaged. The main political goal to which this capacity is to be directed is the traditional social democratic one of improving living standards, defined now in ways that take on board the concerns of 'new social movements'. Crucially, the state can and should focus on improving human resources: on increasing workforce skills, the stock of productive knowledge, and the efficiency of both private and public management. In the context of more competitive world markets and the grudgingly-admitted greater openness to trade and capital movements, these improvements in human resources are viewed as the necessary foundation of international competitiveness.[38] The apparent failure of public ownership, central planning and other 'old' forms of state intervention makes imperative the adoption of a new form of 'mixed economy', in which the proven incentive systems of the private sector are harnessed to the altruistic goals established by the political process.

The sceptics remain convinced, as already noted, that states have the capacity to tame the forces of globalization. A measured reregulation of global trade and finance can be achieved by a mix of national, regional and global initiatives: these can be constructed by convincing financiers and markets that these measures will safeguard the benefits of liberalization and reduce the risk of costly major crises.[39] Furthermore, a recasting of industrial, education and employment policies by a 'developmental'[40] or 'catalytic'[41] state can allow a country to respond effectively to the challenge of global markets and avoid being caught in a low-skill, low-wage, low-investment vicious circle. Since for the sceptics transnational corporations remain bound to their country of origin, they can be harnessed as the flagships of national regeneration.

Reviewing the actual pattern of events over the past thirty years, it is very hard to see much evidence for the feasibility of this political strategy. Initiatives to reregulate global trade and finance, from the 'New International Economic Order' of the 1970s to the Tobin tax, have made no headway whatsoever. Within Europe, the Maastricht Treaty has enshrined the monetarist, free-market core of the EU; despite the existence of a 'social chapter' in the treaty, there is a clear trend towards a levelling-down of welfare and the 'flexible' labour markets championed as much by 'New Labour' in Britain as by the bosses in Germany, France and Italy.[42] Equally telling is the case of Eastern Europe. Here, Amsden's attempt to apply the lessons of South Korea to the restoration of capitalism in the region[43] failed totally to connect with political realities: far from the market 'meeting its match' as she predicted, a pragmatically-moderated neoliberal programme has been remarkably successful in ensuring economic and political stability, in large measure due to the pervasive role of Western capital.[44] As for East Asia, it is far too soon to judge how well the benchmark exemplars of state activism, South Korea and Japan, will weather the storm. Can the South Korean debacle be blamed on the liberalization and opening of its financial sector, and on the weakening of the state's powers of economic direction, in the last ten years? Or did these developments simply indicate that the state-business arrangements were now 'catalyzing' the breakneck expansion of South Korean capital abroad, rather than the development of the national economy?

In the end, however, the globalization debate yields such unsatisfying political conclusions because its conceptual apparatus is so impoverished. The sceptics *assume* the degree of state autonomy that is necessary for their political prescriptions to have credibility. Clearly, if the state is (a) powerful, and (b) dominated by the democratic will, then globalization and its discontents can be readily thrown aside in favour of a more acceptable agenda of national economic and social progress; what is more, there is then no need to contemplate the messy and thus far unproductive strategy of building an international movement. However, there are strong arguments against this Panglossian position.

III. A CRITIQUE: BRINGING CAPITALISM BACK IN

As I have already indicated, the root problem with the sceptical critique of globali-zation is its view of the state, and in particular the autonomy of the state. Although this is a view shared across a number of intellectual traditions in the social sciences, it has been articulated most explicitly in modern international political economy. The 1985 collection of essays edited by Peter Evans, Dietrich Rueschemeyer and Theda Skocpol under the title *Bringing the State Back In* epitomizes this view.[45] The editors aimed to go beyond what they saw as overgeneralized neo-Marxist and neo-Weberian views, on state autonomy and on state strength respectively, through detailed case studies which could reveal the more significant structures and processes at work within states and between states and social groups. Although they frequently stressed the open-ended nature of these explorations, the ultimate aim was to develop 'state-centered explanations'[46] which would in turn help to develop effective state policies: for example, Rueschemeyer and Evans explicitly tried to identify the conditions for 'effective state intervention'[47] in economic and industrial development.

Cammack has argued strongly that this volume was part of a project designed to break with the Marxist or neo-Marxist approach to the state in the Third World, which in turn had developed in the 1960s and 1970s out of the theories of im-perialism and underdevelopment.[48] Marxist debates on the state in the 1970s had moved beyond the limitations of traditional structuralist and instrumental views, and explored a wide range of cases and issues using more flexible concepts, for example that of 'relative autonomy', that could handle the contingent and variable aspects of capitalist state institutions and practices. One result of this was a consid-erable overlap in research agendas and debates between neo-Marxists and more orthodox social scientists in many fields. In the 'final analysis', however, all varieties of Marxist analysis see the state through the prism of the class nature of capitalism. While those who adopted the neo-Marxist approach and sought to change the state from within quickly found themselves marginalized or ejected,[49] most mainstream social scientists found it easier to distance themselves from a class approach.

The collapse of the Soviet Union and its satellite states in Eastern Europe made this task much easier. In the short term, this was readily accepted as prima facie evidence of the failure of Marxism, which had remained the official ideology of the Soviet bloc: the attempts, by Western anti-Stalinist Marxists and by East European 'third way' advocates alike, to establish a bridgehead for democratic socialism were quickly routed by the triumphant march eastwards of the 'free market'. The most that socialists could hope for, apparently, was to work for an amelioration of capitalism, without even the long-term perspective of revolu-tionary transformation that earlier generations of reformists, from Bernstein to Crosland, had explicitly retained.

However, the neoliberal triumph has been short-lived. The demise of the Soviet model led first to expressions of the need for an alternative bogeyman with which to scare the citizens of the 'free world': radical Islam, eco-terror-ism, drugs, economic migration, all variants on the theme of 'the barbarian at the gates'. But it was soon apparent that capitalism itself retained all its historical capacity to wreak destruction upon humanity, whether in its birth-pangs in the rubble of communism, in the industrialization of China, in the persistence of mass unemployment in Western Europe, or in the financial crises that engulfed Britain in 1992, Mexico in 1994 and East Asia in 1997-8.

From this standpoint, what is abundantly clear is that globalization is intrinsically a *capitalist* process. In the context of globalization, it makes no sense to analyze the state in abstraction from capitalism, because the concrete conditions and events that confront states at present arise from economic and social processes organized along capitalist lines. This is not to say that all, or indeed any, such events can be reduced to the inevitable outcome of some sort of mechanical unfolding of history. But in the face of widespread and repeated phenomena such as high levels of cyclical and structural unemployment; financial crises caused by over-lending and inadequate regulation; the subordination of education and culture to commercial forces; the dismantling of public systems of social security in favour of private pension rackets; the ever-widening gap between rich and poor; bitter struggles over trade union rights; environmental threats arising from uncontrolled commercial exploitation of nature; – need I go on? Can *any* of these be adequately understood as the out-come of 'autonomous' state actions and processes? Of course not; which is why in *practice* the theorists of 'stateness' have to bring in through the back door the factors that they dismiss at the front door as smacking of 'economic determinism' or 'class reductionism'. This is brought out very clearly in a recent essay by Peter Evans, which is subtitled 'reflections on stateness in an era of globalisation'.[50]

Twelve years after *Bringing the State Back In*, Evans reviews the challenge that glo-balization in its neoliberal form poses to the state, but he continues to claim from the East Asian cases 'the possibility of a positive connection between high stateness ... and success in a globalising economy'.[51] Like other sceptics, Evans emphasizes the ideological dimension of globalization, which is carried through into formal injunctions to individual states through Anglo-American dominance in the inter-governmental organizations of the IMF, WTO, etc. However, an 'economically stateless world' cannot provide the stability and order that transnational investors re-quire, and the complexities and risks of global finance impress this need ever more firmly upon them: 'While globalisation does make it harder for states to exercise economic initiative, it also increases both the potential returns from effective state action and the costs of incompetence'.[52] In addition, the 'new institutional eco-nomics' of the information age means that attacks on the state as 'rent-seeking' are blunted by the increased economic importance of public goods, whose availability depends on public enforcement of property rights and/or on public provision. Even a revived role for 'civil society', Evans argues, does not mean a correspond-ingly reduced role for the state, because of the need for 'state-society synergy': civic associations require a capable and involved state if they are to act effectively in society. Thus, for both 'external' and 'internal' reasons, Evans concludes that a 'return of the pendulum' back towards 'stateness' seems likely.

But what is the *content* of this stateness? This is where capitalism suddenly enters as a concept, slipping in through the back door, for as a result of the economic dominance of transnational business, it seems to Evans that the state can only be restored to a positive role if that role is restricted to 'activities essential for sustaining the profitability of transnational markets'.[53] The welfare state remains diminished, and indeed delivering services and security to business 'means devoting more resources to the repression of the more desperate and reckless among the excluded, both domestic and international'.[54] In other words, the state is being restructured around a specifically *capitalist* project of 'development', in which private profits are promoted at the expense of poor people and poor countries. Evans concludes by finding some hope that social interests other than business elites just might create 'state-society synergies' with 'beleaguered state managers and politicians disenchanted with leaner, meaner stateness';[55] indeed he finds this 'no less implausible than the alliances that were actually forged between labour organisations and the state during the early decades of the twentieth century'.

Thus the trajectory of Evans' work leads back from an abstract emphasis on the developmental role of the state, to an acknowledgement that the actual thrust of state activities is determined at present by the power of the business elite, in other words the capitalist class; and that a real alternative to the dominance of neoliberalism depends on the political mobilization of 'citizens and communities'. What remains, however, is the need to link this more systematically to an analysis of whether and how the economics of capitalism have changed.

If we start from the capitalist nature of globalization, the first task is to characterize briefly the main features of global capitalism today, abstracting from its divisions into nations. Precisely because of the global integration of production, markets and finance, the common dynamic of this system is more pervasive, and certain important features can therefore be seen to apply everywhere. Central to this common dynamic has been a shift of economic and political power towards capitalists across much of the world. In the developed capitalist countries, the century or so up to the 1970s saw significant gains for workers, in the context of persistent national rivalries, world wars and the secession of the Soviet bloc from world capitalism. The latter decades of this period also saw an end to formal colonialism and the beginnings of a genuinely global and potentially democratic political order.[56] Since 1970, global integration has incorporated the former Second and Third Worlds firmly back into the capitalist fold, not merely by forcing open national markets and directing local production to the world market through debt peonage, liberalization and privatization, but also by incorporating local business and bureaucratic elites into the political, social and cultural world of the emerging global capitalist class. Above all, the greater mobility and penetrative capacity of capital has forged powerful weapons for rolling back the gains of workers in all countries. Pursuing this in more detail, I suggest eight features, the first four being 'microeconomic' features, while the remainder emerge at some more aggregate level:

1. Decline in labour's market power

Changes in technology and in patterns of demand have seriously affected the market power of labour. The concept of technological unemployment remains an ideological one, designed to scare workers into concessions: in the long run, accumulation in capitalist economies is based on employing labour, not on employing 'technology'. However, in advanced industrial societies, employment and production have shifted towards non-material 'service' activities, some of which are knowledge- and skill-intensive, and away from manual manufacturing tasks. The shift in demand has been magnified by the threat of job flight for manual workers in particular. The reality or threat of mass unemployment has enabled employers to weaken the organizations of labour either directly, or through legislative changes. None of this is gainsaid by the experience of certain countries such as South Korea or South Africa where at times industrial expansion has enabled significant increases in union membership and real wages. At the same time, the role of wages in normal cyclical rhythms of accumulation continues: thus in the U.S.A., although the expansion of the 1990s was unprecedentedly long, labour shortages eventually started to hit profits.

2. Reassertion of control over labour

There have been substantial changes in capitalist management, which has developed and refined both carrots and sticks, from the shopfloor to the boardroom, aimed at increasing the productivity and intensity of labour. Much – far too much – has been made of the idea of a new 'post-Fordist' era, of smaller-scale, flexible production systems in which workers have to be reskilled and re-empowered in return for providing sophisticated, high-quality products: this bears as much relation to the realities of workplace domination and control as the ideology of the free market does to the real world of monopoly and *caveat emptor*. In substance, the changes in recent decades centre on the reassertion of management control over labour through a refined mix of the strategies of 'direct control' and 'responsible autonomy'.[57] Nonetheless, despite the apparent sophistication of production and management systems, they still depend as always on the compliance of workers.

3. Corporate finance and control

The global tide of privatization has opened up vast new markets for private capitalists, as well as handing over to them control over vital physical assets: not only in the transport, telecommunications and energy sectors, but in heavy industry, finance, tourism and increasingly now in health, education and social services. This has been accompanied by a dramatic extension of the corporate form of capitalist ownership and finance, in particular the shift from narrow ownership coupled with bank fi-

nance towards equity finance.[58] This shift is partly a response to the increased competitiveness and volatility of markets, since wider equity finance allows the 'insider'
interests (including core banks) to off-load risk onto outsiders. However, when
taken in conjunction with well-orchestrated panics over public pension provision,
it also mobilizes at low cost the lifetime savings of workers, helping to tie the latter
in to the practice and ideology of capitalist ownership.[59]

4. Capitalist competition reasserted

In the post-1945 'golden age', both conventional industrial economics and the
heterodox traditions of institutionalism, Keynesianism and neo-Marxism, argued,
albeit with different terminologies, that competitive capitalism based on entrepreneurial small business had been progressively replaced by monopoly structures
and practices. Scale economies and the high cost of innovation required market
dominance, supernormal profits and price leadership, relegating the individual
entrepreneur to marginal sectors or a strictly subordinate and dependent role.
The last thirty years have provided ample grounds for restoring the classical view
(of Smith, Marx or later Schumpeter) that competition is not about market equilibrium and prices, but about the search for sources of market power and profit.
The giant corporations of today are not stagnant managerial bureaucracies, but
dynamic and flexible profit-seekers – and transnational expansion has been a
central concrete form of this competitive accumulation.

5. The economic role of the state

Although the neoliberal assault on the state has done little in most countries to
reduce its absolute weight in the economy, as conventionally measured by ratios
of public expenditure to national income, it has generated fundamental changes in
the way the public sector is financed and managed. The key monetarist ideas, that
'bloated' public finances were inflationary and 'crowded out' private investment,
reflected the growing realization in capitalist circles that there was, otherwise, no
logical limit to the enlargement of the public sector: ultimately, Keynesianism and
the welfare/warfare state might turn out to be proto-socialist, rather than just a
modified form of capitalism.[60] The enforcement of monetarist targets for public
spending and debt, whether through the judgements of currency and financial
markets or at the behest of lenders, has halted the ratchet-like trend of expansion
in the public sector, with well-known consequences. Equally important is the shift
in power within states towards finance ministries, central banks and cabinet offices, with spending departments obliged to realize 'efficiency gains', that is cuts,
on a permanent year-by-year basis.[61] This has fed down through service providers
in the form of financial and bureaucratic controls, applied in a way that strikingly
resembles Soviet-style central planning, with all its familiar outcomes: a fixation
on a limited range of quantitative targets at the expense of quality or content, the
substitution of individual for collective incentives, relentless cost-cutting, demoralization, corruption and waste.

6. States and markets in global capitalism

As already discussed in section 2, this restructured economic role of the state has been generalized and enforced both through financial markets, and through inter-governmental bodies and processes. However, it also results from the process of economic integration itself. Competition for world markets ensures that, as long as states continue to exercise territorial jurisdiction in economic matters, they will continue to try to respond to the needs of 'their' national business sectors: hence the promotion of 'neo-mercantilist' policies, typically by industrial ministries (supported by the defence sector on security grounds). On the other hand, the more that accumulation by the national business sector is itself internationalized – through exporting, outward investment, technology imports, or whatever – the more it will need to relate also, directly or indirectly, to other states, and the more different states will need actively to manage the resulting common interests and conflicting goals. This reality, of a multiplicity of competing states and capitals, is mostly analyzed through bargaining models,[62] but such an approach may conceal the extent to which states are so politically penetrated and dominated by business[63] that they cannot be seen as having independent objectives to be pursued by bargaining. Indeed, it is precisely in conforming to the agenda of business – transmitted through markets as well as political processes – that states have 'restructured' themselves away from their Keynesian and welfarist goals. In the post-colonial underdeveloped countries and in the restored capitalisms in Eastern Europe, new comprador bourgeoisies emerge, as internationalization forces national capitalists to link up (in a subordinate position) with powerful transnational interests: as McMichael argues, 'globalisation' has replaced 'modernisation' as the dominant ideology of development.[64]

7. Transnational politics and regional groupings

Post-war Keynesian-welfare and post-colonial states, focused on national economic management and development, formed a transnational political order in which – in contrast to the interwar period – a range of multilateral intergovernmental organizations were developed with the purpose of structuring and regulating inter-state relations. This inter-state system in principle provided an economic and security environment which supported national capital accumulation: in particular, through the Bretton Woods institutions, adjustment mechanisms which could help all countries to avoid a return to the trade wars and depression of the interwar years. Despite apparent principles of equality among states, the system's installation and maintenance depended crucially on US hegemony. The mushrooming of global trade, investment and finance from the 1960s placed extra demands on this inter-state system at exactly the time when that hegemony was being challenged in the economic sphere by Western Europe and Japan. For some twenty-five years, calls for a fundamental redesign of international institutions have been resisted in favour of *ad hoc* changes of their agenda, supplemented by an updated form of traditional 'great power' diplomacy, of which the G5/7/8 'economic summits' are the most

visible part. The existence and importance of these transnational political structures
bears out the view of globalization sceptics that the state has not withered away; on
the other hand, repeated forecasts that trade and currency tensions would lead to the
breakdown of inter-state cooperation and a return to interwar-style protectionism
have proved wide of the mark. Regional groupings represent an attempt to create
more durable and legitimate transnational political structures. Far from indicating an
alternative to 'universal' global integration, they rest on exactly the same economic
foundations: the greater intensity of economic integration between neighbouring
countries generates greater pressure to find collective solutions.

8. The new imperialism

From around 1870, formal colonial empires and informal hegemonic powers
formed an imperialist system, in which less developed and militarily weaker regions were politically and economically subordinated to one or other of the competing imperial powers. Formal political independence did not of itself change
anything in countries locked into a traditional primary-producer role in the international division of labour, and in any case informal spheres of influence came
to be exercised through bodies such as the British Commonwealth, the Alliance
for Progress in the Americas, and regional US-led security bodies like NATO.
In the 1960s and 1970s, neo-Marxist and dependency writings broadly captured
the continuance of imperialism, based on economic and political subordination,
and generating still-increasing gaps in living standards between developed and
underdeveloped regions. More or less radical policies of national development in
those decades often challenged directly the power of foreign capital through na-
tionalizations, forms of economic planning, and discriminatory monetary, fiscal
and trade policy instruments, but with little success. In the 1970s, the growth of
global capital markets appeared to offer a 'non-political' substitute for official aid
flows, but did nothing in itself to change the chronic tendency towards balance
of payments crises in the Least Developed Countries.

   The shift towards so-called export-oriented industrialization accelerated as the
problem of external debt spread to engulf most of the non-oil-producing Third
World: in the 1980s, this provided the right circumstances for a major economic,
political and ideological offensive aimed at 'opening up' the markets and resources of
the Third World again to foreign capital. As the annual reports of the UNCTAD's
Division on Transnational Corporations and Investment have charted,[65] there have
been almost universal moves to liberalize controls on trade and FDI, including controls on foreign ownership of banks and other financial institutions, and of minerals,
energy, transport and communications companies. It is these foreign investments
that form the core of the new imperialism. As Sunkel argued long ago, once these
investments become central to development strategy, they serve to tie local capitalists, managers, politicians and bureaucrats to the economic interests of parent TNCs
and other foreign investors.[66] This is supported by the extensive role of the IMF and
the World Bank in designing and enforcing 'structural adjustment' policies; by the

regular participation of the elites in transnational political forums both official (IMF etc.) and unofficial (e.g. the annual Davos conferences); by the continued education of these elites in the leading business and other graduate schools of the USA and Western Europe; and by routine corruption and kleptocracy, as notoriously in Indonesia.

IV. CONCLUSION: RESPONDING TO GLOBALIZATION

What conclusions, then, does the 'globalization debate' lead to when recast in this light? First, in the last thirty years or so national economies have become significantly more internationally integrated, and as a result national governments have lost much of the autonomy that they enjoyed in economic policy-making. This has restored the salience of world market forces in shaping economic outcomes, and encouraged a halting and *ad hoc* multiplication of intergovernmental institutions and processes. Secondly, the vast majority of the largest privately-owned firms, in all sectors and countries of origin, operate transnational networks of production, and in turn generate lower-level networks of trade and production that engage a significant proportion of formal-sector workers everywhere. Thirdly, notwithstanding the continued differences in national legal and regulatory systems, a growing proportion of workers find themselves entering labour markets that are *de facto* global. Fourthly, nation-states are an integral part of the process: they have accommodated and even accelerated this global integration with policy changes that have shifted the balance of economic and political power towards employers and owners, and away from the majority of workers and their dependants.

For a century, despite a lot of lip-service to internationalism, socialist and progressive movements of all kinds have functioned primarily at the national level and below: this has been true as much of trade unions and other organizations of 'civil society' as of political parties. Given the resulting legacy of institutions, practices and political cultures, and the gains in economic justice and political democracy realized through national struggles during that century, it is hardly surprising that the immediate reaction to the perceived threat of globalization is framed at the national level. Accustomed as most of us are to the formal structures and processes of electoral democracy, we seek to bring the issue on the agenda of our organizations, and we look to national government to orchestrate a response. We look for single-issue alliances to build support for such responses, for example linking trade unions, environmental groups, and consumer organizations in challenging pro-business measures of privatization and deregulation.

The problem is that, when we get to the national level, we find that the state has become increasingly structured around an agenda that intrinsically excludes or subordinates our concerns. On the national terrain, for example, a weakened labour movement may, as in the UK, find itself excluded, as tripartite structures are abandoned as part of a general assault on labour. On global trade and investment issues, crucial debates and decisions have moved to little-known and relatively inaccessible intergovernmental bureaucracies, allowing 'our' governments to say that their hands are tied: indeed, in heavily-indebted countries these un-elected bureaucracies take over key governmental policy functions.

In these circumstances we have two choices, if a straightforward reactive resist-ance along customary lines fails (which is clearly not always the case). First, we can accept the limitations of national politics and seek to identify new and effective policy aims and instruments. This is what is offered, in very different ways, by the reconstituted social-democratic parties of the left, and the conservative-nationalist parties of the right. For the latter, globalization has cruelly undermined their vision of a nation united against its enemies, because big business insists on being free to operate on a world stage. The revival of conservative-nationalism in Europe and elsewhere is built on a populist response to this, and traditional big-business parties alternate between resistance and concessions as they seek to limit the appeal of the renewed far right.[67] But social-democratic parties, including the ex-'communist' parties of Eastern Europe, have recovered electorally after the long onslaught of ne-oliberalism, essentially by accommodating to it. As well as accepting fiscal and mon-etary constraints and rejecting protectionism, they now offer a 'new New Deal' that enshrines the world market as the ultimate arbiter of what is and is not produced, and incorporates the political ideology of individualism into everyday life at work and at home.[68] Amid all the talk of joint private/public ventures, of new ways of regulating the private sector and of 'supplementing' public welfare provision, in the end this amounts to a political sea-change, in which the fundamental interests of business – a cheap and appropriately-trained workforce, gullible consumers and 'responsive' regulators – form a protected core in the political agenda, while every-thing else depends on 'what we can afford'. Above all, 'we' have to accept the 'real world' by pursuing the common national goal of world market competitiveness, through improving the productivity of labour: the main consequence of this being an inexorable pressure to 'level down' wages and conditions, whatever is said about the virtues of 'reskilling', 'increasing value added' and so on.

Alternatively, we can seek to develop a transnational collective response. This is still often enough rejected as a desirable but hopelessly unrealistic aim. Yet if we be-lieve that effective social movements arise when the activities of participants create shared circumstances and immediate interests, as well as beliefs, then deeper global integration is precisely creating the basis for transnational social movements. This is certainly the case for labour movements today.[69] Quite apart from the more spec-tacular demonstrations of solidarity, such as over the Renault-Vilvoorde closure, and in support of dockers in Liverpool and Australia, to an increasing extent routine collective bargaining is undertaken in a global context. The threat of transfer of jobs to overseas affiliates hangs over local and national negotiators in all the more mobile industries, while public sector workers are told that the world's financial markets will not tolerate the increase in public spending that would result from higher pay increases.[70] Most recently, the campaign against the OECD's Multilateral

Agreement on Investment brought together international NGOs concerned with environmental protection and poverty, trade unionists seeking to maintain labour standards, and protection-minded national business sectors. Although it can be argued that the crucial factor in temporarily halting the MAI was the unwillingness of President Clinton to risk splitting the bizarre coalition of interests that make up the Democratic Party in a mid-term election year, the campaign began with, and was continued by, a grass-roots transnational alliance rooted in shared interests.

None of this is to deny that the development of alternatives to present-day global capitalism requires an enormous political effort at the local and national levels. If capital is to be tamed, let alone supplanted as the main organizing concept in our political economy, we obviously have to craft alternative forms of economic and social organization in each state as well as across states.[71] But a transnational dimension to this work is also both necessary and feasible.

NOTES

1   E.g. C.P. Kindleberger, ed., *The International Corporation*, Cambridge, Mass.: MIT Press, 1970; R.Vernon, *Sovereignty at Bay*, New York: Basic Books, 1971.

2   E.g. H. Magdoff, *The Age of Imperialism*, New York: Monthly Review Press, 1969; R. Murray, 'Underdevelopment, international firms and the international division of labour', in Society for International Development, *Towards a New World Economy*, Rotterdam: Rotterdam UP, 1972; H. Radice, ed., *International Firms and Modern Imperialism*, London: Penguin, 1975.

3   M.Waters, *Globalization*, London: Routledge, 1995, p.2.

4   E.g. J-J. Servan-Schreiber, *The American Challenge*, New York: Athenaeum, 1968; C. Tugendhat, *The Multinationals*, London: Eyre and Spottiswoode, 1971; C. Levinson, *Capital, Inflation and the Multinationals*, London: Allen & Unwin, 1971, in addition to those already cited.

5   Indirectly in cases where an intranational transaction is induced by or contingent upon an international transaction.

6   P. Hirst and G.Thompson, *Globalisation in Question*, London: Polity, 1996.

7   D. Gordon, 'The global economy: new edifice or crumbling foundations?', *New Left Review* 168, 1988; Hirst and Thompson, *Globalisation in Question*; W. Ruigrok and R. van Tulder, *The Logic of International Restructuring*, London: Routledge, 1995; R. Wade, 'Globalisation and its limits: reports of the death of the national economy are greatly exaggerated', in S. Berger and R. Dore, eds., *National Diversity and Global Capitalism*, Ithaca, NY: Cornell University Press, 1996; J. Zysman, 'The myth of a "global" economy: enduring national foundations and emerging regional realities', *New Political Economy* 1(2), 1996; L.Weiss, *The Myth of the Powerless State*, London: Polity, 1998.

8   J. Perraton, D. Goldblatt, D. Held, and A. McGrew, 'The globalisation of economic activity', *New Political Economy*, 2(2), 1997.

9   See e.g. H. Hasegawa and G. Hook, eds., *Japanese Business Management: Restructuring for Low Growth and Globalisation*, London: Routledge, 1998, part I.

10   Similar arguments were advanced some years ago, for example by T.H. Moran,

Multinational Corporations and the Politics of Dependence: Copper in Chile, Princeton: Princeton UP, 1974 in his concept of the 'obsolescing bargain': fixed investments (in this case in the copper industry) would give host governments the leverage needed to strike a better deal with investors.

11 K. Polányi, *The Great Transformation,* Beacon Hill: Beacon Press, 1944.

12 F. Fröbel, J. Heinrichs, and O. Kreye, *The New International Division of Labour,* Cambridge: Cambridge UP, 1980; J. Nash and M.P. Fernandez-Kelly, eds., *Women, Men and the International Division of Labour,* Albany: SUNY Press, 1983.

13 Thus *Business Central Europe,* June 1998, blames the low level of FDI in Estonia on its lack of government incentives (p.10), and praised the announcement of 'long-awaited' new incentives in the Czech Republic (p.25).

14 On the internationalization of state structures see S. Picciotto, 'The internationalisation of the state', *Capital & Class,* 43 (Spring), 1991.

15 R. Gilpin, *The Political Economy of International Relations,* Princeton: Princeton UP, 1987, p. 389.

16 B. Warren, 'The internationalisation of capital and the nation state: a comment', *New Left Review,* 68, 1971; D. Gordon, 'The global economy: new edifice or crumbling foundations?', *New Left Review,* 168, 1988; Weiss, *The Myth of the Powerless State.*

17 Weiss, *The Myth of the Powerless State,* pp. 190-2.

18 E. Helleiner, 'Post-globalisation: is the financial liberalisation trend likely to be reversed?', in R. Boyer, and D. Drache, eds., *States Against Markets: the Limits of Globalisation,* London: Routledge, 1996.

19 This point is taken up again in the next section.

20 J.A. Hart, *Rival Capitalists: International Competitiveness in the US, Japan and Western Europe,* Ithaca: Cornell UP, 1992.

21 Weiss, *The Myth of the Powerless State.*

22 E.g. H. Chorney, 'Debts, deficits and full employment', in Boyer and Drache, eds., *States Against Markets.*

23 Hirst and Thompson, *Globalisation in Question,* pp. 163-7.

24 R. Murray, 'The internationalisation of capital and the nation state', *New Left Review* 67, 1971; S. Gill and D. Law, *The Global Political Economy: Perspectives, Problems and Policies,* London: Harvester Wheatsheaf, 1988; D. Drache, 'From Keynes to K-Mart: competitiveness in a corporate age', Boyer and Drache, eds., *States Against Markets.*

25 For example, contrast the rosy view of Germany's current prospects in Weiss (*The Myth of the Powerless State,* ch.5) with that of Streeck (W. Streeck, 'German capitalism: does it exist? Can it survive?', *New Political Economy,* 2 (2), 1997).

26 Interestingly, Rodrik argued in a recent study, published by the prestigious and 'mainstream' Institute for International Economics in Washington, that globalization had 'gone too far', and could not be guaranteed to give rise to unequivocal welfare benefits either within or between nations (D. Rodrik, *Has Globalisation Gone Too Far?,* Washington: Institute for International Economics, 1997).

27 Except of course when global or regional 'powers' choose to override this principle and 'intervene'.

28 L. Panitch, 'Globalisation and the state', in this volume.

29 W. Carlin and D. Soskice, 'Shocks to the system: the German political economy under stress', *National Institute Economic Review,* 159, 1997.

30 C. Berggren and M. Nomura, *The Resilience of Corporate Japan*, London: Paul Chapman, 1997.

31 H-J. Chang, *The Political Economy of Industrial Policy*, Basingstoke: Macmillan, 1994; D. Lo, *Market and Institutional Regulation in Chinese Industrialization*, Basingstoke: Macmillan, 1997.

32 D. Ashton, and F. Green, *Education, Training and the Global Economy*, Aldershot: Edward Elgar, 1996.

33 R. Wade and F. Veneroso, 'The Asian crisis: the high-debt model versus the Wall Street-Treasury-IMF complex', *New Left Review*, 228, 1998.

34 This proposition is developed more fully in general terms in H. Radice, '"Globalisation" and national differences', *Competition and Change*, 3(4), 1998, and in the case of Europe in Radice, 'Britain under "New Labour": a model for European restructuring?', in H.R. Bellofiore, ed., *Which Labour Next? Global Money, Capitalist Restructuring and Changing Patterns of Production*, London: Edward Elgar, 1999.

35 For example, Japan's industrial finance was largely stock-market-based before World War II, while the USA's was significantly bank-based prior to the Great Depression.

36 For example, both Japan and Germany were banned from military research after the Axis defeat. This may be more important in explaining their subsequent industrial dynamism than certain institutional features of their 'innovation systems' which only emerged later on.

37 For an extreme example, see Wade and Veneroso's reference to 'anecdotal evidence' that the bribery of key officials by Japanese and Western financial institutions played a part in South Korean financial deregulation (R. Wade and F. Veneroso, 'The Asian crisis: the high-debt model versus the Wall Street-Treasury-IMF complex', *New Left Review*, 228, 1998, p. 9).

38 R.B. Reich, *The Work of Nations*, New York: Vintage, 1992.

39 See e.g. Hirst and Thompson, *Globalisation in Question*, ch. 9; Wade and Veneroso, 'The Asian crisis'. For Helleiner, the governments that *chose* to liberalize can now choose to rein in global finance – although it may take a 'major global financial crisis' ('Post-globalisation', p. 206) to bring them to make this 'choice'.

40 A. Amsden, *Asia's Next Giant*, New York: Oxford UP, 1989; R. Wade, *Governing the Market*, Princeton: Princeton UP, 1990.

41 Weiss, *The Myth of the Powerless State*.

42 Radice, 'Britain under "New Labour"', in Bellofiore, ed., *Which Labour Next?*

43 A. Amsden, J. Kochanowicz, and L. Taylor, *The Market Meets its Match*, Cambridge, Mass.: Harvard UP, 1994.

44 H. Radice, 'Capitalism restored: East-Central Europe in the light of globalisation', in T. Krausz, ed., *The Change of Regime and the Left in Eastern Europe*, Budapest: Akadémiái Kiadó, 1998.

45 P.B. Evans, D. Rueschmeyer, and T. Skocpol, eds., *Bringing the State Back In*, Cambridge: Cambridge UP, 1985.

46 Evans, Rueschmeyer, and Skocpol, eds., *Bringing the State Back In*, p. 7.

47 D. Rueschemeyer and P.B. Evans, 'The state and economic transformation: towards an analysis of the conditions underlying effective intervention', in Evans, Rueschmeyer, and Skocpol, eds., *Bringing the State Back In*, p. 44 and *passim*.

48 P. Cammack, 'Review article: bringing the state back in?', *British Journal of Political*

Science, 19, 1989; P. Cammack, 'Statism, new institutionalism and Marxism', *Socialist Register 1990*.

49 For an example of this approach, see the British neo-Marxist study of state institutions and policies (London-Edinburgh Weekend Return Group, *In and Against the State*, London: Pluto, 1980).

50 P.B. Evans, 'The eclipse of the state? Reflections on stateness in an era of globalisation', *World Politics*, 50 (1), 1997.

51 Evans, 'The eclipse of the state?', p. 70.

52 Ibid., p. 74.

53 Ibid., p. 85.

54 Ibid., p. 86.

55 Ibid.

56 It seems hard to recall now that in the mid-1970s the so-called Cold War blazed hotly across large parts of sub-Saharan Africa as Washington and London propped up the tottering regime of apartheid in a desperate and finally successful attempt to stave off communism in the region.

57 Andrew L. Friedman, *Industry and labour: class struggle at work and monopoly capitalism*, London: Macmillan, 1977.

58 On the dramatic growth of stock market flotations in Europe, see 'The Euro's warm-up act: IPOs', *Business Week*, 22 June 1998.

59 Needless to say, the *active* functions of ownership – trading and voting stock – are appropriated by the investment intermediaries; although where the prospect of profit is minimal, worker buy-outs (ESOPs in the US) are permitted.

60 The clearest example of this realization came in Sweden (see e.g. S. Wilks, 'Class compromise and the international economy: the rise and fall of Swedish social democracy', *Capital and Class*, 58, 1996).

61 R. Cox, 'Global *Perestroika*', in R. Miliband and L. Panitch, eds., *Socialist Register 1992: New World Order?*, London: Merlin, 1992.

62 E.g. J. Stopford, S. Strange, and J. Henley, *Rival States, Rival Firms: Competition for World Market Shares*, Cambridge: Cambridge UP, 1991.

63 As suggested by Evans ('The eclipse of the state?').

64 P. McMichael, 'Globalisation: myths and realities', *Rural Sociology*, 61(1), 1996.

65 UNCTAD, *World Investment Report 1996: Investment, Trade and International Policy Arrangements*, New York: United Nations, 1996.

66 See, for example, O. Sunkel, 'Big business and "dependencia": A Latin American view', *Foreign Affairs*, 50 (3), 1972; Sunkel, 'The pattern of Latin American dependence', in V.L. Urquidi and R. Thorp, eds., *Latin America and the International Economy*, London: Macmillan, 1973.

67 In Britain the struggle remains within the Conservative Party.

68 G. Albo, '"Competitive austerity" and the impasse of capitalist employment policy', in R. Miliband and L. Panitch, eds., *Socialist Register 1994: Between Globalism and Nationalism*, London: Merlin, 1994; G. Albo, 'A world market of opportunities? Capitalist obstacles and left economic policy', in this volume.

69 For recent assessments of the present state of international trade unionism, see A. Breitenfellner, 'Global unionism: a potential player', *International Labour Review*, 136 (4), 1997, and H. Ramsay, 'Solidarity at last? International trade unionism approaching

the millennium', *Economic and Industrial Democracy*, 18 (4), 1997.

70 Unionized workers in the City, Britain's financial centre, are routinely threatened with the loss of business to other European financial sectors.

71 Albo, 'A world market of opportunities?'; L. Panitch, 'Rethinking the role of the state in an era of globalization', in J. Mittelman, ed., *Globalization: Critical Reflections, International Political Economy Yearbook*, Vol. 9, Boulder, CO: Lynne Riener, 1996.

GLOBALIZATION AND 'THE EXECUTIVE COMMITTEE': REFLECTIONS ON THE CONTEMPORARY CAPITALIST STATE

Constantine Tsoukalas

INTRODUCTION

The old Marxian question is still unanswered and unanswerable: how can it be that an increasing majority of non-owners continue to lie under the democratic dominance of a shrinking minority of property owners? Why should the many accept the continuing domination of the few? More specifically, how does an increasingly inegalitarian democracy remain viable? The mechanisms that secure the continuity of the system thus appear as the most crucial of political issues. The fundamental role of the state in ensuring the reproduction and political co-hesion of capitalist class societies remains the most important question of political theory.

The most critical issue is the articulation between class domination and political power. One must consequently continue to ask the same old questions even as one tries to understand what is distinctively new about the current period. In what sense is the problem of the relations between the state apparatus and capital different than it was in the 1970s? And to what extent has the relative autonomy of the state been modified? Can one observe new specific forms of reproduction of social rela-tions within both dependent social formations and those belonging to the capitalist 'core'? And how is the new situation reflected on the level of social practices and class struggles?

These questions are, I believe, of enduring significance. It is my contention that

This essay was first published in *Global Capitalism vs. Democracy, The Socialist Register 1999.*

some tentative answers to them can be offered by drawing on Nicos Poulantzas' analysis of what he identified as the new phase of imperialism.[1] In this period, inter-imperialist antagonisms are present not only in 'interstate' political confrontations but also, and I would add mainly, *within* all countries concerned, dependent or not. The phenomenon of 'induced reproduction' of imperialist antagonisms is crucial in this connection. No longer can one speak, in Lenin's terms, of a geographical partition of the globe into more or less defined zones of imperialist influence and dominance. The growing mobility of capital and new productive and information technologies have led to a concomitant mobility and fluidity of the economic bases of accumulation and exploitation. Direct exploitation of labour can potentially be pursued by capital in various social formations simultaneously but under very different conditions.

This tendential 'de-territorialization' and destabilization of exploitative forms, already anticipated in the 1970s but considerably accentuated since, has been accompanied by a universal rise of the rate of exploitation which has been countering the tendency of the rate of profit to fall. At the same time, the period of national Keynesian welfare states and differentiated norms of redistribution has come to a close, in the face of a new orthodoxy intent on reversing all welfarist trends on a universal scale. In all developed countries, including the metropoles, and even more so in dependent formations, economic inequality is rising rapidly, and simultaneously socially accepted 'tolerance levels' of unemployment, poverty and misery have been rising everywhere. When, in countries like Spain, a quarter of the active population is registered as unemployed, one may well ask at what point the 'acceptable' or inevitable begins and ends, and whether there are 'normatively determined' limits to exploitation and misery. What seemed to be socially unthinkable some years ago is now accepted as a matter of course. On the level of political representation, internalized 'social equilibria' are being rapidly supplanted by what are now seen as 'socio-technological equilibria'. Ethical controversies and policy considerations are being recast in terms of, and in some cases supplanted by, purely functional, performative standards of judgement.

In what follows, I touch very briefly on four specific points. First, the question of the precipitous decline, or even structural impossibility, of a 'national bourgeoisie' capable of retaining a relatively autonomous basis of capital accumulation, and of the new resulting internal equilibria in the dominant power blocks. Second, the growing fragmentation of the labouring population into numerous, mobile, differentiated and largely antagonistic fractions, with all that this implies for the process of dislocation and disorganization of traditional forms of class struggle. Third, the new functions of the capitalist state which, in its increasingly authoritarian form, assumes overall reproductive responsibility by means of a growing regulation of the de-regulation process. This is generating an unprecedented fusion, or confusion, of the state's economic and ideological functions. Fourth, the new developing forms of articulation between the various state apparatuses and the professional political personnel occupying their summits, on the one hand, and the representatives of big capital on the other.

THE NATIONAL BOURGEOISIE

All these issues are linked to the traditional territorial fragmentation of the world into relatively coherent 'national' social formations in the specific context of which capitalist social relations are materialized and reproduced. Obviously territoriality itself has not evaporated. Indeed, the internationalization of relations of production can by no means be understood to imply that economic activities take place in a trans-territorial class vacuum. Exploitation must always take place somewhere: in other words, within the territories of specific societies organized as sovereign states. Whatever the organizational forms taken by accumulation, their concrete operationalization must remain, by definition, 'domestic'.

Thus, irrespective of the processes and mechanisms employed by capitalists in their search for profit, the main question to ask must concern the various forms of social activity of the bourgeoisie, or fractions thereof within the given domestic socio-economic environments. If the constitution of domestic power blocks and their internal antinomies and political antagonisms can only be properly understood in conjunction with their trans-territorial entrepreneurial capacities, they must nonetheless also always operate within definite borders, however loose their dependence on internal markets may be. Even if capital may be controlled in the ether, it must be accumulated on earth.

In this respect, Poulantzas proves to have been quite prophetic. The pertinent question is in what sense can the 'nationally' operating capitalist forces be 'national' at all? Conversely, we are obliged to ask ourselves about the limits of accumulative autonomy of the dominant fractions of capital within national formations. Poulantzas underlined the gradual decline of traditionally autonomous national fractions of the capitalist class. Against the prevalent positions of the Left in the early 1970s, not only did he pin down the decline and historic supersession of the accumulative autonomy of national bourgeoisies, but he also insisted on the necessity of a new concept, the 'interior bourgeoisie'. In contrast both to the 'national' bourgeoisie and the 'comprador' bourgeoisie, the new concept served to denote the emerging and thereafter dominant fraction of a domestically operating capital which was already permeated by, and was thus reproducing, 'external' inter-imperialist contradictions. In other words, it was becoming obvious already in Poulantzas' time that there could no longer be a dominant fraction of the domestic ruling classes which might continue the accumulation process within the narrow horizon of the domestic market.

Indeed, it is by now clear that with the partial exception of the US, Japan, and to a lesser extent some European countries, there can be less and less question of autonomous national bourgeoisies. Globalization has brought about a further restriction of the accumulative autonomy of immobile domestic capital. This is evi-

dent in the proliferation of new developments that are undermining the traditional
organization, technologies and strategies employed by national firms. The spread of
horizontal and vertical joint supranational ventures, the prevalence of trans-territorial technological and information networks, and the total liberation of trade and
capital movements have transformed the competitive horizon of domestic capitalists. In this changing environment, the contradictions and antagonisms of international capital are now directly present within national socio-economic formations.
Transnational concentration has reached previously unheard of levels. At the end of
the 1960s the 200 largest 'multinational' firms controlled 17 per cent of the Gross
World Product. By now, their activities are estimated to be of the aggregate order
of eight trillion dollars annually, almost one third of the planet's revenue.

Nevertheless, a major problem remains unresolved. The dominant discourse on
'globalization' tends to neglect the fact that the process is neither unambiguous nor
conceptually clear. On the one hand, it refers to forms of trans-territorial mobility,
to the vertical or horizontal integration of productive activities and to mechanisms
of international capital circulation. On the other hand, globalization refers to new
joint forms of control and to new strategies of capital accumulation. The two facets
are certainly interrelated, but not identical. Organizational trans-territorialization
does not necessarily bring about any kind of supranational trans-territorial control.
Metropolitan imperialist centres that remain ideologically, politically and economically bound to their national contexts compete for world hegemony. Even if accumulation tactics are de-localized, power strategies are still organized on the basis
of definable inter-imperialist antagonisms, all the more so as long-term advantages
seem contingent upon a relative military, economic, political and symbolic strength
that can be represented and made use of only on the level of organized national territories. In this sense, deterritorialization is by no means incompatible with intensified inter-imperialist struggle.

Indeed, to the extent that national states are not abolished, there can be no deterritorialized imperialism. If the fragmentation of organized political systems can be
instrumental in permitting and encouraging mobile and de-localized forms of accumulation, at the same time these organized state entities provide the framework
for the universal pursuit of collective power. In this context, new contradictions
have given birth to new and complex capitalist strategies. On the organizational
level, growing mobility has brought about a world-wide free market, which is
reproduced by means of a conjunction of purely economic flows and the interplay
of hegemonic interventions of national territorial interests. It may well be that the
dominant capitalist mode of production is gradually putting in place a new original
political superstructure that more perfectly corresponds to the perceived long-term
interests of the competing metropolitan nations. If the relative autonomy of small
and dependent states has traditionally been challenged by direct diplomatic, political
or military interventions, by now utter dependence vis-à-vis the core countries is
being enhanced and strengthened through the intermediation of what is conceived

as a universally globalized capital which is free to impose its allegedly transnational will. Together with exploitation, imperialism is hiding behind the 'neutral' logic of a supposedly uncontrolled transnational market logic. This may well be one of the most important overall ideological effects of the globalization discourse.

Once more following Poulantzas, it is now even more true that the contradictions between fractions of capital within national states are 'internationalized'. As a consequence, the disarticulation and heterogeneity of national bourgeoisies is further accentuated. Indeed, it may be doubtful whether the very term corresponds to a specific social reality. All dominant domestic forms are by now tendentially internal in Poulantzas' sense. The recent dismantling of national plants by Renault, a public and therefore by definition national firm, is a striking sign of the new era. Poulantzas' interior bourgeoisie may well prove to have been only a transitional form of organization in a period when the internationalization of capital was not yet completed. It is clear that the last remnants of these autonomous national bourgeoisies have been almost totally infeodated to mobile and potentially de-localized 'inter-national' capital. Even if ultimate control remains in the hands of firms and cartels maintaining strong national affiliations, and this is obviously the case in the strongest metropolitan capitals, both investments and profits are potentially increasingly de-localized.

A manifestation of this new situation is the total repudiation of policies advocating import substitution. 'National' capital cannot be protected any more, for the simple reason that there is no material domestic structure that must be protected. Domestic deregulation is only an induced effect of international deregulation. Characteristically, the further liberalization of international trade institutionalized by the Uruguay round – and, incidentally the complete collapse of protectionist 'anti-imperialist' third world solidarities in the UN and elsewhere – was imposed against residual protectionist tendencies both in the US and in Europe. Within the intercapitalist front, national bourgeoisies are being increasingly marginalized and defeated both economically and politically.

A word of caution is called for, however. It would, of course, be totally unwarranted to maintain that new supranational agencies directly reflecting the interests of world capital like the International Monetary Fund or the Group of Seven have supplanted territorial state sovereignty, directly imposing the concrete terms of national economic interventions. Far from constituting themselves independently as new sources of autonomous political and economic power to which states are forced to submit, these agencies reflect state-sponsored processes of globalization. In this sense, the nation-state remains as always the central terrain of class struggle.

The case of Europe is instructive on this point. Despite the rhetoric of integration, European member states are far from having fused into a single ideological and organizational structure giving birth to a coherent and relatively homogeneous system of class relations. There still is no European working class nor a European national bourgeoisie. If the treaty of Maastricht imposed a certain number of common fiscal and economic policies, it carefully refrained from anticipating the eventuality of common social policies. The overall responsibility for reproducing internal class relations and equilibria resides with national states. The Maastricht 'criteria' only refer to quantitative macroeconomic standards of economic, monetary and fiscal 'performance'. Despite the rhetoric on the dangers of social exclusion, the European Union does not demand that its members succeed in reducing unemployment, restricting poverty or minimizing social exclusion. In no sense does the impending emergence of a monetary union imply the construction of a 'social Europe'. Social coherence, systems of exploitation and class conflicts remain purely internal affairs. There still can be only one kind of political sovereignty: state sovereignty. And this is precisely the reason why the most pertinent political question today remains that of the relative autonomy of the *national* state.

Nevertheless, there can be no doubt that the internal forms of sovereign domestic political decision-making have been substantially modified. More than anything else, the free trade, austere public budgets and tight monetary policies called for by the Maastricht treaty reflect the new limits of the autonomy of responsible bourgeois states and the power blocks they are called upon to represent. They also reflect an incapacity, self-induced or otherwise, to imagine autonomous forms of domestic planning and economic intervention. But they also express a continuing antagonism between ideologized crystallizations of power.

Indeed, the potential mobility of capital is so overwhelming that all locally-bound investment decisions are increasingly dependent on the adequacy of domestically-secured rates of profit. Domestic productivity and exploitation rates can in practice not be raised other than by further squeezing 'social costs'. If they are to survive the growing competition the dominant fractions of internal capital (in alliance or not with fractions of mobile world capital) must always be able to disinvest and de-localize their activities, if need be. A territorially restricted capital can no longer compete with its mobile counterpart. And this is the reason why all capital is now capable of blackmailing the domestic system within which it chooses to pursue the accumulation process. Any substantial increase in the 'social costs' of redistribution will result in the threat of capital flight.

The political responsibility of states is consequently geared mainly towards maximizing domestic productivity and exploitation rates on the terms of mobile capital. Once more with the partial, but significant, exceptions of the great American metropolis and Japan, investment forms adopted by big capital evoke the particular independence of the historically de-localized shipping industry. By dint of the fact that 'flags of convenience', which permit exploitation rates that are not burdened with any but minimal social costs, are eminently present and available, wages and labour security will tend to be restricted everywhere. Free inter-territorial mobility brings about a 'free market' of labour power which is indirectly reflected in the general fall in the relative remuneration of labour. All the more so with the collapse of 'existing socialism', now that the 'political risks' of subversion – risks which impeded free universal mobility – have been effectively minimized on a world scale.

THE FRAGMENTATION OF THE LABOURING POPULATION

Transformations in the labour process and working class organizations have accompanied these processes of capitalist restructuring. Scientific developments in cybernetics, automation and computer science since the 1970s have contributed to an enormous increase in the productivity of labour and have rendered a growing fraction of the working population functionally redundant. By now, 'primary' labour markets are hardly distinguishable from 'secondary' ones. Structural unemployment and deregulation have afflicted all branches, even the most central and technically advanced. In parallel fashion, the continuous rise in life expectancies and longer periods of education have increased the percentage of people technically and structurally excluded from the production process. The absolute and relative cost of social welfare, including education, was constantly rising as a result; a development which was rationalized in terms of a 'fiscal crisis of the state'. Thus, the combination of the overaccumulation of capital, growing intercapitalist competition and soaring social costs led to a universal trend towards a 'renegotiation' of the overall terms of labour contracts and for a concomitant reorganization of the exploitation patterns in the world economy.

The combined effect of a global reduction in growth rates and the deterritorialization of productive activities acted to disarticulate and disorient working-class organizations everywhere. 'De-proceduralization' of labour conflicts undermined solidarities and further disorganized class affiliations, threatened as they were by the adverse socio-psychological effects of the new technologies which transformed the subjective representations of organized productive units. Even more to the point, the gradual but uncontainable increase of unemployed and unemployable masses led to a further fragmentation of the working class. Consequently, technical and economic progress has been internalized in increasingly non-political terms: working class organizations which had been previously led to believe that they would actively and permanently participate in the decision making process, and thus negotiate the overall terms of income distribution, were once more pushed to the sidelines. While still nourishing hopes for uninterrupted progress towards petty consumer paradises, they suddenly found themselves to be more or less ousted from the power game. Internal political systems were subsequently pressured to accept and regulate redistribution norms according to the dictates of the free market. However, this was only one of the aspects signalling the spectacular retreat of responsible public initiatives into new forms of regulative inertia. States have been progressively unburdening themselves of the task of shaping both the present and the future. The responsible 'pastor-state' is being rapidly dismantled.

The working class faces a genuine dilemma in its struggle to defend what is left of its postwar gains in the real and social wage. In the best case, organized labour may succeed in clinging to some gains from the previous era, such as free education and medicare. In the worst case, labour seems obliged to accept, however reluctantly, that with further redistributional demands considered an impediment to 'competitiveness', the gloomy present must be permanently traded off against the doubtful hope of a sunnier future, or at least the doubtful security of the status quo. The uncertain temporal dimension of labour struggles is absolutely novel both in its strategic implications for, and in its tactical effects on, the ideology of the Left. Flexible representations of time, flexible labour forms, flexible individual strategies and the flexible internalization of social roles necessitate a flexible class consciousness and equally flexible forms of mobilization.

Thus, anomic and recurrent labour pressure seems to be perfectly compatible with what is left of redistributional and reformist demands which are now ostensibly tied to domestic capital accumulation. Disorganized and uncoordinated activities have tended towards a further political and social fragmentation of the labouring class. Indirectly, the long-term strategy of the bourgeoisie, which has always aimed at dividing the working class into fractions, has thus met with a good deal of success. As a side effect, post-fordist organizational realities have led to a growing and cumulative political segmentation and fragmentation of workers and dispossessed alike. Meanwhile growing numbers of desperate and largely unemployable masses are pushed towards adopting unorganized individual survival strategies. Predictably, the new forms of informal survival are closely tied to 'post-modern delinquency' practices. New 'illegalisms' are being constantly promulgated within societies where increasing police controls and extending penitentiary systems are becoming more and more crucial mechanisms not only of social control, but also of class regulation.

It is obvious that the political and ideological 'retreat' of working class struggles since the 1980s is a 'pertinent effect' of the new phase in the process of reproduction of class relations. It is an effect which is not isolated within the strictly economic sphere, but is also determined by the remarkable ideological and political forms of the overall victory of the bourgeoisie. If nothing else, the new political direction indicates not only that prevailing global relations of production are accepted as portrayed by the discourse of globalization, but also, significantly, that the unilaterally imposed norms of income distribution within concrete social formations may extend to a temporal horizon that seems to be indefinitely receding into a distant future.

THE NEW FUNCTIONS OF THE CAPITALIST STATE

Within this context, the tendencies described by Poulantzas in the early 1970s have been largely consolidated. The economic functions of the state are being progressively amalgamated with its repressive and ideological functions. In this respect, the rise of technocratic 'developmental' authoritarianism may precisely be understood in light of the fact that the 'interior' field in which it is called upon to operate is already circumscribed by the contradictions of the dominance of mobile inter-national capital. More and more, the main economic functions of the state must therefore be geared towards ensuring the institutional and ideological conditions of the internationally-imposed deregulation of economic and labour relations, as well as to contributing to the general acceptance of the alignment of public policies to the norms of international competitiveness. As already mentioned, above and be-yond the project of developing the national economy, the demand for unregulated competitiveness must reign supreme. In this sense, the most pressing ideological task of the state is to convince everyone of the need to de-institutionalize and 'de-substantialize' all previous forms of consensual negotiation of redistribution – i.e. to *dis*-incorporate social classes.

It is thus no accident that, irrespective of the ideological and political 'colours' of the government in power, it is only within the strongest core countries (e.g. Germany, France, Sweden, Canada) that the new authoritarian techno-orthodoxy may still be somewhat resisted in order to maintain existing equilibria. Weaker links in the imperialist chain, even if formally run by social democrats (e.g. Italy, Spain, Greece), are obliged to accept induced forms of labour division and deregulation much more unconditionally. As things stand, it is only in the few countries that constitute the hard imperialist core that domestic class contradictions can still be politically negotiated. Wherever 'national economies' are weak, states feel obliged to deflect or simply neutralize redistributive demands.

In this respect, the ideological functions of the state are of crucial importance. Never before has the ideological notion of the 'international competitiveness of the national economy' been more compulsively central. Under the auspices of the state, all ideological apparatuses (schools, media, parties, mainstream intellectuals, trade unions, etc.) are systematically geared towards the dominant developmental tenets, characteristically modified to suit the new imperatives. If long-term development is synonymous with deregulated competitiveness, the very terms in which the so-cially desirable is defined are fundamentally modified. In lieu of an 'autonomous', 'sustained' and 'autocentred' national development – the overriding myth of the 1960s and 1970s – international 'productivity' and 'competition' now appear as the new objectivized gods.

The first preoccupation of state intervention is thus to 'convince' people of the developmental ineluctability of 'modernization' via technocratic deregulation. The restitution of the inherent 'sovereign rights' of the market lurks behind all public rationalizations. It is no accident that in contrast to the social-democratic period, which relied on social, political and ideological arguments, the burning issue of 'nationalizing' or 'de-nationalizing' industries and utilities is now seen uniquely in terms of its repercussions on quantitative economic 'performance'. Deregulation is the new dominant theme, and unlimited performative deregulation is not only a specific form of active intervention but also the main ideological tenet that must prevail. Intervention in the de-regulating process is, however, an internally contradictory process. The constant public attention needed to bring about appropriate institutional and legal deregulatory reforms calls for increasingly authoritarian forms. The state is present to ensure that the 'national economy' is organized so as to compete with the other 'national economies' under the best possible terms. Furthermore, this general assertion is made acceptable precisely because of its alleged technical validity. The obvious Hobbesian metaphor may be expressed in military terms: states are at 'war', each to protect its national economy; the true enemy being, however, not other states, but each state's domestic subjects (i.e. its working class).

In this context, the concrete effects of competitiveness on the forms of class struggle, and even the question of who gains and who loses, may appear as irrelevant and 'ideological'. Regardless of the 'nationality' of the bourgeoisie which is to profit from market deregulation, it should be encouraged to make full use of its class prerogatives. The main agents of class struggle are a deterritorialized and integrated bourgeoisie versus a territorially tied and fragmented working class. This 'geo-social' imbalance is only the latest expression of the structural power asymmetry between capital and labour. And the exacerbation of these asymmetrical terms seems to impose new structural limits on the 'accepted' forms of class conflict, as they must be secured, imposed and legitimated by the state.

In this sense, as Poulantzas was the first to note, the internationalization of capital 'neither suppresses nor by-passes nation states, either in the direction of a peaceful integration of capitals "above" the state level (since every process of internationalization is effected under the dominance of the capital of a definite country), or in the direction of their extinction by the American super-state'. On the contrary, national states provide the necessary mechanisms and 'take charge of the interest of the dominant imperialist capital in its development within the "national" social formation'.[2] Indeed on the material level, deregulation, labour fragmentation, productivity and profit maximization can only be ensured within a juridically-given territorial context. In this sense, far from dispensing with national states' functions and services, the extended reproduction of the accumulation of international capital is totally dependent on their constant intervention.

Thus, the institutional and economic prerequisites of capital accumulation rest on the national states' capacity to guarantee the new forms of accumulation internally. It is precisely in this sense that the political and ideological cohesion of social formations, still materialized only by and through states, provides the basis for reproducing the (interchangeable) coherent socio-economic and legal environments necessary for any productive organization. The jurisdictional fragmentation of sovereign political formations can consequently be seen to correspond ideally to the interests of de-localized capital. Whereas the organized state remains a necessary mechanism for securing the external conditions of production and reproduction, these conditions are far better served if all states are separately induced to reproduce their internal institutional and ideological order on the universal deregulatory model. On the contrary, the eventual appearance of a universal democratic 'Super-State' could lead to the resurgence of political autonomies liable to curtail unlimited capitalist power.

The fragmentation of relatively autonomous sovereign territorial political jurisdictions thus corresponds to the interests of deterritorialized capital. If nothing else, this justifies Poulantzas' assertion that one should not *stricto senso* speak of 'state power': the 'post-modern', 'post-industrial' and 'post-fordist' 'national state-system' provides a perfectly suitable institutional and ideological setting for ensuring the reproduction of trans-territorial forms of accumulation.

RELATIONS BETWEEN THE PERSONNEL OF THE STATE AND CAPITAL

Finally, the state of affairs described above has some further important implications for the objective forms of articulation between political personnel and big capital. This is one point at which the question of relative autonomy may be concretized and empirically substantiated. One of the central objects of discussion between Miliband and Poulantzas in the 1970s referred to the theoretical relevance of relations between the personnel occupying the 'summits' of the state and big capital respectively. While Miliband insisted on the importance of demonstrating the bourgeois class origin of political personnel and their special class links to the management of big firms, Poulantzas completely disregarded class origin and underlined the objective character of relations between the ruling class and the state apparatus. Poulantzas was mainly preoccupied with the structural determination of state interventions; he considered that whatever motivations, behavioural tendencies and personal links there might be between political personnel and big capital, the operation of these objective relations was a simple effect of the objective cohesion of public apparatuses, necessitated by their overall function.

On the epistemological level I would tend to side with Poulantzas. Recent developments, however, may suggest new objective reasons why the 'personal links' between capital and political personnel are henceforth not only empirically ascertainable, but in another way, structurally determined, if not inevitable. Regardless of their class origin, and independently of whatever class allegiances they might feel, those at the summits of state bureaucracies are increasingly tied to the private sector. The objective cohesion of the state apparatus, including that of political parties, calls for new 'particularistic' forms of structural articulation between high public office holders and private capital. Indeed, it is my contention that, in a convoluted and indirect way, the new internalized functions of the capitalist state described above have contributed towards a growing political and economic dependence of political personnel on capital.

Very briefly, this emerging tendency may be suggested in the form of a number of points.

(i) The universal domination of competitive instrumental rationality has led to a restriction of the economic policy options of most states. The growing disillusion-ment and depoliticization of the population at large is an immediate consequence. Most developed countries seem to be advancing in the steps of the US where the crystallization of political antagonisms do not immediately correspond to clear class alternatives.

(ii) An important result of this new conjuncture is the dwindling 'internal' basis for financing political parties. Less and less are labour and professional organizations capable of mobilizing their members in collective actions aimed at intervention and struggle on the political level. Hence the prevalence of fragmented and individu-alistic free-rider attitudes – described as 'natural' by liberal organizational theorists – in growing sectors of social life. Inevitably, contributions of funds and energy by individual militants are being drastically curtailed.

(iii) In a related development, political conflict is concentrated on secondary de-bates and cannot directly reflect well-established and internalized class issues. To the extent that earlier collective images animating political struggle have been rapidly eroding, political discourse is suffering an increasing loss of substance. The social alternatives opened up by democratic political antagonisms must be constantly reit-erated on the level of collective representations. In this sense, one may legitimately speak of a growing 'theatricality' of internal political conflict, still organized in par-ties. Political competition, in which parties constantly struggle to increase electoral and ideological influence, is developing into a subsystem ever more detached from any social and class foundations.

(iv) However, de-substantialized controversies are becoming more and more expensive, in both absolute and relative terms. On the one hand, organization costs have soared far beyond available organizational resources. On the other hand, the very fact that the issues separating the main contenders for political power are becoming far less visible increases the importance of what is now termed 'political communication'. The everyday political game of propaganda and public image-making is now an integral part of political life. Elections increasingly are won or lost not according to the relevance of issues that are increasingly beyond the grasp of the population at large, but as a result of the success or failure of pervasive public relations activities. Persons and parties are thus forced to rely on expensive media coverage and on the services of highly-paid professionals. On all fronts, the costs of democratic competition are accumulating.

(v) If direct contributions are dwindling and costs are soaring, the democratic political-electoral game must be suffering an increasing deficit. To the extent that the 'political costs' necessary for the reproduction of the political system cannot be covered by the voluntary micro-contributions of individual party members, and external financing becomes a functional necessity, the question of new sources of 'political money' must inevitably be raised.

(vi) At the same time, an increasing amount of public-decision making consists of making contracts with big business. Privatization, military expenses, public works, and all kinds of political choices, translating into contracts with the private sector, represent a growing fraction of public budgets. Obviously, deregulation refers to the capital-labour relation and not to the importance of public contracts which, if anything, have been growing in inverse proportion to the restriction of economic activities directly organized under the auspices of the state. It is no accident that inter-territorial 'bribes' are now not only widely acceptable but also accorded tacit official approval: in most European countries, 'unsuccessful' bribes are considered to be a legitimate business cost to be taken account of in domestic tax exemptions. Even if it is 'internally' frowned upon, transnational corruption is officially legitimated as part of the game. Inevitably, the articulation between 'domestic' public decisions and 'deterritorialized' private profits is thus more structured and continuous than ever before.

(vii) Like all forms of capital, state-linked big business reproduces on the domestic scale all the contradictions and antagonisms of de-localized international capital. Competition for particularistic state favours and contracts is becoming wider and deeper. The 'interior' bourgeoisies, together with their international linkages, are engaged in constant (oligopolistically organized) struggles in the expanding international market for public works, contracts, licences and interests.

(viii) Against this background, bids from national and international firms tend to be accompanied by more or less open offers of pay-offs. The question of *'functional corruptibility'*, endemic in dependent countries, has rapidly become an objective structural feature of most, if not all, state structures. Indeed, the gravity of the problem is reflected in the fact that, like the USA, most European countries have recently implemented severe restrictions on electoral costs. Public financing of parties and elections is only one of the solutions that has been proposed. However, numerous studies have demonstrated that official public funds can account for only a fraction of soaring political costs. Political costs are virtually unlimited and uncontrollable. Whether this implies a growing structural corruption of political personnel – a fact which not only seems obvious but is amply corroborated by empirical studies – or whether this constant input of resources from the private sector to public and party decision-making is used exclusively to promote the organizational interests of parties and collective public entities, is irrelevant to my argument. The main point to underline is that, objectively, political personnel and parties seem obliged to solicit and 'accept' large private 'contributions' in order to reproduce themselves as communicationally viable candidates for public office. Apart from the question of 'corruption' and all the normative issues associated with it, it is a fact that new systemic factors are pushing the political structure towards an increased dependence on unofficial and usually hidden forms of financing. 'Personal links' are in this way structurally determined.

This development, in turn, exacerbates the general disillusionment with democratic forms. If general depoliticization results in a growing dependence of political organizations on an uninterrupted flow of resources originating in the private sector, and to the extent that this new objective link between politicians of all shades and their respective (or common) economic 'sponsors' becomes public knowledge, the depoliticization process will become cumulatively more pronounced. 'Lobbies' and 'sponsorships' are both functionally and organizationally integrated. By dint of their very success, the new forms of articulation between capital and top state personnel thus seem to be undermining general political credibility and further exacerbating both the financial deficit of the political game and its resulting financial dependence on capital.

CONCLUSIONS

What may be inferred from the above is that what has changed is the specific *form* of articulation of a particular branch of the state – indeed the most important and powerful of them, the elected political summit – and not the *principle* of the relation of articulation itself. The new dominant forms of capital accumulation on a world scale are precisely reflected in the new forms of relative autonomy of national states. The international tendency towards restricting the external regulation of capitalist competition has called for a concomitant circumscription of public decision-making processes within new limits. The symbolic and functional presence of national states is more necessary than ever for the cohesion of social formations at the same time that their economic and ideological interventions are far more 'deregulating' than before. This poses new dilemmas for the successful reproduction of the state.

It may well be that one of the growing contradictions within the contemporary capitalist state resides in the novel discrepancy between the professed aims of the political personnel responsible for the regulation of deregulation, on the one hand, and the established state bureaucracy entrusted with the symbolical, juridical and ideological cohesion of national social formations on the other. Antagonistic relations between government and traditional public organizations – such as schools, local administrations, and health and welfare institutions – seem to be emerging on a scale that transcends the predictable response to threats to public services. Privatization and rationalization touch the core of what was the main institutional and political manifestation of the overall relative autonomy of a state apparatus guaranteeing social cohesion. The new obsessive doctrine of a quantifiable 'productivity' applied to all organized state functions – from the judicial to administrative and from the military to educational – introduce a universal technical-economic measure of assessment to functions that were traditionally legitimized though their autonomous value. In a convoluted way this may be seen to effectively diminish the relative autonomy of the state. Obviously, to the extent that market logic is introduced directly into the evaluation of public functions, not only is the internal system of organization tendentially transformed, but more to the point, public services and functions are becoming detached from their original functions. Whereas the desirability of free urban public transportation was still an open issue in the 1970s, by now the debate is centred uniquely around the question of the possibility of running public transportation in 'efficient' ways. The very principle of redistribution serving the needs of social reproduction is blurred by the notion that all services and mechanisms, private or public, must 'naturally' bow to the technical prescriptions of profitability and competitiveness.

This development suggests another potential contradiction between the elected summits of the state personnel, who must direct the regulation of deregulation, and the rest of the state apparatus which remains responsible for the day-to-day social and symbolic cohesion of society. On the level of representations, this contradiction may be summed up in the ostensible incompatibility between public 'neutrality' and particularistic 'preferentiality'. These incommensurable principles must be actively reinterpreted by the state to open up new possibilities for a resolution. The state must be capable of taking preferential deregulatory decisions while simultaneously preserving the mask of bourgeois respectability. This is precisely what happens when the state summits and the organized political subsystem form direct financial links with capitalists in ways that uphold their assumed autonomy, while the principal normative 'separation' between private and public still reigns supreme. The ideological consistency of the system must confront the growing discrepancy between the 'neutrality' of the state and the functional dependence of its summits. Techno-authoritarian discourse provides a way out. But the price to be paid is the growing delegitimation of democracy. More than ever before, the social contract is reduced to an increasingly unconvincing procedural legality.

For all intents and purposes, it is capital itself that assumes the soaring costs of re-production of the entire political subsystem in the narrow sense of the word: a new kind of 'faux frais', or false political cost, is thus emerging as a structural prerequisite for the smooth functioning of the state system. This fact largely explains why, as a matter of course, big capital offers direct and simultaneous financial support to all serious contenders for elected political power, regardless of ideological shade. For the representatives of the internal bourgeoisies – divided as they are among themselves – the issue is not so much one of maintaining political personnel on their direct payroll, but rather, one of sustaining a system of political representation that is dependent on direct inflows of uninterrupted capital 'subventions'.

One may conclude that while relative state autonomy still remains important, this autonomy is more and more structurally 'selective'. In the contemporary international setting, the overall function of national states is being rapidly reconfigured by 'pseudo-autonomous' forms of articulation between the political and the economic. But this 'pseudo-autonomy' is not reflected in the same way throughout the various branches of the state apparatus in all their growing interrelation and complexity. Henceforth, if the mass of the state apparatus, including the judiciary, is still governed by the overall class contradictions, and thus continues to intervene in the interests of overall social reproduction, state 'summits' must assume the ambivalent but now essential role of imposing the required forms of deregulation.

Under these circumstances, one might well speak of a 'differentiated' relative autonomy, reflected in the internal contradictions between the various 'branches' of the state apparatus. It is precisely these contradictions which mark the character of the present phase. Indeed, if state summits function in ways that bring to mind the most schematic of Marxist formulations – one is more and more tempted to return to instrumentalist conceptions – its overall role must still consist in securing a minimum of social cohesion under the hegemony of the dominant class, a cohesion the costs of which are by now mainly 'political'. In addition, one might add, the political and ideological dangers emanating from the political personnel's incapacity to reproduce itself in a visibly autonomous way is counterbalanced by the further fetishization of the professed technical and ideological neutrality of other branches of the state apparatus. The more obvious it becomes that the specific objective forms of articulation between the state summits and the bourgeoisie are increasingly ambiguous and suspect, the more it is ideologically fundamental to cling to the illusions of public meritocracy and technocratic neutrality. If possible, these internal contradictions between branches of the state, in respect of the forms of their 'relative autonomy', must be masked behind a wider techno-authoritarian discourse covering the entire function of what is still considered to be the public sphere.

I hope to have shown here that the newly crystallized forms of articulation between the political and the economic must be re-examined in view of the global effects of a growing non-correspondence between the 'national' scale of political-ideological organizations and struggles on the one hand, and the 'inter-nationalized' and deterritorialized scale of capital accumulation on the other. In this respect, the national state, still the fundamental instance ensuring the reproduction of social cohesion, has been led to modify spectacularly the form of its specific interventions as well as its functional role in neutralizing the dominant forms of class struggles, both on the economic and on the political-ideological level. In this context, new contradictions between the various components and functions of the state apparatus have appeared, endangering its internal cohesion. As a consequence, the ideological and political prevalence of the new dominant 'techno-authoritarianism' assumes a paramount importance.

One of the main political side-effects of the present conjuncture is that it has become clear that working-class struggles have entered a new phase and face unprecedented challenges. The contradiction between the national and international loci of class struggles has led to a growing disorganization and demoralization of the victims of exploitation. Obviously, I cannot suggest the ways in which these new trends may be overcome. But it seems to me beyond doubt that it is impossible for the various fragments of the working class to advance towards new strategies and tactics unless the political implications of complex new forms of state intervention, and the concomitant question of the modes of its relative autonomy, are once again given the highest priority.

NOTES

This is an abbreviated and revised version of a paper prepared for the symposium on 'Miliband and Poulantzas in Retrospect and Prospect', City University of New York Graduate Centre, 24-25 April 1997.

1   Nicos Poulantzas, *Classes in Contemporary Capitalism*, London: NLB, 1974.
2   Ibid., p. 73.

CONTRADICTIONS OF SHAREHOLDER CAPITALISM DOWNSIZING JOBS, ENLISTING SAVINGS, DESTABILIZING FAMILIES

Wally Seccombe

W.R. Timken Jr., fourth in a venerable family line of industrialists, heads a bearing and steel company in Canton Ohio. The city's biggest employer, the Timken company is very advanced technologically with an excellent reputation for high quality products; yet in another sense it is an old-fashioned firm. As the *New York Times* reports, Mr. Timken is a paternalistic boss.[1] Born and raised in Canton, he worked for the firm for two decades under his father's tutelage before taking it over, and he has no intention of moving the company anywhere. Proudly, he shows the *Times* reporter a letter his grandfather sent to his sister in 1922 stating:

> Money should be conscientiously used to some extent right here in Canton where all of it came from. I recognize our bounden duty to do something for Canton and the thousands of men and women here who have toiled and made the many millions each of us have.

Here is a frank acknowledgment that capital's wealth derives from labour, plus a firm commitment to the company's workers and their home town – both antiquated sentiments in today's world of free-floating 'shareholder value' and jet-setting CEOs with several residences but no fixed address.

Wall Street brokers don't look at modern capitalism in the way Mr. Timken does. He is a representative of fixed, productive capital rooted in Canton for four

This essay was first published in *Global Capitalism vs. Democracy, The Socialist Register 1999*.

generations; they head up circulating capital, zipping around the world in cyber-space, seeking places to park some notional cash today in order to take off with much more of it tomorrow. The Street doesn't like Mr. Timken's company very much. The *Times* reporter explains:

> The rap on the Timken Company from Wall Street analysts is that it could be even more profitable if it would only be more aggressive about downsizing its work force of 18,000, if it were not so preoccupied with striving to produce the top quality bearing and steel products in the world and if it was less worried about its responsibility to the people of Canton. 'The company is so focused on quality and its reputation and pleasing its customers', said Tobias Levkovich, an analyst at Smith Barney, 'to some degree it hurts the profit margins'.

The money managers contrast Timken with another firm headquartered in Canton, the Diebold Company. Diebold is North America's leading maker of au-tomated teller machines, so there is an obvious affinity with Wall Street's business. The ATM extends the computerization of financial transactions, displaces more labour from the circulation of wealth, and enlists the savings of the masses in the business of capital accumulation in a much more direct way than the traditional sav-ings account ever did. It's a marvellous instrument for asserting the dominance of circulating over fixed capital, part of a much larger process that is installing money managers at the head of the banquet table in the new digital economy. But the main reason Wall Street analysts love Diebold is that the company has cut costs and made a bundle in the last decade, opening several lower-paying factories in the South, moving hundreds of decent-paying manufacturing jobs out of Canton.[2] If Diebold awards its top executives with stock options, as four in five large U.S. corporations do today, then the company's soaring stock-price will have personally enriched them in a multi-million dollar way for shedding employees in Canton.

When the bull market began its record-setting run in 1982, the Dow Jones Industrial Average stood at 776; sixteen years later, it has just broken through 9000 as I write. Hoping to moderate the market's steep ascent and thus avert a crash, Federal Reserve Chairman Alan Greenspan warned in December of 1996 that American investors had fallen prey to 'irrational exuberance'. Since then, the Dow has risen 65%. No-one knows how long this will last or whether the mar-ket's frothy bubble can be gently deflated. When the Crash of October 19, 1987 knocked 22.6% off the Dow in a single day (the largest one-day drop in its history), most money managers agreed, with the chastened wisdom of hindsight, that the market was overvalued and due for a major correction. So what are these sages saying today, with the Dow in orbit at three and a half times the peak it reached prior to Black Monday? Not much. Most are too busy raking in the loot to fret about the minority of nay-sayers in their ranks who warn that the market is seri-ously overvalued.

The persistent rise of equity markets is a euphoric bet by investors on the stellar future of 'shareholder capitalism' and its capacity to keep driving up profit margins. Psychologically, the willingness to bet is related to many factors, above all the free-market elation that swept across the Western world with the collapse of Communism. And conversely – the doubts lurking beneath this giddiness – there is a nagging feeling that the deregulated future is shaping up as a very scary place. Millions of middle-aged baby boomers (the author included) fear that by the time we lose our jobs, retire, or require extensive hospital care, the supports provided by the welfare state won't be there in a reliable form. We'll be left, with our families, to fend for ourselves. This ominous prospect makes it prudent to start investing our personal savings in a retirement fund during our peak earning years while we are still in a position to do so.

The meteoric rise of stock markets has been spurred by the computerization of long-distance financial transactions and the deregulation of cross-border capital flows. In the past decade, trade has expanded at twice the rate of GDP, foreign direct investment at three times, and cross-border share-transactions at ten times.[3] In 1970, transactions in bonds and equities across U.S. borders represented 3% of the nation's GDP; by 1996, 164%.[4] In the post-war era of fixed-rates (before the U.S. went off the gold standard in 1971), the vast bulk of foreign exchange was directly related to trade, tourism and foreign direct investment. Today, these activities account for a small fraction of the flow; nine-tenths of it is orchestrated by fund managers speculating on currency swings, or by firms and investors trying to defend themselves against such swings through the use of derivatives and hedging strategies. Money is changed between currencies today at the mind-boggling rate of $1.5 trillion on an average business day, double the volume of five years ago. Daily turnover on the world's foreign exchange markets often exceeds the total reserves of the major central banks.[5] The resulting currency gyrations have made it much more difficult for governments to coordinate their macro-economic policies and almost impossible to predict or control the terms-of-trade between countries – two essential conditions of international financial stability. When things go horribly wrong – as they have most recently in East Asia – the global money traders shun countries and denounce governments that they had embraced just yesterday, diverting attention from the ways their own speculative machinations precipitate financial chaos. This exculpatory exercise follows predictably from the first article of neo-liberal faith – that 'the markets' are never wrong.

Freed from substantial government restraint, the anonymous power of circulating capital has 'turbo-charged' Anglo-American capitalism and spread its neo-liberal currents around the world.[6] Working in concert with other forces, the tidal wave of near-money sloshing around in cyberspace is shifting the balance of power:

- altering the prevailing patterns of capital accumulation, the pecking order among the agents of capital, and the organizational form of large corporations;

- turning the balance of class power against labour by intensifying job insecurity on the one hand, while luring the family nest-eggs of fully employed workers into a compensatory bet on the continued appreciation of financial assets on the other, thus confounding their class interests.

The paper examines these changes in turn.[7]

Fund managers and the triumph of shareholder capitalism

As the hired guns of circulating capital, money managers champion 'shareholder capitalism'. They snap up the shares of companies whose top executives aggressively slash the payroll, shut-down unprofitable plants, sell off sideline businesses and use the profits extracted by ruthless cost-cutting to boost dividend pay-outs and repurchase company shares. In most cases, radical pruning 'works', at least in the short term: profit margins rise and the net gain is passed through to shareholders. But what if CEOs have longer-term, fixed-capital priorities — such as offering employees job security and training opportunities, signing multi-year contracts with local suppliers, and retaining earnings for longer-range R&D investments? This is 'stakeholder capitalism' (a term of derision on Wall Street) wherein executives eschew the immediate advantages of layoffs, outsourcing and spot-markets in favour of deepening the firm's relationships with its employees, suppliers and local communities in the belief that these *in situ* commitments will benefit the company and its shareholders in the long-run. The *modus operandi* of the major Japanese corporations has been more reflective of stakeholder priorities, and we know what a reversal of fortune has occurred between American and Japanese capital in the past decade. Following Wall Street's lead, the world's money managers are increasingly inclined to shun companies that insist on preserving the stakeholder model.

Initially, incumbent executives and board-insiders rebuffed the demands of the brokers and fund managers, resenting the latter's intrusion on *their* turf. During the 1980s, they fought back with poison pills, golden parachutes, staggered board terms, and a raft of other measures designed to make managers harder to dump and companies unappealing targets for hostile takeover bids. By 1990, about half of America's largest companies had adopted such measures.[8] But even as corporate executives tried to defend their traditional prerogatives, money managers increased their leverage through a judicious combination of carrot and stick — if a company's share-price outperformed the market average, its top executives would reap millions through performance bonuses and stock options; but if it lagged behind its competitors for long, they might be shown the door.

The directors of publicly-traded companies whose stock 'underperforms' are no longer prepared to be patient with CEOs who seem shy about 'making the tough decisions' to cut costs and streamline operations. And if they won't pull the trigger, institutional investors with big blocks of shares will press for changes at the top, or failing that, ally with the firm's competitors to oust entrenched managers. The waves of mergers and acquisitions that have fuelled the escalation of North

American stock-markets since the early 1980s have been based upon identifying companies that are *not* aggressively maximizing shareholder value, taking them over, turfing out the old managers and bringing in executives prepared to do whatever is necessary to restore the company's profit margins.

Slimming corporations and fattening shareholders

Under intense pressure from fund managers to boost shareholder value, corporate executives have embarked upon a crash-course in divestment and re-engineering – spinning off sideline businesses, shutting down losing divisions and shifting production to regions with lower labour costs. They've become so keen to cut costs that radical pruning is undertaken by thriving firms as well as those who are floundering. A 1992 survey of 530 large firms in the U.S. found that three-quarters had downsized in the past year, and one in four had divested, merged or acquired businesses. The great majority were making money.[9]

When drastic cuts are made by desperate corporations awash in red ink, the workers and communities hurt by job losses regret management's decisions but generally find them understandable. When, however, downsizing is undertaken by the managers of prosperous firms with flush balance sheets, their actions are more likely to provoke disbelief and outrage. Slashing the payroll of profitable companies breaks with past practice and violates an implicit understanding that most workers felt they had with their employers. Robert Reich, former Secretary of Labor in the Clinton Administration, comments:

> The norm had been, until relatively recent years, that if a company was highly profitable, workers could be assumed to have steady employment. Indeed, if company profits increased, workers' benefits and wages would increase with them.... That is no longer the case ... Highly profitable companies now shed thousands, if not tens of thousands, of workers. In doing so, companies are in certain cases doing nothing more than redistributing income from employees to shareholders.[10]

Successive waves of corporate streamlining in the eighties and nineties have reversed the post-war trend towards vertical integration and horizontal conglomeration. Capital markets today impose a 'conglomerate discount' on the parent company's stock, exerting enormous pressure on firms to eliminate intertwined ownership structures and 'fix, sell or close' money-losing subsidiaries.[11] Wall Street's new mantra is: 'Back to basics, refocus on the core business'.[12] After two decades of such 're-engineering', most major North American corporations are leaner than they were in the 1970's. Slimmer, but not smaller. Despite the glib talk by futurists and management gurus about the virtues of nimble 'networking' corporations, downsizing does not normally entail shrinking the corporation. What gets shrunk is the number of employees in relation to company revenues. From 1971 to 1991, the world's 500 largest multinationals increased their revenues by seven times without increasing the number of workers they employed globally.[13]

Neo-classical economists argue that in most cases downsizing raises the efficiency of firms and boosts their profit margins, with the gains being passed through to shareholders. While ostensibly refraining from moral judgment, the implication is that whatever makes private corporations more efficient must be good for almost everyone. The normative premise lurking in the mainstream paradigm is revealed when the social devastation that results from corporate culling is referred to as an 'externality'; this is tantamount to telling laid-off workers, their families and by-passed communities: 'gee, we're sorry you got in the way, but Progress stops for no-one these days'. Marxists view corporate downsizing from the dynamic stand-point of 'many capitals' in competition with one another, not from the micro-economic standpoint of the (ideal) firm. From this perspective, corporate purging is an essential corrective to capitalism's recurrent 'tendency to over-production'.[14] In the competitive quest to increase market-share, firms rush to expand their produc-tive capacity. Sooner or later, entire industries becomes glutted with more product than can be sold at a profit. In the face of brutal price competition, the only way firms can restore sagging profit margins is to discharge surplus capacity by laying off workers, shutting down older production facilities and driving less efficient firms out of business. Short of wars and depressions, financial markets are vital to the Darwinian process of revitalizing the economy by culling laggards from the flock. While investment floods new business ventures and 'leading edge' technologies, it abandons the fixed capital embodied in older plants and less efficient enterprises, compelling uncompetitive firms to renovate, sell out, or die. Marxists would there-fore agree with neo-classical economists that destroying surplus productive capacity by means of aggressive downsizing is perfectly rational from the standpoint of firms. Yet we would explain capitalism's tendency to devastate the lives of those it expels and leaves behind not as an incidental by-product of rising efficiency, but as the *systematic* result of firms treating labour-power as an expendable commodity while maximizing returns to shareholders under rigorously competitive conditions.

The holy terror and IBM's born-again experience

The recent history of IBM provides a textbook case of the process at work with the stock market riding herd. As its mainframe business sagged and IBM stumbled badly in the PC and server markets, the company's stock got mauled, falling from an all-time high of $175 per share in August of 1987 to an eighteen-year low of $41 just six years later – a loss of 77% in the midst of a rising market. IBM's board finally 'got the message': the only way to regain the market's confidence and save the proud behemoth from slow death-by-disinvestment was to dump John Akers, the CEO, and parachute in a turnaround specialist, breaking with the company's longstanding tradition of promoting top executives from within.

After hiring an executive search firm to shop the top job round the upper ech-elons of corporate America, the recruiters approached Louis Gerstner, a free-agent with a fierce reputation after brief stints as the top boss at American Express and

RJR Nabisco. Some IBM board members were worried that the candidate knew almost nothing about the computer industry, but the chief-recruiter prevailed: 'Lou was tougher than nails. Hard things needed to be done. I knew he could do them'. The candidate turned down an initial offer, but the recruiting team persisted. In a breathless *Fortune* magazine cover-story on the devout Christian (entitled 'The Holy Terror Who's Saving IBM'), Betsy Morris explains how Gerstner was persuaded.

> The recruiters told Gerstner that he had a moral imperative to take the job. He must do it for the good of the country. That worked. Said one individual involved: 'It appealed to his ego, his larger self – this concept of serving society as well as making money and being successful'.

Emboldened by higher purpose, Gerstner negotiated his terms. The main sticking point was that the board offered him a stock-option on a measly 500,000 shares and the candidate felt he was worth a million. With the promise of 'future considerations', he accepted the job.

When Gerstner took over Big Blue in April 1993, he arrived with his retinue of loyal disciples in tow, executives who had moved with him from company to company in his tours of duty. In a firm with an old-fashioned reputation for life-time employment and corporate loyalty, tough-as-nails "Lou and crew" finished off a massive downsizing that slashed IBM's payroll almost in half, from a high of 406,000 employees in 1986 to 219,000 by 1994. Predictably, they turned the stock-price around in the process.

> Heedless of criticism inside and outside the company, Gerstner began to cut costs, restructure and weed out disbelievers. He jolted the culture with shock therapy....
> He slashed long-term debt from $14.6 to $9.9 billion, managed nonetheless to buy back $10.7 billion in stock, and goosed IBM's share price to $168, $6.75 below its all-time high.[15]

The company's PR department claims that under Mr. Gerstner's leadership IBM is going all-out to regain its dominant position on the 'cutting edge' of information technologies. A glance at the balance sheet tells a different story. From the end of 1994 to March 31, 1997, IBM shelled out $13.2 billion buying back its shares, while spending only $9.9 billion on research and development. In April 1997, Gerstner raised IBM's dividend a further 14% and announced that the company would repurchase another $3.5 billion shares.[16] The stock rose $8 on the news, and went on to reach an all-time high in May 1997. These spending priorities have already shrunk the company's net worth by 15% and do not bode well for its global competitiveness in the long-term. But IBM shareholders are not complaining. These fair-weather friends have made a bundle as Big Blue's share-price has risen five-fold under Gerstner's leadership; they will continue to hold the stock only as long as the company appears set to make them more in the near future.

For his part, Mr. Gerstner's book-value profit on the company's stock recovery was a tidy $69 million, and the board has granted him an option on another 300,000 shares. While he proclaims the public benefits of private greed, some IBM executives are more reticent.

> At a dinner with top executives and their spouses … Gerstner rubbed some people the wrong way by blatantly talking about how much they'd all reap as a result of the dramatic run-up in IBM's stock.[17]

Perhaps they were reminded of the biblical story of their boss's Lord-and-Saviour driving the moneychangers from the temple.[18]

The bull market in stock options and share buy-backs

Exempting executive suites from the cost-cutting frenzy, corporate boards have jacked up the compensation of their top managers at a dizzying pace – 500% from 1980 to 1995. A study of 365 of the largest American corporations revealed that the average compensation of CEOs had bounded 30% in 1995 and another 54% in 1996. While lecturing their employees about the need for 'team-work and shared sacrifice', these hypocrites made 209 times that of an average American factory worker in 1996, up from 44 times in 1965.[19] Money managers are quite prepared to bestow their blessings upon the seven and eight-figure incomes top CEOs rake in annually, as long as the company's share-price is rising in line with its competitors. (The incomes of top fund managers, after all, are roughly comparable.) However, when a firm's profits sag and its share-price languishes, today's fund managers do not hesitate to publicly question the worth of its CEO. This generates bad press, pointed questions from shareholders at annual meetings, and attracts the unwanted attention of takeover sharks who smell blood in the water – all of which may shorten the tenure of bosses who fail to keep their company's share-price competitive.

The leap in executive pay has been driven by a shift in remuneration from basic salary to stock options. Ever since Berle and Means' classic study of the joint-stock company highlighted the separation of managers from owners, mainstream economists have fretted about the firm's 'agency problem' – how to ensure that managers consistently place the shareholders' interests above all other considerations. The stock option is designed to address this issue by providing managers' with a direct incentive to act in ways that will benefit shareholders; the 'virtuous circle' is closed when investors snap up the firm's stock, lift its share-price and enrich the option-laden executives whose priorities have pleased them.[20] In the past decade, this inducement has become a very sweet carrot indeed. The senior executives of publicly-traded American companies now receive about 40% of their pay in stock options, and in the largest corporations, the proportion is much greater. While the average salary of the twenty highest-paid U.S. executives in 1996 was a paltry $9.1 million, their stock-option gains averaged $72.8 million.[21]

In floating the huge stock options they offer their top executives, corporate boards usually prefer to repurchase stock in the market rather than issue new shares; in this way, they avoid adding to the outstanding shares in circulation and 'diluting shareholder value'. In effect, boards send the company's cash on a farewell tour through the stock-market (usually to rapturous applause) rather than handing it over directly in the form of salary hikes or bonuses. In 1996, the firms listed in the S&P 500 index announced repurchase schemes worth $145 billion; this represented an 87% leap over the prior year, which is especially remarkable in light of the sky-high prices the bull market placed upon them.[22]

It is easy to understand why top executives loaded with stock options would push repurchase schemes; but why have company directors gone along for the ride?[23] Under what circumstances does it make sense for directors to drain the operating capital of companies in order to boost their stock-prices? The answer seems to be: when firms have more cash on hand than they can productively invest and fear disgruntled shareholders.[24] There is no doubt that company coffers are now brimming with cash; since the recession of the early 1990's, profit margins have rebounded sharply. But high profit-rates in earlier periods did not trigger a buy-back binge of this magnitude. What is different now? Managements used to feel that it was prudent to retain the bulk of corporate earnings to fund major investments in future years or simply to cushion the firm's passage through the next recession. Nowadays, they act more like worried store-owners who empty out the cash register when they close up shop at night, leaving the till standing open in plain view of the street. To be seen hoarding earnings is asking for trouble from dissatisfied fund managers demanding higher dividend pay-outs, or worse, from corporate raiders vowing to 'unlock shareholder value' through a takeover bid. Far better to use the money to appease shareholders and inoculate them against takeover fever.

The wave of share buy-backs reflects an unusual conjunction of factors – exceptionally high returns to capital coupled with persistent constraints on expanding productive capacity. The source of the latter impediment is sluggish consumer demand, directly related to capital's success in cutting payroll costs and intensifying workers' insecurity. Since the mid 1970's, real wages have stagnated and workers have become increasingly worried about losing their jobs. With saving-rates at an all-time low, people are concentrating on paying down mountains of personal debt and are no longer spending with reckless abandon. The upshot is that many product markets have become glutted. In this economic climate, major investments in new plant are too risky; so companies have opted instead to spend the surplus reacquiring their shares, boosting stock dividends and shopping for other companies. During the past fifteen years, U.S. non-financial corporations (in aggregate) have financed their investments *entirely* from retained earnings, while pouring additional billions into the market in the form of dividends, buy-outs and share-retirements, well in excess of new-share issuance and initial public offerings.[25] One recent study estimates that capital expenditure has dipped beneath 70% of cash-flow, a near-record low.[26] This shifts capital-value massively from the sphere of production into the sphere of exchange. As share-prices go into orbit and the average daily trading volumes on North American stock exchanges escalate, the total number of shares in circulation is actually contracting. Since households have also been injecting their savings at a record pace (more on this below), wealth is not flowing through North American capital markets in either direction; it is accumulating in the sphere of exchange as a vast swirl of speculative liquidity seeking higher returns.

Mergers and acquisitions: shopping for a mate

When corporations have more cash on hand than they know what to do with, they can always go shopping. From 1981 to 1995, U.S. non-financial firms laid down 34% of their total capital expenditures buying one another. The 'M&A' binge which helped to drive the stock markets skyward shows no sign of abating. The 1980's were billed as the decade of 'merger mania'; yet in 1997, the fourth year in a row of record highs, the value of U.S. deals reached $957 billion, 12% of GDP. This is almost three times the volume of 1988, the peak year of the prior decade.[27] The merger waves of the 1980's were typified by hostile takeover bids sprung on ambushed companies by corporate raiders – notorious outsiders such as T. Boone Pickens, Carl Icahn and Ronald Perelman – who pursued their objectives by means of proxy fights and leveraged buyouts funded by junk bonds. While shotgun marriages still occur, the asset-strippers of the previous decade have been replaced by more respectable suitors, such as the CEOs of Johnson & Johnson, Hilton Hotels, Citicorp, and the Royal Bank of Canada. They are more inclined to sit down with their prospective partners behind closed doors and work out 'a good fit'. Executives often see an opportunity for strategic mergers when seeking to make their companies major players in rapidly evolving markets that neither firm has the capacity to fully exploit on its own.

As soon as companies announce deals, they are assessed by financial analysts from the top brokerage houses who broadcast their views instantaneously. The widely-publicized verdicts of the more prominent analysts are vital to the rapid formation of a consensus in capital markets, where windfalls are reaped by making the same move as everyone else but doing so just ahead of the pack. If the leading analysts declare that a proposed merger 'makes sense' – has a realistic chance to make money for shareholders in the not-too-distant future – the executives who cooked up the deal are rewarded by sharp jumps in their companies' stock prices.

While the typical merger deal is hailed from the office towers as 'a match made in heaven', down below on the shop floor, the company announcement reads much more like the weather advisory of an approaching tornado, threatening to suck up earth-bound creatures and spit them out onto the street. After watching other firms go through mergers and takeovers, workers anticipate that the consummation of their company's deal will provide top executives with a one-time chance to jettison contractual obligations, suspend the seniority principle, cull redundant staff in overlapping departments, and sell off subsidiaries that bosses now view as peripheral to the amalgamated company's core business. From the vantage point of employees, today's 'civilized' mergers do not look very different from the asset-stripping shoot-outs of a decade ago.

Pouring personal savings into financial markets

We shift our attention now from firms to households on the other side of capital markets. As real interest rates slowly descended through the 1990's, vast numbers of baby boomers concluded that they were no longer making enough money on their savings in the standard safe-havens of bank accounts, guaranteed investment certificates and Treasury Bills. So they opted to take greater risk in the pursuit of higher returns by shifting funds into equities and bonds, mainly via mutual funds. If investors are willing to ignore the broader social fallout and calculate their interests narrowly, this appears to be a good bet. Historically, the world's major stock markets have risen much more than they have fallen. The chances of coming away from the table with more money than one bet in the first place is vastly better here than in any casino. And since the odds are in the investors' favour, the longer they play, the more money they are likely to make – the exact opposite of gambling in a casino. It stands to reason, then, that people with savings and a mounting anxiety about the future of public provision would be willing to 'put their money down' on private capital. The only surprise is the sheer number and size of the bets being made. Once we take that into account, the stock market's blast-off is explicable in terms of the prosaic laws of supply and demand – a torrent of cash chasing relatively few investable assets. Since the start of 1995, the total value of shares owned by American households has surged by almost $5 trillion.[28]

Does the deluge of cash pouring into financial markets mean that households are spending less and saving more? Not at all. From the mid 1970s, when the real incomes of wage-earners stopped rising, most families dipped into their savings and went into debt in order to sustain their living standards. American households now save 3.8% of their disposable income, the lowest level in 58 years.[29] The share of disposable income they must pay to service their debts has reached the unprecedented level of 18%.[30] The indebtedness of Canadian households is only slightly less onerous. By 1996, the household savings rate of Canadians hit a 50 year low at 4.6% of disposable income.[31] In short, the tidal wave of new investment reflects a major *reallocation* of savings and not an increasing propensity to save. This is what economists call 'disintermediation'. Middle and working-class savers used to let the banks put their money to profitable use; now they are much more inclined to invest their own savings. The trend is transforming finance capital and hitching the fortunes of Main Street to Wall Street as never before.

The great bulk of the new money flooding into capital markets has been channelled through collective instruments such as mutual funds, pensions, insurance portfolios and trusts. This is a new trend. Wealthy Americans have always preferred to hire brokers, place their own bets, and hold shares individually. In 1985, individual investors held 57% of the shares of America's largest corporations and 'institutional investors' the remaining 43%. Nine years later, these proportions were reversed as vast numbers of middle- and working class households poured their savings into the capital markets. Mutual funds in particular are growing at a torrid pace. In the 1990s, the asset-value of U.S. mutual funds quadrupled in seven years, reaching $4.6 trillion in 1998.[32] 66 million U.S. citizens now have mutual fund accounts and for the first time ever, Americans have more value tied up in mutual funds than they hold on deposit in the nation's banks (at $4.2 trillion). Pension funds have also grown rapidly and by the late 1990s were valued at $3.5 trillion.[33] The same trends are occurring north of the border. In 1986, Canadian mutual fund assets stood at C$20 billion; by April 1998, they totalled C$329 billion. Mutual funds and pension plans combined now hold a majority of the country's publicly-traded shares.[34] On both sides of the border, most of the new investment is going into equities. In 1990, U.S. stock funds accounted for less than a quarter of mutual fund assets; seven years later, over half. In Canada, the portion climbed from 37% in 1992 to 52% by 1996.[35]

When dispersed investors pool their savings in mutual and pension funds, they concentrate formidable power in the hands of fund managers. By and large, the latter exercise this power 'passively', simply playing the markets. There is no legal barrier to fund managers becoming active shareholders. A minority of pension managers have led the campaign for 'shareholder activism' and taken seats on cor-porate boards; a few have even become embroiled in takeover battles. But most money managers have too many stocks in their portfolios to get involved with specific companies; they prefer to sit at computer terminals and place their bets anonymously.

While money managers are capitalism's new magnates, wielding tremendous power *in* financial markets, they must submit to the discipline *of* those markets, held hostage by the same 'numbers game' they run on corporations. The price-perform-ance of mutual funds is listed every day in the papers. Comparative historical data are readily available, and there is a rapid proliferation of guide-books by free-lance analysts who specialize in rating mutual funds for prospective investors. The latter are free to redeem their units at a day's notice and shop their savings around. Many unit-holders are impatient for results and mirror the restless attitude that money managers display towards companies. In fact, the short-term dispositions of both are linked, for when investors rush to withdraw their money from a fund, they force the manager to sell holdings to pay them off. Fund companies put their managers under intense pressure to deliver results and attract more money to their funds. The ones who lag behind their competitors may find themselves ousted and replaced by newer hot-shots on a roll – just like the underperforming CEOs they pressure.

In an era of resurgent 'shareholder power', mutual funds make the link between investors and companies more tenuous than ever. The unit-holders of a mutual fund do not actually own shares in the companies in the fund's portfolio; legally, the fund's trustee holds them (in segregated accounts) on behalf of the unit-holders. The decision to invest one's savings in financial markets is thus divorced from on-going decisions as to where to invest it; this is a significant change in the history of capitalism.[36] Mutual fund investors are like money-travellers who decide which re-gion of the world they would like to visit and pick a tour-operator who offers an at-tractive package-deal in the area. When they arrive at the airport, the operator takes over, planning the itinerary and hiring someone to drive the electronic tour-bus, deciding which sites to visit along the way. At this point the analogy breaks down, because at least the travellers on a real tour-bus take an interest in the sites they visit. In the case of most pension contributors and mutual-fund investors, ignorance is bliss. They have no idea what companies the fund currently holds in their name; that's what they hired the manager to worry about. The fund manager executes the trades that drive their imaginary bus through cyberspace, whistling cheerful tunes (in the form of quarterly fund reports) designed to persuade the paying customers not to rush for the exits when the road gets bumpy.

Labour's capital goes to market

Corporate assets are held much more widely now than they have ever been. At the time of the 1929 Crash, only 3% of American households held shares; before the October 1987 crash, 25% did; now roughly 45% do.[37] Pensions have grown very substantially. In 1975, 45 million U.S. workers were enrolled in private pen-sion plans with $259 billion in assets; by 1998, almost twice as many workers were included in pension plans with assets of $3.5 trillion, roughly 60% of the country's GDP. In 1957, 818,000 workers across Canada were enrolled in pensions worth C$2.3 billion; by 1996, 5.1 million workers (42% of the paid labour force) were registered in plans worth C$485 billion, equal to 62% of the country's GDP.[38]

While the base of the financial pyramid has been spreading out and down, the richest households still hold a disproportionate share. In the U.S., the wealthiest 10% of households claim 81% of stocks and 88% of bonds that are individually held (with pooled investments being much more broadly spread).[39] The property foundations of the capitalist class remain firmly in place. Since the overall distribution of wealth and income has become even more unequal in the past two decades, the Right's claim that we have entered an era of 'people's capitalism' is risible. Yet it would be equally foolish, from the Left, to conclude that nothing much has changed from a class perspective. Deferred labour income has become a *major* source of new money flowing into capital markets and the traditional dividing line between wage-income and capital accumulation has been blurred.

The new money flooding into financial markets shows up in data on household wealth, where financial assets are growing rapidly even in relative terms. In 1980, Canadian households held 20% of their assets in financial investments; a decade lat-er, 30%. I have no current figure, but it is undoubtedly much higher now, perhaps

40%. In the U.S., financial assets now represent 43% of total household wealth. This is a 50 year high, and may well be an all-time record. The shift from physical to paper assets is related to the sag in the real estate market. Millions of working people have chosen to invest their savings in mutual funds rather than paying down the mortgage; thus far, it's been a profitable choice. American households today have more equity tied up in the stock market than they do in their own homes.[40]

Precisely because they are not rich, small investors tend to worry about how their investments perform. The more insecure they feel concerning their jobs and the public provisions of the welfare state, the more they count on private investments to help fund the future expenses associated with aging, retirement and their children's post-secondary education. People invest hope in capital markets together with their hard-earned cash. Will the finance minister's new budget be tough enough to please the bond market? Will the economy's growth slow down a bit so that the central bank doesn't raise short-term interest rates? Will the share-price of company X perk up when the CEO announces plans to restore profitability by shutting down several plants? These prospects may sound ominous to workers, but they please investors. Wage-earning investors have a foot in both camps. The main financial concern of younger employees is to take home enough pay at the end of the week to cover current expenses; as they reach middle-age, workers become increasingly concerned with the future. They wonder when they can afford to retire and worry that their families will sink into poverty when the paychecks suddenly stop. Acting prudently, many middle-aged workers save and invest so that they will have an additional source of income to supplement pension benefits and social security payments when they retire.

Pension plans and workers' binary class interests

Twenty years ago, the management consultant Peter Drucker wrote a book entitled *The Unseen Revolution: How Pension Fund Socialism Came to America*. He saw the rise of employee pensions as having major implications:

> The shift to an economy in which the 'worker' and the 'capitalist' are one and the same person, and in which the 'wage fund' and the 'capital fund' are both expressed in and through 'labor income' is a radical innovation and at odds with all received theory. That the 'capital fund' is created out of labour income – and payments into a pension fund, whether made by employer, employee, or both, are 'deferred wages' and 'labor costs' – is perfectly sound Marxism. But it is totally incompatible with both classic economic theory and Keynesian neoclassicism. That this 'capital fund' is in turn channelled back through 'labour income' – which is what pension payments are – is again perfectly sound classical theory. But it is totally incompatible with Marxism, even at its most revisionist.

The worker and the capitalist have not become 'one and the same person' and the U.S. is today more thoroughly capitalist than ever. But Drucker was nonetheless prescient in drawing attention to an important structural change in the American economy that neither neo-classical economists nor Marxists could readily acknowledge. The ensuing two decades have deepened the intermingling of class incomes across the life-course that he highlighted in the 1970s.

The channeling of labour savings into capital markets is a two-edged sword. Conceivably, unions could seize control of their own pension funds and put them to co-operative use. Concerted strategies along these lines are certainly possible. Several bold and exemplary attempts have been made; they deserve to be more broadly studied and discussed by the Left.[41] But let us also be clear that there are formidable obstacles in venturing down this road; the resistance to capital redeployment is not confined to the rich. Millions of working people are counting on these funds to provide retirement income, and they have reason to fear the harsh verdict of the financial markets on non-maximizing capital investment.

Consider the Ontario Teachers Pension Plan. With $54 billion aboard, the OTPP directs one of the largest pools of capital in Canada; the Plan owns 3% of the TSE 300, the Toronto Stock Exchange's top three hundred companies. As with most pension funds, its managers are prohibited by the Plan's constitution from having any investment objective other than risk-adjusted maximization. As the OTPP's President insisted in his 1993 Annual Report:

> A number of teachers have suggested that corporate governance be extended to social investment. The purpose would be to prohibit investment in companies that, in some people's perception, produce 'socially unacceptable' products or behave un-acceptably in terms of environmental conduct, labour relations, human rights, and other political and social matters. The teacher's pension plan is not, in our view, a political pool of capital... The plan exists solely to provide members with retirement income and related benefits ... Fiduciary duty requires us to resist suggestions to al-ter the plan's investment policy to advance the social and political ideology of some people at the expense of all plan members.[42]

'Social and political ideology', in this context, means any policy that is poten-tially at odds with the Plan's duty to accumulate capital as quickly as possible on a risk-adjusted basis – any strategy, in other words, that runs counter to the reigning neo-liberal orthodoxies of our day. For teachers who are relying on the Plan, and very little else, to furnish them with income upon their retirement for the rest of their lives, the President's warning to beware of 'social investment' sounds omi-nous.

The OTPP's money managers are renowned as 'shareholder rights' advocates. Asked about the wave of corporate downsizing, the Plan's chief investment officer says:

> Companies aren't put together to create jobs. The number-one priority is creating shareholder wealth ... When we buy shares in a company, we treat it as if we're owners of the company. We believe the board of directors ... has a duty to maxi-mize the share value for us. If its not going to be looking after our interests first and

foremost, then we will invest elsewhere.[43]

Holding a huge portfolio of Ontario bonds, OTPP's managers are also hard-line fiscal conservatives. Their stance contrasts sharply with the teachers' unions who were major organizers of the Days of Action, a series of city-wide strikes and demonstrations against the Ontario government's deep cuts to social services. At the 1996 demonstration in Hamilton, teachers' comprised more than half the turnout which police estimated at 100,000. The follow-up demonstration in Toronto was even larger, and the province's teachers once again turned out in massive numbers. They then led the charge against an odious Bill 160 (removing power from local school boards and vesting it with the Minister of Education) with an all-out province-wide political strike for two weeks which sustained widespread public support and shook the government. In the meantime, the OTPP's managers – to judge by their previous statements – probably commended the Harris government behind the scenes for it's drastic spending cuts on the grounds that they were 'investor-friendly'.

This 'mixed message' cannot be plausibly ascribed to the divergent ideologies of union leaders and money managers; both are representing teachers and can reasonably claim to be acting on their behalf. The truth is that teachers have conflicted class interests, as have other workers with substantial pension funds circulating through financial markets. How would we estimate the balance of teachers' interests across the labour-capital divide? A clear majority of the plan's 155,000 active teachers are entitled to retire with a full pension in the next fifteen years.[44] As retirement approaches, the financial health of the OTPP becomes much more important than modest changes in their present rates of pay. In the meantime, relatively few young teachers have been hired since 1975. For the first time in 1997, pension benefits paid out exceeded contributions from active teachers. As the Annual Report explains:

> The growth in pensioner population relative to the active teaching population means that we will have to depend more on investment income than is the case today. These demographics underscore the importance of implementing a diversified investment policy that maximizes long-term investment returns so that we can pay the pensions promised without increasing the contributions.[45]

'Maximizing returns' has entailed entering the equity markets in a big way. From 1990 to 1996, roughly three-quarters of the OTPP's asset-expansion has come from investment income and capital appreciation. The OTPP pattern is not unusual in this regard. In the past fifteen years, investment income has swelled Canadian pension funds at roughly *twice* the rate of contributions from employers and workers combined.[46]

If the dreaded bear market finally shows up in North America and sticks around for long, many pension funds that have struggled to remain viable will be threatened with depletion. Without a sustained boost from investment income, the retirement benefits of the baby-boom generation cannot possibly be funded by the contributions of the 'baby-bust' generation following in its wake. The younger cohort is much smaller to begin with, and its entry into the full-time labour-force has been delayed by chronically high levels of youth unemployment and prolonged schooling. Most have been unable to obtain regular employment on a year-round basis and to become steady contributors to pension plans until their mid to late twenties.

There is a widespread perception among the elderly today that they are now receiving in benefits simply what they paid in during their working lives, plus a modest investment income. In most cases, this is inaccurate. If they have contributed to pay-as-you go plans which favour early cohorts, and if they collect benefits for more than a decade, they will use up their own contributions; from then on, their pension benefits and social security checks will be paid for by active employees and taxpayers. As the ratio of beneficiaries to contributors increases, the 'medical breakthroughs' that have prolonged life will prove to be costly for the children of the elderly, both in terms of their responsibilities for direct-care and financial assistance. If the stock market holds up over the next two decades, investment income will probably fill the growing retirement gap for most members of the older generation and the situation will be alleviated. If it does not, North Americans seem bound to experience an inter-generational financial crunch as the boomers retire in droves. Under these deflated circumstances, the primary institution of inter-generational support and solidarity – the family – will come under increasing strain.

Deregulating capital, destabilizing families

Conservatives are loath to admit it, but the 'shareholder capitalism' they herald is fast undermining the traditional family they hold sacred. While they prefer to blame the family's ills on sexual permissiveness, moral degeneracy and creeping welfare-socialism, the truth is that unregulated capitalism is hard on families, even small, nuclear and 'sub-nuclear' families. In shortening all forms of commercial contract, the free market militates against the long-term obligations to one's partner, parents and children that enable families – in whatever form – to endure and provide reliable support, binding three generations together over the life-course. The more atomized, turbulent and rootless economies become, the more difficult it is to justify costly childbearing, long-term monogamy, or taking time off work to care for one's elderly parents. In eroding the subsistence-base of the economy and commodifying every consumable, unfettered capitalism devalues the unpaid work done at home – overwhelmingly women's work – that provides for such elementary family pleasures as sitting down and eating a home-cooked meal together.

In a liberal-democratic state, the right to move around the country and compete for any job available is the foundation of free labour. But there is a vast difference between having the right to change jobs and being compelled to chase jobs all over the place simply in order to subsist. Quitting work and being sacked are not only very different experiences at the time, they have very different long-term consequences for people's lives and their capacity to keep families and communities together. Anything that renders employment more dislocated, temporary and irregular, anything that makes the future stream of labour income less reliable, destabilizes wage-earning families. The most obvious disruption is job loss, especially in conditions of mass unemployment where the competition for scarce jobs is intense. Across the OECD states (with the notable exception of the U.S.), the jobless rolls have grown enormously since the early 1970s. In Canada, the average rate of unemployment has risen for four straight decades. People who lose their jobs have a much harder time finding another. The average bout of unemployment was 14 weeks in 1974; by 1994, it had reached 24 weeks.[47] In the meantime, the contraction of the labour force in many industries has gone hand-in-hand with the scheduling of substantial overtime. Paying individuals in a shrunken workforce time-and-a-half is apparently cheaper than keeping more workers with benefits on the payroll. While the Right often blames this social perversity on high payroll taxes, it is worth noting that Marx observed the same combination 130 years ago:

> The overwork of the employed part of the working-class swells the ranks of the reserve, whilst conversely the greater pressure that the latter by its competition exerts on the former, forces these to submit to overwork and to subjugation to the dictates of capital.[48]

Recently, free-market advocates have been urging governments to make their labour markets more 'flexible'. This would be a blessing for working families if it meant that employees had more discretion in determining their working hours. But rather than flexibility *for* workers, more often it is a case of an obligatory flexibility *of* workers, bending to employers' demands in order to keep their jobs. What conservatives really mean by labour flexibility is that it ought to be easier *for employers* to:

- lay-off workers at any time;
- replace permanent staff with part-time workers who do not qualify for benefits;
- contract out corporate functions to specialized firms who hire unorganized workers on short-term contracts and pay them much less;
- schedule more overtime to avoid recalling laid-off workers or hiring new ones; and
- transfer production to regions with fewer employment regulations and lower labour costs.

When companies are free to treat workers as dispensable commodities, they make the labour market *less* flexible for employees. Household routines are disturbed by changes in the way firms contract with labour and schedule shifts.[49] Just-in-time production schedules are organized to fill customer orders, tighten inventory levels, and secure technological efficiencies in batch processing. The result is that staffing plans must be finalized later – just-in-time – and workers are provided with less advance notice of their shift-schedules. In consequence, family events become that much harder to plan. Intensified competition in consumer markets fosters extended selling hours. As stores stay open later and Sunday shopping proliferates, retail employees must work more evening and weekend shifts. In Canada, nine-to-five days and the five-and-two week comprise a shrinking proportion of all employment. In 1976, 65% of Canadian workers put in a standard work-week; by 1995, only 54% did.[50]

Changes in the labour market are shaking up the life-course as well. As the pace of technological change accelerates, occupational skills become outmoded more quickly and career employment paths are more difficult to sustain; promotional ladders are disrupted by corporate downsizing, mergers, takeovers, and plant closures. As middle-aged workers who have worked for the same company for years lose their jobs, employers and politicians propose 'retraining' and 'life-long learning' as antidotes to a growing sense of insecurity. Young people in their late teens and early twenties find it increasingly difficult to enter the full-time labour force and become self-supporting adults; between 1990 and 1995, the average income of Canadians aged 15 to 24 fell 20%.[51] High levels of youth unemployment have forced many young adults to return to school when their job prospects appear dismal and to live with their parents far longer than either generation would have wished. The whole process of growing up and 'settling down' – finding a mate, living together, forming families and having kids – is delayed, disrupted, rendered uncertain and reversible.

The mass influx of married women into paid work – due in part to disruptions in male employment – has eased the financial pressure on households; but it has done so by adding considerably to women's work-loads and making the preservation of families more difficult in other ways. In multi-earner households, all members who are presently employed or are seeking jobs must be able to find suitable work close to home. The decision of one member to move to another location in order to accept a job offer there either splits the family or forces the rest to pull up stakes in order to stay together as a household, quitting their jobs and leaving schools and friends behind. 'Long-distance' families proliferate, where a breadwinner (usually male) migrates and leaves his family behind, often hoping to sponsor their eventual reunification at some point in the future.

The deregulation of the working day and the shift to a two-earner norm have complicated family time-management, exacerbating the trade-off between making money and 'making time'. The more hours the members of a household need to devote to paid work, the harder it is to set aside family-time together. When the work schedules of two or more members of the household cannot be synchronized, family meals together during the week are rare and sleep-times are disparate.[52] The domestic work that directly sustains family life is thus forced to adapt to the pre-determined timetables of work and school. Since women still do the great bulk of unpaid family work even when they work outside the home, it falls to them, much more than to men, to try to reassemble what the demands of the external world have pulled apart – making-do with disjointed meal-times, feeding the kids while preparing to eat later with husbands, caring for people who are coming and going at odd hours. As it becomes much more difficult to co-ordinate the family's life together, time-management issues become a major bone of contention between spouses.

Employers may recognize and quite genuinely care about their employees' need to safeguard family-time. But when their own profit-maximizing imperatives are competitively enforced and driven by the short-term interest of shareholders, they find it extremely difficult to accommodate the family needs of their workers. For their part, wage-earners realize that as individuals they can best compete in the labour market by being responsive and flexible, willing to pull up stakes on short notice to go wherever the best job opportunities present themselves. As committed family members, however, they strive to forge out of this unsettled landscape as much residential stability and community rootedness as they can. Employees who focus on making more money and climbing the corporate ladder tend to sacrifice involvement with their families; conversely, familial devotion inhibits the aggressive pursuit of market opportunities. Women have long been aware of this conflict; men who are trying to spend more time with their families now realize the magnitude of the problem.

At the core of the neo-liberal ideal of unfettered capital mobility and flexible labour markets lies an abstract individualism that makes it extremely difficult to keep families intact and communities pulling together. In the words of Edward Luttwak, 'turbo-charged capitalism … rewards acrobats at the expense of working stiffs who also happen to be fathers and stable members of the community'.[53] Listen to the voice of one working stiff, a steelworker in Hamilton, Ontario, on the way in which de-regulated capitalism is taking its toll on family life:

> You don't know if tomorrow you are going to have a job.… You don't know if your family is all of sudden just going to pack and leave on you because they are fed up with it. You know my kids will come home and I'll come home after like twelve hours of fighting and arguing with guys down there… and a kid looks at you and goes 'Dad'. You go nuts on him, eh. And you think 'Christ, if I don't get out of here I'm going to kill somebody… I'm going to beat up on the kids'… And that's why there is so much problems.… because the parents can no longer cope.[54]

Conclusion

As corporate profits and household savings continue to flood into financial markets at an unprecedented pace, the global structure of capital becomes increasingly top-heavy and unstable. A vast sea of speculative liquidity is now sloshing around the world in cyberspace, swollen out of all rational proportion to the base of productive capital whose future earnings it presumably foreshadows. Driven by greed and fear (the ruling emotions of financial markets), this protean superstructure is increasingly prone to unpredictable booms and busts, as strong herding tendencies develop and the normal two-way flow of funds can easily turn into a one-way stampede overnight. In the boom phase, the tide rises and the sea expands; investment flows from the financial centers of New York, London and Tokyo into 'emerging markets' as money managers sing the praises of the newest 'economic miracles'. As soon as their glib prognostications are shattered by some unexpected piece of bad news, however, they rush for the exits, fleeing to the relative security of their own, better regulated, financial markets.

As the governments and peoples of East Asia have recently discovered, the mass exodus of anonymous investors can bankrupt a capital-poor country in a matter of days, depreciating its currency, ballooning its foreign debt, depressing its urban property markets and draining liquidity from its debt-ridden financial institutions. An avalanche of deflationary pressures soon force desperate governments into the arms of the World Bank and the IMF whose officials typically insist – as a condition for lending them emergency funds – that governments push through fiscal austerity measures and 'structural reforms' designed to bring their economies into closer conformity with the preferred neo-liberal model. The resulting pain imposed on the broad mass of the population is declared to be unfortunate, but in the long run will do them a world of good, since 'tough medicine' is needed to 'restore the confidence of foreign investors' – the *sine qua non* of national prosperity in 'the new global economy'. In the meantime, the calamities that have suddenly befallen the country (whose virtues were widely touted until recently) are now discovered to stem from (take your pick) political corruption, 'entrenched cronyism', government mismanagement, or the nation's baffling cultural resistance to market incentives – anything but the international financial system.

Looking at the same destructive whirlwind from a very different vantage point, the readers may be wondering why the deferred labour income of wage-earners from rich countries is fuelling finance capital's bonfire-of-the-vanities and burning the working people of poor countries – in Latin America yesterday, in East Asia today, and who-knows-where tomorrow. Seeking to explain working-class conservatism in rich countries, Lenin once argued that the upper strata of wage-earners had been bought off by the 'enormous superprofits' of imperialism, based upon the 'superexploitation' of the producers in poor countries. This enabled capitalists in the developed world:

to bribe the labour leaders and the upper layers of the labour aristocracy ... This stratum of workers-turned-bourgeois ... who are quite philistine in their mode of life, in the size of their earnings and in their entire outlook ... are the real agents of the bourgeoisie in the workers' movement.[55]

Shorn of its moralizing tone, this materialist analysis seems relevant in the current context. Ironically for Lenin – a fierce opponent of 'revisionism' – his argument subverts the strategic cornerstone of Marxist orthodoxy: that the proletarians of *all* countries have a compelling interest in uniting to overthrow capitalism.

Marx did not foresee that the savings of wage-earners would one day become a major source of capital formation. He treated wages simply as a fund for 'individual consumption'. Most working-class families in his day were mired in a day-to-day struggle for existence and Marx largely ignored the inter-generational dimensions of working-class reproduction. Fixating narrowly on workplaces as the sole sites of wealth-creation and class-based power, he left households – with their intimate dependency-based forms of domestic power – out of account. But households are the incubators of labour-power and the ultimate source of society's future wealth; we can never adequately grasp the intricate value-flows back and forth between the sexes, between the generations, and, finally, between labour and capital if households are not present in the analysis.

The problem we face today is not so much Marx's blind-spot, but the failure of contemporary socialists – staring this demographic reality in the face – to come to grips with it. With all its shortcomings, Marx's analysis of capitalism contains profound insights that can assist us in this effort. Consider, for example, his subtle notion of 'the metamorphosis of the value form' as explicated in *Capital*, wherein the surplus value pumped out of 'living labour' in the sphere of production disguises its origins as it becomes money-capital and then shows up mysteriously in the sphere of exchange as an alien, unruly force that acts back upon workers to secure their submission to capital in the anonymous form of 'market discipline'. Marx sees the extraction of surplus value as a double-barrelled alienation – the separation of labour from its *wealth*, and the loss of working-class *power* over the disposition of money-capital in the process.

The potential strengths of this analysis are vitiated when we focus too narrowly on exploitation 'at the point of production' and gloss over the distinct circuits of capital. As I have tried to show, the labour-savings circuit is configured very differently than the more familiar corporate-profit loop. It is schematic and misleading to assume that the latter furnishes an adequate blueprint for apprehending the broader crisscrossed field of capital accumulation, especially when this terrain spans the globe (in space) and encompasses all three generations (in time).

The wealth that wage-earners hand over to money managers through pension and mutual funds derives from wages, not from profits; ultimately it returns to workers (their spouses and children) in the form of investment income. These funds join the general pool of investment-capital and for the most part are managed no differently than other investments. But legally they remain labour's capital; they can therefore be reclaimed by their 'rightful owners' and put to alternative uses much more readily than other forms of capital can. By contrast, the wealth that employers extract from labour which shows up as profit on the company's balance-sheet is more decisively alienated and much harder to reclaim. Might labour's collective access to 'its own' capital-pool open up a new front of anti-capitalist struggle and provide a powerful point of leverage for an alternative economic strategy? The potential gains of extricating labour's capital from the alienated orbits of circulating capital and placing these funds at the service of labour-friendly co-operative endeavours are considerable. So too are the difficulties in doing so. While the legal barriers do not seem formidable (wherever alternative investment objectives are democratically determined and fund managers are held accountable), the chief obstacle in my view is the perfectly understandable desire of most workers to maximize their investments in preparation for a retirement of unknown duration where the provisions of the welfare state look increasingly uncertain. Non-maximizing deployment threatens this interest. However, the consequences of unions failing to exert collective control over their pooled savings and simply leaving pension fund managers alone to 'to do what they do best' are also considerable. Under a profit-maximizing investment strategy, the beneficiaries are deeply implicated in the private accumulation process, since this part of their future income-stream derives from capital's success in raising the rate of exploitation and favouring shareholders over workers.

The politics of the next few decades will be incomprehensible without paying careful attention to demographic trends and inter-generational wealth-flows. A huge cohort of baby boomers are now contemplating their retirement in the not-too-distant future. How will they live out their senior years? With an inexorable decline in the ratio of working-age contributors to elderly beneficiaries in pension plans, there are serious doubts as to whether there will there be sufficient savings available in *any* form to prevent former wage-earners and their spouses from falling into abject poverty in their senior years.

Beyond the vexed issue of private pensions lurks the even thornier question of the public retirement funds promised by governments to their senior citizens upon reaching a specified age. In the face of projected shortfalls in these programs, the path of least resistance is to look for ways to raise the rate of return on their assets. In the U.S., for example, Republicans in Congress have been pushing for Wall Street's preferred 'solution' – to privatize Social Security by paying out the plan's accumulated assets to citizens who elect to opt out, so that they can invest their share as they see fit while releasing the government from its obligation to provide for them in old age. Predictably, those whose future retirements will be cushioned by other sources of wealth can afford to take this risk and might well gain personally from it, while the poor who are completely dependent upon public provision would almost certainly stand to lose, either by taking private risks that they could ill-afford, or by sticking with a shrunken government program that was no longer defended with any vigour by the affluent. How will the Left respond to this challenge? Clearly there are huge stakes involved in the struggle over the nature of society's publicly-funded retirement contract with its senior citizens.

In an aging society, the needs of the dependent elderly place increasing demands on families and the welfare state. This raises unavoidable questions about the proper distribution of responsibilities for direct care and financial support between next-of-kin and public agencies on the one hand, and within families on the other (between daughters and sons, cohabiting members and kin living elsewhere, childhood families and in-laws, close friends of the sick and their own kin, etc.). The sinews of friendship and kin solidarity will be sorely tested in a money-driven society where market relations encourage a narrow calculus of personal interest and the sphere of interpersonal obligation has been steadily reduced, among most Westernized cultures, to the cohabiting members of the nuclear family. In sum, issues of class, gender and generation are all entangled on this terrain. How these issues get fought out, and the alliances that are forged to deal with them, will be critical to the prospects of reviving a broadly-based progressive politics in the early decades of the Twentieth Century.

NOTES

1   Michael Winerip, 'He's Out of Step, but That's Fine with Canton's Biggest Employer', *New York Times*, December 2, 1997, p. A1.

2   *New York Times*, December 2, 1997, p. A10

3   *The Economist*, October 18, 1997, p. 79.

4   *International Capital Markets, 1950-1995*, OECD publication, 1997, pp. 13-16; Joel Seligman, *The Transformation of Wall Street*, rev. ed., Boston: Northeastern University Press, 1995, p. 569; Stephany Griffith-Jones and Barbara Stallings, 'New global financial trends: implications for development', in *Global Change, Regional Response*, Barbara Stallings, ed., Cambridge: Cambridge University Press, 1995, pp. 144-57. See also, Andrew Walter, *World Power and World Money*, rev. ed., London: Harvester Wheatsheaf, 1993; Jonathan Michie and John Grieve Smith, *Managing the Global Economy*, Oxford: Oxford University Press, 1995.

5   William Greider, *One World, Ready Or Not, the Manic Logic of Global Capitalism*, New York: Simon & Schuster, 1997, p. 234; *The Economist*, September 20th, 1997, p. 24.

6   'Turbo-charged' is Edward Luttwack's apt term. Cf. *Harper's Magazine*, May 1996, p. 38.

7   While these effects have been manifest far beyond the shores of North America, I shall confine myself here to the U.S. and Canada, and leave the global ramifications to be examined in a subsequent text.

8   Michael Useem, *Investor Capitalism: How Money Managers are Changing the Face of Corporate America*, New York: Basic Books, 1996, p. 65. For a closely-grained review of this battle, see the second chapter, 'When Investors Challenge Company Performance'.

9   On these trends, see Michael Useem, *Executive Defense: Shareholder Power and Corporate*

Restructuring, Cambridge: Harvard University Press, 1993; Michael Useem, *Investor Capitalism*; Neil Fligstein and Peter Brantley, 'Bank Control, Owner Control or Organizational Dynamics: Who Controls the Large Corporation?', *American Journal of Sociology*, 98, 1992, pp. 280-307; Gerald F. Davis and Suzanne K. Stout, 'Organizational Theory and the Market for Corporate Control: A Dynamic Analysis of the Characteristics of Large Takeover Targets, 1980-1990', *Administrative Science Quarterly*, 37, 1992, pp. 605-33; Mary Zey and Brande Camp, 'The Transformation from Multi-divisional Form to Corporate Groups of Subsidiaries in the 1980s', *The Sociological Quarterly*, 37(2), pp. 327-51.

10 Harper's Magazine, May 1996, p. 38.

11 In the words of Jack Welsh, the CEO of General Electric, one of the few North American conglomerates that investors still like.

12 David Sadtler, Andrew Campbell and Richard Kroch, estimate that the market value of companies spun off from their parents in Britain and the U.S. rose from $17.5 billion in 1993 to more than $100 billion in 1996. See Andrew Campbell, Richard J. Koch and David Sadtle, *Break-Up! When Large Companies are Worth More Dead than Alive*. New York: John Wiley and Sons, 1997.

13 Michael Useem, *Investor Capitalism*, p. 164.

14 Cf. 'Excess Capital and Excess Population', Marx, *Capital*, Vol. 3, Moscow: Progress Publishers, 1971, pp. 250-9. Neo-classical economists have finally recognized this tendency – in their terms, the risk of firms overinvesting due to a surging cash flow in excess of potential investments with positive net present value. (See Michael Jensen, 'Agency Costs of Free Cash Flow, Corporate Finance, and Takeovers', *American Economic Review*, 76, 1986, pp. 323-9.) But whereas Marxists situate the contradiction of excess capital investment at the macro-level, as a destructive effect of the competitive scramble for market share, neo-classical economists remain wedded to the theology of market equilibrium, identifying the problem as an 'agency cost' of managers who fail to maximize shareholder value.

15 Betsy Morris, 'The Holy Terror Who's Saving IBM', *Fortune*, 135(7), April 14, 1997, p. 71.

16 From 1995 to April 1998, IBM spent about $20 billion reacquiring its own shares. Despite revenues and profit margins that came in well below market expectations in 1998, the stock continues to set records because management continues to demonstrate its absolute devotion to shareholders by buying back more shares and raising dividends. See 'IBM plans steps to lift the share price', in the *Globe & Mail*, April 29, 1998, p. B11.

17 Ibid., p. 80.

18 Mark 11:15

19 'Executive Pay, It's Out of Control', *Business Week*, April 21, 1997, pp. 58-66.

20 Adolf Berle and Gardiner Means, *The Modern Corporation and Private Property*, rev. ed. New York: Harcourt and Brace, 1932/1967. For a more recent rumination on the perennial issue of 'corporate governance', see Margaret Blair, *Ownership and Control: Rethinking Corporate Governance for the 21st Century*, Washington: Brookings Institute, 1995.

21 Calculated from the table on pages 58-9 of *Business Week*, April 21, 1997. Canadian trends lag behind, but are headed in the same direction. In a report on the 1997 annual

incomes of the CEOs of Canada's largest firms, the top ten (in total compensation) averaged C$890,000 in basic salary, C$2.4 million in performance bonuses (mostly related to share-price appreciation), and C$9.5 million in stock-option gains. *Globe & Mail*, April 18, 1998, p. B6. Stock options permit managers to purchase shares from their companies at a bargain price. They must be exercised to generate the gains recorded in the compensation totals being cited here.

22 *The Economist*, June 28, 1997, p. 77.

23 The correlation between repurchase announcements and share appreciation has been noted in several studies. See Robert Comment and Gregg Jarrell, 'The Relative Signalling Power of Dutch-Auction and Fixed-Price Tender Offers and Open-Market Repurchases', *Journal of Finance*, 46, 1991, pp. 1243-1271; David Yermack, 'Good Timing: CEO Stock Option Awards and Company News Announcements', *Journal of Finance*, 52, 1997, pp. 449-476.

24 In the language of neo-classical economists, firms run the risk of overinvesting when they have a cash flow in excess of that required to fund all projects that have a positive net present value. The buy-back disgorges the excess and mitigates the 'agency conflict' inherent in managers placing other objectives before the paramount one of maximizing shareholder value. For an empirically-based analysis of these trends, see George W. Fenn & Nellie Liang, 'Good News and Bad News About Share Repurchases', a 1997 discussion paper distributed by the U.S. Federal Reserve, and available on the Fed's web-site.

25 Doug Henwood has shown that 'far from turning to Wall Street for outside finance, nonfinancial firms have been stuffing Wall Street's pockets with money', in *Wall Street*, New York: Verso, 1997, p. 73.

26 This estimate is based on the industrial companies in Standard and Poor's 500 Index, as reported by Tom Galvin, chief equity strategist at *Donaldson Lufkin & Jenrette*: 'Stingy capital spending pays off in stock prices', *Globe & Mail*, March 23, 1998, p. B6.

27 *Globe & Mail*, 'Mergers Hit Fever Pitch', Dec. 22, 1997, p. B1; Charles V. Bagli, 'A New Breed of Wolf at the Corporate Door', *New York Times*, March 19, 1977, p. B1; 'America Bubbles Over', *The Economist*, April 18, 1997, p. 67.

28 *The Economist*, March 28, 1998, p. 68.

29 'Last of the Big-Time Spenders', *Toronto Star*, August 5, 1997, p. D1 and Maria Ramirez, 'Americans at Debt's Door', *New York Times*, Oct. 14, 1997. See also, *New York Times*, Feb. 11, 1998, 'Share of Wealth in Stock Holding Hits 50 Year High', p. A1.

30 Maria Ramirez, 'Americans at Debt's Door', *New York Times*, Oct. 14, 1997.

31 The savings decline may well be halted or reversed in the next decade, as baby boomers save in earnest for their retirements; but thereafter, it seems destined to resume its fall as the proportion of the population 65 years and older rises sharply. The prospect of an aging population draining the global pool of capital-savings in the next fifty years is clearly ominous, and has attracted the attention of the West's major research institutes. See, for example, Barry Bosworth, *Savings and Investment in a Global Economy*, Washington: The Brookings Institute, 1993; and the 1997 OECD report *Future Global Capital Shortages: Real Threat or Pure Fiction?*, Paris: Organisation for Economic Cooperation and Development, 1996.

32 As of March 1, 1998.

33 Michael Useem, *Investor Capitalism*, p. 26; *New York Times*, Sept. 25, 1997, p. C2.

34 *Globe & Mail*, January 3, 1997, p. B9; *Toronto Star*, January 16, 1997, p. E1.

35 *Globe & Mail*, March 18, 1977, p. B1.

36 See Robert Clark's 'The Four Stages of Capitalism: Reflections on Investment Management Treatises', *Harvard Law Review*, 94, 1981, pp. 561–82.

37 This includes assets held by individuals, plus pooled investments such as mutual funds and pensions. *The Economist*, March 28, 1998, p. 18.

38 See E. Philip Davis, *Pension Funds, Retirement-Income Security and Capital Markets, An International Perspective,* Oxford: Clarendon Press, 1995; David A. Wise, ed., *Pensions, Labor and Individual Choice*, Chicago: University of Chicago Press, 1985; Statistics Canada, *Pension Plans in Canada 1996*, Ottawa: Statistics Canada, Pensions Section, 1997, Cat. No. 74–401.

39 Henwood, *Wall Street*, p. 67. Unlike the thousands of authors who write homages to Wall Street and supply hot tips that promise to make you a million, Henwood, the editor of the *Left Business Observer*, is a trenchant critic of the Street who proudly offers no advice on playing the market. I found *Wall Street* an illuminating read, particularly Henwood's analysis of the self-sufficiency of non-financial corporations who, far from sucking investment money in, have been paying it out, 'stuffing Wall Street's pockets'. My main objection is that he belittles the magnitude and importance of the flood of wage-earners' savings into the markets in the past decade via mutual funds and pensions. This permits him to preserve the comforting left-wing delusion that financial markets simply redistribute income among the wealthy and have not snagged a *rentier* interest among the ranks of the fully employed working-class.

40 *New York Times*, February 11, 1998, pp. A1, C4.

41 Some of the more promising ones are reviewed by Richard Minns in 'The Social Ownership of Capital', *New Left Review*, 219 (September) 1996.

42 Quoted from the President's Address, cited in the OTPP's mailing to members, *Highlights of the 1993 Annual Report*, Ontario Teachers Pension Plan Board, p. 12.

43 *Globe & Mail*, March 23, 1996, p. B1.

44 Under the former agreement, about half of all active teachers were due to retire in 15 years. But just as this text was being finalized, the teachers' federations agreed to a new early-retirement deal with the government that will increase this proportion considerably.

45 *1996 Report to Members*, Ontario Teachers Pension Plan Board, p. 9.

46 See *Trusteed Pension Funds, Financial Statistics, 1994*, Ottawa: Statistics Canada, 1996, Cat. No. 74–201, p. 15.

47 Globe & Mail, January 3, 1997, p. A4.

48 *Capital*, Vol. I, Moscow: Progress Press, 1971, p. 595

49 See Manfred Garhammer, *Time and Society*, 4(2) London: Sage, 1995.

50 From a *Statistics Canada* study by Mike Sheridan, Deborah Sunter and Brent Diverty, reported in the *Globe & Mail*, September 2, 1996.

51 'Canadians got poorer in the 90s', *Globe & Mail*, May 13, 1998, p. A5.

52 The commodification of food and the devaluation of the home-cooked meal proceed apace. Over forty cents of every dollar Americans spend on food now goes to restaurant meals and take-out. Cited in Jane Brody, *New York Times*, June 16, 1998, p. B10.

53 *Harper's Magazine*, May 1996, p. 38.

54 'Down there' is Stelco's Hilton Works, and '12 hours' refers to the plant's new shift-schedule. This interview is from a study conducted by the author with Meg Luxton, June Corman and David Livingstone.

55 From the preface to 'Imperialism, the Highest Stage of Capitalism', Lenin, *Selected Works*, Volume 1. Moscow: Progress Publishers, 1963, p. 677.

MATERIAL WORLD:
THE MYTH OF THE 'WEIGHTLESS ECONOMY'

Ursula Huws

'The Death of Distance',[1] 'Weightless World',[2] the 'Connected Economy',[3] the 'Digital Economy',[4] the 'Knowledge-Based Economy',[5] the 'Virtual Organization'.[6] All these phrases were culled from the titles of books published in the six months prior to writing this essay, in spring, 1998. They could have been multiplied many times: 'virtual', 'cyber', 'tele-', 'networked' or even just 'e-' can, it seems, be pre-fixed interchangeably to an almost infinite range of abstract nouns. Without even straying from the field of economics, you can try 'enterprise', 'work', 'banking' 'trade', 'commerce', or 'business' (although the device works equally well in other areas: for instance 'culture', 'politics', 'sex', 'democracy', 'relationship', 'drama', 'community', 'art', 'society', 'shopping' or 'crime').

A consensus seems to be emerging – in economics as in other fields – that something entirely new is happening: that the world as we know it is becoming quite dematerialized (or, as Marx put it, 'all that is solid melts into air') and that this somehow throws into question all the conceptual models which have been developed to make sense of the old material world. We are offered a paradoxical universe: geography without distance, history without time, value without weight, transactions without cash. This is an economics which sits comfortably in a Baudrillardian philosophical framework, in which all reality has become a simulacrum and human agency, to the extent that it can be said to exist at all, is reduced to the manipulation of abstractions. But these books have not been designed as contributions to postmodernist cultural theory; far from it. Frances Cairncross's *Death of Distance*

This essay was first published in *Global Capitalism vs. Democracy, The Socialist Register 1999*.

comes with a glowing testimonial from Rupert Murdoch on the front of its shiny blue dust-jacket, while Diane Coyle's *Weightless World,* not to be outdone, carries an endorsement from Mervyn King, executive director of the Bank of England, on its back cover. These are not academic inquiries into the nature of the universe; they are practical manuals for managers and policy-makers. A new orthodoxy is in the making, an orthodoxy in which it becomes taken for granted that 'knowledge' is the only source of value, that work is contingent and delocalizable, that globalization is an inexorable and inevitable process and that, by implication, resistance is futile and any assertion of the physical claims of the human body in the here-and-now is hopelessly old-fashioned. The implications of this emerging 'common sense' are immense. Capable of shaping issues as diverse as taxation, employment legislation, levels of welfare spending, privacy rights and environmental policy, these notions serve to legitimize a new political agenda and set the scene for a new phase of capital accumulation.

The task I have set myself in this essay is to re-embody cyberspace: to try to make visible the material components of this virtual world. In this, I find myself rather oddly positioned. Having been arguing for over two decades for greater importance to be given in economic and social analysis to white-collar employment, and to the ways in which information and communications technologies have facilitated its relocation, it seems perverse, to say the least, to respond to this sudden new interest in the subject by saying, in effect, 'Well, hang on a minute. Are things really changing all that much? How 'dematerialized' are most developed economies? To what extent is service employment really expanding? What contribution does 'knowledge' make to economic growth? And how global are most economies anyway?'.

In addressing such questions a delicate path has to be picked. On the one hand it is necessary to subject the claims of the proponents of the 'new economics' to some empirical tests. Before throwing out the bathwater, in other words, it is wise to check it for babies. On the other, it is necessary to avoid the opposite danger of assuming that nothing has changed: that because something cannot be measured accurately with existing instruments it does not exist at all. I cannot claim to have walked this path to its conclusion. However I hope here to have flagged some of the more important landmines to be avoided along the way. If I have not found solutions, I hope I have at least identified some problems.[7]

At the risk of appearing pretentious, it does seem necessary to set the problem in its epistemological context. The current hegemonic position of postmodernism in most university departments (with the partial exception of the 'hard' sciences) has created a number of obstacles to addressing such questions.[8]

First, and most obviously, postmodernism throws into question the very scientific project itself. Even to admit to trying to discover the 'truth' about what is happening is to run the risk of being accused of vulgar positivism. If one accepts that all facts are contingent and socially constructed there is no rational basis even for selecting the data with which to test an argument, let alone for claiming any special validity for one's own discoveries. This is not the place for a detailed discussion of how – or indeed whether – it is possible for a scholar to find a third route, which avoids both the hard rocks of crude positivism and the swampy morass of relativism to which such an approach inevitably leads.[9]

Second, by insisting that all science is socially constructed, postmodernism makes it very difficult to produce a stable concept of the body – the flesh-and-blood body which gets on with the business of circulating its blood, digesting, perspiring, shedding old cells, lactating, producing semen, menstruating and a myriad other functions (including, no doubt many that a positivist might describe as 'yet to be discovered') regardless of what its inhabitant is thinking. The problem is urgent: how to resolve the crude dualism which is set up when 'the biological' is counterposed to 'the social' (or 'nature' to 'culture', 'body' to 'mind', 'manual work' to 'mental work', 'the material' to the 'ideological', that which is studied to the scientist, and so on). But postmodernism has yet to produce a definitive resolution to this difficulty. Baudrillard's solution is to regard the human body itself as just another culturally constructed simulacrum.[10] An alternative model, proposed by Donna Haraway, is to acknowledge the ways in which science and technology have penetrated the natural by proposing that the body cannot be viewed independently from its cultural surroundings but has, in effect, become a cyborg.[11] In both of these approaches the body is reduced to a cultural construct, which has the effect of rendering its materiality difficult to grasp and analyze. This is relevant in this context because without a concept of the body as something distinct and separate from capital (or any other abstraction) any theorizing about the weightless economy will be circular: one is, in effect, trying to see the place of labour in the capital accumulation process having already written out the possibility of being able to define (and measure) that labour.

The post-modernist approach has also led to a third problem which is pertinent in this context: the conception of 'culture' as series of discourses, endlessly renegotiated and reproduced by all those who participate in them. This, combined with the focus on semiotic analysis to analyze these discourses, makes invisible the fact that cultural products such as books, films, 'science' or advertisements – and the 'ideas' they contain (at least to the extent that these are a conscious result of mental effort) are also the products of human intellectual and physical labour. Without some means of modelling, and measuring, this labour (whether waged or not), it is extremely difficult to make analytical sense of the 'weightless economy'.

Having outlined some of the difficulties, let us go on to examine the main tenets of the 'weightless economy' school. Three quite distinct themes emerge in this literature: dematerialization; the 'productivity paradox' and globalization. Although these are capable of being separated from each other conceptually, they tend in practice to be discussed together.

One of the leading proponents of the dematerialization thesis is Danny Quah,[12] a Harvard-trained econometrician who is a professor at the London School of

Economics. His central argument is that the economy is becoming increasingly dematerialized with intangible services increasingly replacing physical goods as the main sources of value. He distinguishes two aspects of dematerialization which he regards as having macroeconomic importance: 'The first is simply increased weightlessness deriving from the growth of services – as opposed to, say, manufacturing in particular, or industry in general. The second is dematerialization deriving from the increased importance of IT'.[13]

Let us look first at the growth in services. It has been an article of faith in most of the literature, at least since Daniel Bell first coined the term 'post-industrial society' in the early 1970s, that a, if not the, major trend of the 20th Century has been the rise of services at the expense of agriculture and manufacturing.[14] The most usual measure of this rise is service employment, and it is readily illustrated by graphs (usually derived from census data) showing employment in services soaring heavenwards as the century progresses, whilst employment in agriculture and manufacturing falls dramatically. Before going on to a more detailed discussion of service employment, it is worth noting several difficulties with this representation.

First, the standard industrial classification system, which is used as a basis for assigning workers to sectors, fails to take account of the major changes in the division of labour which accompany technological change and the restructuring of economic activity, both in terms of ownership and of organization. Thus, for instance, the 'decline' of agricultural employment, which is visible in terms of the numbers of people actually working on the land, can only be demonstrated by leaving the mechanization of farming and the commodification of food production out of the picture. If you were to include, for example, all the people employed in making tractors, fertilizers and pesticides, and all the people engaged in packing and preparing food, and those involved in its distribution to supermarkets as part of the agricultural workforce, the graph would slope much less steeply. Similarly, the decline in manufacturing employment is usually demonstrated within a particular national context, or that of a group of nations (for instance the OECD nations, NAFTA or the EU). This fails to take account of the manufacturing employment which has simply been relocated to another part of the globe (although it may still be carried out by the same companies, based in the same countries and retaining their service employment there). Finally the growth in service employment over the course of the century can only be demonstrated convincingly by leaving out domestic servants, whose numbers have declined steadily as employment in other forms of service work has risen.[15] In Great Britain, for instance, domestic service accounted for 40% of all female employment in 1901, but had fallen to 5.2% by 1971.[16]

These qualifications aside, there are deeper difficulties involved. Any analysis which uses as its raw material aggregated data on 'service activities', whether these are derived from employment statistics, output data or other sources, is in effect collapsing together several quite different types of economic activity, involving contrasting and contradictory tendencies. While it may be possible to make out a case that dematerialization is taking place in some of these, it is my contention that in others precisely the opposite tendency is occurring, and that in the long run this tendency of commodification, or the transformation of services into material products, is the dominant one in capitalism.

The aggregated category 'services', which Quah and others use as the basis for their calculations, can be broken down into three distinct types of activity. The first of these consists essentially of a socialization of the kinds of work which are also carried out unpaid in the home or neighbourhood. It includes health care, child care, social work, cleaning, catering and a range of personal services like hairdressing. It also includes what one might call 'public housekeeping' such as the provision of leisure services, street cleaning, refuse collection or park-keeping. Even 'live' entertainment – and the sex industry – can plausibly be included in this category. (Under the standard industrial classification scheme (SIC) it is mostly classified under 'hotels, catering, retail and wholesale distribution', 'miscellaneous services' or in the public sector, although it is not coterminous with these categories.)

Whether or not outputs from these activities or employment in these sectors are visible in the economic statistics varies according to a number of factors including demographic structure, the degree of political commitment to providing public services, cultural variations, the extent of female participation in the workforce and what Gøsta Esping-Andersen has described as 'de-commodification', defined as 'the degree to which individuals or families can uphold a socially acceptable standard of living independently of market participation'.[17] These activities become visible in the public accounts when they are first socialized and enter the money economy: when, for instance, it becomes possible to attend a public concert instead of singing around the piano at home, to take an ailing baby to a clinic or to get one's legs waxed at a beauty salon. Conversely, they revert to invisibility if they are not available in the market. If, for instance, a political decision were made to abandon the state provision of school meals, employment of school meals staff would decline, but this would not necessarily mean that the labour of preparing such meals had disappeared; it would in all likelihood simply have re-entered the sphere of unpaid domestic work.

I have argued elsewhere that it is not simply the boundary between paid and unpaid labour which is permeable and shifting here; this kind of 'service' activity is also in an active process of commodification.[18] The general tendency is for new technologies to be used, not to dematerialize these activities but to materialize them (albeit in some cases with more and more 'knowledge' embedded in the new commodities). Thus we have a historical progression from washing clothes in the home as an activity either carried out unpaid or by the labour of paid domestic servants, via the provision of public laundries (staffed by 'service' workers) back into the home where it is now once again generally carried out as unpaid work but using an ever-burgeoning variety of new commodities such as washing machines, detergents, tumble dryers, fabric conditioners and steam irons. These undeniably material goods are made in factories and transported physically from these factories by various means to a growing proportion of homes throughout the world. The need to purchase them serves as one of the many ties pulling the 'underdeveloped' portions of that world ever more tightly into the cash nexus.

Washing, of course, is not the only activity which has been commodified in this way. One could point with equal justification to the processed food industry or the drugs industry as examples of commodified domestic labour. A random perusal of the advertisements in the room as I write this article throws up 'lunch-box-sized individual fruit-flavoured portions of fromage frais' (packaged in foil tubes!), 'panty-liners with flexible wings', 'under-eye moisturizer' and a 'universal remote control'. Not only can all of these commodities be traced readily back to their origins in unsocialized activity it would also be fair to say that none of them, with the possible exception of the moisturizer, would have been conceivable a generation ago; the ability of capitalism to generate new commodities can seem almost magical, as though they are being conjured out of the air in a perfect reversal of the 'dematerialization' hypothesis. We must remind ourselves, however, that their raw materials come from the earth and that the only magic involved is human inventiveness and labour.

A few statistics on the consumption of these raw materials underline the point: in the UK, iron consumption has increased twenty-fold since 1900; the global production of aluminium has risen from 1.5 million tonnes in 1950 to 20 million tonnes today.[19] In the decade 1984-1995 (during a period in which we should have seen the 'weightless' effect becoming visible, if the theorists are to be believed) aluminium consumption in the UK rose from 497,000 tonnes to 636,000; steel consumption increased from 14,330.000 to 15,090,000 and wood and paper consumption more than doubled, from 41 million to 93 million tonnes.[20]

This inexorable drive towards the creation of new commodities is perhaps the central drive in the history of capitalism; the physical production of material goods being the simplest way of deriving value from living labour. It is not, of course, the only way. There are profits to be made, for instance, from running private nursing homes, or contract cleaning agencies, from servicing computers, arranging conferences or organizing rock concerts. However – partly because of the limitations on the extent to which human productivity in these areas can be enhanced by automation and the consequent dependence on a geographically fixed and skill-specific workforce – it is easier and in the long run more profitable to be in the business of manufacturing and/or distributing endlessly reproducible material commodities. Thus while most of the major opera houses in the world require a public subsidy to stay open, selling Pavarotti's Greatest Hits on CD is hugely lucrative. Similarly, commodified medicine, in the form of mass sales of patented drugs, seems likely to remain much more profitable than employing doctors and nurses. These products do, of course, 'contain' knowledge (in the first case in the form of the composer's score, the performance of the conductor, orchestra and singer, the skills of the producer and studio engineers, the intellectual labour of the scientists and technicians who developed recording technology in general and CD technology in particular, and so on; in the second case *inter alia* in the form of inputs from doctors, scientific researchers and laboratory technicians). Except where this knowledge is paid for on a royalty basis, however, this can be regarded as 'dead' labour, whose cost is amortized in the early stages of production, producing a steadily increasing profit margin which grows with the size of the production run.

We can see, therefore, that in at least some parts of the service sector, the trend is one of materialization, rather than dematerialization. What of the others?

A second category of service activity could be classified as the development of human capital – the reproduction of the knowledge workforce itself. Into this category come education and training and some kinds of research and development. This sector is not immune from commodification – witness the standardization of courses and the development of products such as interactive CD-ROM to deliver instruction. David Noble has argued that the introduction of intranets (a combination of computers linked together on an internal telecommunications network) into universities is ushering in a new era of commodification in higher education. In his words,

> The major change to befall the universities over the last two decades has been the identification of the campus as a significant site of capital accumulation, a change in social perception which has resulted in the systematic conversion of intellectual activity into intellectual capital and, hence, intellectual property. There have been two general phases of this transformation. The first, which began twenty years ago and is still underway, entailed the commoditization of the research function of the university, transforming scientific and engineering knowledge into commercially viable proprietary products that could be owned and bought and sold in the market. The second, which we are now witnessing, entails the commoditization of the educational function of the university, transforming courses into courseware, the activity of instruction itself into commercially viable proprietary products that can be owned and bought and sold in the market.[21]

The content of these new commodities is abstract, in the sense that it has been abstracted from the lecturers, researchers and graduate students employed in this sector. Unlike past forms of commodified scholarship, such as text-books, these newer means of abstraction rarely acknowledge the authors' ownership by means of royalties. Nevertheless, they do not differ fundamentally from the process whereby the design of a carpet is abstracted from a skilled weaver and embedded in the programming instructions for an automated loom. What it is important to keep sight of here is that the workforce has not disappeared. Even if the more original and creative (and perhaps hence the most troublesome) workers could somehow be emptied of all the knowledge that their employers find useful and got rid of, a workforce – including original and creative people – would still be required, however deskilled and intensified the rest of the work process had become, to replenish the stock of intellectual capital, produce new educational commodities and administer the new standardized courses, in standardized doses, to the next generation of students.

The systematization of education which has taken place in recent years bears a close resemblance to the systematization of other forms of non-manual work. For instance, the way in which the assessment of students' work may be transformed from a mystified and subjective process of exercising individual professional judge-ment to the ticking of boxes on a standard marking scheme is not unlike the way a bank manager's assessment of a client's eligibility for a loan or mortgage increas-ingly turns on the administration of a standard questionnaire, with standard built-in criteria, in which the decision is effectively made by the software programme.

This sector, then, is one where enormous changes are taking place in the labour process (and, with it, the capital accumulation process) in association with the in-troduction of the new information technologies. It does not, however, appear to raise any new problems which are not soluble within the framework of the 'old' economics.

The third category of service activity is the one which most concerns Quah and the other economists of the 'weightless' school. This is the 'knowledge work' which is either directly involved in the production of physical commodities, or in-volved in the production of new commodities which are entirely weightless. In the former category, an oft-cited example is that of the fashion shoe, only a fraction of the price of which is attributable to the raw materials and the cost of physical manu-facture and transport. The main value, it is argued, comes from the 'weightless' attributes of the shoe, derived from its design, its brand image, the way in which it is marketed and so on. As Diane Coyle puts it, the 'buyer is paying for what they do for her image rather than something to protect her feet'.[22] Notwithstanding the extra money a purchaser is prepared to pay for a high-status product, it is still, at the end of a day, a material object which is being purchased, and from which the manufacturers derive their profit. The snob value of a Nike running shoe in the 1990s is not different *in kind* from that of a sought-after Paris bonnet in the 19th century;[23] the main difference lies in the fact that the former is mass-produced while the latter was individually made. In the former case, the 'knowledge' has been ab-stracted from a specialist knowledge-worker in a reproducible form; in the second it lay embedded in the skill of the milliner whose bodily presence was thus required to produce each new bonnet.

The emergence of the specialist knowledge worker is thus a product of the in-creasingly specialized division of labour in manufacturing.[24] In this process, as the physical business of production becomes more and more capital-intensive, through automation, the manual processes of assembly become progressively deskilled, ena-bling the work to be done ever more cheaply. In the case of sports shoes, this is often by the use of extremely low-paid labour in developing countries. In 1995, for instance, it was reported that twelve thousand women were employed in Indonesia making Nike shoes, working sixty hours a week and many earning less than the government's minimum wage of US $1.80 a day. It was estimated that raising their wages to US $3.50 per day would still bring the labour cost component of a pair of shoes to less than US $1 a pair. In 1993, by contrast, Michael Jordan alone received over US $20 million from Nike for allowing his name and image (and by implication his sporting achievements) to be associated with their product – equivalent to more than the total labour cost for all the 19 million pairs of Nike shoes made in Indonesia.[25] Traditional economics allows us to understand the very small proportion of the cost of the final shoe attributable to the labour involved in its manufacture as the super-exploitation of a vulnerable group of workers; the 'new' economics simply renders them invisible. Yet it is difficult to see the division of labour in the production process as anything intrinsically new; rather it can be seen as the continuation of a process which has been evolving for at least the past century and a half.[26] Michael Jordan may be earning considerably more, but his contribution to the value of the final product is not different *in kind* from that of the little girls who posed for the Pears Soap advertisements at the turn of the twentieth century[27] or the members of the royal family who give their official blessing and the use of their coats of arms to pots of marmalade.

What is perhaps new is the large-scale introduction of new technologies not just into the process of *production* of commodities but also into their *distribution*. The creation of global markets for mass-produced commodities has generated imperatives to increase the efficiency of this distribution workforce and, indeed, to introduce entirely new ways of reaching potential customers and persuade them to buy. In some cases this has produced the rather paradoxical effect of recreating the illusion of a return to the customization of products associated with the era before mass production. Thus, for instance, there are now web-sites into which you can input your measurements to enable you to order a pair of blue-jeans tailored to your own precise individual dimensions (provided, of course, you are prepared to select from a menu of standard styles from a single manufacturer). The computerization of parts of the production process has been combined with the use of the new communications technologies to create a direct interactive link between customer and producer. This also has the effect of cutting out various intermediaries (such as the wholesaler and the retailer) and of reducing the manufacturer's risk of over-producing, or producing the wrong product, almost to zero: only that which has already been ordered by the customer need ever be produced. In this case, however, there is still a material commodity which has to be manufactured, packed, and delivered over real physical distances to its customer.

In other cases, the commodity being distributed is less easy to pin down in its material form. An example of this might be the use of a call centre for activities like selling airline tickets, providing directory enquiry information, arranging financial transactions, providing assistance on software problems or dealing with insurance claims. Again, the sophisticated use of new technology makes it possible to personalize these services, however remote the site from which they are delivered. Software can, for instance, be programmed to use the area code from which a call is originated to direct the caller to an operator who will reply in the right language or even the appropriate regional accent, thus creating an illusion of local response whatever the actual location or time zone. The same digital trigger (the caller's telephone number) can also be used to ensure that the caller's personal file is visible on the screen to the operator before the first 'hello' has even been uttered, making it possible to generate a highly personalized response and, indeed, an illusion of intimacy, as well as maximizing the operator's productivity by avoiding any waste of time in taking down unnecessary details.

The use of computer-generated scripts which pop up on the screen to be read verbatim by the operator can reduce the skill requirements to a minimum. This sort of work is also amenable to a high degree of remote monitoring and control. Studies of call centre workers in the UK – already an estimated 1.1% of the workforce[28] in a market estimated to be growing at the rate of 32% per annum across Europe[29] – have found that the work is highly controlled, relatively low-paid, frequently involves round-the-clock shift-working and produces a very rapid rate of staff turnover, with 'burn-out' typically occurring after 12 to 20 months on the job.[30] The evidence suggests that, far from constituting some new kind of knowledge worker, formerly unknown to economics, these are the Taylorized, deskilled descendants of earlier forms of office worker (such as bank tellers, insurance salespeople, booking clerks and telephone operators) even though the work may be taking place at different locations and under different conditions of employment. There seems to be no good reason why the value which they add to the products or services being delivered (which may, or may not, be of a tangible nature) cannot also be measured by the traditional means.

This brings us to the other kind of knowledge work in this category discussed in the 'weightless economy' literature – the kind which produces no material end-product whatsoever. This may take the form of algorithms (such as a software program), intangible financial products (such as a life insurance policy), creative works (such as a film script) or speculations (such as an investment in futures). Again, none of these is new in itself: a musical score, the perforated roll of paper which contains the 'instructions' for a pianola, a chemical formula, the blueprint for a machine or indeed a recipe book, represent essentially the same kind of algorithm as a computer program, for example. And various forms of gambling, usury and insurance seem to have been around for as long as money. In the seventeenth century, one of the earliest uses of official statistics (in this case the *London Bills of Mortality*, from which the merchant John Graunt constructed life expectancy tables) was for the calculation of annuities.[31] And writers, poets, dramatists, visual artists, scientists, inventors and musicians have been producing 'intangible products' for centuries. When we read of rock musicians borrowing money on the world's stock markets against their future royalty earnings this may seem like some new semi-magical way of generating income out of thin air, but is it really very different from the way in which impecunious young aristocrats in the 18th century settled their gambling debts by the use of IOUs drawn against their future inheritance? Danny Quah argues that weightless products defy the traditional laws of economics because they are simultaneously infinitely expandable, indivisible and inappropriable. In other words a new idea can only be discovered once; once discovered it can not only be used over and over again without being 'used up', and even if there are formal restrictions, in the form of patents or copyright, on so doing it can in practice be freely reproduced.[32] While it is certainly true that the new communications and reproductive technologies have made the rapid dissemination of ideas easier than ever before, this again does not appear to be a new phenomenon. Surely these features have always been present when new discoveries have been made (such as the use of penicillin to heal infection, or the theory of gravity, or the discovery of electricity)? And the copying of ideas is as old as the history of fashion.

It is possible to argue about the exact relationship of these abstract products to material reality. In some cases they may act as proxies for material goods (as in the case, for instance, of a mortgage, which can be exchanged for a house, or an insurance policy which can be exchanged for a new car or indeed a credit card transaction which can be exchanged for goods or cash). In other cases (for instance in the case of a piece of music or a poem) it is more useful to envisage them in relation to the human desires they satisfy.

If we are to avoid constructing a purely abstract universe, constituted entirely of 'knowledge' (in which disembodied entities inhabit a virtual space, are sustained by virtual inputs, and produce virtual outputs – a universe without birth or death, a universe where infinite consumption is possible without the generation of waste), it is useful to retain an awareness of this underlying materiality. From an economic perspective, I would argue, it is important to retain a more specific awareness of the materiality of the worker and his or her labour process. It is only by examining this process in some detail that it becomes possible to tease out the specific contributions made at each stage to the 'value' of the final commodity. Such an analysis can also illuminate the process which Marx identified whereby labour is progressively abstracted and incorporated into capital in its specific relation to 'knowledge' work in an economy increasingly dependent on the use of information and communications technologies.

In brief, we could say that in the 1990s the division of labour has evolved to a point where a substantial part of the labour force is engaged in 'non-manual' work; is, in other words, engaged in the generation or processing of 'information' (even though this work nevertheless involves the body in a series of physical activities, such as pounding a keyboard, which have implications for its physiological well-being). The development of computing technology has made it possible for this information (or 'codified knowledge', as it has been conceptualized by David and

Foray[33]) to be digitized and for some aspects of its processing to be automated, and the development of telecommunications technology has enabled this digital information to be transmitted from one place to another with great rapidity and at very low cost. These technologies in combination have made it possible for many of these processes to be standardized, as a result of which it has become possible for the workers to be monitored by results, and for the task to be relocated to any point on the globe where the right infrastructure is available together with a workforce with the appropriate skills.

We must now ask ourselves what, precisely, is the relationship of this workforce to capital? How is the value of the final commodity constituted? In relation to its material content, Marx has already given us the answer: there is the dead labour of past workers embodied in the machinery used to make it, and in the extraction of the raw materials and the capital used to set the enterprise up, and the appropriated living labour of the workers who process it. In relation to the intangible content, there is also the dead labour of the people whose past work made the idea possible; but there is also living labour in two quite distinct forms.[34] The first of these is the routine labour of deskilled workers who are essentially following instructions. We might call these 'process' knowledge workers. These may be involved either in the production process (for instance coders working on the development of software, graphic designers laying out web pages, copy-typists inputting data, managers supervising the purchasing of raw materials or the organization of the production process, quality controllers checking the final output) or in the distribution process (such as call centre staff or invoice clerks). Although when it is casualized some form of payment by results (or piece-rate) may be applied, it is normally paid by time, as is the case with manual work. Even if the activity is outsourced, the wage or salary bill is verifiable and it is thus a relatively straightforward task to relate these labour costs to the output in order to calculate the value added.

Then there is also another kind of knowledge work, which we might call 'creative' or 'originating' labour (some of which may be contributed, with or without acknowledgement, by the 'process' workers) which generates new intellectual capital, in the form of ideas, designs, programs or more definable (if not tangible) intellectual products such as words, music or images. The contribution made by this work is harder to calculate. The ideas may be appropriated from a waged workforce (in most countries, ownership of intellectual property produced by employees is automatically assigned to the employer). However they may be produced by freelances or other independent individuals or organizations under agreements which assign all or part of the ownership of rights to the creator. In such cases, the right to use the intellectual product may involve the payment of fees or royalties or the negotiation of complex licensing agreements. Alternatively the ideas may simply be stolen. Intellectual property rights can be legally asserted not just in the outputs of workers who are conscious of their roles as generators of valuable ideas, for instance as writers, artists or inventors. They also apply to the tacit knowledge of people who have no awareness of the alienable nature of what they own. The music of tribal peoples, for instance, may be appropriated to be used on CDs or film soundtracks; their visual art may be photographed and printed on tee-shirts or wrapping paper, or scanned in to give an 'ethnic' feel to the design of a web page; their sacred artefacts may be used as 'inspiration' for a new range of designer clothes or jewellery. It does not stop there: supermarkets developing 'own range' 'ethnic' convenience foods will generally insist that the subcontractors who prepare the food for them give them an exclusive right to use the recipe; the handed-down knowledge of the family or community thus becomes appropriated as privately-owned intellectual capital.[35] Even more extreme is the patenting of human genetic codes for research purposes, a development of the practice of patenting the DNA of various plants and animals (with a slight tweak to ensure its uniqueness) for use in new drugs and genetic engineering products.[36]

It is no accident that the ownership of intellectual property is currently one of the most hotly contended issues both at the level of international trade agreements and at the level of workplace negotiation. In the UK, for instance, the National Union of Journalists has found itself in recent years in a series of disputes with large employers over the right of freelance journalists and photographers to retain ownership of copyright in their own work. Many employers, including the supposedly left-of-centre *Guardian* newspaper, now make it a condition of employment that all rights, electronic or otherwise, become the property of the newspaper.[37] On one level, this can be regarded as a simple dispute between labour and capital, with workers fighting for a larger share of the products of their labour. However the concept of ownership is rather different from that which pertains in a typical factory. It is now over two centuries since workers effectively gave up their right to a share in the ownership of the product of their labour in return for a wage. The knowledge worker who insists on a royalty, or on the right to re-use what s/he has produced, is not behaving like a member of the proletariat; s/he is refusing alienation.

Nevertheless, the worker's right to ownership of the 'idea' (as opposed to the right to be paid for the time put in on the processing of that idea) is profoundly ambiguous. The knowledge worker usually occupies an intermediate position in what might be seen as the knowledge food chain. Ideas do not come from nowhere: they may be copied, consciously or unconsciously, from others; they may draw on what has been learned from teachers, or from books, or from observations of people who do not regard themselves as creative; or they may have arisen from the interactions of a group of people working together as a team. A journalist or television researcher generally obtains inputs from interviews with 'experts' (who may or may not be salaried academics or writers with an interest in plugging their books); there is no rational basis for deciding whether the end result should 'belong' to the journalist's employer, the journalist, the 'expert', or someone further down the chain, for instance the 'expert's' research assistant, or a person interviewed by the research assistant in the course of carrying out the research, or indeed the parents of the person interviewed by the research assistant who inculcated the views expressed in the interview. An analogous intermediary position could be said to be occupied by the scientist doing research on disease resistance in rice who obtains information from South-East Asian peasants as part of the process which eventually leads to his or her employer registering a claim to ownership of the new strain which is developed; or by Paul Simon incorporating tribal music into 'his' work; or by the photographer who records the face of an elderly Jamaican fisherman to use to advertise a canned drink.

In the final analysis it is market strength which determines who can claim what share of the cake, but the analysis of how the 'value' is formed is complicated by these considerations. The fact that it is complicated to model does not render the task impossible. In order to do so, it is necessary to take account of the fact that real people with real bodies have contributed real time to the development of these 'weightless' commodities.

This brings me to the second issue which occupies such a large place in the weightless economy literature: the so-called 'productivity paradox'. The starting point for this discussion is the belief that growth rates, measured in GDP (gross domestic product) and TFP (total factor productivity) have in most developed countries remained obstinately low since 1973 – well below their post-war levels up to that date. This year is chosen as the watershed partly because it was in 1973 that the oil crisis generated a number of dramatic hiccups in the economic statistics, and partly because it more or less coincided with the beginnings of what has been various described as the 'knowledge economy', the 'information economy', the 'second industrial revolution' or the 'computer revolution'. If, as is widely argued on both the left and the right of the political spectrum, the introduction of these new technologies can unleash human potential, making workers more productive and creating a host of new products and services, then this ought to have led to a surge in economic growth. The apparent evidence that it has not done so is one of the main factors leading to the belief that a new economics is required. However the paradox may not be as surprising as it first appears.

First, the evidence itself: productivity is normally measured by the relationship between the value of outputs and that of the inputs of labour and capital. As Danny Quah has pointed out, if we are to judge by the statistics alone, the most productive group of workers in the world are French farmers.[38] The implication is that apparently high productivity can simply be an effect of artificially high prices of final outputs. This suggests that part of the explanation for the 'productivity paradox' may lie in the very sharp reduction in prices which has accompanied the process of computerization.

But do the empirical data support this definition of the problem? In this connection, Neuburger has convincingly shown that although there was a sharp drop in *output*, labour productivity did not exhibit a correspondingly sharp fall, and in some OECD countries did not fall significantly at all.[39] Moreover for the UK he has also shown that the present system of public accounts would only reveal the kind of productivity gains delivered by information technology in about ten percent of the sectors comprising the total economy.[40] Nonetheless a paradox does seem to exist, even if not in nearly as extreme a form as generally supposed. So what might be the explanation for it? Is political economy really incapable of providing one?

Here, I can only indicate some of the main possible solutions to the puzzle out of the many which have been proposed. One has to do with the effects of globalization. It is very difficult for nationally-based systems of accounting to deal accurately with the transactions taking place in a globalized economy. Where high levels of output are recorded in one country, but some of the inputs may have been in the form of very cheap labour in another, and complex adjustments have to be made to allow for such factors as fluctuating exchange rates and transfer pricing practices within large transnational companies, then some slippage may take place which affects the GDP figures positively or negatively.

There are also many ways in which the extra productivity produced by information technology may not reveal itself in output figures. It may increase the efficiency of *unpaid* rather than paid labour, for example by making it much quicker and easier for a library user to identify a book, or a customer to withdraw cash from a bank. To the extent that information technology encourages the development of self-service this will not be reflected in the figures. It could be argued that a firm which improves its service to customers will thereby gain market share and that this will ultimately feed through into increased output figures, but this does not take account of the generalized effect which takes place when the whole sector has adopted this new technology; customer expectations will have risen but no single firm has a competitive advantage. Jeff Madrick has, in addition, raised a number of other technical issues, including a possible oversupply of services, that may have affected the statistics in the USA.[41]

There are also very specific problems here associated with the public sector: improvements in efficiency and quality of service resulting from the introduction of new technologies into public administration or the delivery of public services may well lead to a better quality of life but this will not be reflected in the output figures, since national accounts do not at present capture in any direct way things like cleaner air, healthier children, happier cyclists or less confused form-fillers. It is sometimes argued that the nature of Britain's publicly-funded National Health Service creates a consistent bias in the national accounts leading to an underestimation of GDP.

A study of the public sector also raises some more fundamental questions relating to the socialization of domestic labour (discussed above in the context of service employment). Part of the apparent fall in productivity from the 1970s onward might be a direct effect of the greater labour force participation of women during that period, and hence an increase in the need for a market supply of childcare and other services previously provided in the home.[42] A group of Norwegian researchers used a social accounting framework to decompose GDP growth into productivity gains and 'reallocation' gains resulting from the transition from unpaid household production to the labour market. They concluded that 'about one-fourth of the growth in GDP in Norway over the period 1971-90 can be attributed to the transition of household services from unpaid to paid work'.[43]

Neuburger's own explanation for the 'productivity paradox', insofar as it exists, is an interesting one. He hypothesizes that during the 1970s there was a qualitative improvement in working conditions across most of the OECD countries and that the increased cost of inputs (reflected in lower productivity growth figures) represented a real gain for labour, in the form of improved health and safety at work, a better working environment, longer holidays and other achievements. In most developed countries, 1970-76 was, after all, as well as being a time of considerable trade union militancy, the period in which equal pay, protection against discrimination, maternity rights, protection against unfair dismissal, the right to a safe working environment and a number of other rights were, at least formally, enshrined in employment protection or anti-discrimination legislation. Although much of the legislation was difficult to implement and many workers fell through the net it did, according to Neuburger, lead to some measurable redistribution from capital to labour, and the productivity figures provide the evidence for it.

These issues of productivity and growth are, then, evidently complex; but we can at least conclude that they cannot be understood in relation to technology alone, but must be analyzed in their full social and historical context.

A third strand in the discussions about the weightless economy concerns globalization. Perhaps one of the most dangerous illusions fostered here is the notion that the new information technologies mean that anything can now be done by anyone, anywhere: that the entire population of the globe has become a potential virtual workforce. The issue of globalization is crucial because it raises very directly the question of how the virtual economy, insofar as it exists, maps on to the physical surface of the globe we inhabit.

Although it is full of euphemistic descriptions of the 'death of distance' or the 'end of geography', the literature on the subject is surprisingly short on empirical evidence.[44] At one extreme, sceptics such as Paul Hirst and Grahame Thompson go so far as to assert that a global economy cannot be said to exist in any meaningful sense, and even maintain that the world economy is somewhat *less* global now than it was before the first world war.[45] At the other extreme is a large literature, much of it by postmodernist geographers, which takes the presumption that globalization is taking place as its starting point, and is concerned to develop an understanding of the social, cultural and economic implications of this. The empirical evidence on which it draws is, however, slight, rarely going beyond the anecdote or case-study writ large.[46] Few systematic attempts have been made to establish the scale of relocation of information-processing work across national boundaries.[47]

It is in fact extraordinarily difficult to obtain a statistical picture of the changing international division of labour. Apart from the difficulty of distinguishing between final outputs and intermediate ones, the traffic in jobs will not necessarily even appear in an easily identifiable form in the trade statistics, because of the range of different contractual arrangements which might apply, each of which is visible in a different way in the national accounts. Material goods must be transported in a physical form across national boundaries, and are therefore generally recorded in import and export statistics; but information sent over the internet leaves no such trace and there is no easy way to assess the value of such traffic. It is, of course, possible to measure its *volume* but, despite the arguments of Luc Soete and others who propose a 'bit tax',[48] this is not a good indicator of value: a computer program which has taken thousands of skilled person–hours to write will typically be much smaller in volume (measured in bits) than a video clip or scanned–in photograph in whose generation only a few moments of unpaid time have been invested.

The fact that something is difficult to measure does not, of course, mean that it does not exist, and it is clear that the widespread use of computers for processing information, and of telecommunications for transmitting it, *has* introduced an enormous new range of choices in the location of information–processing work.

However it would not be correct to infer from this that these choices are entirely untethered from the material. First, and most obviously, they depend on a physical infrastructure. The process which was formalized in the liberalization of the telecommunications market following the ratification of the World Trade Organization pact of 15 February 1997 by 68 countries has opened up most of the world as a market for the major telecommunications multinationals and involved a rapid spread of infrastructure and a sharp fall in telecommunications costs. But this process has been highly selective; it certainly cannot be said to have given all the world's population access to the 'information society'. In many developing countries whole communities are effectively without any telephone access whatsoever and even those lines which exist are of poor quality. The optical fibre cable which is required to transmit high volumes of information quickly, and which provides a vital underpinning for many 'weightless' activities, is so far only available in selected parts of the globe, mainly in large cities, such as Singapore, where high usage, and hence profitability, is anticipated.

Even 'wireless' communications are dependent on material goods, like satellites, to continue functioning. On May 20th, 1998, Americans were reminded sharply of this when there was a malfunction in the onboard control system and a backup switch of the Galaxy IV satellite, owned by PanAmSat. The satellite reportedly provided pager service to more than 80% of US pager users, and also carried NPR, several television networks, and Reuters news feeds. Whilst CBS services were quickly switched to Galaxy 7, pager users, including many hospitals, were left without any service.[49]

Telecommunications infrastructure is not the only material prerequisite for participation in the global weightless economy. There is also a need, continuously renewed because of its rapid obsolescence, for hardware: for personal computers, mobile telephones, modems, scanners, printers, switches and the many components and accessories involved in their manufacture and use. Not only do the costs of these differ in absolute terms from country to country, but so does their cost relative to basic income and subsistence. Mike Holderness has pointed out that 'a reasonable computer costs about one year's unemployment benefit in the UK or about the annual income of three schoolteachers in Calcutta' and that the annual subscription to Ghana's only internet host is about the same as the entire annual income of a Ghanaian journalist.[50]

The notion that anyone can do anything anywhere is therefore in practice constrained by a number of spatial factors. It is also, of course, constrained by the fact that not all human activities are delocalizable in this way. The majority of jobs are, and seem likely to remain, firmly anchored to a given spot, or series of spots, on the world's surface because they involve the extraction of the earth's raw materials, their processing, the manufacture of material commodities (which is delocalizable, but within limits), transport, construction, or the delivery of physical services (ranging from health care to garbage collection).

That said, it is undeniably the case that more and more work *is* delocalizable. The reasons for this are many. First, there are the changes in the division of labour which have increased the proportion of jobs which simply involve processing information. Second, the digitization of that information has vastly increased the extent to which it can be accessed remotely, removing the need for physical proximity to sources and eliminating transport costs. Third, the standardization of tasks associated with computerization has enabled a growing proportion of activities to be monitored remotely (replacing management of the work process with management by results) which in turn allows them to be outsourced or located at a distance from the manager. Fourth – partly because of the hegemonic power of companies like IBM and Microsoft – there has been a convergence of skill requirements across occupations and industries, with a few generic skills (such as a knowledge of Word or Excel) replacing a large number of machine-specific, firm-specific or occupation-specific skills which have in the past both constrained the mobility of workers and created a dependence on their skills among employers, effectively anchoring them to the places where those skills were available. Fifth, as already noted, there has been both a rapid diffusion of the infrastructure and technology and a sharp fall in its cost.[51]

This should, in principle, have enabled any region in which the right combination of infrastructure and skills is present to diversify its local economy and enter the global market in information-processing work on an equal basis with any other region. By removing the strategic advantages of some regions (created by such things as economies of scale or proximity to markets) it should have levelled the playing field. It is this idea which underlies much of the optimistic rhetoric about the ability of new information and communications technologies to regenerate remote regions. However the results of empirical research reveal that things are not so simple. The very fact that employers now have a huge range of alternative locations to choose from appears, paradoxically, to have increased, rather than decreased, the degree of geographical segregation in the global division of labour. Although its specific components may have changed, comparative competitive advantage is more, rather than less important, with each location having to compete separately for each type of activity. No longer constrained to have most of their information processing activities on one site, corporations are now free to seek out the best location on an activity by activity basis, with the whole world to choose from. Thus a company might decide to get its manufacturing done in Mexico, its research and development in California, its data entry in the Philippines, its software development in India and establish two call centres, one in New Brunswick, Canada, and one in the Netherlands. In each case, the site would be selected on the basis of the availability of skills and the advantageousness of other local labour market conditions, tax regime, etc. If the market became more competitive, or local workers started demanding higher wages or better conditions, or the local tax regime changed, it might switch: it might, for instance, go to Indonesia for manufacturing, to the Dominican Republic for data entry, to Russia for programming or start using homeworkers for some of the more routine call centre functions. Even within countries, this increasing geographical specialization (generally accompanied by polarization in incomes and standards of living) can be observed. Some recent research I carried out in the UK revealed a steadily growing gap between those regions which were successful in attracting high-skilled 'creative' knowledge work (mostly concentrated in an affluent 'green' corridor to the west of London) and those which had succeeded only in attracting routine back-office functions and call centres (almost exclusively in declining industrial areas).[52] Remote rural areas with poor infrastructure had failed to attract either type of employment.

Such findings cast serious doubt over many of the claims made by economists of the 'death of distance' school. They suggest that location has actually become *more* rather than less important. Some places seem likely to be able to build on their comparative advantages to increase the gap between themselves and the rest of the world; others seem likely to be able to find niches for themselves in the new global division of labour, by exploiting things like language skills, time zone advantages, cheap labour, specialist skills, or good infrastructure; still others will be left entirely out in the cold. The dream of a fully diversified local economy in any given area seems likely to remain unrealizable except for a few privileged pockets.

And what of the future of knowledge work? It seems likely that two existing tendencies will intensify. On the one hand, there is likely to be a continuing erosion of the traditional bureaucracy (as first anatomized by Max Weber at the beginning of the century) with its stable hierarchies, rigid rules, orderly – if implicitly discriminatory – promotion patterns, 'jobs for life', process management and unity of time and space, in favour of an increasingly atomized and dispersed workforce, managed by results, insecure and expected to work from any location. If they are not actually formally self-employed, this group of workers, which will include a high proportion of the 'creative' knowledge workforce, will increasingly be expected to behave as if they are. On the other hand, there is likely to be the creation of what is in effect a new white-collar proletariat engaged in the more routine 'process' knowledge work, closely monitored with Taylorized work processes and stressful working conditions. Geographical segregation will make it difficult for members of the second group to progress to the first.

The geographical distribution of intellectual labour (the movement of jobs to people) is only one aspect of globalization, of course. In analyzing the forms of capital accumulation which prevail as the century draws to a close it is also important to look at the global division of labour in terms of the physical movements of migrant workers (the movement of people to jobs) and in terms of the development of mass global markets.

In order to do so, however, it is not necessary to develop a new economics of weightlessness. On the contrary, we must reinsert human beings, in all their rounded, messy, vulnerable materiality – and the complexity of their antagonistic social relations – at the very centre of our analysis.

NOTES

1   Frances Cairncross, *The Death of Distance: How the Communications Revolution will Change our Lives*, Boston: Harvard Business School Press, 1997.

2   Diane Coyle, *Weightless World: Strategies for Managing the Digital Economy,* Oxford: Capstone Publishing, 1997.

3   Christopher Meyer and Stan Davis, *Blur: the Speed of Change in the Connected Economy*, South Port: Addison-Wesley, 1998.

4   Don Tapscott, ed., *Blueprint to the Digital Economy: Wealth Creation in the Era of E-business*, New York: McGraw Hill, 1998 and Don Tapscott, *The Digital Economy: Promise and Peril in the Age of Networked Intelligence*, New York: McGraw Hill, 1995.

5   Dale Neef, ed., *The Economic Impact of Knowledge (Resources for the Knowledge-based Economy)*, Boston: Butterworth-Heinemann, 1998.

6   Bob Norton and Cathy Smith, *Understanding the Virtual Organization,* New York: Barrons Educational, Hauppage, 1998.

7   In doing so, I have been helped immeasurably by discussions with the economist Henry Neuburger who has brought more sceptical rigour to these questions than anyone else I know. He is not responsible, of course, for any inadequacies in my arguments, for which I take full blame.

8   There is some encouraging evidence that this may have peaked, and that the old modernisms are beginning to reassert themselves. Nevertheless, we now have several generations of students already in or about to enter the intellectual labour market who have been taught to view the world through postmodernist lenses, and whose practices will be influenced by these views.

9   The critical realism of Roy Bhaskar seems to offer the most promising way forward currently on offer – see Roy Bhaskar's own *A Realist Theory of Science,* 1975, repub-

lished by London: Verso Books in 1997 (Verso Classics 9) and *Dialectic: The Pulse of Freedom*, London: Verso Books, 1997; Andrew Collier, *Critical Realism: An Introduction to Roy Bhaskar's Philosophy*, London: Verso Books, 1994; and the interesting discussion of Bhaskar's work in Meera Nanda, 'Restoring the Real: Rethinking Social Constructivist Theories of Science' in Leo Panitch, ed., *Socialist Register, 1997*, Rendlesham: Merlin Press, 1997.

10   Jean Baudrillard, *Simulacra and Simulation (The Body, in Theory: Histories of Cultural Materialism)* translated by Sheila Faria Glaser, Chicago: University of Michigan Press, 1995.

11   Donna J. Haraway, *Simians, Cyborgs, and Women: The Reinvention of Nature*, London and New York: Routledge, 1991.

12   Web address: weightlesseconomy.com.

13   Danny T. Quah, 'Increasingly Weightless Economies' in *Bank of England Quarterly Bulletin*, (February) 1997, p. 49.

14   Daniel Bell, *The Coming of Post-Industrial Society*, New York: Basic Book, 1973.

15   I do not have the resources while writing this article to demonstrate this conclusively on a national scale. However in 1979-80, with the invaluable help and guidance of Quentin Outram, I carried out a detailed study based on data from the decennial Censuses of Employment supplemented in more recent years by data from Census of Employment, of service employment by occupation and industry (i.e. including those 'service' workers whose employers were categorized in 'manufacturing' or other non-service sectors) in one part of Britain – West Yorkshire. While doing this work – which focused particularly on women's employment – we were greatly struck by the almost exact parallel between the decline of domestic service and the expansion of other forms of service employment between 1901 and 1971. The report, which was published under the title *The Impact of New Technology on Women's Employment in West Yorkshire*, by Leeds Trade Union and Community Resource and Information Centre, 1980, did not, unfortunately, draw attention to this finding.

16   C.H. Lee, *British Regional Employment Statistics, 1841-1971*, Cambridge: Cambridge University Press, 1979.

17   Gøsta Esping-Andersen, *The Three Worlds of Welfare Capitalism*, Cambridge: Polity Press, 1990.

18   First in Ursula Huws, 'Domestic Technology: liberator or enslaver?' in *Scarlet Women*, No. 14, January 1982, reprinted in Kanter, Lefanu, Shah and Spedding, eds., *Sweeping Statements: Writings from the Women's Liberation Movement* 1981-1983, London: The Women's Press, 1984; then in Ursula Huws, 'Challenging Commodification', in Collective Design/Projects, ed., *Very Nice Work If You Can Get It: The Socially Useful Production Debate*, Nottingham: Spokesman, 1985. The argument is summarized in Ursula Huws, 'Consuming Fashions', *New Statesman & Society*, August 1988 and, most recently, in Ursula Huws, 'What is a Green-Red Economics?: The Future of Work', *Z*, (September) 1991.

19   Tim Jackson, *Material Concerns: Pollution, Profit and Quality of Life*, London: Routledge, 1996.

20   Department of the Environment *Digest of Environmental Statistics*, information supplied by Friends of the Earth.

21   David Noble, 'Digital Diploma Mills: The Automation of Higher Education', article

distributed on the internet with the author's permission by the Red Rock Eater News
Service (pagre@weber.ucsd.edu), October, 1997.

22 Diane Coyle, 'Why knowledge is the new engine of economic growth', *Independent*,
23 (April) 1998.

23 I am indebted to James Woudhuysen for this comparison.

24 Harry Braverman's *Labour and Monopoly Capital: The Degradation of Work in the Twentieth
Century*, New York: Monthly Review Press, 1974 remains the classic account of this
process.

25 'There is No Finish Line – Running Shoes: the Follow-Up', *News from Irene*, 22
(March) 1995, pp. 33-36.

26 The publication of Charles Babbage's *On the Economy of Machinery and Manufactures* in
London in 1832 is as convenient a starting point as any to select for the systematic and
conscious introduction of processes designed to reduce labour costs in manufacturing
to a minimum.

27 Selected annually in a 'Miss Pears' beauty contest which continued certainly up to the
1950s, when I was a child, and quite possibly for many years afterwards.

28. Sue Fernie and David Metcalf, 'Hanging on the Telephone', in *Centrepiece: the
Magazine of Economic Performance*, 3(1) (Spring) 1998, p. 7.

29 Research by Datamonitor, quoted in Una McLoughlin, 'Call centre staff development', *T*, October, 1997, pp. 18-21.

30 Incomes Data, *Pay and Conditions in Call Centre*, IDS Report, 739 (June) 1997,
Geraldine Reardon, 'Externalising Information Processing Work: Breaking the Logic
of Spatial and Work Organization', United Nations University Institute for New
Technologies Conference on *Globalised Information Society: Employment Implications*,
Maastricht, October 17-19, 1996; and Sue Fernie and David Metcalf, 'Hanging on the
Telephone', in *Centrepiece: The Magazine of Economic Performance*, 3(1) (Spring) 1998.

31 Martin Shaw and Ian Miles, 'The Social Roots of Statistical Knowledge' in John Irvine,
Ian Miles and Jeff Evans, eds., *Demystifying Social Statistics*, London: Pluto Press, 1981,
p. 30.

32 Danny Quah, 'Policies for the Weightless Economy', Lecture to the Social Market
Foundation, London, April 21, 1998.

33 David and Foray, 1995, incompletely referenced citation in Luc Soete, 'The Challenges
of Innovation' in *IPTS Report* 7, Seville: Institute for Prospective Technological
Studies, September, 1996, pp. 7-13.

34 Luc Soete distinguishes three forms in which knowledge becomes embedded in a
commodity (or, in his language 'contributes to growth') These are 'easily transferable
codifiable knowledge', 'non-codifiable knowledge, also known as tacit knowledge
(skills)' and 'codified knowledge'. See Luc Soete, 'The Challenges of Innovation' in
IPTS Report 7, Seville: Institute for Prospective Technological Studies, September,
1996, pp. 7-13. This typology is extremely useful for analyzing the components of
value added but less so for keeping the labour process in focus.

35 This is certainly the practice in the West London district of Southall, which houses a
large population from the Indian subcontinent and one of whose major industries is
the preparation of curries and other Indian foods for British supermarket chains. See
Ursula Huws, *Changes in the West London Economy*, London: West London Training
and Enterprise Council, 1992.

36 The excellent bi-monthly *GenEthics News: Genetic Engineering, Ethics and the Environment,* chronicles new instances of this in every issue.

37 This is documented in the National Union of Journalists' monthly magazine, *The Journalist.*

38 Danny Quah, 'As Productive as a French Farmer', *Asian Wall Street Journal,* September 29th, 1997.

39 Henry Neuburger, 'Thoughts on the Productivity Paradox', unpublished paper, undated, p. 1. Arguing that measurement of total factor productivity is circular, he selected labour productivity as providing a more robust indicator.

40 Henry Neuburger, loc. cit., p. 9.

41 Jeff Madrick, 'Computers: Waiting for the Revolution' *The New York Review of Books,* March 26th, 1998.

42 Sue Himmelweit, discussion of ONS Households satellite accounts, Royal Statistical Society, November, 1997, quoted in Henry Neuburger, 'Thoughts on the Productivity Paradox', loc. cit.

43 Iulie Askalen, Olav Bjerkholt, Charlotte Koren and Stig-Olof Olsson, 'Care work in household and market: Productivity, economic growth and welfare', paper submitted to the IAFFE-sponsored session at the ASSA meeting, Chicago, 3-5 January, 1998. I am indebted to Sue Himmelweit for bringing this important research to my attention. Henry Neuburger has partially tested this hypothesis in the UK by modelling – in the form of household satellite accounts – two areas of activity, childcare and catering, using both input and output measures. He concluded that 'conventional GDP by omitting unpaid child care understated growth in the 1960s and overstated it in the 1970s'. See Henry Neuburger, 'Modifying GDP', unpublished paper, undated, p. 2. For an interesting discussion of the development of satellite accounts and social accounting matrices, see Neuburger, 'Measuring Economic Activity', unpublished paper, undated. The evidence is clearly complex and contradictory, but such studies do point up the incomplete picture gained from the conventional accounting procedures.

44 I have discussed this literature at some length in Ursula Huws, *Teleworking: an Overview of the Research,* Joint publication of the Department of Transport, Department of Trade and Industry, Department of the Environment, Department for Education and Employment and Employment Service, London, July, 1996; and Ursula Huws 'Beyond Anecdotes: On Quantifying the Globalization of Information Processing Work', United Nations University Institute for New Technologies Conference on *Globalised Information Society: Employment Implications,* Maastricht, October 17-19, 1996.

45 Paul Hirst and Grahame Thompson, *Globalization in Question,* Oxford: Polity Press, 1996, p. 27.

46 I have discussed this problem in 'Beyond Anecdotes: on Quantifying the Globalization of Information Processing Work', in *Globalised Information Society: Employment Implications,* United Nations University Institute for New Technologies Conference, Maastricht, October 17-19, 1996.

47 I am currently engaged, along with the United Nations University Institute of Technology, in the design and implementation of a study which will, for the first time, provide reliable empirical evidence of the extent of teleworking and teletrade in services in Malaysia, with a sister study in Bombay.

48. Luc Soete and Karin Kamp, *The "BIT TAX": the case for further research,* MERIT, University of Maastricht, 12 August, 1996.

49 Richard I. Cook, MD, Cognitive Technologies Lab., Department of Anaesthesia and Critical Care, University of Chicago, quoted in RISKS-FORUM Digest 19.75, forwarded by Red Rock Eater News Service (pagre@weber.ucsd.edu), May, 1998.

50 Mike Holderness, 'The Internet: enabling whom?, when? and where?', *The Information Revolution and Economic and Social Exclusion in the Developing Countries,* UNU/INTECH Workshop, Maastricht, October 23-25, 1996.

51 I have summarized these, and other related factors, in a number of publications including, Ursula Huws, *Follow-Up to the White Paper – Teleworking,* European Commission Directorate General V, September, 1994, also published as *Social Europe, Supplement 3,* European Commission DGV, 1995; Ursula Huws, *Teleworking: an Overview of the Research,* Joint publication of the Department of Transport, Department of Trade and Industry, Department of the Environment, Department for Education and Employment and Employment Service, July, 1996; and Ursula Huws, 'Telework: projections', in *Futures,* January, 1991.

52 Ursula Huws, Sheila Honey and Stephen Morris, *Teleworking and Rural Development,* Swindon: Rural Development Commission, 1996.

THE NATURE AND CONTRADICTIONS OF NEOLIBERALISM

Gérard Duménil and Dominique Lévy

A sudden change in the rules governing the functioning of capitalism occurred at the end of the 1970s. This change can only be understood in relation to the deterioration in the economic performance of the major capitalist countries during the 1970s, and the failure of the initial set of policies which had been adopted in order to stem the deterioration. The slowdown in the growth of labour productivity, lower accumulation and growth rates, rising unemployment, inflation, and the increased macro-instability (booms and recessions) marked the contours of what can retrospectively be called *the structural crisis of the 1970s and 1980s*. The Keynesian policies which had contributed to the prosperity of the 1960s were tried again at first, but accelerating inflation undermined them. At the same time, the growing difficulties of the so-called socialist countries freed the ruling classes of capitalist countries from a fundamental political concern. These developments created the conditions for a sharp reversal of policies which occurred at the end of the 1970s. A prominent element in this transformation was the change in monetary policy in 1979, the dramatic rise of interest rates in the last year of the Carter Administration, that we denote as *the 1979 coup*. Rapidly, with the election of Margaret Thatcher in the United Kingdom and Ronald Reagan in the USA, the overall political import of the new course became clear: repression of workers' claims for better living standards and working conditions, an attack

This essay was first published in *A World of Contradictions, The Socialist Register 2002*.

on the welfare state, acceptance of unemployment, deregulation (especially of financial activities), etc. More than 'policies' in the narrow sense of the term were at issue. This new framework of rules to which the functioning of capitalism was subjected, is now known as neoliberalism, a return to liberalism in a new configuration.

After twenty years of neoliberalism, how should its performance be assessed? The costs of neoliberalism in terms of unemployment were huge. Initially, it prolonged the effects of the structural crisis. In the USA the unemployment rate peaked in the mid-1980s; in Europe an even more lasting wave of unemployment developed. The Third World was devastated by the debt crisis; monetary and financial institutions were shaken even in the USA; large monetary and financial crises signalled a new financial instability in the world economy. Speculation grew in the stock markets of large capitalist countries, adding to the threat of financial collapse. But today, inflation is down. The unemployment rate declined gradually in the USA, until it returned to the levels of the 1960s, and over the last few years a similar decrease has been under way in Europe. Despite the threat of recession, by the turn of the century growth was an object of pride in the USA and the envy of other countries. The speculative bubble was shrinking and the threat of a major collapse had so far not materialized.

In the overall assessment of neoliberalism, much complexity is created by the differences between the performance of various countries – notably the USA, Europe, Japan, and the periphery. Why was unemployment more severe in Europe than in the USA? In the growth of the US economy during the second half of the 1990s, what is most significant: the virtues of neoliberalism, or US hegemony? Or to frame the question differently: can the 'performance' of the USA be generalized to a broader set of countries?

This essay concerns neoliberalism, neoliberalism under US hegemony: its place in the history of capitalism, the social significance of the new rules that it imposes, its social costs and associated risks, its *future*. We have already discussed elsewhere the costs and benefits of neoliberalism.[1] Its resilience is certainly the most difficult issue to tackle. Can we detect within neoliberalism *internal contradictions* that cast doubt on its ability to survive, both economically and politically? In other words, what is the nature of the new order of capitalism: a mere transition made possible by the crisis and the defeat of the labour movement, or a new era? These questions raise the issue of the interpretation of Keynesianism. Were the Keynesian years an exception following the Great Depression, or did they suggest the possible contours of another capitalism, or even a first step of capitalism beyond its own rules? Thus the definitions of capitalism, of Keynesianism and of neoliberalism are all at stake in this discussion.

This essay should, then, be understood as a contribution to a broad, very ambitious, debate. It addresses two types of issues. The first section is devoted to explaining the dynamics of capitalism, its periodization, and the interpretation of neoliberalism. The perspective is that of the Marxist analysis of history, what used to be called historical materialism (relations of production and productive forces, classes and class struggle, and the state), and Marx's economic analysis in *Capital* (historical tendencies, crises, money and finance, etc.). The periodization of capitalism underlying this investigation combines three levels of analysis: (1) the transformation of the relations of production (the ownership and control of the means of production); (2) the historical tendencies of technology and distribution (notably trends in the profit rate); (3) the succession of specific power configurations (the domination of various fractions of the ruling classes and their compromises with other classes). We broadly characterize neoliberalism as a specific power configuration, the reassertion of the power of capitalist owners, after years of controls on finance: a new discipline imposed on all other classes (on managerial and clerical personnel as well as productive workers), and an attempt, or set of attempts, to implement a new social compromise.

The second section discusses various fields in which the long-run sustainability of the neoliberal order may be questioned, depending on neoliberalism's ability to: (1) establish a new social compromise in an environment of rising inequality (associating broader social strata to the growing prosperity of the few, really or fictitiously); (2) ensure the stability of the economy (avoiding various forms of crisis: recession, and monetary and financial crises); (3) ensure significant accumulation and growth. In the last of these is implied the ability to finance sufficient accumulation, in a system where profits are largely distributed to rich households (*via* interests payments and dividends) and, to date, are not ploughed back into non-financial corporations; to spread the benefits of the new social order outside of the USA, at least minimally (to prove that these benefits are not exclusively the result of the USA's global hegemony); and to maintain a steady growth rate (beyond the gradual deflation or bursting of the 1990s financial bubble). The long-run sustainability of the neoliberal order also depends (4) on prolonging the more favourable trends of technical change that have been apparent since the mid-1980s.

A concluding section briefly outlines the possible future of neoliberalism: the more or less likely forms of its perpetuation and possible alternatives – conditions which might lead to its gradual or sudden disappearance; and the compatibility of neoliberalism with the continuing transformation of the relations of production.

Despite its broad perspective, the paper should not be understood as a *thorough* critique of capitalism. Its scope is still limited. We do not relate the pursuit of growth and technical change to the preservation of the planet, or rule by the owners of capital to the misery of many countries of the periphery, to gender and race exploitation, or to the gradual assertion and diffusion of ways of life and ideologies along lines which will be extremely difficult to reverse.

I A HISTORICAL PERSPECTIVE[2]

1.1 A Marxist framework of analysis

At the centre of Marx's and Engels' interpretation of history in the *Communist Manifesto* are the fundamental dialectics of productive forces and relations of production. Relations of production may stimulate or inhibit the development of the productive forces, and the development of the productive forces creates the conditions for the transformation of the relations of production. This framework is applied twice: first to the transition between feudalism and capitalism, and then to the development of capitalism itself (heralding the transition to socialism).

Each configuration of relations of production corresponds to a specific class pattern. This is obviously true in the comparison between feudalism and capitalism, but also holds during the various phases of a given mode of production. For example, the rise of the banking system and, more generally, of financial capital, is reflected in the maturation of a specific fraction of the ruling classes.

This division of the ruling classes into various fractions is particularly clear in *The 18th Brumaire*. There, Marx distinguishes between *landowners, the aristocracy of finance*, and *large industrialists*. Together, they govern under various *regimes*, which we call *power configurations*: the Restoration, the Monarchy of July, the Republic, or the Empire. They can rule jointly (as in the Republic or Empire) and possess a larger (as in the Republic) or narrower (as in the Empire) degree of freedom to openly express their internal contradictions. The hegemony of one specific group can be more (as in the Restoration and Monarchy of July) or less clear. More generally, because of the always gradual character of the transitions between various modes of production (such as between feudalism and capitalism), the ruling classes of successive modes of production may coexist (as they did under the Old Regime). In such configurations, the nature of the various groups is always evolving and hybrid forms may exist.

In these historical dynamics *class struggle* is crucial. In the broad sense of the term, it includes both the opposition between ruling classes and dominated classes, and the tensions between the various fractions of the ruling classes. The state is the organized expression of the power configurations, the locus of their formation and preservation, and the instrument of coercion that goes with this power.

Concerning the economics of capitalism, Marx developed in *Capital* the thesis that under capitalism technical and distributional changes tend to follow specific patterns of evolution, which we call *trajectories à la Marx*. These trajectories combine: (1) the growth of output, capital, and employment; (2) the rise of labour productivity, the real wage, the capital-labour ratio (various *compositions of capital*), and the decline of the profit rate. These tendencies express the difficulty of sustaining the growth of labour productivity without resorting to increased amounts of capital investment (what we call the *difficulty of innovation*). The decline of the profit rate creates the conditions for large crises: recessions, unemployment, speculation, etc.[3]

This economic framework of analysis is closely related to the above historical framework. Although Marx had not developed these tools when he wrote the *Communist Manifesto* with Engels, it is the existence of these historical tendencies which accounts for the recurrent structural crises and business–cycle fluctuations characteristic of capitalism. In various respects, Marx's *Capital* makes explicit the basic insights of the *Manifesto*, and its assessment of capitalism's catastrophic future.

1.2 The dynamics of capitalism

1.2.1 The ownership of the means of production, management, and modern finance

Central to capitalist relations of production is the *private ownership of the means of production*. This includes simultaneously: (1) ownership in the narrow sense of the term – the power to purchase and sell means of production, including labour power, and (2) the right and the ability to manage them. This fundamental relationship was profoundly altered at the end of the nineteenth century. The main development, whose early forms had already been analyzed by Marx, was the separation between ownership and management (the two above components), and the concentration of ownership within financial institutions. These transformations cannot be separated from the emergence of modern finance.

These transformations of capitalist ownership reached new heights in the USA in the wake of the structural crisis of the 1890s. The crisis followed a period of decline in the profit rate. It degenerated into a crisis of competition, with enterprises attempting to stem the collapse of their profit rate by various forms of horizontal alliances. This was the period of cartels and trusts. Antitrust legislation forbade any form of agreement in which firms were preserved as independent entities sharing, for example, markets or profits. Simultaneously, company law was enacted allowing mergers and the formation of holding companies. A huge merger wave followed at the turn of the century, known in the USA as the *corporate revolution*.

Within corporations, management was delegated to large pyramidal structures of managerial and clerical personnel. They undertook what Marx used to call the *functions of the functioning capitalist* – i.e., in contemporary terminology, *management* in a rather broad sense of the term (actually, all unproductive labour). These functions are those required in order to maximize the profit rate. This second transformation is known as the *managerial revolution*.

Large corporations were formed under the control of finance, whose modern configuration – consisting of financial institutions tightly linked to non-financial corporations – was simultaneously emerging.[4] It was accompanied by a dramatic development of financial mechanisms, a huge wave of 'financial innovation'. Paralleling the rise of credit mechanisms, and beyond the mere financing of transactions, the amount of money increased tremendously, especially in bank accounts.[5] Although the term is not used, one could call this a *financial revolution*.

This new configuration of twentieth century capitalism represented a considerable transformation of capitalist relations of production, a new aspect of what Marx had called the *socialization* of production (in contrast to production relations adequately embodied in individuals, such as the individual owner-manager). This social trait of capitalism was constantly reinforced during the twentieth century. Under neoliberalism it reached new heights with the development of huge financial institutions, such as mutual and pensions funds, and the transfer of still more capitalist tasks to salaried personnel. The managerial revolution has now reached the core of the capitalist system – i.e., finance.

1.2.2 Accumulation, the purchase of labour power, and the macro-economy

In addition to ownership (in the juridical sense of the term) and management, there are also 'macro-economic' components to the capitalist exercise of the private ownership of the means of production. Two major aspects must be identified. (1) In a capitalist economy, capital accumulation may require savings from profits, but capital can also be 'created' by the banking system, *via* credit mechanisms and the issue of money. The total amount of this creation is crucial, since inflation may result from excess credit, and capital in the form of securities and cash may be devalued.[6] More generally, independent of its destination, accumulation or consumption, excess credit poses a threat to previously accumulated capital, both by inflation and by the possible destabilization of financial institutions. (2) In controlling the valorization process of capital (a component of management), the purchase of labour power is of particular importance. As analyzed by Marx, the *periodic replenishment of the reserve army of labour* plays a central role in the determination of the cost of labour, and hence of profits, periodically imposing strong pressures on wages, pressures which tend to compensate for the rise of wages during periods of overheating (*overaccumulation*).

Capitalism gradually developed centralized institutions and mechanisms charged with the control of the macro-economy, with major consequences for the issuing of money, the level of activity, and employment. As in the case of the juridical forms of ownership and management, *centralized* macro-economic policies actually modified the exercise of the private ownership of the means of production, in the direction of an increased *socialization*. The emergence of such mechanisms actually raises the issue of their *aims*. In whose interests do they work?

In the late nineteenth century, this control was ensured by large private financial institutions (in the USA, mostly large New York banks in the *National Banking System*). The main concern was the stability of the purchasing power of money in terms of gold, and the stability of the financial system.[7] The stabilization of the macro-economy gradually became an objective *per se*. The shock of the Great Depression and World War II inaugurated the era of Keynesianism with the involvement of the state (the central bank) and new aims. The capitalist class saw this as an encroachment on its power, since these aims included full employment and affected price stability (the preservation of accumulated capital). The recognition of the right to work and the establishment of the welfare state after World War II considerably modified the wage relation, as labour power was gradually treated less and less as an ordinary commodity. Under neoliberalism, however, the earlier objectives of finance were restored, with a renewed contempt for the problem of unemployment and an overriding concern for price stability. There has been and there will be no reversal of this 'macro-economic' component of the private ownership of the means of production; only the specific macro-economic targets set within it are at issue.

1.2.3 Maximizing the profit rate

The profit rate is a key variable in the functioning of capitalism and the mechanisms involved undergo significant transformations. The *maximizing of the profit rate* performs, in its own way, a number of necessary economic tasks. It determines the efficient use of inputs and resources; it guides the selection of the most efficient techniques and the choice between various fields of investment (among firms and industries). It also drives the efforts made by individual firms to stimulate demand.

There is an important political component embedded in the undertaking of these functions. In particular, the first function (economizing in the use of resources) implies: (1) the forms and degrees of the pressure exercised on workers, given their resistance and the existing set of regulations; and (2) a similar impact on the environment, on the rules regulating its preservation (given the resistance of various fractions of the population). There is obviously an international aspect to this search for profits too, which accounts for the *imperialist* features of the leading capitalist countries (their rivalry and their domination over the periphery).

The maximizing of the profit rate is an expression of the capitalist nature of the relations of production, but this capitalist feature also depends on: (1) the contours of various fields partially insulated from the profitability criterion (e.g. defence, education, health, research); (2) the private appropriation of the surplus as the income of a class of owners; (3) the concentration of wealth among the few; (4) the effects of regulations and policies (as particular components of the general functions of the state), macro-economic policies, taxation (the taxation of firms and upper income brackets), etc.

1.2.4 Classes and power configurations

The transformation of relations of production described in the previous three sections is connected to the parallel evolution of class patterns.

The managerial revolution resulted in the rise of the so-called *new intermediary classes* of managerial and clerical personnel, distinct from the traditional petty bourgeoisie. The transfer of the capitalist functions to salaried workers was, however, realized in a highly 'polarized' fashion, with the concentration of conception, initiative, and authority at the top of the hierarchy (managerial personnel), and execution of tasks at the bottom (clerical personnel). *This polarization represents a new class relation.* This opposition is distinct from the separation of the capitalist owner from the productive worker in Marx's analytical framework in *Capital*. The position of the productive worker vis-à-vis the means of production was also modified. As the delegation of capitalist functions progressed, the control of the productive worker over the labour process was further diminished.

The complexity of the contemporary class pattern of capitalism is an expression of the coexistence of these fundamental class contradictions: (1) between capitalists and productive workers – the traditional capitalist relation; (2) between managers and all categories of 'managed' workers, productive and unproductive – a new class contradiction.[8]

Thus, two fractions of the ruling classes coexist (cooperate but also fight, to various degrees). At the top of the social hierarchy are capitalist owners and managers, just like the aristocracy and bourgeoisie in the Old Regime described by Marx.

The power of the ruling classes is usually tempered by compromises. Two aspects can be distinguished within such compromises. One concerns the content and extension of cooperation among the fractions of the ruling classes, such as management and capitalists, within various state or parastatal institutions. There is an *interface* between these classes, the world of boards of directors where owners still engaged in some form of management collaborate with top managers, who are also owners to a certain extent. This interface is crucial to the preservation of a type of capitalism where ownership and management are basically separated. The other aspect concerns compromise with broader fractions of the population. At issue are the participation of larger sections of salaried workers in prosperity, when it exists, and the stringency of the discipline recurrently imposed on these groups, etc.

As recalled in section 1.1, the state is the locus of the formation and preservation of power configurations. This is true of the cooperation between the fractions of the ruling classes, as well as of the compromise with broader segments of the population.

The degrees of *hegemony* and *compromise* exercised by capitalist owners are of primary importance in the definition of power configurations. Since the beginning of the twentieth century, with the emergence of modern finance and the delegation of management to salaried personnel, the hegemony of capitalist owners can be described as that of *finance*, meaning by this, financial institutions and individuals holding large portfolios of financial securities.[9] This hegemony is always tempered by the alliance with top management, but during such a hegemony the rules of the owners are basically endorsed by top management. Schematically, two such periods of hegemony have existed, one at the beginning of the century and another since the 1980s. They were separated by the *Keynesian compromise*, in which finance was 'repressed' to a certain extent, and in which top management, in its private and public components, was 'reunited' to some extent with the other fractions of management. Keynesianism limited the prerogatives of finance concerning what we called above the 'macro-economic' facet of capitalist ownership; it encouraged sectional behaviour by managers and established a rather broad compromise among wage-earners; it extended the field of activities freed from the necessity to maximize the profit rate (i.e. 'the market').[10]

Actually, the emergence and stabilization of neoliberalism would have been impossible without the convergence of top management and capitalist owners, a modification in the content of the compromise characteristic of the interface. The *right turn* of the 1980s, analyzed by Thomas Ferguson and Joel Rogers,[11] and the consolidation of neoliberalism, cannot be reduced to the rise of the reactionary forces which originally backed Ronald Reagan. President Reagan simply adjusted his policies in line with other business groups.

1.2.5 *Historical tendencies and crises*

A central component of Marx's analysis in Volume III of *Capital* is the description of the patterns of evolution which in section 1.1 we called *trajectories à la Marx*, whose central feature is a declining profit rate. Such declines lead to structural crises. In our opinion, this framework of analysis is still very relevant to the study of capitalism, with the proviso that structural crises failed to cause the collapse of capitalism but instead stimulated its transformation, making possible fresh upswings in the profit rate.[12]

As shown in Figure 1, the succession of various phases in the USA since the Civil War is particularly evident in the profile of the *productivity of capital*. The dotted line represents the trend characteristic of the average technology, abstracting from the effects of the business cycle. The fluctuations around this

Figure 1: Secular trends of capital productivity (dollars of product per dollar of fixed capital): USA (private economy)

trend mirror the movements of the average level of activity. Note the fall into the Great Depression, and the levels reached during World War II. Unless otherwise specified, the series in the figures are the results of authors' computations on the basis of national accounting frameworks.[13] A first phase of decline is apparent in the late nineteenth century leading to the structural crisis of the 1890s; a gradual recovery is observed, evident from the 1920s; the Great Depression apparently interrupted this movement as a result of the sharp and lasting contraction of the activity, but actually accelerated the elimination of the backward fractions of the productive system; a second period *à la Marx* is observed during the second half of the 1960s, 1970s, and early 1980s; the trough was attained during the great recession of 1982; eventually there is a new trend upward.

These movements are related to the transformations in the relations of production described earlier. We interpret the upswing in the first half of the century as an effect of the *managerial revolution*, which resulted in increased efficiency in the use of capital (in all components of activity: within the workshop, with Taylorism and the assembly line, but also in commercial activities, and in inventory and liquidity management). In our opinion, a new revolution in management is presently under way, whose effects have become apparent since the mid-1980s. The 'marginal efficiency' of managerial innovation was probably declining, because of its costs. The new revolution can be described as a revolution within management itself. Information technology allows for gradual improvements in efficiency and diminishing costs, but it is clear that other organizational elements are also involved. More and more sophisticated management must avoid any bureaucratic bias.

1.2.6 *Imperialism and US hegemony*

In our opinion, *imperialism* has been, to various degrees and under various forms, a permanent feature of capitalism. A chronology of its successive stages should be established. Since the 1960s and 1970s, and the dissolution of the colonial empires, it survives in the collective dominance of the major capitalist countries. Among these countries, one is dominant: the United States. The notion of *US hegemony*, as we use it, refers to this configuration: the imperial collective domination of the major capitalist countries of the centre over the periphery under US leadership.

1.2.7 *Periodizing capitalism in the twentieth century*

A basic problem in the periodization of capitalism is the existence of various competing criteria.[14] The transformations of relations of production (with their multiple elements), class patterns, power configurations, technical trends and crises, as well as stages of imperialism, all are potential alternative criteria.

These alternative criteria are linked in many respects, but they also possess a significant degree of autonomy concerning both the mechanisms involved and the timing. For example, the transformations in macro-policies and the establishment of the Keynesian compromise, following the Great Depression and World War II, occurred during a period of continuing favourable trends in technology and distribution (see above, section 1.2.5); the depression resulted in part from the rapidity of technical change, but also from the slow adjustment of macro-policies and institutions. The various criteria delineate different periods, and their combination easily degenerates into the multiplication of sub-periods. Structural crises and wars are convenient markers.

1.3 *Neoliberalism and the new capitalism*

How can neoliberalism be interpreted in the context of capitalist transformation?

Before entering into a more technical analysis, the following general comments may be made concerning the nature and content of neoliberalism.[15] (1) Concerning the relations of production, neoliberalism cannot be analyzed as a movement away from the overall process of socialization and the delegation of management to salaried personnel. It actually accelerated this transformation in some respects, while blocking it in others. What is at issue is only the modification of earlier trends. First, as in the first period of the hegemony of finance, in the early twentieth century, neoliberalism strengthened the separation between ownership and management. It accelerated the development of large non-financial corporations managed by business staffs; salaried management grew within financial institutions (like mutual and pension funds). The new pro-merger attitude of the government helped this development. Second, the behavioural 'bias' of managers and public officials is important here. This is what is key in the new pro-finance model of corporate governance, regulations, and policies: moving away from managerial autonomy within corporations, and away from the Keynesian compromise and the state. Neoliberalism meant the unambiguous reassertion of the maximization of the profit rate in every dimension of activity (see above, section 1.2.1). (2) In spite of the rise of managerial and clerical personnel engaged in financial activity, neoliberalism cannot be defined in terms of specific class patterns. This general observation must, however, be qualified in some respects. An important point is that there will be no 'euthanasia of the rentier' (if such a process was ever underway). In addition, reliance on extreme social inequality may prolong or extend the most acute forms of exploitation for a fraction of productive workers, and simultaneously enlarge the proportion of personnel engaged in personal services. Neoliberalism reinforces the tendency of capitalism to keep the lower strata of wage workers where they are, rather than advance them into the upper strata. (3) Unemployment will be used, as was traditional in capitalism, as a lever to control labour costs and to discipline wage workers. The stability of prices will ensure the preservation of the wealth of the holders of monetary and financial assets. Neoliberalism is thus a form of 'aggressive' capitalism. (4) The new more favourable patterns of technical change of recent decades, if maintained, might open a new path for capitalism. These trends became apparent under neoliberalism but they are not intrinsically characteristic of it. They are, to a large extent, managerial achievements. Their sustainability is an issue. Moreover, neoliberal or not, the capitalism of the future is not immune to new trajectories *à la Marx* and the accompanying structural crises. This point is politically important because of the way propaganda tends to classify all 'favourable' aspects of contemporary capitalism as features of neoliberalism. (This underlines the importance of a careful approach to periodization.)

Two definitions of neoliberalism can, then, be given. (1) In a narrow sense, the term *neoliberalism* can be used to designate a course of events, a set of 'policies', that occurred during the 1980s and 1990s, with the potential to lead to a new phase of development. It can be interpreted *as an attempt, in the 1980s, by a class of capitalist owners, to restore, in alliance with top management, its power and income after a setback of several decades.* Some of the features recalled above are analogous to nineteenth century capitalism, but it goes without saying that the notion of restoration does not imply that the new course of capitalism is identical to any events experienced in the past. (2) In a broader sense, the term *neoliberalism* can be used to designate a new capitalism, with certain characteristics of sustainability: *the historical outcome of the restoration of the power and income of a class of capitalist owners in the context of advanced managerial capitalism.*

The difference between the two patterns could be significant. It could even be so large that the term *neoliberalism* comes to appear inappropriate to designate longer-term developments.

II CONTRADICTIONS?

Do any of the traits of the last twenty years put in question the sustainability of neoliberal capitalism? Can we detect any internal contradictions? In this second section, we basically consider the US economy, which we compare with the average of three European countries (France, Germany, and the United Kingdom),[16] and with France alone.[17] (Japan should obviously be considered in a more extensive study.)

2.1 *Ruling and compromising*

2.1.1 *The wealth of the wealthiest*

Rising inequality has often been described as a characteristic of neoliberalism. There is obviously an international component to this feature, and the gap between the most advanced countries and the poorer countries of the periphery is well known.[18]

Even at the centre of the capitalist world economy, the lower fractions of the population were injured by neoliberalism. Unemployment reached double-digit levels, briefly in the USA after the change in monetary policy, and remained close to such levels in Europe for fifteen years. Simultaneously, the wealthiest fraction significantly improved its income and wealth.

There is a specifically *financial* aspect to these flows of income and wealth

Figure 2: Share of total wealth held by the top 1% of wealth holders (%): USA, households

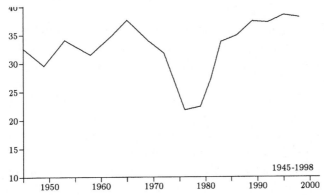

Wealth includes real estate (housing), securities and cash, and consumer durables.
Source: the data are from E. Wolff, *Top Heavy*, The New Press: New York, 1996, supplemented by more recent estimates.

toward the richest. It is clearly apparent in the large amounts of interest and dividends paid by non-financial enterprises, one set of households and the state, to financial institutions and, basically, another set of households. The dramatic rise of the stock market from the mid–1980s added to this increasingly unequal distribution of wealth.[19] The astounding 'compensation' of top managers has also been frequently emphasized.

This rise in the income and wealth of the wealthiest part of the US population followed a period of real setback and can to some extent be described as a recovery. During the first phase of the structural crisis of the 1970s low profits, low distributions of dividends and low interest rates, combined with large inflation rates, had considerably reduced the income of the ruling classes. As shown in Figure 2, the fraction of the total wealth in the USA, held by the richest 1% among households, fluctuated between 30 and 35% during the first decades after World War II. This percentage declined to 22% in 1976. Neoliberalism reversed this.

These observations illustrate a few aspects of the notion of 'aggressive capitalism' introduced earlier. Confronting the decline of their income and wealth, the ruling classes politically modified the course of capitalism. From the mid-1980s onwards they were able to impose tight controls on the growth of wage costs and to enlarge, to an astonishing extent, their own 'siphoning off' of profits. They restored their position dramatically, even *prior to* the appearance of the new upward trend in the profit rate.

One may question the sustainability of this course of development in the long run. In the first place, the stagnation of wages (manifested in the increasing share of profits despite the slow growth of labour productivity) has played an important role in the recent recovery of the profit rate, and the growth of the cost of workers' benefits has been gradually reduced. Two basic trade-offs are involved, between: (1) wage costs and profits; and (2) income transfers favourable to finance and accumulation.

Secondly, the struggle of wage-earners for better working conditions and living standards suffered a double blow: its defeat during the structural crisis and the assertion of neoliberalism; and the collapse of any alternative to capitalism in the 'socialist' countries (actually a long history of gradual disillusionment), and the failure of all social-democratic or Keynesian reformist ways out. The discouraging consequences of these setbacks will not last for ever. Unless the present techno-logical advance is prolonged, creating durable conditions for a relaxation of these trade-offs, it will become more and more difficult to repress labour.

In order to preserve their privileges, the ruling classes have two options: either the establishment of a new social compromise of their own (to align larger segments of the population with the prosperity of the wealthiest), or a shift towards a more and more authoritarian regime.[20]

2.1.2 'All capitalists'

Neoliberalism broke the solidarity of wage-earners and destroyed the compro-mise which had set limits to the power of finance, which had characterized the Keynesian years. The leading social role in the old power configuration had been played by managerial personnel (managers, engineers, professionals) within both private corporations and state and parastatal administration. The arrangement affected wage-earners in general *via* the commitment to full-employment, larger access to education, and the welfare state in general. In spite of the controls over finance, the relationship with finance was also one of compromise. The primary limitation to the earlier pre-eminence of finance concerned the control of credit, by regulations and new monetary policy targets (see above, section 1.2.2), while other aspects of financial activity (notably the allocation of capital) were less affected, notwithstanding the limits placed on horizontal mergers and restrictions on the financial activities of the commercial banks, and on international move-ments of capital. This raises the question of what new compromise might be substituted for that which prevailed during the Keynesian years.

It is easy to understand that crucial to the neoliberal program of restoring the power and income of capitalist owners within advanced managerial capitalism is their relationship with management. A key element is *top management*, beginning with what we call the *interface* between ownership and management. As already mentioned, the reliance on top management has been a prominent feature of neoliberalism from its inception, and it was strongly associated with the new flow of income toward finance. This feature is so congenial to neoliberalism that it can hardly even be described as a social compromise. Such a 'compromise' would, in any event, belong to the first category outlined above in section 1.2.4: coopera-tion between the various fractions of the ruling classes.

But the establishment of a broader compromise, including the middle classes,

Figure 3: FDIC-insured commercial banks (–) and savings and loans institutions (---) that were closed or received FDIC assistance: USA

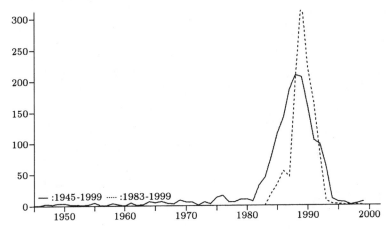

FDIC: Federal Deposit Insurance Corporation

is crucial to the survival of neoliberalism. The slogan is 'everyone is a capitalist'. Its main practical components are: (1) the distribution of shares to wage-earners, as a supplement to their wages; (2) stock options; and (3) pension funds. The effectiveness of these devices is increased by tax incentives. Institutions such as pension and mutual funds, which developed before neoliberalism, expanded to unprecedented levels and will remain a central element in the neoliberal edifice, associating the upper half of households with the fate of capital. In the establishment of this compromise, the dramatic rise of the stock market from the mid-1980s onwards acted like a bonanza. The middle classes who had some financial assets actually subscribed to the view that the most lax capitalist rules increased their living standards, and that class barriers could be gradually overcome. This favourable period is over.

2.2 (De)Stabilizing the economy

The purpose of this section is to discuss the (in)stability of capitalism dominated by neoliberalism. Is neoliberalism a system especially prone to monetary and financial crises? Does such a propensity put its survival in question? In this discussion, we will distinguish between domestic and international issues.

2.2.1 Domestic issues: financial crisis and macro-stability

In the USA the rise of neoliberalism created a significant financial crisis during the 1980s. It is not the purpose of the present study to recount the development and various phases of this crisis.[21] The amplitude of the event is illustrated in Figure 3, which shows the number of banks and savings associations which failed or were rescued. The figures speak for themselves. The crisis resulted from the sharp rise of real interest rates in the early 1980s, deregulation, and defaults. The

Figure 4: Yearly growth rate of output for each quarter (%): USA

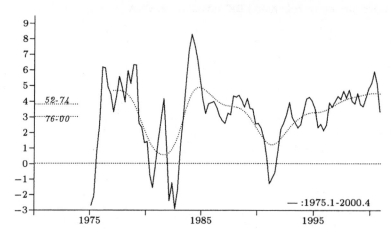

The variable depicted is the growth rate of each quarter in comparison to the same quarter one year earlier. The dotted line is a trend line abstracting from shorter-term fluctuations. The short horizontal segments describe the average growth rates for the two periods 1952-74 and 1976-2000.

feedback effect on American banks of the crisis of the debt of the so-called *Less Developed Countries* was considerable. Most other advanced capitalist countries were also affected to various degrees. This financial crisis was an expression of the deepening of the structural crisis and the implementation of neoliberalism, and can be interpreted as a transitional phenomenon. A primary lesson is that after the early reluctance to act by the Reagan administration, which claimed that the 'market' would take care of the situation, the US government and monetary policy did much to stop the problems of the financial system spreading to the real economy.

This sharp disturbance of the working of financial institutions at the centre must be contrasted with the relative stability of the macro-economy (a rather stable rate of growth) from the mid-1980s onwards. Figure 4 depicts the yearly growth rate of output for each quarter since 1975 in the USA. One can see in this figure the negative growth rates of output in the recessions of 1980 and 1982, and the peak in 1983, which coincided with the emergence of neoliberalism. But growth was markedly stable during the rest of the period, with the exception of the 1993 recession. Thus, beyond the initial period of dramatic disturbance (the transition years), neoliberalism can claim to have made a contribution to macro-economic stability. Despite the decline which began in 2000, this is an object of pride in the USA.[22]

The analysis of these developments refers to basic macro-economic mechanisms. The crucial issue, in these respects, is one of stability (see box opposite).

It is important to keep in mind that, despite the abandonment of some of the rules established after the Great Depression, the transformation of the institutional framework in the early 1980s *strengthened* the power of the central bank. As indicated in its name, there were two facets to the US *Deregulation and Monetary Control Act* of 1980. New prerogatives were given to the central bank, which were required by the need to exercise strong pressure on the economy, targeted at the elimination of inflation. The commitment to intervention under more dramatic circumstances also remains strong (as shown by the government's reaction to the banking and savings and loans associations crises in the 1980s). *With respect to macro-policy, neoliberalism did not destroy but reinforced the institutions of Keynesianism, except that the targets were changed – price stability rather than full employment.*[23]

Overall, the comparison between the two periods of financial hegemony is telling. There is continuity in the targets: (1) the stability and survival of monetary and financial institutions, and (2) the stability of the general level of prices. The major difference is that during the second, neoliberal, hegemony, the tools of Keynesian macro-economic policy were inherited and effectively used by and for finance.

BUSINESS-CYCLE FLUCTUATIONS
MONETARY AND FINANCIAL (IN)STABILITY

Under 'ordinary' conditions, i.e., in the absence of exceptional shocks and destabilization of monetary and financial institutions, demand levels, in contemporary capitalism, are controlled, during the phases of the business cycle, by monetary policy (in particular, in the USA, by mortgage credit for housing purchases).[24] The stability of the general level of activity shows that these mechanisms are still very powerful, perhaps more efficient than ever. There is little inflation and capacity utilization rates are, in the average, 'normal' (i.e., fluctuating around a figure slightly above 80%). One may say, more technically, that *local stability* is generally ensured.

'Ordinary' conditions are not always present. A sudden and large shock, such as a collapse of the stock market and the accumulation of defaults on bad debts, could *destabilize* the economy, affecting the demand behaviour of households and the supply and demand behaviour of firms. A recession may follow, destabilizing demand and output levels. As was the case in the USA during the 1930s and the early 1980s (during the monetary and financial crisis), and as is presently the case in Japan, such shocks affect the functioning of the banking system, a key driver in the mechanisms of monetary policy. This may render monetary policy inefficient for some time and be manifested in sharp fluctuations upward and downward, or a collapse of activity. In the latter case, a public deficit (borrowings by the government, one channel in the issue of money) is required, though not necessarily sufficient.

2.2.2 *International issues: instability and US hegemony*

The most dramatic crises of neoliberalism were the international monetary and financial crises of the 1980s and 1990s, beginning with the debt crisis of the *Less Developed Countries* in 1982; then the crisis of the Mexican economy in 1994, those of South-East Asia in 1997, of South America and Russia in 1998, and most recently of Turkey in 2000-01. Independently of the rise of real interest rates, the central *financial and monetary* factors of the crises of the 1990s were: (1) the international mobility of capital, which was gradually established as a prominent component of the new neoliberal order; and (2) flexible exchange rates and the strange combination of flexibility and rigidity (the pegging of some currencies to the dollar) prevailing on international currency markets.

The international institutions of Keynesianism, the IMF and the World Bank, also survived the transition to neoliberalism, but, like the central banks of capitalist countries, the targets of their activity were redirected. They became the agents of the diffusion of the neoliberal order throughout the planet, with the additional concern that regional perturbations should not jeopardize stability at the centre.

Already, the Bretton Woods agreements had failed to create a genuine international bank, with its own, independent, currency. A special role had been given in the final agreement to currencies potentially 'as good as gold', i.e., the dollar. When the dominance of the USA was undermined for the first time at the end of the 1960s, the rules established at Bretton Woods began to unravel. The so-called 'crisis of the dollar' did not undo the dollar's pre-eminence.[25] On the contrary, its hegemony was maintained in a new institutional context, that of flexible exchange rates and gradually liberated flows of capital. Indeed the most conspicuous, almost caricatural form, of US hegemony is the gradual dollarization of the world economy.

In spite of this similarity the situation is in important respects different from that prevailing domestically within the major capitalist countries, particularly the USA. Contrary to what occurred domestically, no strong framework has emerged with responsibility for maintaining the international monetary and financial stability of the world economy. Regardless of the class content of the reasons for this, it poses an important threat to international stability. It is a serious contradiction within neoliberalism, linked to the transition away from many of the components of the Bretton Woods agreements (periodically adjustable rates of exchange, limitations on the mobility of capital during periods of crisis, etc.). Its most threatening aspect is the failure to impose a regulatory framework limiting the movement of capital whenever and wherever necessary, and, more generally, to regulate international financial and monetary institutions and mechanisms.

A major reason for this failure to establish an independent set of international institutions was the USA's determination to preserve its hegemony. There are strong similarities between the resistance of private finance in the early twentieth century to the emergence of adequate mechanisms for macro-economic stabilization, and the resistance of the USA both to the establishment of such an international framework after World War II and to the transformation of monetary and financial institutions in the wake of the crisis of the dollar.

2.3 *Accumulating capital*

2.3.1 *Slow accumulation*

The accumulation of capital under neoliberalism is slow, and the transfer of income to finance is threatened by this sluggishness. This is the conclusion which follows from a quantitative analysis of growth rates within the major capitalist countries, and it raises the question of the compatibility between rapid accumulation and the large transfers of income toward financial institutions and rich households that are characteristic of neoliberalism. Note that the contrary view is presently dominant. The neoliberal creed is: (1) the USA is the leading neoliberal country; (2) its economic growth is rapid, faster than in other advanced capitalist countries; therefore (3) neoliberalism means investment (capital accumulation) and growth. In Europe, an additional proposition is: (4) Europe must emulate the USA.

But basic observations contradict this dogma. Figure 5 shows the rate of accumulation in the USA and the average of three European countries since the 1960s. The two curves show a declining trend, and the different patterns of evolution in Europe and in the USA, especially since the mid-1980s. Despite the fluctuation upward in the 1990s in the USA there is no neoliberal miracle guiding accumulation. The rate of accumulation moves cyclically: most likely, the last points in the series for the USA will appear as a peak, and it is not yet possible

Figure 5: Rate of accumulation (%): France, Germany, and United Kingdom (– • –), and the USA (–)

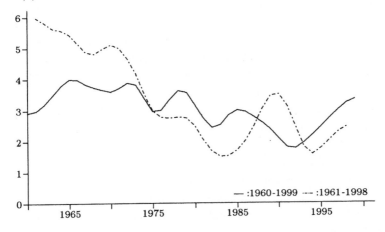

The unit of analysis is the total private economy. The accumulation rate is the growth rate of the fixed capital stock, net of depreciation. The series has been slightly smoothened to abstract from short-term fluctuations.

Figure 6: Rates of net savings (—) and net investment (- - -) (%): USA

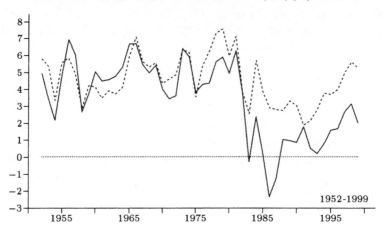

Investment is that of enterprises. In this context, net means after subtracting the depreciation of fixed capital. Savings are the difference between the total net product and all purchases of goods and services (including the purchase of residential capital by households) other than the investment by enterprises. (Capital gains are not counted as a component of income.)

to detect the trend upward which should follow from the rise in the profit rate. Figure 6 shows the rate of net investment in the USA. It shows that investment only recovered to its pre-neoliberal levels in the late 1990s.[26]

It is a common feature of neoliberalism, in both the USA and Europe, that very large fractions of profits are paid in interest and dividends. Consequently, despite the restoration of the profit rate since the mid-1980s, the rate of retained profits (after all payments, including interest and dividends) remains low, as does the accumulation rate (which is tightly linked to the rate of retained profits). This is illustrated in Figure 7, in the case of France. One can note: (1) the strong recovery of the profit rate prior to the payment of interest and dividends, significantly above its levels of the early 1970s; (2) the rising rate of transfer of profits to finance, with the effect that the rate of retained profits remains below the level of the 1970s; (3) the close correlation between the rate of retained profits and the rate of accumulation.[27] A central feature of neoliberalism is that the investment of non-financial corporations is self-financed. In the USA this has been the case since World War II, and continues to be so. In France heavy reliance on borrowing disappeared with neoliberalism. Whatever the complexity of the actual channels, things unfold within neoliberalism as if the profits pumped out of the productive sector of the economy do not return to it. This is a central contradiction of 'actually existing neoliberalism': its inability to promote strong accumulation. This does not deny, however, the role of finance in the allocation of capital among various activities (its propensity to finance promising innova-

Figure 7: Rate of profit before the payment of interest and dividends (–), rate of retained profits (after these payments) (---), and accumulation rate (·····) (%): France, non-financial corporations

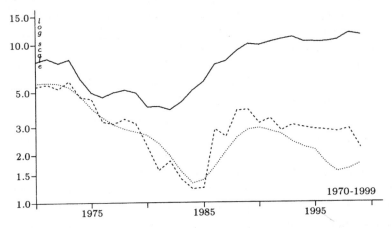

The accumulation rate is the growth rate of the stock of fixed capital, net of depreciation. Profits, in both definitions of the profit rates, are divided by net worth. This figure uses a logarithmic scale on the vertical axis, and the distance between the curves are, thus, proportional to the ratios among the various rates. The burden of interest and dividends payments is measured by the distance between the two series (---) and (–).

tions, possibly beyond what is appropriate).

This feature of neoliberalism is puzzling. It is certainly possible to imagine a configuration of capitalism in which large flows of profits are transferred to capitalist owners, *via* the payment of interest and dividends, and then returned to the non–financial sector in the form of new loans and newly issued shares. But this has not been the case so far. It is rather intuitive that high real interest rates discourage borrowing, but these trends suggest, more surprisingly, that in the relationship between the productive sector and the stock market *maximizing the market price of corporations* has been more important, or at least more successful, than relying on financial markets to finance accumulation. (The repurchase of their own shares by corporations is, of course, negative accumulation.) No other feature of neoliberalism shows so clearly that its ruling classes are parasitic, and the capability of neoliberalism to meet the requirements of accumulation will be crucial in the long run.[28]

2.3.2 *Advanced capitalist countries: Growth under US hegemony*

A basic flaw in the neoliberal creed (see section 2.3.1 above) is the second proposition in the neoliberal mantra: the growth differential between the USA and Europe and Japan. Attributing this to the beneficial effects of neoliberalism overlooks the advantages of the USA's hegemony, in particular the pre-eminence of the dollar, its so–called *seignorage*.[29]

As is well known, US accumulation was not financed, after the beginning of the 1980s, by domestic savings but by foreign savings. As shown in Figure 6, the rate of savings of all agents in the USA dropped suddenly in those years to about zero, exactly at the inception of neoliberalism. No other country could have afforded the external deficits (and the corresponding imports of capital) resulting from the gap between domestic investment and savings.[30]

It is difficult to balance US domestic factors and international determinants in explaining this unusual situation. On average, profit rates do not appear larger in the USA than in Europe,[31] and it is not clear that foreign capital was attracted by larger profitability levels in the USA. Capital flows to the USA seem to be more a consequence of US domestic policy, given the attraction of the privileges attached to hegemony.

One specific domestic feature of the US economy is that credits to households continued to rise throughout the 1990s.[32] This is certainly a crucial factor in the explanation of the very high spending levels (consumption plus purchases of residential capital by households) in the USA, and hence the very low levels of domestic savings. This is where the absence of external constraint and reliance on external deficits is crucial.

Thus neoliberalism, when assessed from the viewpoint of major capitalist countries (without bringing the periphery into the picture), already appears to be a very hierarchical system. The lesson that the USA, as the leading example of neoliberalism, is supposed to teach seems quite dependent on the USA's hegemony. A new balance of power, in favour of Japan and, to a lesser extent, Europe, would fundamentally challenge the alleged virtues of neoliberalism in relation to accumulation and growth. The US example does not demonstrate the ability of neoliberalism to achieve growth, first, because US accumulation is not strong (see section 2.3.1 above) and, second, because much of the USA's superior performance can be imputed to their world hegemony rather than to their comparative advance along the neoliberal route.

2.3.3 *Prosperity and the bubble*

In the analysis of the growth of the economy an important role is often attributed to the stock market rise of the late 1990s, in particular in the USA,[33] and this could be seen as grounds for questioning the ability of neoliberalism to maintain continuously growing levels of demand.[34] If this view were sound it would indeed signal a significant contradiction in the functioning of capitalism under neoliberalism.

The parallel between the last two decades and the beginning of the twentieth century, and the occurrence of the Great Depression, plays an important role here. The 1920s and the last fifteen years of the twentieth century have much in common: (1) new trends in technology and distribution; (2) audacious monetary and financial innovations; (3) a merger wave; and, probably not coincidentally, (4) a sharp rise in stock market indices. Keynesian economists see a connection between demand and stock indices in relation to the Depression, contending that a contraction of demand followed from Wall Street's collapse at the end of 1929.[35] This line of argument implies that activity had been previously stimulated by the rise of the stock market (as a result of a *wealth effect*).[36] The same would presumably be true of the recent prosperity in the USA, at least during the 1990s.

A preliminary difficulty with this interpretation of contemporary spending levels in the USA is that the speculative boom was common to most advanced capitalist countries, with the obvious exception of Japan, and was not stronger in the USA than in Europe. For example, a bubble of exactly the same amplitude and timing existed in France, and demand was not stimulated to the same extent as in the USA. But our disagreement is even more fundamental.

There is no questioning the fact that the rise of the value of the portfolio of shares held by a fraction of households affects their spending and borrowing behaviour, but monetary policy is still powerful (see section 2.2.1 above, and Box) and can adjust the levels of demand against the pressure of other determinants (i.e., ex post). In the absence of a rise of the stock market, monetary policy could have performed its tasks even more easily. The same will be true after the current market adjustment, provided that the monetary and financial framework is not unsettled in the process.

Much confusion is created by the coexistence in the USA of the stock market bubble, the rise of household credit, and external deficits. A quite unusual chain of events has been at work: (1) loans stimulate the spending of households (consumption and purchase of housing) – possibly, for a fraction of the population, through the inducement of the rising stock market; (2) the additional total spending (i.e., spending of households plus investment by firms) is purchased from abroad without significant inflationary consequences for domestic prices; (3) the normal utilization of productive capacity, *via* the control of price stability, is assured with great care by monetary policy.

Overall, it appears that a speculative bubble is a predictable development in the context of a merger wave, the recovery of the profitability in a segment of the economy, and deregulation of financial mechanisms. But we do not believe it is a necessary component of the formation of demand in general, or under neoliberalism in particular. A large crisis could follow from the bursting of the bubble if the necessary macro-policies were not implemented – if the shock radically destabilized the banking system, or if the crisis reached cumulative international proportions – but such developments are distinct from the mechanisms which govern the formation of demand when the conditions for stability are ensured, as was the case during the second half of the 1990s. The bubble is not a condition for the survival of neoliberalism. Quite the contrary, a 'soft landing' may be a condition for the continuation of the new course of capitalism. Without the bubble, neoliberalism would be neither more nor less apt to secure accumulation and growth.

2.4 *Improving technology*

It becomes more and more clear that about in the mid–1980s a period characterized by more favourable conditions of technical change began (see section 1.2.5). In Europe as in the USA the declining trend of the productivity of capital was not only interrupted but reversed (see Figure 1), and profit rates tended to rise. The prevalence and prolongation of these trends is crucial to neoliberalism and the future of capitalism in general. A gradually more efficient technology is a necessary condition for steady and lasting growth, together with its international diffusion (obviously with the limitations inherent to capitalism), and the implementation of a new social compromise. The question must, therefore, be posed of a possible link between neoliberalism and the features of technical change.[37]

We believe that a deep-seated transformation of management is presently underway, as in the early twentieth century, once again in the wake of a structural crisis (see section 1.2.5). The similarity between these two episodes is large. The managerial revolution of the early twentieth century was tightly linked to the preceding merger wave (the 'corporate revolution'); both finance and management were involved (in the context of the separation between ownership and management). The same is true of the transformations of the last two or three decades of the twentieth century. Obviously, the new technologies benefited from earlier R & D, and appear basically to have been a managerial achievement, the work of engineers and specialists. The previous merger wave, the *conglomerate* wave, had managerial features, related to the prevailing antitrust legislation, but under neoliberalism finance changed the rules and a pro-merger attitude was adopted.[38] Finance allowed for the restructuring of the economy, modifying the juridical framework and its application, and provided the necessary coordination and funding; and it imposed stricter profitability criteria. As is typical in capitalism, the task was undertaken under the pressure of a profitability crisis, i.e., ex post, with high costs for large segments of the population, but finance can claim to have made a contribution.

That finance played a role in the restructuring of the economy during the crisis of the 1970s and 1980s does not imply that it possesses the ability to prolong these trends. Their continuation is, however, crucial to the future of neoliberalism and capitalism in general. We have no prognosis to offer in this respect. The pattern of events in the twentieth century suggests only that specific risks accompany rapid technical change, as shown by the Great Depression, while on the other hand the benefits of a technical and organizational revolution may last several decades.

III BEYOND NEOLIBERALISM?

This last section uses the basic distinctions introduced in this study – between the transformation of relations of production, tendencies and crises, and power configurations – to discuss the future of neoliberalism.

3.1 Tendencies and crises

A common feature of all significant changes in the period covered in this essay is their relation to crises. This basic function of economic 'violence' remains a core feature of capitalism.

A first, very dramatic, development, which might contradict the neoliberal dream, would be that *history repeats itself.* This first transition scenario is that of great *instability.* The favourable course of technical change, opening a new phase of capitalism and financial hegemony, as in the beginning of the twentieth century, is suddenly and provisionally interrupted by a major depression, like that of the 1930s. The Great Depression was the *crisis of the recovery from the structural crisis of the late nineteenth century under financial hegemony*, with a significant monetary and financial component. The entire sequence of events could be reproduced: (1) structural crisis (that of the 1970s); (2) new favourable trends (presently underway), and a new hegemony of finance (as is also the case now); (3) a major crisis (recurrently announced); (4) a second period of controls on finance and a new social compromise.

If the path of technical change is less rapid, or if the favourable trends observed during the last fifteen years come to an end or are reversed, difficulties will be felt *via* 'significant' crises. They will be aggravated by social tensions (caused, for example, by stagnating wages or the difficulty of financing retirement plans) and international confrontations (which may impose new monetary and financial rules). Instead of maintaining its prerogatives, finance will have to gradually retreat. The transfer of profits in its favour will be limited and new regulations will be imposed. Neoliberalism faces this potential scenario in the medium run.

A spectacular development would be the occurrence of a new structural crisis (such as that of the 1890s and 1970s). History would then repeat itself yet again and a new power configuration would be imposed in the wake of such a crisis (as was the case in the transition between the 1970s and 1980s), but the new element would be that finance would be in command, instead of repressed.

3.2 Relations of production

At an even more profound level of analysis, the crucial issue is one of relations of production. The history of capitalism reveals their gradual transformation in the direction of an increased socialization: (1) the growing size and a larger interdependency of individual units of production, the central coordination of macro-policies and the definition of regulatory frameworks, the concentration of ownership and allocation of capital, the social control of education, research, etc.; (2) the delegation of the functions implied by the accomplishment of these tasks to specialists within non-financial corporations and financial institutions. Neoliberalism was possible, because it did not interrupt these developments but strengthened them. In all instances, the issue was the definition of *targets*: managing *firms* and the *macro-economy* in the interest of the owners, with much contempt for the costs borne by other classes or countries.

It is not clear that neoliberalism can measure up to the task of furthering this socialization in all of its components, as listed above. The question is, therefore, posed, whether there is a fundamental contradiction between this historical task and the narrow perspective of the interests of the owners. This essay set out a number of significant limitations. (1) The current forms of capital ownership still guarantee a large degree of initiative for finance which is incompatible with the quest for monetary and financial stability. First, they still allow the collective retreat of financial investors whenever they are confronted by potential losses (as manifested in international financial crises and collapses of the stock market). Macro-policies are only efficient under 'ordinary' conditions, and monetary and financial disturbances jeopardize their effectiveness. Second, the other facet of ownership – the allocation of capital among industries and firms – is still largely subject to the very volatile expectations of major financial institutions, such as pension and insurance funds, motivated solely by the interests of their customers, again with potentially negative macro-consequences. (2) Despite the involvement of finance in the definition of the new more favourable course of technical change in its first stages, neoliberalism has not resolved one of the major contradictions of capitalism: the capability to maintain a steady course of technical change. This would require new levels of the socialization of R & D and the implementation of innovation, i.e., a more profound transformation of relations of production beyond the basic profit-maximizing requirements of individual firms or corporate alliances.

3.3 Power configurations: alternative issues

3.3.1 Neoliberalism: the end of history?

Some of the contours of the capitalist dream of the ruling classes under neoliberalism are easy to infer from the events of the last two decades and the associated propaganda. Capitalism is the end of history. The owners of capital consolidate their position and income, and govern in close collaboration with top management. A broader compromise is established with the upper middle classes, who benefit from slowly rising purchasing power, health insurance, and pension funds; they share the benefits of a rising stock market (after a 'soft landing') and high interest rates. Accumulation rates are reasonable and crises are limited in extent. This is made possible by the continuing favourable shape of technical change. The hierarchy of wage-earners remains strong, but the situation is under control. Thanks to the export of capital to peripheral countries, segments of the population in the periphery are gradually moving toward a status similar to that of the lower income brackets of the centre; small elites collaborate with the ruling groups of the major capitalist countries. The USA leads the way, followed by Europe and Japan (finally adjusted to the benefits of neoliberalism), and, at some distance, by the more cooperative other countries.

A more conflictual course of events is, however, more likely, and probably foreseen by the shrewdest advocates of neoliberalism. Distributional tensions will remain significant, and social conflicts will have to be confronted. The rivalry among major capitalist countries and anti-imperialist struggles by forces in the periphery will remain significant. Stability will be basically ensured, but at the cost of recurrent crises. Capitalism must transform itself, but the fundamental features of the power configuration will be preserved. The problem will be to lead the international race and ensure the continuing pre-eminence of the ruling classes.

3.3.2 Beyond neoliberalism: the pursuit of history?

An alternative outcome is that the neoliberal power configuration will be destabilized, following one of the alternative scenarios outlined earlier. Just as the structural crisis of the 1970s paved the way for the come-back of capitalist owners, a logical consequence of our analysis is that a new compromise will then have to be struck between the leading managerial classes and the rest of the labour force (or at least some fractions of it). Depending on the form and extent of class struggles, the managerial and popular components of the configuration of power will be more or less accentuated – anywhere from a new form of Keynesianism to some more radical transformation.

Regardless of its precise social content, there are certain tasks essential to capitalism that any new compromise will have to carry out. The first historical setback to finance introduced the socialization of the *control of the macro-economy*, in the broad sense of the term (stabilizing business fluctuations and ensuring the stability of financial mechanisms and institutions). Redirecting these tools toward new (to some extent 'earlier') targets will not be the most difficult task to achieve. On the agenda for 'post-neoliberalism' are new degrees of socialization to achieve more efficient technical progress and accumulation. (Possible directions for this were suggested during the decades of the Keynesian compromise, but none of them was successfully implemented, neither the preservation of the favourable path of technical change, nor strong accumulation – hence inflation, hence unemployment.) The economics of a new compromise will be largely determined by its politics. Capitalism is not the end of history.

NOTES

1   G. Duménil & D. Lévy, 2001, 'Costs and Benefits of Neoliberalism. A class analysis', forthcoming in *Review of International Political Economy*, 8 (4).2000, *Crise et sortie de crise. Ordre et désordres néolibéraux*, Presses Universitaires de France, Paris.

2   A more detailed analysis can be found in G. Duménil & D. Lévy, 'Periodizing Capitalism. Technology, Institutions, and Relations of Production', in R. Albritton, M. Itoh, R. Westra, A. Zuege, *Phases of Capitalist Development: Booms, Crises, and Globalization*, London: Palgrave, 2001.

3   We analyzed these mechanisms, in particular the patterns of technical change

and the relationship between declining profit rates and crises in previous works (G. Duménil & D. Lévy, *The Economics of the Profit Rate: Competition, Crises, and Historical Tendencies in Capitalism*, Aldershot: Edward Elgar, 1993; 'Technology and Distribution: Historical Trajectories à la Marx', *Journal of Economic Behavior and Organization*, 2000 (forthcoming)). See also: D. Foley, 'Endogenous Technical Change with Externalities in a Classical Growth Model', Department of Economics, Graduate Faculty, New School University, New York, forthcoming in *Journal of Economic Behavior and Organization*.

4   Hilferding analyzed one of its possible configurations (R. Hilferding, *Finance Capital: A study of the Latest Phase of Capitalist Development*, London & Boston: Routledge and Kegan Paul, [1910] 1981).

5   G. Duménil & D. Lévy, *La dynamique du capital. Un siècle d'économie américaine*, Paris: Presses Universitaires de France, 1996 ch.22.

6   There is also a problem concerning the allocation of this capital among capitalists.

7   To avoid bankruptcies, financial panics, and the suspensions of payments.

8   Our reference to a *Marxist framework of analysis* can be seen as a combination of *fundamentalism* and *revisionism*. The consideration of new class patterns is a central element of this revisionism. The analysis of exploitation and the relationship between productive and clerical workers is typical of the problems faced by contemporary Marxism. Two basic attitudes can be distinguished: (1) a strict adherence to Marx's framework – surplus-value is extracted from productive workers (when this difficulty is not simply ignored, other groups are classified as *petty bourgeois*); (2) an implicit revision – a new proletarian or working class is defined including production and clerical workers. Our viewpoint is closer to this second attitude, but we make explicit the conceptual leap that it implies.

9   This is an 'institutional' definition of *finance*. It can also be defined in the strict sense as a class. The notion of *finance capital*, meaning a tight and hierarchical relationship between industrial capital and banking capital, is usually attributed to Rudolf Hilferding (*Finance Capital*). American sociologists attempted to identify among capitalists (shareholders and members of boards of directors), in the postwar US society, a specific subset of *financial capitalists*, whose ownership and power span financial and non-financial corporations (M. Soref & M. Zeitlin, 'Finance Capital and the Internal Structure of the Capitalist Class in the United States', in M. Mizruchi & M. Schwartz, eds., *Intercorporate Relations. The Structural Analysis of Business*, Cambridge: Cambridge University Press, 1987. See also K. van der Pijl, *The Making of an Atlantic Ruling Class*, London & New York: Verso, 1984).

10 In some countries large segments of the productive system were placed under the control of state officials.

11 T. Ferguson & J. Rogers, *Right Turn. The Democrats and the Decline of American Politics*, New York: Hill and Wang, 1986.

12 This is a second illustration of the combination of *fundamentalism* (in the reference to the tendency for the profit rate to fall) and *revisionism* (in the identification of phases of restoration). We share this view with Ernest Mandel (*Long Waves of Capitalist Development. The Marxist Interpretation*, Cambridge and Paris: Cambridge University Press & Éditions de la Maison des Sciences de l'Homme, 1980).

13 A recent description of the series can be found in G. Duménil & D. Lévy, *Crise et*

sortie de crise. Ordre et désordres néolibéraux, Paris: Presses Universitaires de France, 2000.

14 The paper excludes phenomena which are often used as markers in the periodization of capitalism, such as the transformations of *competition*, notably the notions of competitive and monopoly capitalism. This choice is deliberate since we question the relevance of this distinction. The transformations of competition can be considered in combination with other phenomena, as in Lenin's analysis of imperialism, or in isolation.

15 The notion of 'liberalism' itself is already quite ambiguous. See, for example, the introduction to J. Weinstein, *The Corporate Ideal in the Liberal State, 1900-1918*, Boston: Beacon Press, 1968.

16 In 1995, the output of these three countries represented 70% of that of the USA.

17 This analysis borrows from Duménil & Lévy, 'Costs and Benefits of Neoliberalism'; *Crise et sortie de crise*, 2001

18 UNPD, *Human Development Report*, Bruxelles: De Boeck, 1999.

19 In the measurement of financial income (interest and dividends received plus capital gains), it is important to correct for the impact of inflation.

20 Immanuel Wallerstein sees in the growing demand for democratization one of the contradictions (in addition to the exhaustion of the reserves in cheap labour and ecological resources), which will provoke the final outbreak of capitalism, presently on the verge of entering its last Kondratieff cycle (I. Wallerstein, 'Globalization or the Age of Transition? A Long-Term View of the Trajectory of the World-System', *International Sociology*, Vol. XV(2), 2000).

21 Federal Deposit Insurance Corporation, *History of the Eighties. Lessons for the Future*, Washington: FDIC, 1997

22 We abstract from the slowdown of the US economy which began in 2000 (Figure 4). Independently of other more dramatic developments (always possible in the present context of threatening financial instability and which would affect the world economy), the USA could enter a new recession (while Europe has not to date).

23 The balance of external accounts is a target to be taken into account in Europe, but not in the USA (section 2.3.2).

24 A theoretical exposition and modeling can be found in the third part of G. Duménil & D. Lévy, *La dynamique du capital. Un siècle d'économie américaine*, Paris: Presses Universitaires de France, 1996.

25 L. Panitch, 'The New Imperial State', *New Left Review*, March-April 2000.

26 Because of the shortening of the service life of fixed capital, it is necessary to consider the rate of *net* investment, and not of *gross* investment as is often done.

27 The small gap during the 1990s reflects the desperate attempt by firms to get out of debt, manifested in rates of self-financing larger than 100%.

28 It is important to keep in mind that the financing of future retirement plans depends on growth (and technical progress), not on its institutional form, redistribution among wage earners or pension funds. Pension funds could only contribute to the solution of this problem, if they led to larger savings and growth rates, which is not presently the case. What is at stake in the alternative between redistribution and funds is a more or less egalitarian framework.

29 P. Gowan, *The Global Gamble. Washington's Faustian Bid for World Dominance*,

London: Verso, 1999. We will abstract in this section from other aspects of the dominance of the USA, such as its position in trade or financial international agreements, political pressure or military intervention.

30 Obviously, the rate of exchange of the dollar is also at issue. With the exception of the sharp fluctuation upward in the early 1980s, the real exchange rate of the dollar remained comparatively low, in particular with respect to the yen, but this weakness did not offset the trade deficit.

31 Labour costs remain higher in the USA than in Europe, and available measures contradict the view that a technical gap could offset these differences.

32 The comparison with France shows the significant difference in the patterns of evolution. During the 1970s and the first half of the 1980s, the ratio of the total debt of households to their disposable income fluctuated in both countries between 60% and 70%. This rate of indebtedness grew in 1990, but while it declined during the following years in France, it went on rising in the USA, reaching the unprecedented level of 95%.

33 R.J. Gordon, 'Technology and Economic Performance in the American Economy', Working Paper, Conference of the *Centre Saint-Gobain pour la Recherche en Économie*, 2000.

34 F. Chesnais, 'La "nouvelle économie": Une conjoncture propre à la puissance hégémonique américaine', in Séminaire Marxiste, *Une nouvelle phase du capitalisme?*, Paris: Syllepse, 2001.

35 In our opinion, this interpretation is dubious: (1) The stock market fell after industrial production; (2) the depression continued well after the restoration of the stock market.

36 In such models, the wealth of final consumers is a variable in their demand function, besides their income.

37 At issue here is the degree of autonomy of the various levels of analysis: relations of production, tendencies and crises, and power configurations.

38 G. Duménil, M. Glick, & D. Lévy, 'The History of Competition Policy as Economic History', *The Antitrust Bulletin*, Vol. XLII(2), 1997. The basic characteristic of conglomerates was *diversification*, as the law limited mergers of firms engaged in the same activity.

THE GROWTH OBSESSION

Elmar Altvater

In pre-capitalist and pre-industrial times economic growth was dependent on population growth which, in turn, depended on the supply of goods and services for subsistence and reproduction. But since the Industrial Revolution GDP growth has been propelled by the dynamic development of the productive forces, i.e. by increased (labour) productivity. From the second half of the nineteenth century, average growth rates increased remarkably. This growth, however, has been extremely uneven over time and in space, and has failed to narrow the inequalities between peoples and regions in a globalizing world.

Ignoring all evidence to the contrary, a recent World Bank report reached the remarkable conclusion that 'growth is good for the poor', i.e. that faster growth is not widening but closing the gap between rich and poor – and, moreover, not as the effect of a 'trickle-down' process; the report alleges the existence of a '1-to-1-relation' between growth and poverty-reduction.[1] The World Bank report is thus very optimistic with regard to the distributional effects of economic growth.[2] Yet even this bizarre (and strongly contested) conclusion does not touch upon the all-important question of whether economic growth is sustainable, economically as well as socially and ecologically. The following sections discuss the economic, ecological and financial limits to growth and address the question of why quantitative growth is so crucial for the capitalist system.

This essay was first published in *A World of Contradictions, The Socialist Register 2002*.

I. GROWTH TRIUMPHANT?

In the history of industrial capitalism, and in particular during the second half of the twentieth century under the rule of 'Fordism', economic growth can be said to have been 'triumphant'[3] – owing to the ever more efficient mobilization of productive resources. Between 1950 and 1973 (the year of the collapse of the Bretton Woods system and the 'oil crisis'), nearly everywhere in the world growth rates reached levels unprecedented in human history, tempting Richard Easterlin to predict that '[t]he future ... to which the epoch of modern economic growth is leading is one of never ending economic growth, a world in which ever growing abundance is matched by ever rising aspirations'.[4] Yet the assumption that physical inputs can expand indefinitely and produce an ever growing real output is, as McMichael says, 'ecological nonsense – nothing physical can grow indefinitely'.[5] The statement 'growth forever' therefore only makes sense if the growth that Easterlin and other growth-enthusiasts have in mind is mere monetary growth (known as inflation), or a purely virtual 'new' economy (without transportation, material production, and physical consumption of resources). And indeed these notions are often invoked in arguments that try to reconcile ecological sustainability with the requirements of a capitalist growth economy.[6]

Yet in both recent economic history and contemporary economic theory enthusiasm for growth is anything but a marginal phenomenon. For one thing, it follows from the 'Eurocentric logic'[7] of quantitative growth, i.e. of an acceleration in time and expansion in space ('time-space-compression', as David Harvey calls it)[8] that is responsible for the contemporary process of globalization. It is important to note, however, that in this line of thought it is not simply 'growth' that matters but *efficient* growth. Capital does not like disorderly growth; it needs growth which serves the end of profitability. Conversely, profitability is the motor of growth. Therefore, not only the growth rate of GDP counts but also the profit rate and the accumulation rate. This raises complicated theoretical and methodological questions, especially in the era of globalization when it is no longer the national economy (or a given sector, such as manufacturing) which defines the arena for the formation of an average rate of profit.[9] Since surplus profits can be generated by both advanced productivity and low labour costs, the same profit rate may result from very different constellations of productivity, wages, and capital-labour relations. The social implications of 'growth' become indeterminate under these conditions.

Furthermore, in this line of thought the performance of the 'real economy' is usually interpreted without reference to financial globalization. This approach is seriously flawed because monetary capital is more mobile and flexible than ever before. Investment decisions (and therefore also growth rates) are not only determined by (industrial) profit rates but also by the global interest rates on financial assets. Since under conditions of financial globalization accumulation no longer necessarily takes place in the real economy, the relation between surplus value, profits, accumulation and real GDP-growth has become much looser. Under certain circumstances it is now more profitable to accumulate financial assets than to invest in real projects. Thus, prices of financial assets are inflated whereas commodity-prices (in particular in manufacturing, as shown by Duménil and Lévy)[10] are deflated – at least relative to the price-index of GDP. The broken link between real and monetary accumulation manifests itself as a paradoxical 'inflationary deflation'.[11]

A second general reason why most social scientists and politicians obsessively preach the ideology of triumphant growth is the idea that economic growth increases employment, incomes and taxes, and in this way provides resources for the alleviation of social conflicts, the expansion of development assistance, the eradication of poverty, the implementation of environmental standards, and so on. Steady growth was indeed the backbone of the corporatist 'Keynesian class compromise' associated with the 'Fordist' mode of regulation that character-ized developed capitalism during the postwar period; and it is also assumed to offer a remedy for backwardness in the less-developed world – the argument of 'modernization' theory. Thus a recent article dedicated to the benefits of the 'Washington Consensus' declares: 'Without investment there is no economic growth, and without economic growth there is no sustainable economic policy …'.[12] The idea that there could be a mode of social cohesion other than the capi-talist one based on high economic growth is, naturally, not considered.

Given these two mutually reinforcing general reasons for the obsession with growth, it is not surprising that disseminating policy proposals for the stimulation of growth is a common preoccupation of economists, whether they work within the Keynesian tradition or are of a more neoclassical and neoliberal persuasion.[13] Even many ecological economists also believe that it is not economic growth, but economic *stagnation*, that harms the environment.[14] This may not be entirely false with respect to 'dirty', i.e. visible and perceptible, pollution. However, 'clean' life style-pollution, e.g. the emission of greenhouse gases or the 'externalization' of ecologically destructive effects into remote areas or into the far future (nuclear waste), is without doubt also a side-effect of growth and welfare creation.[15]

In addition, as Immanuel Wallerstein has pointed out, growth-mania is of a systemic nature. It is enshrined in the institutions which allow the system to function as a 'totality': 'Capitalism as a historical system is defined by the fact that it makes structurally central and primary the endless accumulation of capital. This means that the institutions which constitute its framework reward those who pursue the endless accumulation of capital and penalize those who don't.'[16] Since the accumulation of capital is driven on by (the anticipation of) profits, Wallerstein's statement really summarizes the 'grand narrative' of the modern capitalist system: the processes of profit-making, accumulation, and institutional regulation, which give a degree of security to the system, simultaneously produce insecurity on all levels of social and individual life.

Wallerstein is confident that the contemporary long cycle of accumulation which has lasted for over a century will soon come to an end, and that capitalism will then enter a stage of systemic crisis. It is true that growth mania has no real ground in the real economy. But the continued construction of institutions that emphasize growth and further instil the profit motive in individual capitalists needs to be understood as an attempt to maintain social, economic and political stability and avoid a radical, 'paradigmatic' change. Whether it is dressed up as 'modernity' or 'post-modernity', whether it appeals to a 'Third Way' or a 'new economy', or as a rationale for overcoming backwardness, growth mania is nothing but a conservative reaction to the tendency to 'systemic crisis' identified by Wallerstein.

II. DISEMBEDDING

The transition to a 'growth economy' in the nineteenth century was just one aspect of the ongoing 'great transformation' of pre-capitalist social forms into a capitalist market economy.[17] The combination of commodification processes, the circulation-facilitating function of money and the ready availability of fuels formed a perfect 'trinity' that sparked capital's acceleration in time and expansion in space, i.e. accumulation and growth.[18] Markets have existed ever since people began to exchange products, but until the capitalist mode of production emerged markets remained 'slow' and growth rates low. Capitalism established a social, economic, political, cultural foundation, and the requisite sources of energy, which allowed for the mobilization and development of productive forces on a hitherto unknown scale. In the course of the 'primitive accumulation of capital', economic growth emancipated itself from the limited energy supply afforded by living labour. Thereafter, throughout the history of capitalism, workers have been replaced by means of production fuelled by (mainly) fossil energy. This process has been analyzed as the 'real subsumption of labour' or the 'production of relative surplus value'.[19] Capital and its institutions went through a process of 'autonomization' ('*Verselbständigung*') vis-à-vis society (e.g. population growth, human needs) and social control. This was the process conceptualized by Polanyi as the 'disembedding' of the market from the social system;[20] the former then imposed its logic – i.e. the rule of commodities, money and capital – on the latter.

Today, we have to be aware that, firstly, the process of disembedding was by no means an event unique to the nineteenth century; and, secondly, that the continuing process of disembedding embraces money in its many different forms and functions. Money not only circulates goods and services in 'ordinary markets'; as credit it obeys not only the rules of the real economy but also the 'logic' of a disembedded financial system operating on a global scale, partially disconnected from the real economy and increasingly serving to finance not only real (domestic and foreign) investment but also speculation.

Modern financial instruments are almost entirely disconnected from the real economy. As a result, it is possible for growth rates of turnover of financial assets to be many times higher than the growth of any indicator of 'real' activity. However, the disembedded financial sphere has certainly not become irrelevant to the functioning of the real economy or society. On the contrary, globally formed interest rates on financial assets require matching real growth rates and in this way exert a severe pressure on the real economy. This sets new *economic* limits to growth.

III. ECONOMIC LIMITS TO GROWTH

Economic growth is the result of a process of the transformation of energy and matter. In Marxian terms this is the concrete and use value aspect of growth. From this perspective, it should be evident that growth has its limits. After all, planet Earth's stocks of energy and matter are limited. We will discuss this in the next section. But economic growth is also the outcome of a social production process ruled by money (through the interest rate) and capital (through the profit rate). In the long run, capital requires a 'geometric' growth of inputs in order to maintain stable (relative) growth rates. Because the long-run geometric growth of absolute quantities is an absurd idea, high rates of (real) economic growth can only be sustained for a certain period of time. Nevertheless, the maintenance of high interest rates requires nothing less than the realization of precisely this absurdity and the dominant growth discourse presents it as a socially and economically feasible objective.

Statistical evidence (see Table 1) shows that (a) the absolute increases of GDP in highly developed countries remained positive and rather stable since the beginning of the 1960s (with merely cyclical fluctuations); and that (b) in the 1990s real increases were not only smaller in absolute terms, but were also achieved on the basis of an already higher level of real GDP. Growth rates inevitably declined.

Table 1: Absolute increases of real GDP (1991 prices) in billions of national currency, annual averages

Period and Country (Currency)	1960-69	1970-79	1980-89	1990-96	1960-96
USA (US$)	110.05	120	140.83	120.13	122.72
Japan (YEN)	11.98	9.68	12.18	7.02	11.27
Germany (DM)	46.92	45.52	36.64	76.3**	46.15*
France (FF)	140.1	139.31	123.3	68.35	134.19
Great Britain (BP)	8.26	8.85	13.37	6.88	9.56
Italy (LIT)	29.94	29.61	24.97	9.13	28.25

* 1960-1989 only

** Since 1990 unified Germany; Germany until 1989 West Germany only; Italy: 1000 bn Lira; Japan: 100 bn Yen

Source: Council of Economic Advisers (Sachverständigenrat zur Begutachtung der gesamtwirtschaftlichen Entwicklung, Jahresgutachten 1997/98, table 3*; author's calculations)

In Germany the highest increase in real GDP occurred in 1968, after the 'small' crisis of 1966–67; DM 102 billions translated into a real growth rate of GDP of 7.46%. In 1988 the same absolute increase would have produced a growth rate of only 4.43%. The increase actually achieved in that year equalled no more than DM 83.4 billions. The real growth rate was 3.62%, still rather high by historical standards. In the USA, the highest absolute increase in GDP (US$ 327.4 billion) during the period under investigation occurred in 1983; the real rate of growth for that year was 7.00%. In 1996 the same real increase would have produced a growth rate of 4.99%. In reality, GDP in that year grew only by a (still respectable) 2.76%.

In his long-term analysis of economic growth, Angus Maddison has measured the impact of labour productivity, hours worked and capital productivity on the annual average compounded growth rate. He shows that 'over the long term, working hours of the average person fell by half; labour input increased less than population…'. His findings clearly underline the positive relation between labour productivity and economic growth. '[L]abour productivity', he continues, 'rose a good deal faster than GDP per capita. From 1820 to 1992 Japanese labour productivity rose 46-fold compared with a 28-fold increase in per capital GDP'.[21]

But although labour productivity has obviously been the main motor of growth in the last century, a look at the growth figures since 1950 reveals that (1) total factor productivity fell in all countries under consideration, that (2) the capital-labour ratio increased until the mid-1970s and has decreased since then, and that (3) the capital coefficient increased (i.e. 'capital productivity' declined remarkably). The impact of the factors mentioned on the profit rate is negative. For the profit rate depends positively (1) on a distribution of income in favour of capital, i.e. on low real wages per worker; (2) on an increase in labour productivity; and negatively (3) on a growing capital-labour ratio (which, in value terms, indicates the rising organic composition of capital). In the long run, the profit rate tends to decline (as Marx showed), but of course this decline is cyclically modified. Therefore, during the last decade of wild deregulation, flexibilization and mobilization of all factors of production (i.e. of high pressures on individual and social wages, a redistribution of income in favour of capital, and decreasing costs of constant capital (especially of raw materials)), the profit rate went up sharply. Nevertheless, Wallerstein's expectation of a 'global profit squeeze'[22] is plausible in the long run.

Since the 1960s, in the industrialized countries rates of productivity growth, although declining, have still been higher than the rate of growth of manufacturing output.[23] The consequence has been the dismissal of workers and the emergence of an 'employment gap'. Growth tends to become 'jobless growth' – a development that can only be counteracted by a reduction of working time or the creation of jobs in the public and non-manufacturing private sector. The historical reduction of working hours per person described by Maddison reduces society's growth potential, but at the same time it provides a partial solution to the problem of the 'employment gap'. In Europe between 1973 and 1992 the number of people in employment rose from 138 to 148 million, while there was a 5% *decrease* in the number of hours worked – from 242 to 232 billion.[24]

Table 2: Annual percentage changes of output per hour and output in manufacturing in 10 industrialized countries, 1979-1995

Country	USA	Can	Japan	Bel	Fr	Ger	It	NL	Swe	GB
Manufacturing output	2.1	1.7	3.4	2.0	0.7	0.4	2.3	2.0	2.1	0.7
Output per hour	2.6	1.7	3.4	3.9	3.1	2.2	3.8	3.3	3.3	4.2

Source: Christopher Sparks and Mary Greiner, 'U.S. and foreign productivity and labor costs', *Monthly Labor Review*, February 1997, p. 29.

Table 2 summarizes the long-term development of productivity (output per hour worked) and growth (output in manufacturing). From the end of the 1970s until the mid-1990s, only Japan and Canada achieved an output-growth equal to productivity-growth; all other industrialized countries display the pattern which Maddison discovered as a long-term tendency from the early nineteenth century until the 1990s. The picture, however, changes when long-term GDP-growth is compared with growth rates of GDP per person employed, because the growth rate of labour productivity in services as compared with manufacturing is generally lower. The growth of 'unproductive labour'[25] has the effect of diminished productivity increases. Owing in particular to the growing weight of financial services in production and sales (for instance in the motor-car industry it has reached about 70%), 'unproductive' labour partly offsets the productivity increases achieved by 'productive' labour[26] and hence also the resulting widening employment gap. But because of the introduction of new communication-technologies into the service sector, this sector is likely to display higher rates of productivity growth in the future – a scenario already announced by the advocates of the 'new economy' – so there are no guarantees that the service sector's capacity to absorb a substantial part of the labour force can be sustained in the long run.

There are no easy solutions for the employment gap in dynamic capitalist societies. That is, structural unemployment must be considered an inevitable consequence of a strongly-performing economy. It is not, however, a state of affairs that people happily and voluntarily resign themselves to. The Left has always pursued 'alternative' (i.e. non-market) policies for achieving full employment. As the space for such alternative projects has sharply contracted, increasingly often the only remaining choice is for people to 'exit' from the system of paid employment. This can take the form of a passive acceptance of unemployment and its consequences or the active organization of new forms of labour. The latter way out refers to nothing but the 'informal sector' which is growing in all parts of the world and thus reducing the employment gap. The ILO notes that more than 80% of new jobs created in Latin America and Africa in recent years have been in the informal economy.[27] We return to the 'informal sector' in section 5 below.

IV. ECOLOGICAL LIMITS TO GROWTH AND PRODUCTIVITY

High productivity increases constitute one of the basic features of industrial capitalism in general and of the Fordist system in particular. For this reason, productivity growth forms the starting point of Adam Smith's analysis of the 'origins of the wealth of nations': specialization and a deepening of the division of labour help to increase the output per working hour, and this causes income and wealth to rise.[28] David Ricardo extended the argument to the international division of labour, based on free trade. His 'law of comparative advantage' still serves as one of the most important theoretical foundations of modern economics, and is even enthusiastically embraced by the modern, Eurocentric globalization literature.[29]

Leaving aside the effects of efficiency gains, productivity can only be increased by putting more fixed capital into circulation and by consuming ever larger quantities of matter and energy.[30] Of course, the reproduction of capital(ism) as a whole remains crucially dependent on (surplus) value which can only be produced by labour. But capital's attempt to emancipate itself from its dependence on living labour by substituting the latter with fossil energy and machinery, establishes a new relationship to nature. Fordism, too, cannot be understood as a mere technical and social innovation. It also includes a new relationship to nature, for both the system of production and consumption and the mode of social regulation are heavily based on the use of fossil energy.[31]

It is clear that the material preconditions of the 'Western life style' cannot be established in all societies on earth without destroying nature to the point where human life on earth is jeopardized.[32] One of the first signs that the limits of environmental space have been reached is that the goods needed for production and consumption become 'oligarchic', i.e. reserved for an oligarchy able to secure its access to these resources with monetary claims. Those who do not possess monetary wealth are increasingly excluded from the consumption of goods and services. Consequently the number of poor people in the world is rising; in 1998 the World Bank counted 2.8 billion human beings living below the international poverty line of $2 per capita per day.[33]

But there are also absolute limits, not all of whose effects can be so easily avoided by the rich. Serious studies of the carrying capacity of global ecosystems and on the concept of 'environmental space' have demonstrated that these set objective limits to the process of economic growth.[34] By now (since the Rio Conference of 1992) it has become common sense that fossil resources are not only limited, but that their excessive use is responsible for the greenhouse effect and other ecological evils. It is in this way that the question of ecological sustainability asserts itself and reshapes the discourse of the social sciences in general and that of the economics of growth in particular. This should be suffi-cient reason to jettison any illusions concerning the benign nature of economic and financial globalization. Moreover, Western liberal (formal) democracy could only be globalized if the 'Western way of life' itself could be globalized. But a situation of genuine globality, i.e. a world society based on equality and reciprocity (if not on solidarity), will never be achieved through *capitalist* globalization.

V. FINANCIAL LIMITS TO GROWTH

The interest rate constitutes a benchmark ('hard budget constraint')[35] for any economic undertaking. If capitalists fail to make a profit at least equal to the prevailing interest rate, their capital will be classified as non-profitable and loans made to them will be termed non-performing. As long as the real interest rate is lower than the real growth rate of GDP and of the 'marginal efficiency of capital' (i.e. the profit rate), returns from productive investments will exceed the monetary price of capital, and therefore borrowers in financial markets are likely to invest their loans in the real economy. This 'Keynesian state of affairs' came to an end, however, at the same time as the 'golden age' of Fordist expansion, namely in the course of the 1970s. Since the beginning of the 1980s, the real interest rates on global financial markets have by far exceeded the average real growth rate of GDP.[36] The real economy is 'depressed' by the financial system. The OECD gives three reasons for this configuration of finance and production: first, the growing fiscal deficits and the accumulation of public debt in the highly developed countries; second, higher inflationary risks and consequently a greater weight of risk factors in the formation of interest rates; and third, the globali-zation of financial markets since the second half of the 1970s, with the result that deregulated market mechanisms rather than public interventions began to exercise the function of credit allocation.[37] The political project of deregula-tion, liberalization, flexibilization and privatization has thus intensified global competition with regard to the stability of currencies and profitability of assets. The growing opportunities of exploiting interplace-differentials of profitability on a global scale, together with technical (information and communication tech-nologies) and financial innovations (from hedge funds to derivatives and offshore financial centres), can be considered as the main impulse of globalization.

There is, however, a fourth reason for the high real interest rates that have prevailed since the beginning of the 1980s which is not recognized by the OECD: the crisis of American hegemony. The US trade balance deficit existing since 1971 (due to the outflow of capital) and the deterioration of the current account since the mid-1970s, together with the breakdown of the fixed exchange rate system of Bretton Woods, exerted downward pressure on the exchange rate of the US dollar, and spurred on inflation. A further deterioration of the (still hegemonic) dollar could only be prevented by means of an increase in US interest rates.[38] The period of high interest rates began in 1979 under the Carter administration and was rigorously continued by the Reagan administration. Its effects on the US exchange rate were positive, but proved devastating for debtors – in the USA (e.g. the Savings & Loans crisis), but above all in the Third World. The combination of high interest rates, rising oil prices and declining commodity prices triggered a Third World debt crisis which has not yet been overcome twenty years later. Table 3 shows the relation between real long-term interest rates and real growth of GDP in highly developed countries.

Table 3: Real growth rates and long term real interest rates in industrialized countries, 1960-1995

	Real GDP (annual growth rates in percent)				Real Long Term Interest Rates (percent per annum)			
	60-73	74-79	80-89	90-95	60-73	74-79	80-89	90-95
USA	4.0	2.6	2.4	1.9	1.5	–0.5	4.9	4.4
Japan	9.7	3.5	3.8	1.9	..	–0.2	4.3	3.9
Germany	4.3	2.4	2.0	2.0	2.6	3.1	4.8	3.8
France	5.4	2.7	2.1	1.3	1.9	–0.3	4.7	5.9
GB	3.1	1.5	2.4	1.0	..	–2.0	3.5	4.7

Source: OECD, *Historical Statistics 1960-1995*, Paris, 1997, p. 50 and p. 108.

According to the traditional Keynesian paradigm, the accumulation of capital is financed with loans provided by 'monetary wealth owners', i.e. by banks and institutional investors. The interest rate compels industrial capitalists to produce a profit that is large enough to service their loans as well as to fulfil their own accumulation requirements. In this way, the interest rate is linked to profits, employment and real capital accumulation, i.e. to the social organization of the accumulation regime and its political regulation. The interest rate itself is subject to regulation by (national) monetary authorities, above all the Central Bank. Although it is still a central premise of Keynesian theory, globalization has by now significantly eroded the ability of national monetary authorities to determine interest rates which are nowadays formed on global financial markets. On the one hand, *arbitrage* between different markets equalizes interest rate (and exchange rate) differentials; on the other hand, the differentials (calculated in 'basis points') are continuously recreated, which triggers new rounds of speculation.

Those who lend out monetary wealth (e.g. shares in firms or funds, or government bonds) thereby become *claim holders*. The international financial system works as a very powerful device for channelling surplus produced anywhere in the world to financial claim holders in the big financial centres. As a result, inequality is rising drastically. However, there are so many intermediaries in the chain between monetary claims, debt service and surplus transfer in real terms that under normal conditions these links are rarely visible for people and become recognizable only in times of a crisis. The financial system seems to be a 'virtual world' without any influence on production and reproduction, i.e. on people's living conditions and the natural environment. It is also often regarded as a kind of 'zero sum game' among players in the virtual world of the stock market: some lose what others gain and vice versa, and nothing real is happening. In reality it is another mechanism whereby financial asset holders gain at the expense of those who do not belong to this enviable species. US figures indicate that between 1989 and 1997, 86% of stock market gains went to the top 10% of households, while between 1983 and 1995 the bottom 40% of households lost 80% of their net worth.[39] These facts are in stark contrast with the World Bank's claim that there is a positive '1-to-1-relation' between growth and poverty alleviation. The 'post-modern' understanding of the financial system as de-linked from the real world of production and distribution is completely inadequate for grasping the contradictions and crisis tendencies generated by the global financial system. Some of these tendencies are addressed briefly here.

(1) Although global markets rely in principle on private initiative, the role of the state is indispensable for the working of the system. Of course, nation-states as well as international institutions provide the framework for the social and economic (world) order. With respect to global finance, however, the role of the state, as a public debtor vis-à-vis private monetary wealth owners, is that of a direct participant. The private financial system is fundamentally flawed because wealth owners (and claim holders) are private agents, whereas debtors in most cases are public institutions – or they become public ones when private debtors default. The debt crisis of the 1980s was, above all, caused by the default on public debt, whereas the debt crisis of the 1990s was one of private debt default. This change was an outcome of the policies of deregulation and privatization which have been pursued by international institutions and national governments alike. The Keynesian (as well as Marxian) notion of debtors as private (industrial) capitalists who service their debt by extracting and realizing surplus value has lost its validity in the era of global financial speculation. The debt service of private monetary claims has become 'socialized': governments are made to pass on the costs to their citizens. This is the reason why public debt has increased so remark-ably in nearly all countries during the last twenty years. Where neither private debtors nor national states are in a position to service private debt, international institutions (notably the IMF) provide new credits on condition that the country in question adopts a policy package of structural adjustment. The primary aim of debt crisis management is to safeguard the assets of claim-holders from industrial-

ized countries, and thus to prevent a 'systemic crisis'. In the medium and long term, these policies channel resources from the citizens of the indebted country to claim-holders in other countries. Thus the redistribution of real wealth (surplus value) between creditors and debtors is organized by official institutions, not just by the market. This is one of the ways in which capitalism contradicts 'free market' ideology; the latter's presentation of capitalist reality contrasts ever more sharply with people's experience of it.

(2) In most cases, so-called 'emerging markets' are characterized by high real growth rates and/or high nominal interest rates, both serving to attract foreign capital. When the growth rate declines or the currency is expected to depreciate, foreign capital immediately exits the 'emerging market' in order not to 'submerge'. The result of such capital flight is a further depreciation of the currency. In the cases of the Asian countries, Mexico, Brazil and Russia, currencies depreciated between 50 and 80%. For several reasons, the effects were devastating: (a) the foreign debt to be serviced, which is denominated in foreign currency, shot up; (b) higher export volumes were required in order to earn constant export revenues; (c) higher import prices put an inflationary pressure on the economy; (d) for those who had hard currency at their disposal, whether citizens or foreigners, asset prices fell. The global extension of financial claims thus turns out to be a much more efficient device for the transfer of real value and the intensification of exploitation than, for instance, the plundering activities conducted under colonial rule from the sixteenth century onwards. The operating mode of the global credit system annihilates the potential comparative cost advantages of free trade. It follows yet again that the 1-to-1-relation between growth and poverty eradication, posited by the World Bank, is false.

(3) While on the one hand financial capital exerts *deflationary* pressures on the prices of commodities, on the other hand it produces an *inflation* of asset prices. This paradoxical situation of an *'inflationary deflation'*[40] is an indicator of the extent to which the global financial system has become disconnected from the real economy. A financial boom takes place alongside overproduction and overcapacity in the real economy: 'There is too much of everything. From cashmere to blue jeans, silver jewellery to aluminium cans ... Asia is the epicenter of the problem. Massive investment made on the assumption of continued high rates of growth resulted in broad overcapacity...'.[41] The postwar configuration of international institutions was tailored for a world of constant and moderate rates of inflation; it was designed to counter the deflationary pressures which had proved so destructive after the great crisis of 1929. During the 1930s, deflationary tendencies had resulted in a nearly complete collapse of the world market and nation-states' subsequent resort to protectionist measures and aggressively autarchic policies. Low nominal interest rates cause stock market quotations to rise.

However, in connection with the deflationary tendencies of product prices and real growth rates, even low real interest rates do not trigger new investment in the real economy because of its low profitability, as the case of Japan shows. Japan 'built massive industrial capacity at home and abroad throughout the 1980s, encouraged by low interest rates. In the late 1980s, Japanese monetary authorities lowered real interest rates to virtually nothing to help Japanese exporters survive a drastic strengthening of the yen in 1986. That policy fuelled a huge stock-market bubble...'.[42] However, the low real interest rates were still too high in relation to the expected profit rate. Overproduction or overaccumulation of capital triggered a crisis which had its origins in the 'real' sphere of the economy but first surfaced in the monetary sphere – as a stock market crisis in Japan and as a financial crisis in Asia, Russia and Brazil.

A situation characterized by these tendencies is extremely unstable and may cause the collapse of companies which suddenly find themselves in deep debt. This is the situation which Keynes referred to as a 'liquidity trap': although nominal interest rates are low, even near zero, nobody borrows because investments are not even expected to produce the minimum profit rate. Under such circumstances, it makes sense for individuals to transfer their liquid funds to places where they can earn higher short-term profits.

Nowadays, owners of monetary wealth, rather than 'traditional' industrial capitalists, determine the process of global accumulation. The real rate of return on capital is of less relevance for investment decisions than monetary interest rates. But the process of disembedding and de-linking have not created a completely autonomous financial sphere. The effects of the global financial system constitute the lived experience of people in countries hit by financial crises. The government of Indonesia speaks of at least 30 million people living below the poverty line. In Thailand poverty and informalization are growing visibly. In Russia hunger and malnutrition have returned on a broad scale. In large parts of the country money has disappeared and a pre-modern barter economy is on the rise – a different kind of 'virtual economy'.[43] Although the empirical data are better for some cases than for others, the tendency in other countries hit by the crisis is basically the same. All this points to the fact that the financial system continues to have a profound impact on real accumulation, labour and political regulation.

VI. CONCLUSION:
GROWTH, NATURE, EMPLOYMENT AND MONEY

The problems discussed above arise because for decades both productivity growth and real interest rates have been considerably higher than real growth rates. These are expressions of the declining profit rate on capital in most parts of the world.[44] Unemployment and inequality are increasing on a global scale. For many, the most obvious and convenient way out of this precarious situation appears to be the stimulation of economic growth. In most policy proposals of national governments, international institutions such as the IMF or the World Bank, research institutes or the media, the stimulation of growth is understood as a panacea capable of resolving each and every global problem. But not only are there economic obstacles to an increase of real growth rates, there are also serious ecological limits to further quantitative growth (which, to be sure, also make themselves felt in economic and social terms). The question then becomes: is it possible to reduce the real interest rate or to curb the growth of labour productivity, rather than to continue to stimulate the real growth rate of GDP?

Lowering the interest rate was Keynes' proposal for the creation of new jobs. If the marginal efficiency of capital (the profit rate) could not be increased, the interest rate should be decreased (the 'euthanasia of the rentier').[45] However, this remedy is premised on the sovereignty of the monetary authorities with regard to the determination of the interest rate. As a result of market deregulation, exchange rate liberalization, and financial innovations, the formation of the interest rate on global financial markets can no longer be significantly influenced by national central banks. And global institutions with an adequate control over financial markets do not exist. Even the reform proposals developed after the Asian crisis of 1997 (e.g. by the 'Global Financial Stability Forum' – see the essay by Soederberg in this volume) do not go beyond recommendations for more transparency, prudent behaviour, improved surveillance, monitoring and safeguards; there is no suggestion for interventions into the working of financial markets.

Germany's former finance minister, Oskar Lafontaine, tried to establish a degree of political control over global interest rates (by capping them) and exchange rates (by introducing target zones). He was well aware that such a project could only be realized in cooperation with the European Central Bank and in coordination with the other G7 (G8)-governments. But Lafontaine's proposals were indignantly rejected by 'the markets', the big TNCs, the 'independent' central bankers, public opinion, members of his own government, and – last but not least – leading mainstream economists. Lafontaine's project was the last attempt to break out of the dominant growth discourse and to reconquer economic policy sovereignty from 'the global markets'.

There is a third possible solution: reducing the rate of productivity growth. However, economic growth takes place through competition and is thus based on individual countries' efforts to improve their competitive position; this, in turn, requires increases in productivity. This means that the discourse of globalization and competitiveness inevitably relies on productivity and the conditions required to improve it. This view was very clearly expressed by the Brazilian President Fernando Enrique Cardoso:

> Globalisation means competition founded on higher levels of productivity. That is to say more output per unit of labour. Unemployment has therefore resulted from the very reason that makes an economy successfully competitive … Flexibility of labour relations should also result in lower costs for the hiring of workers... In countries with large populations such as Brazil and India consideration must also

be given to the operation of the so-called informal economy as far as job creation is concerned ...[46]

The consequence of 'successful' adjustment to the challenges of globalization is thus the creation of a dual economy: a formal part, competitive and highly productive, and an informal part that serves to absorb dismissed workers precisely because it is in general less productive than the formal one.[47] The rise of the informal economy obviously provides a 'solution' for the problem of growing unemployment. Its detrimental effects on labour conditions, wages, social security, health conditions and so on become virtues in the era of globalization and under an accumulation regime or growth model which excludes growing parts of the global labour force from the formal employment system. The percentages of informal labour in total employment in 'Third World' countries range from 30% in Chile to 84% in Uganda.[48] In Latin America, between 1990 and 1996 the share of informal employment in non-agricultural sectors increased from 51.6% in 1990 to 57.4% in 1996.[49] In rural areas the percentage of informal work was even higher; the Brazilian Institute for Geography and Statistics (IBGE) considers as much as 90% of the labour force as informal. In Central and Eastern Europe, too, the transition to a market economy and the crisis of 1997 pushed many workers out of the formal into the informal sector, and even in highly developed European countries, informal labour is also becoming more and more important. The percentage of people employed in the so-called 'shadow economy' constitutes between 7% and 16%, depending on the measure used, not counting the roughly 15% of the labour force which is self-employed.[50]

Informal labour, although normally less productive than formal labour, does not have to be unproductive in the Marxian sense. Therefore, the tendency of informalization may be a (partial) solution to the employment problem which does not exert pressure on the average profit rate. In fact, since wage costs in the formal sector are also influenced by the low level of pay for informal labour, the effect on the average profit rate is in all likelihood positive, particularly in those industries where big corporations take advantage of the informal labour of local suppliers.[51] We need to consider the possibility that globalization offers new opportunities for capital to bully working people. On the one hand, capital will try to increase the profit rate and boost productivity by the continued forced flexibilization of labour and wages. On the other hand, it will push redundant workers into the informal sector where they supply low-paid labour, engage in self-employment for local and regional markets, or organize services compensating for the functions that the welfare state has abandoned under pressure from capital.

The growth of the informal sector thus seems to offer a partial solution to the problem of unemployment. Much, though, depends on the measure of productivity that is applied. Normally, this is labour input (in hours worked) against saleable output. This measure is not arbitrary; it is an outcome of 'occidental rationality', the prevailing definitions of property rights, and the associated tendency to compare competitiveness in highly integrated world markets in monetary terms. Nevertheless, there is another measure that would make sense: labour input over the whole life cycle of a product including repairing, tuning and updating the product, and including the *non-traded outputs* of production, i.e. externalized pollution. A procedure of this kind could extend the rules of 'least cost planning' already used in energy markets to the markets for other products. Unfortunately, this measure would not be voluntarily accepted by 'the markets'. Markets and competition enforce acceleration, whereas environmental sustainability requires a policy of deceleration, i.e. restraining productivity increases.

Since the stimulation of growth fails to address the problems of unemployment, inequality and economic instability, a more viable solution could be provided by a combination of new forms of regulation of global financial markets in order to reduce the real interest rate, and a deceleration of productivity growth by means of an expansion of informal sectors and/or a transition to ecologically more sustainable production (and consumption) patterns (and lifestyles). Public awareness of the economic, financial, ecological, and social problems raised by globalization and possible solutions to them still has to be created – e.g. by social movements and NGOs. Without it, the illusory faith in 'growth triumphant' is bound to live on and fuel further deregulation measures – while failing to overcome the crisis. At the end of the day, growth will stagnate or decline, the environment will deteriorate further and the poor will remain poor and grow ever more numerous – all because of the simple-minded notion that growth rates can be advanced even while the limits of the environmental space have been reached and the real economy is depressed by real interest rates higher than the sustainable rate of real GDP growth. In an era of globalization, the conventional paradigm of economic policy is in need of radical rethinking. Such a paradigmatic shift, however, will necessarily have to be accompanied by practical efforts to re-embed the global economic system in qualitatively new social relations and forms of political regulation, on both local and global levels. It is to a transformation of this kind that the movements against de-civilized capitalism, from Seattle to Genoa, aspire.

NOTES

1   David Dollar and Aart Kraay, *Growth is Good for the Poor*, Development Research Group of the World Bank, http://worldbank.org/research, downloaded June 2000.

2   This position has been quoted broadly by newspapers, underlining the necessity of economic growth as a solution for everything. For instance: 'there is no getting around the fact that economic growth must be the point of departure for all improvements in living standards...' (Maza Livanos Cattaui, 'Globalization Holds the Key to Ending World Poverty', *International Herald Tribune*, 30 June 2000). Similarly, the argument of Keith Marsden, published in *The Wall Street Journal Europe* (19 July 2000): 'To reduce poverty, grow the economy.' Not everybody in the World Bank

shares the view outlined by Dollar and Kraay and supported by the new chief econo-mist Nicholas Stern. The editor responsible for the World Development Report 2000 Ravi Kanbur resigned from his office because he could not agree with the optimistic (and in many ways opportunistic) interpretation of Dollar and Kraay (Alan Beattle, 'World Bank Stages Intellectual Battle over Globalisation', *Financial Times*, 30 June 2000).

3   Richard A. Easterlin, *Growth Triumphant: The Twenty-first Century in Historical Perspective*, Ann Arbor: The University of Michigan Press, 1998.

4   Ibid., p. 153. This statement seems to be a repetition of quite similar futurological predictions of perennial growth by Herman Kahn and his Hudson Institute in the 1960s (Fred Moseley, 'The United States Economy at the Turn of the Century: Entering a New Era of Prosperity?', *Capital and Class*, No. 67, Spring 1999, p.26). The emphasis on the desirability and feasibility of growth is an essential aspect of the affirmative discourse of modernity because one of the most important features of modernity is its quantitative expansion in time and space.

5   Philip McMichael, quoted by John Bellamy Foster, 'The Crisis of the Earth. Marx's Theory of Ecological Sustainability as Nature-Imposed Necessity for Human Production', *Organization & Environment*, Vol. 10, No. 3 (September), 1997, p. 126.

6   Paul Ekins and Michael Jacobs, 'Environmental Sustainability and the Growth of GDP: Conditions for Compatibility', in V. Bhaskar and A. Glyn., eds., *The North, The South and the Environment. Ecological Constraints and the Global Economy*, London: Earthscan, 1995.

7   Enrique Dussel, 'Beyond Eurocentrism: The World-System and the Limits of Modernity', in Frederic Jameson and Masao Miyosh, eds., *The Cultures of Globalization*, Durham and London: Duke University Press, 1998, p. 3 passim.

8   David Harvey, *Justice, Nature & the Geography of Difference*, Cambridge, Mass./ Oxford: Blackwell, 1996.

9   This has to be understood as a statement about the main trend in economic devel-opment. There are also counter-tendencies, such as protectionism between trading blocks, and the great divide between those parts of the world captured by the dynamics of globalization and the parts excluded from these.

10   Gérard Duménil and Dominique Lévy, 'Brenner on Distribution', *Historical Materialism*, 4 (summer), 1999.

11   Paul Mattick 'Die deflationäre Inflation', in Elmar Altvater, Volkhard Brandes, and Jochen Reiche, eds., *Inflation – Akkumulation – Krise, I, Handbuch 3*, Frankfurt-Main/ Köln: Europäische Verlagsanstalt, 1976.

12   Moisés Naím, 'Washington Consensus or Washington Confusion?', *Foreign Policy*, Spring, 2000, p. 96.

13   For example, World Bank, *World Development Report 2000/2001: Attacking Poverty*, Washington D.C., 2000.

14   Jügen Blazejczak, ed., *Zukunftsgestaltung ohne Wirtschaftswachstum? – Ergebnisse eines Workshops des DIW im Auftrag von Greenpeace Deutschland*, DIW – Diskussionspapier Nr. 168, Berlin, May 1998; Andrew Glyn, 'Northern Growth and Environmental Constraints', in V. Bhaskar and Andrew Glyn, eds., *The North The South and the Environment. Ecological Constraints and the Global Economy*, London: Earthscan, 1995.

15 For the distinction between 'clean' and 'dirty' pollution, see Elmar Altvater and Birgit Mahnkopf, *Grenzen der Globalisierung. Ökonomie, Politik, Ökologie in der Weltgesellschaft*, Münster: Westfälisches Dampfboot, 1999.

16 Immanuel Wallerstein, 'A Left Politics for the 21st Century? Or, Theory and Praxis Once Again', *New Political Science*, Vol. 22, No. 2, 2000.

17 Karl Polanyi, *The Great Transformation*, Frankfurt am Main: Suhrkamp, 1978.

18 The question of whether this process began, as Polanyi assumes, in the eighteenth and nineteenth century or much earlier, in the course of the long sixteenth century, is an important one; however, this question cannot be answered here.

19 Karl Marx, *Das Kapital*, Marx-Engels Werke 23, Vol. 1, chapter 14.

20 Polanyi, *The Great Transformation*; Anthony Giddens, *Konsequenzen der Moderne*, Frankfurt/M.: Suhrkamp, 1995; Altvater and Mahnkopf, *Grenzen der Globalisierung*, chapter 3, pp. 90-123.

21 Angus Maddison, *Monitoring the World Economy 1820-1992*, Paris: OECD, 1995, p. 40. Data presented and interpreted by Crafts support Maddison's statement; see Crafts, *Globalization and Growth*.

22 Wallerstein, 'A Left Politics for the 21st Century?', p. 147.

23 The German Institute for Economic Research (DIW) calculated an annual average increase of production value in German manufacturing of 1.7% and an average increase of labour productivity (production value per person employed) of 3.7% from 1991 to 1999 (Deutsches Institut für Wirtschafts-forschung, Wochenbericht 14/2000).

24 Mario Pianta, 'Trasformazioni del lavoro: il "terzo settore"', *Parolechiave*, 14/15 dicembre 1997, Roma: Dozelli editore, 1998.

25 For the USA, see Fred Moseley, 'The United States Economy at the Turn of the Century: Entering a New Era of Prosperity?', *Capital and Class*, 67, Spring 1999, pp. 28-9.

26 This is not the place to discuss the Marxist concepts of productive and unproductive labour. For Marx, a worker is productive insofar as he (she) produces surplus value. Unproductive labour, by contrast, does not produce, but merely consumes surplus value. This does not mean that it is useless. Unproductive labour is often necessary in order to sustain a social process of reproduction. The distinction between productive and unproductive labour is not coterminous with that between production and services, or with that between material and immaterial labour. It is, however, obvious that productivity increases can be 'consumed' by unproductive workers, so that there is some margin for the creation of jobs outside the 'productive' sector.

27 Paul E. Bangasser, *The ILO and the Informal Sector: an Institutional History*, Geneva: ILO, 2000 (http://www.ilo.org/public/english/employment/strat/ publ/ep00-9.htm, downloaded 24 October 2000); Victor Tokman, 'La informilidad en los anos noventa: situatción actual y perspectivas', in Jorge Carpio and Irene Novacovsky, eds., *De igual a igual. El desafío del Estado ante los nuevos problemas sociales*, Buenos Aires: Siempro, FLACSO, 1999. For European countries, see Sergio Bologna and Andrea Fumagalli, eds., *Il Lavoro Autionomo di Seconda Generazione. Scenari del Postfordismo in Italia*, Milano: Feltrinelli, 1997; Friedrich Schneider and Dominik Enste, *Schattenwirtschaft und Schwarzarbeit. Umfang, Ursachen, Wirkungen und wirtschaft-spolitische Empfehlungen*, München und Wien: R. Oldenbourg, 2000.

28 Adam Smith, *An Inquiry into the Nature and Causes of The Wealth of Nations*, Chicago: The University of Michigan Press, 1976 [1776].

29 David Held, Anthony McGrew, David Goldblatt and Jonathan Perraton, *Global Transformations. Politics, Economics and Culture*, Cambridge: Polity Press, 1999.

30 In any given production process, the material content of a unit of output may decrease. But in the long run, and on a society-wide scale, the consumption of energy and matter is increasing so rapidly that the carrying capacity of ecosystems has become overstretched. If it were possible to reduce the consumption of matter and energy by simple technical measures, many difficulties during climate and water negotiations would not arise.

31 Elmar Altvater, *Der Preis des Wohlstands*, Münster: Westfälisches Dampfboot, 1992; Elmar Altvater, *The Future of the Market*, London: Verso, 1993.

32 Robert Goodland, Herman Daly, and Serafy El, *Nach dem Brundtland-Bericht: Umweltverträgliche wirtschaftliche Entwicklung*, Bonn: Deutsche UNESCO-Kommission, 1992.

33 World Bank et. al, *Global Poverty Report*.

34 Wuppertal Institut für Klima, Umwelt, Energie, *Zukunftsfähiges Deutschland. Ein Beitrag zu einer global nachhaltigen Entwicklung*, ed. by BUND and Misereor, Basel/Boston/Berlin: (Birkhäuser), 1996; annual reports of the Worldwatch Institute Report (1984 etc.): Lester R. Brown et al., *State of the World*, New York/London: W.W. Norton.

35 János Kornai, 'The Soft Budget Constraint', *Kyklos*, Vol. 39, No. 1, 1986.

36 OECD, *Economic Outlook*, June 1993, Paris.

37 Ibid., pp. 29-31.

38 The macro-economic policy trilemma first articulated by Mundell (that a government can achieve only two of the following three objectives – a fixed or at least stable exchange rate, the free movement of capital, and an independent monetary policy) has been resolved by using high interest rates to protect the exchange rate in the face of a more and more deregulated financial market (i.e. independent monetary policy has been sacrificed).

39 Gates, 'People-ized Ownership Patterns', p. 437.

40 Mattick, 'Die deflationäre Inflation'.

41 Jonathan Friedland and Leslie Chang, 'Spreading Fat Slows Global Economy', *Wall Street Journal*, 30 November 1998. The authors continue their argument by pointing to the fact that China and other new competitors have been throwing masses of cheap goods on already satiated markets. But the main culprit of global overproduction is Japan.

42 Ibid.

43 Clifford G. Gaddy and Barry W. Ickes, 'Russia's Virtual Economy', *Foreign Affairs*, September/October 1998.

44 Robert Brenner, 'The Economics of Global Turbulence', *New Left Review*, No. 229, 1998.

45 John M. Keynes, *The General Theory of Employment, Interest and Money*, London/Melbourne/Toronto: Macmillan, 1964 [1936].

46 The text of the speech can be accessed on the Internet: http://www.brasil.emb.-nw.dc.us/fpst06gl.htm; downloaded 24 January 1999; in Portuguese: Folha de Sao

Paulo, 28 January 1996.

47 ILO, *Employment, Incomes and Equality*, Geneva: ILO, 1972; Alejandro Portes, 'The Informal Economy. Perspectives from Latin America', in Susan Pozo, ed., *Exploring the Underground Economy, Studies of Illegal and Unreported Activity*, Michigan: W.E. Upjohn Institute for Employment Research, 1996.

48 See http://www.ilo.org/public/spanish/region...temas/worker/doc/ otros/iv/ii/i/ index.htm

49 Victor Tokman, 'La informilidad en los anos noventa: situatción actual y perspectivas', in: Jorge Carpio/Irene Novacovsky, eds., *De igual a igual. El desafío del Estado ante los nuevos problemas sociales*, Buenos Aires: Siempro, FLACSO, p. 82.

50 Paolo Perulli, 'Die Bedeutung der informellen Arbeit im postindustriellen Europa', in Elmar Altvater and Birgit Mahnkopf, coord., *Die Ökonomie eines friedlichen Europa, Ziele – Hindernisse – Wege*, Münster: Agenda-Verlag, 2000.

51 This is the theme of a growing number of books, e.g. Kathryn Ward, ed., *Women Workers and Global Restructuring*, Ithaca N.Y: ILR Press, 1990; Altvater and Mahnkopf, *Grenzen der Globalisierung*.

THE AMERICAN CAMPAIGN FOR GLOBAL SOVEREIGNTY

Peter Gowan

INTRODUCTION

The main feature of world politics since the collapse of the Soviet Bloc has been the American state's campaign to rebuild and expand the protectorate systems that formed the basis of American global political dominance during the Cold War. This campaign has, of course, been linked to parallel expansionist efforts by the West European states, and partly cooperative and partly conflictual attempts by the Atlantic powers to organize a new global set of political-legal regimes for reorganizing international economic relationships in ways favourable to the international dominance of American and European business. The purpose of this essay is to explore this campaign for a new protectorate system, though it will also make reference to the connection between this project and the other changes being pushed forward in the international political economy.[1]

I. ORIGINS AND EVOLUTION IN THE COLD WAR

When the Soviet system of military alliances and protectorates collapsed at the start of the 1990s, the American system of protectorates did not follow suit. Instead successive US administrations have sought to revivify and enlarge the American-centred systems into a framework for the structural consolidation of American global power in the twenty-first century. Many, particularly within the American security zones, had imagined that the US protectorates existed only as defensive mechanisms against Communism and Soviet power. But the Soviet collapse showed that, at least as far as the American state was concerned, this was not the

This essay was first published in *Fighting Identities, The Socialist Register 2003*.

case. The origins of the US protectorate system lay in the defeats of Germany and Japan and in the US-led alliance systems to 'contain' Eurasian Communism. But although the protectorate system began as a means for addressing those issues, it became an end in itself for the American state. Indeed, by the 1980s American anti-Sovietism had itself become in large measure a means for preserving and reorganizing the protectorate system itself.

The Origins and Character of the US Protectorate System

The US protectorate system has covered the capitalist core: not only North America, but also the two Eurasian 'rimlands' of Western Europe and East Asia (Japan, Taiwan, South Korea, Australia and New Zealand). Of course, it has extended beyond these zones, but these zones were decisive. It was established in the 1950s as a set of security alliances between the United States and other states under which the US provided external and, to some extent, internal security to the target state, while the latter gave the US the right to establish bases and gain entry for other of its organizations into the jurisdiction of the state. The US was also given effective control over many aspects of the external policies (and some internal policies) of the states concerned.[2]

One important aspect of the system was its 'hub-and-spokes' character which applied also in the West European NATO states: each protectorate's primary military-political relationship had to be with the United States. Attempts by the West European members of NATO, for example, to construct West European caucuses within NATO were slapped down by the United States.[3] This rule against intra-protectorate regional caucusing did not apply to economic politics – hence the institutions of West European integration – but it did apply in military-political affairs.

The protectorate system imposed strict limits on the external orientations of the subordinate states: they could not polarize against the main thrusts of US global policy vis-à-vis the Soviet Bloc and they were expected to respect limits laid down by the United States on their relations with Soviet Bloc countries and Soviet Bloc allies. The US could not only define the enemies of the core. It could also decide when the protectorate zone faced a state of emergency and when it did not: Korea 1950, yes; Hungary 1956, no; Cuba 1962, yes; Czechoslovakia 1968, no; Afghanistan 1979, yes; Poland 1981, yes, and so on.

At the same time, the leadership of the US over its protectorate systems gave it the right to lay down rules for each system without itself being bound by those rules: it claimed the right to invade states deemed hostile, to use covert actions to overthrow governments, to wage proxy wars, mount economic blockades, etc. etc. This right to unilateral action in breach of rules deemed harmful to important US interests applied also in the field of international political economy.[4]

This, then, was a system of US political domination that approached political sovereignty over the way the protectorates related to their external environment in the sense of that term used by Carl Schmitt: sovereign is the power which can define the community's friends and enemies and can thus give the community its social substance (in this case, American-style capitalism); sovereign is the power which can define a state of emergency; and the community's norms apply to the sovereign only in a situation judged normal by the sovereign.[5] Such US political sovereignty over the capitalist core was never total or absolute and at times it was gravely weakened, as during the Vietnam defeat. But it amounted to a qualitatively new type of political order for the core capitalist states.

At the same time, the protectorate system gave the US varying degrees of *direct access* to the *social systems* of the protectorates.[6] US agencies could operate within the protectorate societies to track communist subversion in trade unions, political parties and the media or intelligentsia, and US media and entertainment sectors also gained large openings.[7] And, of course, US firms won wide degrees of access for their exports to and, often, their investments in the protectorates, whose markets were successfully opened by the US during the 1950s.[8]

No less important was the fact that the internal political institutions of the protectorates were harmonized with their external orientations: in those that were liberal democracies the officially acceptable governing parties and mass media organizations were aligned with anti-Communist and anti-Soviet ideology and politics. This gave the US a capacity for mass mobilization on a transnational scale behind its main international political campaigns. Brzezinski has rightly likened this institutionalized anti-Communist political culture to quasi-religious belief systems.[9]

It is very important to note that the protectorate system was never in any sense a juridical empire or principally dependent upon international legal or institutional arrangements. The very fact that it was not, and that states retained their juridical sovereignty as full subjects of international law, was both a key way in which the protectorate system was legitimated *and* a very real source of the ability of the protectorates to continue to be organizing centres of national capitalism.[10]

Coercion and Consent in the Protectorate System

The protectorate system could not, of course, have been established without the coercive occupation of West Germany and Japan at the end of World War II. But at the same time it would be a fundamental mistake to view this system, as it emerged in the 1950s, as the result of coercive diktat produced by US military superiority. The builders of the system – above all Dean Acheson in the last phase of the Truman administration – offered the key states in the system very substantial advantages. The defeated German and Japanese capitalist classes were offered the chance to rebuild their economies as regional capitalist hubs as they had been before 1945, along with re-integration into the state system, though under rather tight US political controls. France and Britain had to accept this US line but were offered other advantages of their own. Britain was allowed to try to hang on to its Empire and given important US support (in the monetary and financial field) for doing so, and was prepared to accept US European dominance in exchange. France and Italy were offered strong support against domestic Communist challenges and France was also offered the role of leading 'European integration' and thus influencing the revival of German capitalism, as well as support in Indo-China. Most of the elites of the dominant classes in these states accepted the US protectorate offers readily and the system remained predominantly consensual during the 1950s and 1960s, apart from the Suez crisis and de Gaulle's withdrawal from the NATO military structure. Serious inter-state tensions pitting groups of protectorates against the US arose only in the 1970s.

And not only did the system offer acceptable national political strategies to the main protectorate states: it was combined with a protectorate-wide political economy regime which offered viable national accumulation strategies to match. At the same time, and very importantly, the protectorate system gained a substantial mass political basis within the protectorates, winning support not only on the centre-right but also within the social democratic movement and large parts of the trade union movements. Gaining and institutionally consolidating this base was partly the result of covert activity in some countries but it was mainly the result of the substantial economic and social gains achieved by labour under the system during the post-war boom. Such gains were undoubtedly an indirect result of the social challenge from Communism after the war. But the American economic paradigm made substantial social concessions to labour viable.

We thus have a paradox: an international political order which qualitatively weakened the foreign policy autonomy of the non-US core states and seriously compromised the internal political autonomy of some of them; but one which at the same time produced widespread consent, either active or passive, amongst a very broad and disparate range of classes in these countries. In this connection, the link between the protectorates' external orientation and the central mechanisms of domestic political domination is particularly noteworthy. The anti-Soviet external orientation proved a very potent mechanism for combating the left internally. The parties of the right, which were the main political mechanisms for confronting working-class movements, were time and again able to use the supposed Soviet threat as their trump card against the left, and by doing so they re-enforced the structure of American dominance. These domestic political structures could also be used by the US against centre-left or centre-right state leaderships on occasion (Willi Brandt 1974, Aldo Moro 1978, etc). The domestic political structure made any kind of direct challenge to US international power difficult to manage domestically: De Gaulle could be considered one, perhaps singular, exception.

Yet the protectorate system also rested upon the American state's coercive military capacities. Indeed this coercive dimension became increasingly important as time passed, and the capitalisms of the protectorates revived and inter-capitalist tensions increased in the 1970s. But these US coercive capacities were exerted on the protectorates *indirectly*: through structuring the state security *environment* of the states concerned, and not at all through threatening the application of US military force against any protectorate. This use of military force to shape the environment of the rest of the core has, indeed, been the secret of American statecraft since 1947. It came into operation once the states concerned had entered a political alliance with the USA against the USSR. Given that political orientation, these states quickly found their entire national military security dependent upon the military political relationship between the USA and the USSR (and/or China). A US-Soviet war, wherever it started, could engulf their region, and if it did it could spell the annihilation of their society. They thus found the security of their state and their population lay entirely outside their own hands.

At times they feared that in a military confrontation with the Soviets the US would allow their annihilation in order to avoid a generalized nuclear war that would destroy the USA. At other times they feared that the USA's brinkmanship might plunge them needlessly into a devastating war. And at yet other times, they feared that the US might strike deals with the enemy which would disadvantage them in some other way. But in all these scenarios the effect of US coercive power on their environment made them cleave to the USA and seek to influence it as their number one priority, and the precondition for influence was that they should be loyal and useful allies.

A second use of US military-political capacity for brigading the protectorates lay in US efforts to gain and maintain control over certain key inputs for the economies of the protectorates, above all oil, but also other strategic minerals. This involved making US political dominance in the Gulf a national security priority of successive US administrations, along with control over sea routes. This was linked to a more general protectorate dependence on the USA's preponderant military influence over the periphery and over the routes to it, for both key economic inputs and for protecting investments and other economic links with the South.

The International Capitalism of the Protectorate System

The protectorate system profoundly altered the character of the capitalist core. In the first place, it ended the possibility of great power wars between core capitalist states. After the Suez debacle, the protectorates' military capacities, still large in world terms, were confined to operations tolerated by the United States. This transformation allowed much more secure exchanges to develop between core capitalisms. And the internal transformation of social relations within the protectorates in the direction of the American 'fordist' system of accumulation opened up the possibility of a vast expansion of their *internal markets*, with the working class not only as the source of expanded surplus value but also as an increasingly important consumption centre for *realizing* surplus value. The centrality of the old imperial patterns of European and Japanese accumulation thus withered.

At the same time, after the war the American state did not try to turn the protectorates into its own capitalist socio-economic empire: it did not make a grab for the key centres of property of the defeated powers or prostrate capitalisms of Europe; and it did not destroy the capacity of other core states to act as *autonomous organizing centres* of capital accumulation. It merely *limited the scope* of this autonomy in Europe, as it sought a range of 'national rights' for its capitals to enter the jurisdictions of European states.[11] The protectorates could still plan and organize their accumulation strategies domestically and internationally. National systems of accumulation were organized through spinal cords of state-financial sector-industrial systems, with commercial banks (often nationalized) playing a central role as transmission belts. And they could use an array of instruments for projecting their capitals abroad.

Where the US proved sensitive and assertive in the economic field proper was in assuring its own control over the international monetary system and in preserving US dominance in what are usually called 'high tech' fields. That included two areas: first, key military technologies – the US has fiercely defended its own military technological dominance over its protectorate allies; secondly, control of the new leading sector technologies – those of what seem to be the new 'infrastructure' (capital goods) industries of the future. Signs of a Japanese edge in some of these areas in the 1980s, for example, provoked fierce hostility from Washington.[12] Linked to this aim to control the high tech sectors has been a determination to drive the high tech sectors it controls through the whole protectorate system to ensure as far as possible that they do form the basis for the new wave of economic transformation across the core. The protectorate status – political dependence – of the rest of the core ensured that the US had great political leverage for precisely ensuring the dominance of its own capitalism in critical areas.[13]

The US protectorate system as it grew up and consolidated itself during the Cold War was the basis for a new type of dominant global power, qualitatively different from British hegemony in the nineteenth century. The US was not the most powerful among a dispersed set of the core capitalist states: it was political master of a core 'brigaded' by it, and it was this relationship with the rest of the core which gave the US extraordinary global power. The basing arrangements, logistics and intelligence facilities supplied by its protectorates, and the institutionalized political alignments of the protectorates internally as well as externally, gave the US truly gigantic capacities for mobilizing massive political force, both ideational and material.

The Reaganite Turn of the 1980s

The great challenge to this system came with the economic and political crisis of the 1970s. The catastrophic defeat and disintegration of American military power in Vietnam was combined with a fierce competitive crisis between the main centres of the triad – the US, Germany and Japan. The US responded to the crisis with big unilateral moves to favour US capitalism against its competitors, such as destroying the Bretton Woods system and imposing a dollar system on the world. The European states attempted to establish a regional political caucus and the US broke it up; and so on.

The Reagan administration attempted a radical reorganization of socio-economic relations within the core and between it and the countries of the South, using the political structures of the protectorate system. The essence of the Reaganite programme was to encourage an offensive against labour and social rights both in the core and in the periphery, so as to strengthen the rights and power of capital in ways that would simultaneously encourage the revival of American capitalism. The earlier post-war development models – the social democratic welfare state, the import-substitution models – were all to be scrapped. So too were the social alliances underpinning these models. Capitalist classes were offered the prospect of enriching themselves domestically through this turn, as rentiers cashing in on the privatization or pillage of state assets and as employers cracking down on trade unions, etc. And the restrictions on the international movement of capitalist property – the systems of capital controls – would also be scrapped, giving capital the power to exit from national jurisdictions, thus strengthening further their domestic social power over labour.

At the same time as these old Cold War restrictions on capitalist property rights were dismantled, capitalist states were expected to make major concessions to American capitalism. They were to support a dollar-centred international monetary system in which the US was free to manipulate exchange rates to suit its exclusive national economic strategy; they were to support the dominance of the American financial system internationally, weakening or preferably breaking the old national spinal cords of state-finance-industry linkages driving national capitalisms; and they were to open up their consumer markets, labour markets and assets to American capitals in the key areas where American capitalism was seeking to build its global dominance: finance, other 'service' sectors, electronics, defence industries etc. – the new 'Uruguay Round' agenda pushed by the Reagan administration from 1981 onwards.

This entire Reaganite turn in US national accumulation strategy was driven forward by a powerful international political campaign, which re-articulated anti-Communism. The USSR was no longer so much an expansionist state: it was an evil empire of controls on 'freedom', controls which also existed in 'socialistic' state structures in the West including social-democratic and development state structures. All such arrangements restricted the freedom of markets and crushed free enterprise with crippling taxation and other restrictions such as 'rigid' labour markets and the like.

But at the same time the Reaganite programme also involved strong elements of inter-state coercion on the part of the US against other core states: fierce coercive pressures on Japan using economic statecraft – driving the dollar down against the yen and brutal confrontations on trade issues; threats of theatre nuclear war in Europe, and threats of aggressive trade war there too.

The Reaganite drive was only a partial success within the core protectorate zones. It succeeded in rallying European elites to halt and start reversing the European social democratic model of capitalism; it gained free movement of capital in the core and in the early 1990s it eventually won a deal on the Uruguay Round, not least because of the new prospects for Atlantic capitals to expand outwards into East and South East Asia as well as the periphery through such a deal.

But it was also marked by failures. The American blandishments for a new rentier capitalism fell on deaf ears in East Asian bourgeoisies. And the Japanese responded to US economic warfare by both regionalizing their accumulation strategy and acquiring leverage over US policy through taking large holdings in the US debt market.[14] And Europe's response combined the shift against the social rights of labour with a new and increasingly political West European regionalism combining the Single Market Programme with a Deutschmark zone on the road to monetary union. These arrangements combined the Reaganite (now called 'neoliberal') turn against labour with a defensive shield against the US dollar system of international monetary relations. There were signs of a remarkable regional alliance of European capitalisms around a common capital accumulation strategy which sat uneasily with a political system requiring loyalty to the American centre.

It is worth noting also that the US activation of the protectorate political structure in the Second Cold War produced a shattering of that structure's mass base in Europe. In the late 1980s enormous peace movements swept Western Europe and popular opinion swung over massively towards the Gorbachev leadership of the USSR. The result was that the Bush administration lost control of European politics in 1989-90: the German government, linked to the Soviet government and riding on a huge popular wave in Western Europe, was able to forge German unification and raise the prospect of an entirely new European political system, replacing the protectorate structures altogether.

II. THE US DRIVE TO PRESERVE THE PROTECTORATE SYSTEM AFTER THE SOVIET BLOC COLLAPSE

With the collapse of the Soviet Bloc, the American policy establishment swiftly decided to struggle to preserve its protectorate system. This political decision has driven or strongly conditioned most of the major political conflicts of the last decade, from the Gulf War through the wars in the Western Balkans to the Bush campaign against 'the Axis of Evil'.

The most blunt evidence of the US decision was the (probably officially inspired) leak of the Defence Planning Guidance document of the Pentagon and National Security Council in early 1992.[15] This indicated that maintaining the protectorate system was the US's *most fundamental strategic goal*. It declared that the 'dominant consideration' in US national strategy would be 'to prevent any hostile power from dominating a region whose resources would, under consolidated control, be sufficient to generate global power'. Those regions were specified as Western Europe, East Asia, the territory of the former Soviet Union and Southwest Asia.[16] This could only mean one thing: stamping out autonomous regionalist challenges to the US protectorate system from the West Europeans and from Japanese or Japanese–Chinese regionalist projects. Put positively, the US was striving to preserve its protectorate systems and to expand them in a new global Pax Americana.

At the time of its appearance the document, written by Lewis Libby and Paul Wolfowitz, drew criticism from some Democrats. As Wolfowitz later explained, Senator Biden, Chair of the Senate Foreign Relations Committee, ridiculed the proposed strategy as 'literally a Pax Americana. ... It won't work'. But Wolfowitz adds:

Just seven years later, many of these same critics seem quite comfortable with the idea of a Pax Americana ....Today the criticism of Pax Americana comes mainly from the isolationist right, from Patrick Buchanan, who complains that 'containment, a defensive strategy, had given way to a breathtakingly ambitious offensive strategy – to "establish and protect a new order".[17]

And Wolfowitz continues:

> One would like to think that this new consensus – Buchanan apart – reflects a recognition that the United States cannot afford to allow a hostile power to dominate Europe or Asia or the Persian Gulf; that the safest, and in the long run the cheapest, way to prevent this is to preserve the US-led alliances that have been so successful .... But in reality today's consensus is facile and complacent .... Still, one should not look a gift horse in the mouth. There is today a remarkable degree of agreement on a number of central points of foreign policy. No one is lobbying to withdraw troops from Korea, as was the case as recently as the late 1980s. No one is arguing that we should withdraw from Europe. American forces under President Clinton's command have been bombing Iraq with some regularity for months now, without a whimper of opposition in the Congress and barely a mention in the press. Even on ballistic missile defence there is today an emerging consensus that something needs to be done – although no agreement on precisely what.[18]

Wolfowitz's claim in 2000 that his central strategic goal of 1991 became the central goal of the Clinton administration cannot seriously be doubted. Anthony Lake, Clinton's first National Security adviser, also stressed the bipartisan nature of core US strategy, declaring that 'Political leaders may change with elections, but American interests do not'.[19] In his first major keynote speech on US grand strategy Lake stressed that the fundamental 'feature of this era is that we are its dominant power. Those who say otherwise sell America short. ... Around the world, America's power, authority and example provide unparalleled opportunities to lead ... our interests and ideals compel us not only to be engaged, but to lead'. (The word 'lead' here is code for protectoratism.) And he continued: 'The successor to a doctrine of containment must be a strategy of enlargement – enlargement of the world's free community of market democracies'.[20]

Lake recognized that in the early 1990s the 'community' of 'market democracies' faced two problems: internal tensions over economics; and a so-called 'military problem', which turned out not to be a military problem at all but the following: 'If NATO is to remain an anchor for European and Atlantic stability, as the President believes it must, its members must commit themselves to updating NATO's role in this new era'.[21] In other words the protectorate system had to be revivified.

This theme of strengthening the US alliance systems was a constant in the speeches of the Clinton administration. In 1996 Lake was still stressing 'acts of construction on the core security issues' and by this he meant first and foremost 'to strengthen and broaden our core alliances as we lay the groundwork for peace in the 21st Century'.[22] And in laying this groundwork for tackling problems around the world, these speeches are striking for what they miss out: not a single word about the UN or any force other than US-led alliances with the US, acting, according to Lake, on the following watchwords: 'Diplomacy where we can; force where we must'.[23] Nothing in these core concepts differs one whit from the concepts of Wolfowitz. And the guiding concepts in Clinton's second term were no different, with Madeleine Albright from Brzezinski's kindergarten playing a central role.[24]

The US drive to revivify its protectorate system was, as Lake indicated in the speech quoted above, linked to a second strategic thrust: the drive for 'economic globalization'. This was an aggressive campaign to reshape international and transnational economic relations within the protectorates, and in the ten 'Big Emerging Markets', in line with the perceived interests of US capitalism. In pursuing this second strand of strategy the Clinton administration announced that economics would no longer be separated from politics within the capitalist core: for the USA, economics was now to be treated as a 'national security' issue. As Andrew Bacevich of Johns Hopkins puts it:

> At the very heart of the Clinton administration's approach to strategy is the concept of globalization. As a rationale for the role of the United States in the world, 'Globalization' today has become the functional equivalent of the phrase 'Free World' during the 1950s and 1960s. It contains an important truth, but vastly oversimplifies that truth. It implies mysteries grasped fully only in the most rarefied circles of government. It suggests the existence of obligations to which ordinary people must submit. It is a powerful instrument of persuasion, the rhetorical device of last resort, to which ... there is no counter.[25]

We will consider later what this second strand of strategy has been about.

No one can, of course, doubt the commitment of the Bush Junior administration to pursue more vigorously than ever the maintenance, strengthening and enlargement of the protectorate system. It entered office determined to give a more activist and coercive accent to this drive at both ends of Eurasia as well as in the Middle East. After a shaky start, these goals were given new focus and impetus by September 11, which was quickly understood by the Bush administration as an *opportunity*, an occasion for achieving precisely what they had wanted to achieve all along. Within four days of the attack Colin Powell and Bush were agreeing that it gave the American state an opportunity to recast global relations as a whole.

III. THE SOURCES OF THE PAX AMERICANA DRIVE

Before proceeding to consider the prospects for consolidating the new Pax Americana we must briefly try to assess what its political and/or social basis is: what combination of forces does it really represent?

Demand-led Supply of Global Order

Some realist American international relations theorists have tried to argue that only the coercive power supplied by a 'hegemon' maintains order within the core capitalist states: without the Leviathan's Pax Americana there will be a

Hobbesian war of each against all. The Pax is thus an American burden with the US supplying the crucial 'public good' of order and cooperation to the system as a whole. The classic statement of this position was John Mearsheimer's famous essay on Europe, entitled 'Back to the Future',[26] arguing that only continued US dominance can prevent Europe from returning to pre-1914 style rivalries.[27]

Yet this interpretation, though having an important grain of truth in the 1950s, had become false by the 1990s, thanks to the transformation of both European inter-state and transatlantic relations. By then, the real problem was that the collapse of the Soviet Bloc had removed the security undergirding of Europe's protectorate status and the West European states were seriously banding together, overcoming the hub-and-spokes patterns of the Cold War security system. The fear of Wolfowitz and others was precisely that Western Europe was coming together dangerously and threatening to throw off the protectorate controls.

The core capitalist countries do indeed engage in constant rivalries to gain advantage in the struggle for shares in global capital accumulation. But they simultaneously engage in efforts to maintain cooperation to preserve arrangements that foster the accumulation interests of all. The idea that intra-core cooperation today depends principally upon protectorate structures policed by an intrusive Leviathan is propagandistic. A particular type of cooperation requires US hegemony, but there are other possible types as well.

American Political Culture

Others detect the source of the US drive for global dominance in the peculiarities of American political culture – the messianic strain in it – suggesting that the US is an exceptional (God given?) state with a manifest destiny to transform the world: the naive assumption that Americans have all the answers to all the world's problems and that resistance to American solutions derives from evil sources.[28]

This strand certainly does exist in American political culture. But so do many other strands that contradict these impulses to global activism, and during the 1990s these other strands have evidently been predominant within the American polity. Since 1989, American voters have been extremely reluctant to endorse any global activist agenda to consolidate a new Pax Americana. This has been a constant source of sorrow and frustration among US state elites. *Only since September 11* has the electorate swung over to support global activism and political assertiveness, and this has been based on the belief that the Bush administration is defending America. The American electorate is not aware that the Bush team is using their fear of terrorism to implement a quite different project for a new global Pax Americana of protectorates.

The State Establishment as 'rent seekers'

David Calleo suggests an interest group source for the Pax Americana drive. He says that 'America's large Cold War military, diplomatic, financial, industrial and academic establishments naturally favoured a new age of triumphant global hegemony. But the rest of the country was not necessarily for it'.[29] This fits with conceptions of a military–industrial complex – industrial groups and the US military along with members of Congress whose constituencies benefit from their operations.

This complex does of course exist. But so do lots of other 'complexes' whose bottom lines or 'maximands' are not directly linked to the military budget. Such groups might be expected to favour a downsizing of Big Military Government and either allocating tax dollars to other fields or perhaps slashing taxes. At the very least such a direct interest group explanation would suggest a big battle within business over the Pax Americana project. Yet that has not been the pattern: consolidating the Pax has become completely bipartisan and consensual outside small nationalist–isolationist circles around Buchanan. Calleo's focus on the various establishments with a direct stake in the Pax does not seem sufficient. Why have the very broadest coalitions of internationally-oriented US business backed this grand strategy?

The Relationship between International Politics and Economics

The general answer lies in the fact that the relationship between international economics and politics is not, in fact, what it is widely supposed to be. There is not, in fact, an *autonomous* and *general* set of norm-based market rules governing international economic exchanges. The legal and institutional arrangements governing international exchanges is extremely extensive but although it is legitimated as governed by clear liberal formulae such as 'multilateralism' and 'free trade', such terms are pure ideological mystification and the rule networks are in reality *thickets of policies* saturated in power relations between states. And these power relations are not at all confined to relationships of economic power: all kinds of political forces are brought into play by states in the shaping and reshaping of international economic rules and regimes.

The ideology of globalization is, of course, geared to obliterating this funda-mental fact. But nobody with any link to the international economic policy of the United States could be fooled by such ideology for a minute. In reality, it 'stands to reason' for all sections of US business with international interests that a political protectorate system must be good for the US if the costs to US business of maintaining it are not cripplingly high.

The Structure of Contemporary US capitalism Depends upon the Protectorate System

But this general argument dovetails with a much more specific one: a consensus within the broad US business class and state policy-making elites that *the real existing structure of US capitalism* depends upon the preservation and extension of the Cold War protectorate systems in the post-Cold War world.[30] A glance at this specific structure of accumulation indicates why:[31]

> (1) The dominance of the dollar rests upon US military-political power.
> This dollar dominance favours US importers and US exporters. It enables
> the US to open its markets to imports from the South almost without trade
> deficit limit, thus ensuring that the US financial sector gains its debt repay-
> ments. The same opportunity for huge trade deficits (equivalent to over
> *1% of world GDP* in 2000) gives the US great leverage over the economies

of East and South East Asia to get them to reciprocally open their jurisdictions to US capitals.

(2) The dominance of Wall Street in the financial sector also rests on both dollar dominance and the fact that the US is the world's dominant military power. This gives the US the benefit of huge flows of funds from all over the world into the US financial market and into the satellite London market dominated by US operators. In the year 2000 the IMF's global accounts showed that the world had an export surplus with itself (sic!) of over 180 billion dollars: this represents just one part of the huge capital flight mainly into the US financial market in a single year. This brings down US interest rates, boosting the whole US economy.

(3) The IMF/World Bank system and the UN system operate largely as instruments of US state policy because of the USA's role as the world's dominant military power. These structures bring a whole host of great benefits to US capitalism, creating new proletarians for US businesses, opening a whole range of markets and doing so very heavily through lending non-American money from other core states.

(4) The protectorate structure gives the American state leverage to protect US ascendancy in a whole range of potentially very important areas from high tech/capital goods to energy resources and prices. It would, in principle, be possible for the other core states to launch a new high tech set of sectors on a world scale focused upon, say, new energy conservation and environmental protection industries. Such a strategic move could produce new waves of capital accumulation across the planet. But insofar as that kind of initiative does not fit with the current structure of US capitalism, US dominance over the security systems of other capitalist powers can block such bold initiatives.

If we take all these features together we can see that their loss would transform social relations within the United States. It would involve the US having to tackle its current account deficits, having to tackle its debt problems, and ending a situation where it relies for its own investment upon sucking in finance from the rest of the world. Tackling such problems would bring American capital face to face with its own working population in a confrontation that would almost certainly result in American workers demanding the kinds of welfare protections and social rights that would make up for the impact of the downsizing of the economic perks of US power.

While interest group pressures, trends in political culture and transnational linkages between capitalist groups across the core all play some part, the current structural relationship between US capitalism and the rest of the world's social systems is surely a critical causal factor behind the broad consensus among US elites for a revival and extension of the protectorate structures.

IV. THE GEOPOLITICAL CHALLENGES FOR A NEW PAX AMERICANA

The Problems for US Grand Strategy

The key military-political problem facing the revived protectorate project lay in Europe. The collapse of the Soviet Union meant that Western Europe was no longer dependent on the US-Soviet military relationship. That freed Western Europe from the underpinnings of protectorate status. It also opened the way for each of the main West European 'spokes' to link up with each other in primary security relationships rather than with the US, creating a West European caucus. The US had to try to re-impose strategic dependency on Europe, re-impose official dominance over military-political issues in Europe and re-impose hub-and-spokes structures. These tasks were far from simple given the fact that Europe might not perceive itself to be remotely threatened either from Russia (especially if its switch to capitalism was combined with strong political and economic linkages with Europe) or from the Middle East. The military-political problem was less acute in East Asia because of the US's ability to play off rivals in the region: China-Japan-South Korea.

The second problem for the US lay in the fact that the whole structure of domestic class political relations within the protectorates tended to re-enforce US hegemony during the Cold War but did not necessarily do so after the Soviet Bloc collapse. During the Cold War, Centre-Right parties fought the Left on the basis of anti-Sovietism and anti-Communism and thus mobilized their domestic social constituencies in ways that fitted in with the overall leadership role of the United States. A large middle-class constituency in the protectorates and their peripheries was thus predisposed to accept US international campaigns articulated through anti-Soviet and anti-Communist themes. With the Soviet collapse, the US lost a powerful undercurrent of transnational socio-political support for its international military-political manoeuvres. US actions violating its own declared rules of international order, which had been tolerated by large transnational constituencies during the cold war, could face serious legitimation problems in the new situation. And this was, indeed, a problem within the USA too until September 11, 2001: there was no readiness on the part of the US electorate to support a sustained global military-political assertion of power by the US state, and this restricted the scope for large-scale US power-plays.

The third general problem for the US lay in the economic field: if the US was trying to rebuild its protectorate system in the context of economic tensions and rivalries within the capitalist core, the erstwhile protectorates could view the attempt to re-establish the protectorate arrangements as part of an attempt to impose new form of exploitative domination over the core. Or to make the same point the other way around, the other core states would desire to throw off protectorate status, or at least to attenuate it, in order to be able to assert themselves more strongly in the field of economic rivalry. In this area of relations the USA was fortunate in facing few acute economic conflicts with Europe, especially once the 'Uruguay round' deal was achieved. Its really big economic target was East and South East Asia where there was a very serious economic problem for the USA: the great economic growth there was occurring in political economies whose assets and markets were very difficult for US capitals to dominate. Clinton's 'globalization' strategy was principally targeted at opening up these economies to US capitals and opening their financial systems to the US. If this problem was not addressed it could lead to another: growing regionalizing tendencies there, with the nightmare scenario lying in China and Japan creating a single regional economic zone. The US thus chose to begin with an aggressive, assertive push to reduce Europe once more to protectorate status, while focusing on the economic problem in East Asia, downplaying the military-political dimension of operations there until after the East Asian crisis of 1997.

The point about US military-political statecraft is fundamental. When the US uses military action it always has political goals. But it is a fundamental error to assume that the main political goals behind the action are concerned with reshaping political relations with the manifest military enemy. Indeed, that part of the political goals may be trivial compared to the way the military action reshapes political relations with protectorate 'allies'. The failure of political analysts to grasp this basic point has often blinded them to what has been going on in contemporary world politics.

Western Eurasia and US Statecraft

The collapse of the Soviet Bloc created one immediate overwhelming political beneficiary: the uniting Federal Republic of Germany. In 1989-90 this caused something close to panic in Washington. The Bush administration toyed with trying to keep the Soviet Bloc in place. There were fears that the Kohl government would go for a German-Soviet redevelopment of East Central Europe – the so-called Herrhausen Plan, although the assassination of Herrhausen (and the attempted assassination of one of the plan's supporters, Lafontaine) led Kohl to abandon the project. There was also the threat of 'Genscherism' – the construction of a pan-European peace and collective security order including the Soviets which would end Washington's political dominance over Europe. But Gorbachev was too focused on the Soviet-US 'partnership' to consolidate this concept, and the Gulf War followed by the Soviet disintegration buried it.

The danger for Germany lay in its West European neighbours ganging up against it in a common front with Washington – the line urged in 1990 by the Thatcher government in Britain. But President Mitterrand took a different course, judging that French power in Europe and internationally could be maximized only as Germany's partner. This choice (challenged by some sectors of French elites) was reinforced by the crucial fact that France and other continental states had already chosen to harmonize their capital accumulation strategies with Germany's through both the construction of a Deutschmark zone and the Single Market programme – the combination forming a neoliberal path: anti-inflation, welfare state downsizing, and restructuring through unemployment. All these elements were combined with a revived political Europeanism. This emergent EU as a *political concert of European capitalisms* was in place when the Soviet Bloc collapsed. (Britain was at this time in limbo and confronting a crisis of national strategy which has really continued throughout the 1990s.) Mitterrand believed that France's role on the UNSC and its military intervention capacity could give it a leading political role as a regional power in alliance with a Germany which led the European concert in the political-economy field. And this approach was necessary for Germany to prevent its European neighbours ganging up against it after unification and to ensure that the East Central European states bordering Germany and Austria were drawn towards Germany (through EU mechanisms of course) in secure ways. For Germany the key to all this was the link with France.

Thus, the Franco–German-led EU concert held together and sought both to strengthen the political dimension of the EU and to project its political (as well as its economic) influence eastwards. Put another way, France, Germany and other EU states *sought to make their political relations with each other at least as important as the relations of each with the United States*. They were moving to replace the Cold War protectorate system of hub-and-spokes subordination to the US with a West European political caucus and to give that a relatively autonomous role in power projection eastwards.

None of this was, of course, remotely motivated by a desire to mount a direct challenge to US economic interests: the EU has continued to be rather accommodating to these. Even more important, the West European capitalist leaderships shared and valued the general, transnational class line of the US international business coalition: 'globalization', downsizing social rights, flexible labour markets, states can't control capital, etc. The European concert only wanted more collectivity, more autonomy, more autonomous political influence eastwards, along with a currency zone and a political definition to match.

But it was, in fact, a very grave threat to the entire US protectorate system for Europe, threatening to wither away NATO and US military-political dominance over Europe. The result is that since 1991 European international politics has been largely dominated by the USA's efforts to reassert its military-political control over Western Eurasia and to reimpose a hub-and-spokes protectorate system, and by West European states' counter-manoeuvres.

We have not the space to survey these battles in detail here. They have been fought out mainly in the Western Balkans.[32] In 1991 the Bush administration thought the EU would split down the middle on the Croatian war. Instead Mitterrand and even Major rallied behind the German position in December 1991. The Bush administration fought back by encouraging the start of the Bosnian war and then by sabotaging the efforts of the EU to lead the process of restoring peace. Finally the French capitulated to the Clinton administration and thus to the idea that the US should lead through NATO on European military-political affairs. The French then sought entry into NATO's military structures on the basis that the European states should be allowed to coordinate their military activities in the Mediterranean and should have a political caucus within NATO. The idea of such a caucus was backed by other West European powers including even the British in 1996. The Clinton administration repudiated such ideas. This led to the Franco-British St Malo declaration involving a direct EU military political role parallel to (though in some kind of relationship with) NATO. The US responded by successfully manoeuvring the West European states into the NATO war against Yugoslavia. The war was very nearly a debacle for NATO and the USA. And immediately after it, the West Europeans feverishly set in place the European Security and Defence Policy involving EU military planning by the general staffs of the West European armed forces and a range of other military-political caucus activities.

In short, ten years of US manoeuvring had not re-imposed the hub-and-spokes protectorate system on Europe. NATO had acquired, in effect, a European caucus, presenting the US with common views on a range of issues. The US response, under Bush Junior, would be to try to sideline NATO as an institutional structure for the War Against Evil, forcing each West European state into a bilateral hub-and-spokes relationship with the US for what the Bush administration hoped would be the new campaigning form of its global protectorate politics.

At the same time, during the 1990s the US achieved what seemed to be one great victory in Europe: it benefited from its Bosnian victory to expand NATO aggressively eastwards towards Russia, thus polarizing Europe versus Russia, notably over the NATO war against Yugoslavia. It simultaneously made NATO the dominant military-political institution of Europe as a whole, excluding Russia. And this exclusion of Russia, turning it potentially hostile, made a future confrontation with it seem possible. This in turn raised the possibility that Europe would once again feel threatened by Russia and thus in need of US military capacity. In short, Europe could return to its Cold War condition of being dependent on the US–Russian strategic relationship.

Or could it? What if Russia remained on the capitalist road, maintained and developed its liberal democratic system and revived economically with a strong political orientation toward Europe (Germany) as against the United States? Paradoxically, German acquiescence in NATO enlargement and in the US war against Yugoslavia could result in a Russian-European linkage. And what political substance could NATO have as an instrument of US power over Europe if Russia could not be 'enemy-ized'?

The US-Russian Relationship

Until 1998 Washington was the dominant influence within Russia and the Clinton administration's policy of a 'strategic partnership with Russian reform' gained victory after victory, successfully urging Yeltsin into confrontation with the Russian parliament in 1993 and working to defeat (through electoral fraud) the still powerful Russian Communist Party. Within this political alliance, the US Treasury established an extremely close linkage with the Chubais clan to do no less than redesign the social relations of Russian economic life and build the new social oligarchy of Russian capitalism, in a close umbilical relationship with US capitalism.[33]

This extraordinary political success not only had devastating effects on the lives of the Russian people and precipitated a collapse in the power of the Russian state: it also enriched Western financial operators with the shift of tens of billions of dollars' worth of property into London and New York. And it was combined with the Clinton administration's ability even to gain the Yeltsin government's acceptance of NATO expansion into Poland in 1997, and to pursue an evidently anti-Russian policy in the Caucasus – a remarkable political achievement.

Yet the Clinton administration proved incapable of following through on these extraordinary triumphs. In the midst of the global financial panic of 1998, the US government was unable to prevent both the collapse of the rouble and the Russian government's repudiation of its government bond debt. The small, economically fragile and pro-Western emergent Russian middle classes faced crippling economic losses. The NATO war against Yugoslavia of 1999 then produced a strong and deep swing of all sections of Russian public opinion against the United States.

Thus, by the time that Bush Junior entered the White House, the US had been unable to find a stable basis for either making itself the key partner of Russia or for polarizing Europe against Russia. Instead, if has found itself in a competition with Europe for Putin's support. Putin's endorsement of Bush's 'war against terrorism' has been combined with a Russian drive to gain effective membership rights within NATO, a bid backed not only by Germany but by a Blair govern-ment proposal that would have given Russia membership rights on some areas of NATO policy. The Bush administration blocked this and the May 2002 NATO-Russia agreement still essentially keeps Russia an outsider in European politics. And the Bush administration's attempt to offer Russia a national strategy which would privilege its relationship with the USA remains fraught with difficulties and obstacles in the energy field, in Eastern Europe and over the Caspian.

The East Asian Theatre

It is difficult to exaggerate the stakes in the US battle to reshape political and thus socio-economic relations in East Asia. These societies, in European terms ranging from large in the case of South Korea to huge in the case of others, have the potential to become the central region of the world economy. The task of US strategy is to prevent China from becoming the centre of a cohesive regional political economy while simultaneously attempting to transform China in ways that will make it structurally dependent upon the USA. All the resources of the American state – economic statecraft, military statecraft and ideological instru-ments – will be mobilized for this battle in the coming years.

One strand of US strategy must be to foster the internal destabilization of the Chinese state in order to produce a regime change. The terms of China's entry into the WTO may be viewed in this context, particularly the requirement that China open its agricultural market to foreign competition. This could place huge pressure on the Chinese peasantry and generate sharp internal social conflicts. A second thrust will, of course, be directed against China's state enterprises and the working class within them, and a third thrust will involve trying to open China for financial/exchange rate warfare on the model of the hedge fund strikes during the East Asian financial crisis.

At a regional level the US is attempting to push Japan into strong regional competition with China, with Japan doing the work of pulling much of South East Asia away from Chinese influence. But it remains far from clear that the Japanese state will accept these US buck-passing efforts. The possibility of Japanese capitalism developing an increasingly strong linkage with China, and the two states reaching agreements on regional preferential trade arrangements, cannot be ruled out. The Japanese social system is thus drifting in both internal and external gridlock and presents both the US and the region with one enormous question mark. Meanwhile the Chinese government pushes forward its regional integration strategy, gaining strong support not only in ASEAN but also, for example, in South Korea, whose Chaebols, fighting for their existence after the US strikes of 1997, could view links with China as a path to their salvation.

US coercive military pressure on China will supplement these thrusts, pushing the Chinese state towards an arms race which imposes strong budgetary strains on the state, decreasing its room for manoeuvre on the domestic social front. The Bush administration evidently wants to supplement this military pressure with confrontational brinkmanship over Taiwan and North Korea. But for a 'contain China' policy on the part of the US to work, Washington would have to be able to swing not only the rest of East Asia but also Russia and Western Europe behind such a drive. And this remains to be achieved. No one can safely predict what the outcome of these confrontations will be, but they will undoubtedly leave a huge mark on world politics in the first part of the twenty-first century.

The Middle East

Control of the energy belt from the Middle East through to the Caspian is a cardinal task for the construction of a new Pax Americana. In this context it is important to stress that such US military-political control is an exclusivist project: it entails the exclusion of strong West European, Russian or East Asian influence in the region. At the same time US control over the energy belt gives it an enormously powerful lever for resubordinating both Europe and East Asia.

Washington has not, up to now, considered that its control in this region is best secured by resolving the conflicts in the Middle East. Quite the contrary: US ascendancy has been secured on the basis of *manipulating* the Israeli-Palestinian and Israeli-Arab conflicts as well as by manipulating other conflicts within the Arab world. By maintaining and buttressing Israeli power, it has made Israel a threat to other Arab states and has thus been able to act as what might be called a 'hegemonic broker'. Only the US has the military-political capacity to restrain Israel. The West Europeans and others are marginalized. And the US has also been able to act as the guardian state over Saudi Arabia and the Gulf in the face of threats to these states from Iran and Iraq.

But since the mid-1990s its Machiavellianism has led the US into a strategic morass. It was outmanoeuvred by the Iraqi government, was unable to gain an international political base broad enough to launch a new war to crush the Iraqi state, lost control of the Israel-Palestinian conflict, and produced mass popular hatred in the Arab world over its support for Israel and its exterminist blockade of Iraq, involving the killing of hundreds of thousands of women and children. And the political base of the US in Saudi Arabia has been steadily undermined both by these policies and by the Saudi regime's own extremist Wahabi ideology.

Thus by September 11, 2001 US policy in the region was adrift and almost entirely isolated internationally. The Bush administration has been attempting to use September 11 to launch a new military-political offensive to regain a more secure position in the Middle East. To achieve this it has set its sights on a war to overthrow the Baathist regime in Iraq. This is a perilous undertaking: the US risks an explosive upheaval in the region involving uncontrollable conflicts. Such an eventuality could set back the drive for a global Pax Americana in a decisive way. And a US military victory over Iraq would risk sucking the US into protracted manoeuvres within the area to restore stability.

Where the US campaign since September 11 has achieved remarkable break-throughs is in Central Asia and in Georgia. With new bases in Uzbekistan, Tajikistan and Kyrgyzstan, and with the introduction of US military forces in Georgia, the US has dramatically strengthened its efforts to gain predominant influence over the Caspian vis-à-vis Russia and Iran. It has also acquired new bases on China's Western flank, thus greatly strengthening its geostrategic capacity vis-à-vis China. But the costs of these advances may also be heavy: the Bush administration has failed as yet to stabilize a new state in Afghanistan, it faces a dangerously unstable Pakistan and has contributed substantially to the sharpening of tensions between Pakistan and India.

Thus the whole vast region from the Eastern Mediterranean to India and China has become a fluid and explosive zone in which the US is being continually chal-lenged to demonstrate its power, to try to manage inter-state tensions or conflicts and to maintain a whole series of often shaky political regimes allied to US inter-ests. And it has to handle all these problems without risking direct engagement in attempting to control populations on the ground militarily – an operation which risks the US getting bogged down in the type of military-political conflict it cannot win.

V. THE US CAMPAIGN AND CAPITALIST WORLD ORDER

For all the American ideological stress on free market capitalism and 'economic globalization', then, we find that the American state, backed by its business class elites, has been engaged during the 1990s in increasingly feverish and increas-ingly militaristic geopolitical manoeuvres to reconstruct the inter-state system as a means to anchor the dominance of US capitalism in the twenty-first century. And its preoccupation with re-engineering patterns of inter-state relations clashes with other fundamental realities of contemporary world politics. Two of these realities need stressing: (1) the fact that world politics in the modern world is transnational mass politics as never before, and that consequently the legitimation of power politics matters; (2) the fact that there are urgent objective issues on the agenda of world society which any political force aspiring to global political leadership needs to address.

On all these fronts, the United States is facing one defeat after another. Paradoxically it is the West Europeans who have hit upon a serious set of ideas for managing these problems, but their ideas clash with the US protectorate project.

Mass Politics and American Military Power

Every military thrust or threat by Washington in its geopolitical manoeuvring attracts the political attention of hundreds of millions of people around the world. Movements of opinion and action at a popular level and with a wide geographical reach have now stretched to unprecedented scope; in the last hundred years the problems of maintaining order and control over populations have become very much more complicated, even if the resources of states for managing their populations have also become more sophisticated.

American military power is incapable of directly controlling populations in the countries of the South, never mind anywhere else. The US must rely upon other states to control their populations. And for these states to carry out that task they have to find political bases for doing so, involving the organization of loyalty rather than naked force. But each American campaign throws these mass loyalty structures at a state level into turmoil. Sometimes this turmoil is pro-American, as was the case in much of Western Europe during the Kosovo war. Sometimes it is anti-American, as in the Muslim and Arab worlds over the Bush-Sharon axis against the Palestinians in 2001 and the first quarter of 2002. But each American campaign is legitimated in different ways from the previous one and seeks different kinds of appeals to different global political constituencies. Principles invoked for one campaign are flagrantly contradicted in the next. Time and again, the efforts of states to gain popular support for one US campaign are undermined by the next US campaign.

Thus in the 1990s US geopolitics has rapidly undermined its own global mass base all over the world, and at this level it has sharply diminishing returns. And this affects not only popular attitudes but the state security concerns of many states, given the fact that their state security is centrally concerned with retaining bases of popular loyalty. The mass mobilizations in the Arab world against the Bush-Sharon axis had exactly this effect, shifting the policies of the Arab states, and this in turn threw the Bush campaign against Iraq onto the defensive, at least momentarily. The American use of a war crimes tribunal as a tactic in its Bosnian manoeuvres, and its legitimation of its war against Yugoslavia in 1999 as a 'humanitarian war' for human rights, was used by the West European states to push forward their idea for a International Criminal Court, an initiative viewed by Washington as a threat to its own military statecraft.

The response of US leaders to these 'blow-back' effects, and to the rapid shrinkage of its global mass political base has, under the Bush regime, been to attempt aggressive gestures of defiance. At the same time it increases pressures on the US to lash out with further military thrusts to prove that it is not intimidated by popular hostility.

All the various aspects of the centrality of mass politics come together in the way in which the US has been relating to international institutions, such as the UN Security Council, the international financial institutions, the WTO and bodies such as NATO, as well as a host of international treaty regimes. Time and again it has simply flouted the institutional norms and rules of these bodies in order to impose its will. This undermines the legitimacy not only of the United States but also of these institutions themselves. And given that these institutions are overwhelmingly designed for protecting the interests of the major capitalist states and their economic operators, US policies are tending to conflict with the collective interests of major capitalist centres.

The Transnational Political Agenda and the US Campaign

The US's military-political campaign has also been combined with an increasingly prominent tendency to oppose, weaken or largely ignore a whole range of global political and policy issues of varying degrees of importance or urgency for other states and for transnational social coalitions. It has been systematically undermining or seeking to weaken a whole network of arms control agreements from the Test Ban Treaty to the ABM treaty, conventions on chemical warfare, landmines, small arms and so on. In the field of international monetary and financial relations it has resisted efforts by the other main capitalist states to stabilize the main exchange rates or to reform the financial architecture to reduce the threat posed by large movements of hot money. Despite its own evident gains from the existence of the WTO, it has made little effort to play an international leadership role within that body, using it instead for short-term and often rather narrow domestic constituency interests. And on issues such as the environment, global poverty and debt, as well as AIDS and the fight against racism, the US has been quite incapable of presenting itself as a global leadership force. Instead it has been increasingly inclined to treat international conference diplomacy on these issues with hostility, or as damage limitation exercises.

The only rationale for this approach to international political management would seem to be that US administrations believe that by using their coercive instruments to pull other major states under their influence they can undermine the social forces taking up these kinds of political issues.

The European Concept of Ultra-Imperialist Hegemony and the US Response

Washington has found itself confronting a fairly coherent set of concepts put forward by the West European states for consolidating a new form of Atlantic/OECD hegemony over the populations and states of the world. The big European idea involves using the structural forms of law that have evolved in the capitalist era as the central instrument of a new hegemony.

Capitalist legal forms have had a binary character, involving a division between municipal (domestic) law and international public law. International law recognizes the juridical sovereignty of states. This implies that states cannot be bound by any legal rules which they have not voluntarily accepted through signing and ratifying international treaties or through ratifying their membership of treaty-based international organizations. At the same time, sovereign states are free to design their municipal domestic legal frameworks as they wish. But these legal forms also contain the idea that when a state does subscribe to an international treaty, its obligations under that treaty trump its own municipal law.

It is this rule which the EU states have picked up and have used as a powerful instrument for socio-political engineering within the EU zone itself. In the past states confronted with this rule had typically been very careful to ensure that their adhesion to international treaties would not restrict their domestic freedom of action to redesign municipal law as they wished in line with changing domestic social balances and requirements. But the Treaty of Rome that founded the EEC in 1958 was highly unusual in taking the form of an international treaty whose substance focused heavily on the regulation of domestic socio-economic legal and institutional arrangements. Inter-governmental negotiations by the executives of EEC member states could produce laws about domestic matters which trumped existing domestic law and which could not be overturned by domestic parliaments. For almost thirty years, the EEC member states did not actually make very much use of this mechanism. But in the 1980s, as they turned towards neoliberalism, the member states began to use it very aggressively and in its strongest form – that of new laws with *domestic* application created by inter-governmental treaty revision conferences of the member states: the Single European Act, the Treaty of European Union (Maastricht), Amsterdam and Nice. The substance of this regulatory effort was directed mainly at class relations within each member state in the field of economic and social policy: anchoring neoliberal policy and institutional frameworks and dynamics within each member state in ways that could not be overturned by parliamentary majorities in any of them.

This principle was then offered by the EU states to the US administration in the Uruguay Round: constructing the WTO as a treaty-based regime which would then trump the municipal law of states adhering to the WTO – locking them in, so to speak, to the open door provisions of the WTO on services as well as trade issues, monopoly rents on intellectual property rights, etc. But this mechanism can be extended far more widely and can be used to lock in states and social formations across a whole range of issues for the kinds of open door regimes that favour the penetration of Atlantic capitals. And the mechanism can be extended beyond political economy issues. Indeed, from the start of the 1990s, the EU has used the mechanism to push forward the reorganization of state political institutions with its Human Rights, Democracy and Good Governance diplomacy. Presented as a juridical method, rooted in a set of ethical norms, this form of diplomacy has actually proved a potent form of power politics. When target states resist EU economic policy goals they can be hit by HRDGG diplomacy, while target states compliant with EC economic objectives can be treated gently in the HRDGG field. This diplomacy thus buttresses EU economic imperialism and legitimates the EU domestically, and at the same time can be used to strengthen the juridical systems of target states so as to provide predictable environments for EU capitals. Last but not least it helps the EU overcome the fact that it is not a democratic structure by making itself an instrument for imposing and invigilating democracy elsewhere!

At the same time, the EU backs such diplomatic instruments with an array of instruments of economic statecraft (above all the granting or denial of market access, a ladder of economic sanctions and aid programmes, sponsorship in the IFIs, etc). And for the EU the ultimate sanction could be the military one, in which the US would play a leading role. Of course this repertoire of instruments is efficacious not only as a means of coercively imposing relations of dominance over target states: it also offers ways for the capitalist classes of the target states to strengthen their own domestic positions in various ways. But the power relation is nevertheless crucial, and it enables the metropolitan centres to expel all kinds of internal problems outwards.

This repertoire of instruments is then offered by the EU to the rest of the OECD world as the kernel of a collective world order project, anchoring the dominance of the richest capitalist countries over the globe for the twenty-first century. But for the EU states such a project would have to be based upon collegial global bodies within which the leading capitalist states would haggle over the precise positive law content of the various legal regimes to be imposed upon other countries. And while the social substance of the regimes would be that of a G7 world order, the main West European states want the (American) use of aggressive military force to be under the discipline of the UNSC. They have carefully ensured that the International Criminal Court does not consider aggressive war against sovereign states to be a war crime or a crime against humanity of any sort. Indeed the EU states support aggression against states whose internal arrangements the EU opposes. But they want such aggression to be sanctioned politically by the UNSC.

Thus the West European concept of a new world order would be a potently coercive one directed to transforming domestic jurisdictions, polities and economies throughout the world. But all the coercive instruments would be legitimated by law.

CONCLUSION

For the American state, this EU project is perceived as a major threat to American global dominance. The entire regime offered by the EU is acceptable only as a sub-system above which stands the American eagle untrammelled by the regimes beneath it to which others may be chained. Under Clinton and Bush Junior the US has therefore exerted increasingly intensive efforts to pressurize or even threaten West European security interests to bring the region back to protectorate status.

The conflicts around these issues are now intensifying. As they do so, various parts of the left, both social liberal and socialist, are beginning to draw together to build a new road forward towards a different kind of world order. The anti-capitalist globalization movement has thrown down a very significant challenge to the ultra-imperialist project of West Europe and, with its added super-imperialist twist, of Washington. The intervention of young peace activists challenging Israeli guns and breaking the siege of the Church of the Nativity with food packages was an inspiring demonstration of real political force. The capacity of gigantic state military force to reshape international politics through terrorizing populations is often underestimated by the Left. But the capacity of popular mass movements to resist and defeat such bureaucratic-technological terror is often underestimated by the Right. It seems that this is a lesson which the American state will yet again have to learn, hopefully before it has plunged, by blustering blunder or by design, millions into the horror of further wars.

NOTES

This is a rewritten version of my Deutscher Memorial Lecture in November 2001.

1   On the political economy side of US protectorate relations see the important article by Leo Panitch, 'The New Imperial State', *New Left Review*, 2 (March-April), 2000. See also Peter Gowan, *The Global Gamble*, London: Verso, 1999.

2   The classic analysis of this process is Samuel Huntington, 'Transnational Organisations in World Politics', *World Politics,* XXV (April), 1973.

3   Geir Lundestsad, *'Empire' by Integration*, Oxford: Oxford University Press, 1998.

4   The US was never, for example, formally a member of the GATT: the Senate never ratified US adhesion.

5   See Carl Schmitt, *The Concept of the Political*, New Brunswick, N.J.: Rutgers University Press, 1976, and Carl Schmitt, *Political Theology: Four Chapters on the Concept of Sovereignty* (Studies in Contemporary German Social Thought), Cambridge, Mass.: MIT Press, 1985). See also Peter Gowan, 'The Return of Carl Schmitt', *Debatte: Review of Contemporary German Affairs*, 2(1) (Spring), 1994.

6   See Barbara Haskel, 'Access to Society: A Neglected Dimension of Power', *International Organisation*, 34(1) (Winter), 1980.

7   Frances Stonor Saunders, *Who Paid the Piper? The CIA and the Cultural Cold War*, London: Granta Books, 1999.

8   Comparative research on the differentiated extents of US penetration in different protectorate societies still remains to be done but it seems likely that the degrees of penetration varied greatly.

9   Zbigniew Brzezinski, *The Grand Chessboard*, New York: Basic Books, 1997.

10 Failure to appreciate this point and its continued relevance vitiates important parts of the argument in Antonio Negri and Michael Hardt, *Empire*, Cambridge, Mass.: Harvard University Press, 2000.

11 'National Rights' in this context means that US economic operators gain exactly the same legal rights to operate within a national jurisdiction as the national operators within that state.

12 On such concerns see Jeffrey E. Garten, *A Cold Peace: America, Japan, Germany and the Struggle for Supremacy*, New York: Times Books, 1992, and Lester Thurow, *Head to Head: the Coming Economic Battle among Japan, Europe and America*, New York:

Wm. Morrow & Co, 1992.

13   As Robert Gilpin has pointed out, West German dependence on US political and military support in the 1960s was crucial in enabling the US to ensure that its businesses were able to establish operations in the Federal Republic in order thereby to become a major force within the European Economic Community (Robert Gilpin, *The Political Economy of International Relations*, Princeton: Princeton University Press, 1987).

14   See Miles Kahler, *International Institutions and The Political Economy of Integration*, The Brookings Institution, 1995, and Miles Kahler and Jeffrey Frankel, eds., *Regionalism and Rivalry: Japan and the U.S. in Pacific Asia*, Chicago: University of Chicago Press, 1993.

15   The obvious motive for the leak was to warn the Europeans of the strength of the US will as Washington drove forward its campaign for an independent unitary Bosnia and thus for a Bosnian civil war just after the triumph of German diplomacy in gaining EU backing for an independent Croatia and Slovenia. On these issues see Peter Gowan, 'The Western Powers and the Yugoslav Tragedy', *New Left Review* 234 (May-June), 1999. On the general debate in US elite circles on grand strategy after the Cold War and on the dominance of the groups advocating US 'primacy', see Barry R. Posen and Andrew L. Ross, 'Competing Visions for U.S. Grand Strategy', *International Security*, 21(3) (Winter), 1996/97.

16   Paul Wolfowitz, 'Remembering the Future', *The National Interest*, 59 (Spring), 2000.

17   Wolfowitz, 'Remembering the Future'.

18   Ibid.

19   Anthony Lake, 'Laying the Foundation for a Post-Cold War World. National Security in the 21st Century', *Speech to the Chicago Council on Foreign Relations*, 24 May 1996.

20   Anthony Lake 'From Containment to Enlargement', School of Advanced International Studies, Johns Hopkins University, Washington DC, 21 September 1993.

21   Lake 'From Containment to Enlargement'.

22   Ibid.

23   Ibid.

24   As Warren Christopher declared after his retirement, 'by the end of the [first Clinton] term, "should the United States lead?" was no longer a serious question': Warren Christopher, *In the Stream of History: Shaping Foreign Policy for a New Era*, Stanford: Stanford University Press, 1998.

25   Andrew Bacevich, *The National Interest*, 56 (Summer), 1999.

26   John Mearsheimer, 'Back to the Future: Instability in Europe after the Cold War', *International Security*, 15(1) (Summer), 1990.

27   John Harper of the Paul Nitze School of International Studies makes essentially the same point: 'Stripped to its bare essentials, the post–World War II transatlantic relationship has been an American protectorate, invited and to an extent shaped by the Europeans themselves. The protectorate has served a double purpose: promoting peace and harmony among the Europeans as well as counterbalancing Russian power' (John L. Harper, 'Bush and the Europeans', *SAISPHERE*, Paul Nitze School

of Advanced International Studies, John Hopkins University, 2001).

28   For a sophisticated culturalist/constructivist interpretation, see David Campbell, *Writing Security: United States Foreign Policy and the Politics of Identity*, Manchester: Manchester University Press, 1998.

29   David Calleo, *Rethinking Europe's Future*, Princeton: Princeton University Press, 2001, p. 176.

30   For an interesting analysis of shifting opinion in US business coalitions see Ronald W. Cox and Daniel Skidmore-Hess, *US Politics and the Global Economy. Corporate Power, Conservative Shift*, Boulder: Lynne Rienner, 1999.

31   These issues are treated at greater length in Gowan, *The Global Gamble*, and also in Peter Gowan, 'Explaining the American Boom: The Roles of Globalisation and US Global Power', *New Political Economy*, 6(3), 2001.

32   This was stressed in the famous 1991 national security document written for the Bush administration by Paul Wolfowitz and Lewis Libby. For more on these issues see Peter Gowan, 'The Twisted Road to Kosovo', *Labour Focus on Eastern Europe*, 62, 1999. See also Paul Cornish, *Partnership in Crisis. The US, Europe and the Fall and Rise of NATO*, Royal Institute for International Affairs and Pinter, 1997.

33   Janine Wedel, *Collision and Collusion: The Strange Case of Western Aid to Eastern Europe 1989-1998*, New York: St. Martin's Press, 1998.

Guide to Additional Readings

Books

Anderson, Perry, 'Force and Consent', *New Left Review*, II/17.

Arrighi, Giovanni and Silver, Beverly, 'Workers North and South', *Socialist Register 2001*, London: Merlin, 2001.

Bartholomew, Amy and Breakspear, Jennifer, 'Human Rights as Swords of Empire', *Socialist Register 2003*, London: Merlin, 2003.

Bello, Walden, *Deglobalization: Ideas for a New World Economy*, London: Zed Books, 2002.

Bond, Patrick, *Against Global Apartheid*, London: Pluto, 2003.

Bonefeld, Werner and Holloway, John, eds., *Global Capital, National State and the Politics of Money*, New York: St. Martin's, 1995.

Brecher, Jeremy; Costello, Tim and Smith, Brendan, *Globalization from Below: The Power of Solidarity*, Cambridge: South End Press, 2000.

Bryan, Dick, *The Chase Across the Globe: International Accumulation and the Contradictions for Nation States*, Boulder: Westview, 1995.

Burkett, Paul and Hart-Landsberg, Martin, 'The Use and Abuse of Japan as a Progressive Model', *Socialist Register 1996*, London: Merlin, 1996.

Coates, David, *Models of Capitalism*, Cambridge: Polity Press, 2000.

Cox, Robert, *Production, Power, and World Order*, New York: Columbia University, 1987.

Dicken, Peter, *Global Shift*, Fourth Edition, London: Paul Chapman, 2003.

Gill, Stephen, *Power and Resistance in the New World Order*, London, Palgrave-Macmillan, 2003.

Gowan, Peter, *The Global Gamble: Washington's Faustian Bid for World Dominance*, London: Verso, 1999.

Grahl, John, 'Globalized Finance', *New Left Review*, II/8.

Harvey, David, *The New Imperialism*, London: Oxford, 2003.

Held, David and McGrew, Anthony, *The Global Transformations Reader*, Cambridge: Polity, 2003.

Helleiner, Eric, *States and the Re-emergence of Global Finance*, Ithaca: Cornell University Press, 1994.

Henwood, Doug, *After the New Economy*, New York: New Press, 2003.

Hirst, Paul and Thompson, Grahame, *Globalisation in Question*, Second Edition, Cambridge: Polity, 1999.

Hoogvelt, Ankie, *Globalization and the Postcolonial World: The New Political Economy of Development*, Second Edition, Baltimore: Johns Hopkins University Press, 2001.

Hudson, Michael, *Super Imperialism: The Origin and Fundamentals of US World Dominance*, London: Pluto, 2003.

Huws, Ursula, *Making of a Cybertariat*, London: Merlin, 2003.

Leys, Colin, *Market-Driven Politics: Neoliberal Democracy and the Public Interest*, London: Verso, 2001.

Mann, Michael, *Incoherent Empire*, London: Verso, 2003.

McMichael, Philip, *Development and Social Change: A Global Perspective*, Third Edition, Thousand Oakes: Pine Forge, 2004.

McNally, David, *Another World is Possible: Globalization and Anti-Capitalism*, Winnipeg: Arbeiter Ring Publishing, 2002.

Moody, Kim, *Workers in a Lean World: Unions in the International Economy*, New York: Verso, 1997.

Moran, Michael, *The Politics of the Financial Services Revolution*, London: Macmillan, 1991.

Panitch, Leo and Gindin, Sam, 'Global Capitalism and American Empire', *Socialist Register 2004*, London: Merlin 2003.

Radice, Hugo, 'Globalization and National Capitalisms: Theorising Convergence and Differentiation', *Review of International Political Economy*, 7(4), 2000.

Robinson, William, *Promoting Polyarchy: Globalization, US Intervention, and Hegemony*, Cambridge: Cambridge University Press, 1996.

Rosenberg, Justin, *The Follies of Globalisation Theory: Polemical Essays*, London: Verso, 2002.

Sassen, Saskia, *Globalization and its Discontents: Essays on the New Mobility of People and Money*, New York: New Press, 1998.

van der Pijl, Kees, *The Making of an Atlantic Ruling Class*, London: Verso, 1984.

Vogel, Steven, *Freer Markets, More Rules: Regulatory Reform in Advanced Industrial Countries*, Ithaca: Cornell, 1996.

Waterman, Peter, *Globalization, Social Movements, and the New Internationalisms*, Washington: Mansell, 1998.

Whitfield, Dexter, *Public Services or Corporate Welfare: Rethinking the Nation State in the Global Economy*, London: Pluto, 2001.

Wood, Ellen, *Empire of Capital*, London, Verso, 2003.

Zuege, Alan, 'Chimera of the Third Way', *Socialist Register 2000*, London: Merlin, 2000.

A Selection of Globalization Web Sites

ZNET
http://www.zmag.org/weluser.htm

Independent Media Center
http://www.indymedia.org/en/index.shtml

Multinational Monitor
http://multinationalmonitor.org/

International Forum on Globalization
http://www.ifg.org/

Focus on the Global South
http://www.focusweb.org/

The Global Site
http://www.theglobalsite.ac.uk/

Global Solidarity Dialogue
http://www.antenna.nl/~waterman/dialogue.html

The Globalization Website
http://www.emory.edu/SOC/globalization/index.html

Global Policy Forum
http://www.globalpolicy.org/globaliz/

Labor Start
http://www.laborstart.org/

LabourNet
http://www.labournet.org/

Common Dreams News Center
http://www.commondreams.org/

The Nation Magazine
http://www.thenation.com/

Red Pepper
http://www.redpepper.org.uk/

Canadian Dimension
http://www.canadiandimension.mb.ca/

Left Business Observer
www.leftbusinessobserver.com

Economic Policy Institute – Globalization Papers
http://www.epinet.org/subjectpages/trade.cfm

Jerome Levy Institute
http://www.levy.org/2/index.asp

Centre for Economic Policy Research
http://www.cepr.org/

NOTES ON CONTRIBUTORS

Gregory Albo is a contributing editor to the *Socialist Register* and Professor of Political Science at York University, Toronto.

Elmar Altvater is Professor of International Political Economy at the Department of Political and Social Sciences of the Free University of Berlin.

Manfred Bienefeld is Professor in the School of Public Policy and Administration at Carleton University, Ottawa.

James R. Crotty is Professor in the Department of Economics and a research associate at the Political Economy Research Institute (PERI) at the University of Massachusetts, Amherst.

Gérard Duménil is a Research Director at the Centre National de la Recherche Scientifique, MODEM, University of Paris X-Nanterre.

Gerald Epstein is Professor in the Department of Economics and co-director of the Political Economy Research Institute (PERI) at the University of Massachusetts, Amherst.

Peter Gowan is a Professor in the Department of Law, Governance and International Relations at London Metropolitan University.

Ursula Huws is a freelance writer and researcher who is also Professor of International Labour Studies at the Working Lives Research Institute at London Metropolitan University and Director of Analytica Social and Economic Research Ltd.

Martijn Konings is at the Department of Political Science, York University, Toronto.

Dominique Lévy is a Research Director at the Centre National de la Recherche Scientifique, CEPREMAP, Paris.

Colin Leys co-edits the *Socialist Register* with Leo Panitch. He is an Emeritus Professor of Political Studies at Queen's University, Kingston, Canada, and an Honorary Senior Research Fellow at University College London.

Leo Panitch is co-editor of the *Socialist Register* and Canada Research Chair in Comparative Political Economy and Distinguished Research Professor of Political Science at York University, Toronto.

Hugo Radice is Senior Lecturer in International Political Economy at the School of Politics and International Studies, University of Leeds.

Wally Seccombe is a founding member and chair of the Everdale Environmental Learning Centre just outside of Toronto.

Constantine Tsoukalas is Professor of Political Science at the University of Athens, Greece.

Alan Zuege is a contributing editor to the *Socialist Register* and is at the Department of Political Science, York University, Toronto.

Also from The Merlin Press:

Socialist Register – Published Annually Since 1964

Leo Panitch & Colin Leys – Editors
2004: THE NEW IMPERIAL CHALLENGE

How should we face the new imperial challenge presented by the US today? How should we understand imperialism and its relationship to globalized capitalism?

Innovative essays on the unique nature of the new US empire and on the new economics of imperialism that both develop and challenge classical Marxist theories.

Contents:

Leo Panitch & Sam Gindin: Global Capitalism and American Empire

Aijaz Ahmad: Imperialism of Our Time

David Harvey: The 'New' Imperialism – Accumulation by Dispossession

Greg Albo: The Old and New Economics of Imperialism

Noam Chomsky: Truths and Myths about the Invasion of Iraq

Amy Bartholomew & Jennifer Breakspear: Human Rights as Swords of Empire

Paul Rogers: The US Military Posture – 'A Uniquely Benign Imperialism'?

Michael T. Klare: Blood for Oil – The Bush-Cheney Energy Strategy

John Bellamy Foster & Brett Clark: Ecological Imperialism – The Curse of Capitalism

Tina Wallace: NGO Dilemmas – Trojan Horses for Global Neoliberalism?

John Saul: Globalization, Imperialism, Development – False Binaries and Radical Resolutions

Emad Aysha: The Limits and Contradictions of 'Americanization'

Bob Sutcliffe: Crossing Borders in the New Imperialism

2003 290 pp. 234 x 156 mm. ISSN. 0081-0606

Hardback 0850365341	**£30.00**
Paperback 085036535X	**£14.95**

Canada: Fernwood Publishing, USA: Monthly Review Press (paperback only); Rest of World & hardback: Merlin Press

David Coates – Editor
PAVING THE THIRD WAY: The Critique of Parliamentary Socialism
A Socialist Register Anthology

The parliamentary road to socialism has held the attention and loyalty of much of the left in the UK for more than a century. But has the strategy worked, and could it yet work? Writings on Parliamentary Socialism inspired by Ralph Miliband provide an important answer to these questions, and in the process throw new light on the history of the British Labour Party.

In this book David Coates brings together original texts, adding critical commentary, annotation and some of his own writings to contributions by Ralph Miliband, John Saville, Leo Panitch, Colin Leys and Hilary Wainwright. Given the centrality of the Third Way to social democratic politics globally, this collection will be of interest to students and practitioners of left-wing politics in all advanced capitalist economies.

Contents:
Introductory Essay
Part 1: LABOURISM AND ITS LIMITS
1. Ralph Miliband: Selections from Parliamentary Socialism
John Saville: Labourism and the Labour Government
Leo Panitch: Social Democracy and Industrial Militancy
David Coates: The failure of the socialist promise

Part 2: FROM OLD LABOUR TO NEW LABOUR
Leo Panitch: Socialists and the Labour Party
Ralph Miliband: Socialist Advance in Britain
Leo Panitch: Socialist Renewal and the Labour Party
Colin Leys: The British Labour Party's transition
David Coates: Labour Governments: Old Constraints

Part 3: MOVING ON
Hilary Wainwright: Once More Moving On and Building New Parties for a Different Kind of Socialism: a Response
David Coates and Leo Panitch: The Continuing Relevance of the Milibandian Perspective

2003 270pp. 234 x 156 mm.
Paperback 0850365120   **£16.95**

Canada: Fernwood Publishing; UK and Rest of World: Merlin Press